D0130388

Social Aspects of Sport

Social Aspects of Sport

second edition

Eldon E. Snyder
Elmer A. Spreitzer
Bowling Green State University

PRENTICE-HALL, INC., Englewood Cliffs, New Jersey 07632

Library of Congress Cataloging in Publication Data

SNYDER, ELDON E.
Social aspects of sport.

Bibliography:
Includes index.
1. Sports—Social aspects. I. Spreitzer, Elmer A.
II. Title
GV706.5.S63 1983 306′.483 82-3698
ISBN 0-13-815639-5 AACR2

Editorial production and supervision by F. Hubert
Manufacturing buyer: Harry P. Baisley
Cover by Wanda Lubelska Design

Printed in the United States of America
10 9 8 7 6 5 4 3

ISBN 0-13-815639-5

PRENTICE-HALL INTERNATIONAL, INC., *London*
PRENTICE-HALL OF AUSTRALIA PTY. LIMITED, *Sydney*
PRENTICE-HALL CANADA INC., *Toronto*
PRENTICE-HALL OF INDIA PRIVATE LIMITED, *New Delhi*
PRENTICE-HALL OF JAPAN, INC., *Tokyo*
PRENTICE-HALL OF SOUTHEAST ASIA PTE. LTD., *Singapore*
WHITEHALL BOOKS LIMITED, Wellington, *New Zealand*

DEDICATED TO THE HONOR OF OUR PARENTS

Murrel and Frances Snyder

Louis and Cleo Spreitzer

Contents

11 The Black Athlete *174*

12 Structural Strains within the Coaching Role and Collective Violence *192*

13 Sports and the Mass Media *211*

14 The Political Economy of Sports *229*

Preface

One objective in writing the first edition of this book was to put under one cover the material we had been using while teaching and researching the sociology of sport. In the intervening years we have continued our teaching and research in this academic area. This edition reflects these ongoing experiences as well as recent developments in the field. We have tried to include material that is of interest to current and future practitioners in the world of sport—coaches, athletic directors, physical education instructors, recreation specialists, sportswriters, as well as educated laypeople. Thus, the content of the book spills over the boundaries of several disciplines—sociology, American studies, popular culture, leisure and recreation, physical education, and child development.

Since the term *sport* is a global concept, we have frequently found it helpful to divide the concept into three subtypes: informal, semiformal, and formal sport. Goals and levels of organization differ within these three spheres; thus the material presented in this volume spans the topics of play, leisure, recreation, physical education, and formally organized sport.

The present work represents a rewriting and expansion of the topics discussed in the first edition. Additionally, we have incorporated new material dealing with cross-cultural variations in sport, social stratification and sport, the black athlete, as well as the economic, political, and religious dimensions of sport. Since we have an ongoing interest in lifelong participation in sport, this topic is given expanded attention in the second edition. In this context we deal with sport as a means of symbolizing a life style, as a leisure-time pursuit, and as a reflection of social patterns inherent in the larger society. Further, societal trends toward equality of opportunity for females in athletics is one of the reasons for our interest in the female athlete.

Our book differs from many other scholarly writings in the sense that we do not attempt to maintain a scientific detachment from the material in order to avoid value judgments. On the contrary, we feel free in our analysis implicitly and explicitly to express values, sentiments, opinions, and recommendations. For example, attention is devoted to both the positive and negative aspects of sport within schools and society. In this context, we offer suggestions—gratuitous though they may be—to coaches, athletic directors, teachers, and parents. Finally, in the preparation of this second edition we want to express our appreciation of our wives and families for their understanding and support.

ELDON E. SNYDER
ELMER A. SPREITZER
Bowling Green State University

Social Aspects of Sport

CHAPTER 1
Introduction

Sport represents one of the most pervasive social institutions in our society. Sport permeates social reality from the societal level down to the individual. Modern sport has its roots deeply embedded in the history of Western society. In classical Greek society the body, developed through vigorous and graceful physical movement, was the epitome of beauty. The importance of physical excellence is readily evident in the sculpture of this period. As Lowe (1977) has noted, the body was perceived ". . . as the source of all good and happiness was the key to spiritual salvation. The more beautiful the body, the better the man or woman in pantheistic terms. The Olympian gods were accorded characteristics that were values of their society—strength, beauty, courage, wisdom, and athletic ability" (p. 4). Although sport in the Greek and Roman eras eventually became predominantly ritualized spectacles (for example, Roman circuses), such spectacles nevertheless attest to the prominence of sport and its reflection in the social and cultural milieu in which it existed. Throughout the Roman Empire, the government erected stadia for entertainment of the citizens. Even to this day, the wide geographical dispersion and the grandeur of these stadia, particularly the Colosseum, are evidence of the breadth and organizational sophistication of the Roman Empire. Game days, festivals, and holidays ("holy days") throughout the Middle Ages continued the practice of competitive games and sport into the modern era.

The prevalence of sport in modern society can be documented in terms of news coverage, financial expenditures, number of participants and spectators, movies, books, themes in comic strips, hours consumed, sales of sports equipment, and time samplings of conversations. In considering the commercial use of sport, television is a good reference. In 1963, the television networks paid $13,900,000 for the rights to broadcast collegiate and professional football. In 1975, the figure had reached $60,000,000. In 1976 the amount networks, stations, and local rights holders paid to get football on television was $201,216,000. Advertisers are paying ABC $85,000 per 30-second spot on a NFL (pro) game and $43,000 on a NCAA (collegiate) game. The rate for a commercial on the Superbowl sponsored by CBS is $275,000 for a 30-second spot. These price tags soon become dated, but the rapidity with which this happens is itself a measure of the public's interest in spectator sports. Attendance at sports events also continues to draw more customers, and the gains and losses between the sports show interesting variations (see Table 1-1). The most dramatic growth is in increased attendance at soccer games. Until very recently, soccer has had wide popularity through the world but has had little acceptance in the United States. With the advent of new television efforts and community youth soccer programs, the sport is gaining in popularity.

TABLE 1-1 Attendance at Selected Spectator Sports and the Gains or Losses in the Last Year

SPORT	ATTEND.	GAIN/LOSS	ATTENDANCE RANK
Horseracing	77,679,954	−1,339,054	1
Baseball	65,356,461	+5,725,452	2
Football (collegiate and professional)	50,075,529	+1,230,000	3
Autoracing	47,700,000	−3,050,000	4
Basketball	40,690,082	+913,000	5
Soccer	23,500,000	+15,000,000	6

Source: Adapted from a media report in the *Bowling Green Sentinel Tribune*, April 29, 1980, p. 17.

The prominence of sport on commercial television is also evident in the frequent use of sports personalities in commercials as well as play-by-play and color analysis of the athletic events. Former athletes Joe Garagiola, Joe Dimaggio, and Bruce Jenner readily come to mind for their appearances in television commercials. Moreover, many other former athletes have left the playing fields to enter show business or television. The list includes such personalities as Don Meredith, Alex Karras, Frank Gifford, Pat Summerall, Tom Brookshier, Tony Trabert, Don Drysdale, Tony Kubek, Julie Heldman, Peggy Fleming, Maury Wills, Carey Middlecoff, Johnny Unitas, Billie Jean King, Cathy Rigby, Arthur Ashe, Bill Russell, and Dick Button. Again, the demand for ex-athletes is due primarily to television's increased emphasis on sports and its expansion of sports coverage. Throughout the 1960s and 1970s professional leagues expanded, new leagues formed, athletic stadia were expanded and refurbished, and new sport palaces were built in such places as Houston (Astrodome), New Orleans (Superdome), Arlington (Dallas–Ft. Worth), Seattle, Hackensack Meadows (New Jersey), Kansas City (Harry S. Truman Sports Complex), and Pontiac (Michigan). Indeed, one could suggest that the athletic stadium is the prototypical architectural form of the modern era similar to the pyramids, temples, cathedrals, railroad stations, and skyscrapers of earlier eras.

We hasten to point out that this trend is not only found in commercial sport. On many college and university campuses, new recreation buildings are being built, primarily designed for informal and recreational sport participation rather than for spectator sports. Additionally, many communities are unable to keep up with the demand for recreation facilities for indoor and outdoor court games, skiing, cycling, jogging, and running clubs.

The pervasiveness of sport is perhaps most evident in the increased participation in sport by some segments of our population. While the majority of the population remains sedentary, significant changes are evident in the increased popularity of sports such as tennis, racquetball, and jogging. According to the U.S. Racquetball Association, in 1970 only 50,000 people played racquetball; today there are 6 to 8 million players. In 1970 some 228,000 racquetballs were sold; in 1979 more than 17 million were sold. Many racquet clubs appeal to the family and social interests of their customers by offering tennis, swimming, and nursery facilities as well as weight training rooms, saunas, whirlpools, game rooms, and snack bars. During the 1970s an estimated 20 million Americans took up jogging—including President Carter. In 1970 the first New York City Marathon drew 176 runners; in 1979 11,533 men and women started the race. Examples of best selling written materials on running include Dr. Kenneth Cooper's *Aerobics*, Dr. George Sheehan's newspaper column on "Running and Being," the books by James F. Fixx (*Complete Book of Running* and *Second Book of Running*), and *Runner's World* magazine. The commercial interests associated with this physical fitness trend are substantial, as exemplified by the competition among companies producing running shoes.

Further evidence of the prevalence of sport in our society is manifested in the sport idioms and figures of speech that are a part of our everyday communication—for instance, "struck out," "scored," "out in left field," "ball park figure," "not in the same ball park," "foul play," "out of bounds," "cheap shot," "dirty pool," "toss up," "fumbled the ball," and so on. Metaphors from the world of sport provide ready-made descriptions, images, and impressions that are used to facilitate communication in nonsport context. For example, Balbus has noted the frequent use of sport terminology in the political sphere.

> State activity is increasingly being cloaked in the rhetoric of the sports world; at times it even appears as if the language of politics is being completely absorbed by the language of sports. Thus the president becomes the "quarterback" who, along with his Cabinet and White House staff "team," pursues "game plan" policies designed to reach the "goal line" and to "win" the political "ballgame." This corruption of the discourse of politics by the discourse of sports alerts us to a possibly profound transformation in the way in which governmental activity in America is defined and understood: to envelop politics with the symbolism of sports is to transfer the meanings which we attribute to the latter to the former. Thus the political ascendency of the sports metaphor may well signal the increasing importance of sports as a legitimating mechanism of the American state (Balbus, 1975, pp. 26–27).

Considering how familiar most people are with sport, the use of such metaphors may indeed promote clarity and precision of communication. However, they may also transfer a sport imagery that distorts other areas of social life. In any event, the proliferation of sport metaphors and figures of speech in nonathletic contexts does document the influence of sport in our society.

Communicating in the language of sport has become so common that it often serves the function of "small talk." Sportstalk of this type is similar to talking about the weather. It opens conversation, regardless of how well people know each other, and allows pleasantries to be exchanged that would otherwise be difficult or impossible. Much of our daily conversation is of this "small talk" variety; in fact sport is the contemporary *lingua franca* of social discourse for a large segment of the population. Perhaps it would be well for communication to be exchanged at a less superficial level, but in a society filled with impersonal relationships, "small talk" may be the best we can hope for in many settings. At least we feel somewhat less lonely and more comfortable when we exchange trite expressions about the Yankees or the success of the local football team. Indeed, we may not have the time or the inclination to discuss more ponderous matters.

The prevalence of sport is also reflected in the play of children, which serves as an early means of socialization into sport activities. Many of these early socialization experiences begin in the family and continue throughout the life cycle in the form of family leisure and recreation. Participation in sport extends into the school setting, with progressive levels of formalization and emphasis on performance continuing through the higher educational levels. In many high schools, colleges, and universities, sport is a major component in resource allocation as well as in status attainment. However, a discordant note in the athletic programs of some major universities gives further evidence of the influence of sport in our society. Alleged academic improprieties among athletes and questionable (not to mention illegal) recruiting practices by coaches suggest that athletic success has become, in some cases, incompatible with the academic goals of higher education (see "The Shame of College Sports," *Newsweek*, September 22, 1980, pp. 54-59). In recent years, with changing sex roles and legal pressures for sexual equality in sport, the interest and involvement of females in sport are burgeoning; sport is no longer a male domain.

The impact of sport is also illustrated by the 1980 Winter Olympic Games at Lake Placid. Eric Heiden's feat of winning five gold medals together with the historic victory of the U.S. hockey team's 4-3 victory over the Soviet Union enthralled the nation, and the entire team became *Sports Illustrated*'s "Sportsmen of the Year." Yet shortly after the exhilaration of these events, on April 12, 1980, the political implications of sport were vividly illustrated when the United States Olympic Committee voted to boycott the Summer Olympics in Moscow. Officially, the decision was in compliance with President Carter's assessment that participation in the games, in light of the Russian invasion of Afganistan, would present a threat to the national security of our country. In summary, we can see that sport is intertwined within the institutional structure of our society at both the macro and micro levels. The prominence of sport in society underscores the desirability of further scientific investigation into this interrelationship.

PARADOXICAL ASPECTS OF SPORT

In Chapter 2, "The Nature of Sport," we focus on some essential characteristics of sport, devoting particular attention to the indeterminancy, duality, intrinsic and extrinsic dimensions. In some respects these dimensions of sport revolve around a series of paradoxes within sport. Elias and Dunning (1972) have discussed a similar notion within the context of sporting events. For example, they note that within an athletic contest there must be a balance of tension maintained between the competing teams. This balance is a kind of fluctuating equilibrium between too much and too little tension. There must be some tension to add excitement and "tone" to the contest, yet this tension must be delicately controlled by the rules to achieve the objectives and continuation of the contest.

It is apparent that the paradoxes can also be considered within a dialetical framework in the sense of a continuous confrontation between opposing qualities. For example, the element of competition in sport provides a healthy tension to the contest. It brings out the motivation to excel and extend oneself physically, emotionally, and mentally. This is self-enhancing, exciting, and exhilarating. Yet, excessive competition contains the potential to destroy sport, since it may lead to violence and to a win-at-any-cost philosophy. Additionally, the motivation to achieve high performances, victories, prestige, national rankings, league championships, and monetary success (extrinsic rewards) demands a very high input of physical, emotional, and material resources. As a consequence, there is likely to be a corresponding loss of the intrinsic fun and joy of participation. Competition, too heavily stressed, turns play into work. Furthermore, the importance of commercial success associated with formal sport is itself a potential threat to sport, since the primary goal of financial solvency may lead to excesses that become a travesty of sport. In this situation, the spectators no longer appreciate the skill, strategy, and excitement of gifted athletes striving for an unpredictable outcome. Rather, they attend to see the blood flow, cheap thrills, and "flash." The essence of sport has been subordinated to entertainment. Even the desire for victory is no longer primary. This characteristic of sport is clearly illustrated in commercial focus of professional wrestling and roller derby. Here, the patent pecuniary interest of the promoters, the induced violence, and distorted humor preclude the appellation of sport. When the audience openly laughs at physical events such as these, it is clear that we have crossed the threshold from sport into parody.

Thus the dialectic within sport needs to be maintained in a delicate balance of tension. Throughout this book, we focus on aspects of play, informal, semiformal, and formal sport. These activities form a continuum with varying mixtures of related paradoxes of sport. Our analysis attempts to delineate these characteristics of sport and their consequences to the participants and interrelated social institutions. We provide our own critiques and analyses of these sport phenomena. Our personal values favor the increased opportunity for people of all ages and sexes to be actively involved in sport. We emphasize the importance of the intrinsic rewards that are associated with autotelic physical activities, yet we recognize the entertainment value of sport for spectators. We admit that the pageantry of sport spectacles is likely to be functional in providing social integration, and we would not deny to talented athletes the opportunity to seek the extrinsic prestige and financial rewards that go with big-time (formal) sport. But we urge the need for balance, lest social resources be diverted to formal and commercialized sport rather than participatory and lifetime sport for the majority of the society. Similarly, we decry the imbalance that goes with the tendency toward passive rather than active participation in sport. We challenge the reader to be aware of these complexities as we deal with the social ramifications of sport in the following chapters.

SOCIAL SCIENTIFIC STUDY OF SPORT

Because sport is a major phenomenon in modern society, one might speculate as to why it has only recently been approached as a legitimate area for study by social scientists.[1] Perhaps one answer to this question lies in the assumption that sport primarily meant physical rather than social interaction and was thus devoid of interest to social scientists. In an insightful essay entitled "The Interdependence of Sport and Culture," Günther Lüschen (1967) points out that even the most simple physical activities, such as walking, are social in nature. In a like manner, the more complex physical activities that are classified as sport involve greater suffusion from the social and cultural milieus. Another explanation for the late entry of social scientists into the analysis of sport may be that the world of sport is often perceived in terms of illusion and fantasy, as a sphere apart from the "real world" (Huizinga, 1938).

The philosopher Paul Weiss (1969) suggests that the relative neglect of sport by scholars is largely due to the dominant tradition in Western philosophical analysis as originally formulated by the Greeks and Aristotle in particular. Sport has been traditionally viewed as a lower form of culture and as not being reflective of the highest levels of human nature.

> Aristotle wrote brilliantly and extensively on logic, physics, biology, psychology, economics, politics, ethics, art, metaphysics, and rhetoric, but he says hardly a word about either history or religion, and nothing at all about sport. Since he was taken to be "the master of those who know" his position became paradigmatic for most of the thinkers who followed, even when they explicitly repudiated his particular claims. . . . The fact that these subjects are studied today by economists, psychologists, and sociologists has not yet sufficed to free them from many a philosopher's suspicion that they are low-grade subjects, not worthy of being pursued by men of large vision (p. 5).[2]

Dunning (1967) has argued that sociologists who define play and sport in terms of fantasy, and who are thus ambivalent about seriously studying the topic, may be reflecting a Protestant Ethic orientation that considers the study of play, games, sport, and leisure as frivolous and unbecoming of a "serious scientist." In response to these sentiments, Dunning emphasizes that "sports and games are 'real' in the sense they are observable, whether directly through overt behavior of

---

[1]For a more technical review of this topic, see Eldon E. Snyder and Elmer Spreitzer, "The Sociology of Sport: An Overview," *The Sociological Quarterly*, 15 (Autumn 1974): 467–87. For an analysis of the relationship between sociology and physical education, see E. D. Saunders, "Sociology, Sport and Physical Education," *Review of Sport and Leisure*, 1 (Fall 1976): 122–38. For an East European perspective, see Andrzej Wohl, "Conception and Range of Sport Sociology," *International Review of Sport Sociology*, 1 (1966): 5–15. We also suggest the readers consult the following sources: Jay J. Coakley, *Sport in Society*. Saint Louis: C. V. Mosby, 1982; D. Stanley Eitzen and George H. Sage, *Sociology of American Sport*, Dubuque: Wm. C. Brown, 1982; John W. Loy, Barry D. McPherson, and Gerald Kenyon, *Sport and Social Systems*, Reading, Ma.: Addison-Wesley, 1978; Günther Lüschen and George H. Sage (eds.), *Handbook of Social Science of Sport*, Champaign, Il.: Stipes, 1981; Wilbert H. Leonard II, *A Sociological Perspective of Sport*, Minneapolis: Burgess, 1980.

[2]From *Sport: A Philosophic Inquiry* by Paul Weiss. Copyright © 1969 by Southern Illinois University Press. Reprinted by permission of Southern Illinois University Press.

people or indirectly through the reports which players and spectators give of what they think and feel while playing and 'spectating' " (1971, p. 37).

There is an increasing realization that sport permeates and articulates with many other social institutions. Furthermore, sport is an important ingredient in people's lives. In the absence of scientific investigation, folk wisdom and assumptions have prevailed as "facts." These include ready-made words, statements, phrases, and slogans that trigger speech and behavior in a kind of stimulus–response fashion and thus by-pass cognitive thought and reflection (Zijderveld, 1979, pp. 12–13). Because sport has become so much a part of our everyday life, this segment of social life is especially vulnerable given the clichés and assumptions (see Table 1-2). Furthermore, as we noted previously, these assumptions are easily transferred as metaphors to other spheres of social life. In a sense, a double falsehood may be perpetrated if a falsehood as it applies to the sport world is transferred as "fact" to other spheres of behavior. Zijderveld (1979) argues that modern society is filled with conflicting norms and values, vagueness, and emotional and moral instability. Thus, our society is clichégenic in the sense that it promotes clichés that provide ready-made but artificial clarity, stability, and certainty.

TABLE 1-2 A Sample of Some Clichés from the World of Sport

It's a game of inches and seconds.	We are rebuilding.
He has all the moves.	We'll surprise a few teams.
He's a pure shooter.	We're a team of destiny.
He's a natural hitter.	We stayed too long with our game plan.
He plays without the ball.	They had the killer instinct.
He plays both ends of the court.	This is a class team.
He can really motor.	We lost the momentum with that play.
He's a blue chip athlete.	We'll take them one game at a time.
He hung the clothesline.	Our staff developed a good game plan.
When the bell rings, he's ready.	It was a team effort.
He's an inspirational leader.	We couldn't establish our passing game.
He came to play.	They wanted it more than we did.
He turned the game around.	We didn't put enough points on the board.
He's the most under-rated player in the league.	They were willing to pay the price.
He's a clutch player.	They put their pants on one leg at a time like we do.

In the world of sport these clichés are readily apparent; for example, one of the most frequently cited functions of sport is that it "builds character." This common assumption has been the theme of many speakers at athletic banquets. On closer investigation, we find that this "truth" is probably more accurately described as a half-truth. Another commonly held assumption is that athletic pursuits detract from academic concerns (resulting in the "dumb jock" stereotype). Research findings are also providing important qualifications to this assumption. The belief that sport provides a model of racial equality and a means for many blacks to become professional athletes is another unfounded assumption. Considerable data have been accumulated that, likewise, raise serious questions about this folk belief. Another commonly held stereotype is that female athletes are physical "Amazons" who tend to be more masculine than most females and are thus likely to suffer from a confusion of sex roles and self-concept. Once again, recent research has refuted these assumptions. Additional questions might be raised regarding the validity of other assumptions such as the following: Sport is a preparation for life; sports are a way to get ahead; the will to win is the will to work. Recent research has begun to raise questions about these assumptions. Scientific investigation moves beyond conjecture to test assumptions in a disciplined manner. New observations and findings about the world of sport frequently demonstrate that previously held perspectives of social reality were distorted.

Berger also argues that the sociological mentality necessarily involves a debunking motif. Regardless of the social scientist's personality, scholarly analysis frequently results in an unmasking of the world that has been taken for granted. This tendency is methodological and not psychological. "The sociological frame of reference, with its built-in procedure of looking for levels of reality other than those given in the official interpretations of society, carries with it a logical imperative to unmask the pretensions and the propaganda by which men cloak their actions with each other" (Berger, 1963, p. 38). The sociological question is not why something malfunctions from the point of view of officials and authorities. Rather, sociologists are more concerned with how a social system works in the first place—that is, in the norms, roles, and structures that hold something together.

Consequently, social scientists see through the facades of social systems and often discover many unofficial conceptions among the participants. In looking behind official definitions of social events, one discovers other layers of reality and latent levels of meaning that are masked in the course of everyday life. The "sociological perspective can then be understood in terms of such phrases as 'seeing through,' 'looking behind,' very much as such phrases would be employed in common speech—'seeing through his game,' 'looking behind the scenes,'—in other words 'being up on all the tricks'" (Berger, 1963, p. 30).

As professional sociologists, the authors of this book have been trained in the intellectual perspective described by Peter Berger. We hasten to add, however, that, as human beings, we value sport and physical activity. In fact, we are delighted that "our avocation and vocation are as one." Consequently, our sociological probes are not for purposes of exposé. They simply represent passionate inquiry from two members of the family of sport. Although we try our utmost to be objective in the appraisal of evidence concerning sport, we do not attempt to conceal our love for human movement in all its many nuances, forms, and textures.

Throughout the course of this book, we consciously note the scientific research that has exposed some of the myths surrounding sport and which in turn has provided more valid information about the world of sport. To question previously held "facts" and clichés is often the initial step in changing people's understandings and consciousness. This function of science provides an important service to humankind. It may, however, threaten those who are committed to (or have vested interests in) the commonly held assumptions and the status quo. While social change is almost always threatening to some people, we hope that this book will give its readers a greater understanding of reality in sport, as revealed by the present state of scientific investigation. A substantial literature is developing on the social and cultural aspects of sport, some of which is cumulative, and much of which goes beyond description toward explanation. We hope that our attempts to synthesize this literature will contribute to a more humane level of sport participation and enjoyment within our society.

Sociology as a discipline attempts to understand and explain social life in a systematic and scientific manner—that is, through controlled observation. As a social scientist, the sociologist of sport places heavy emphasis on the nature of *evidence*. In this framework he or she tries to rely on objective information and seeks to control personal proclivities and preferences. Such restraint pertains, however, only to the practice of sociology and not to the totality of one's life space. Although value judgments should not contaminate the collection and analysis of data, it is clear, nevertheless, that the sociologist makes a value judgment when he or she decides to study the world of sport in a scholarly framework, implicitly saying that sport is worthy of scholarly analysis (I choose to study this topic because it is subjectively interesting and, I hope, objectively significant).

It should also be noted that the social scientist is basically concerned with knowledge for its own sake. This posture might sound like dilettantism in a world where problems cry out for solution. However, nothing is ultimately as practical as a good theory. *Ad hoc* attempts to solve social problems commonly fail; sound policy flows from magnanimity coupled with understanding. Consequently, as sociologists, we are not apologetic about being preoccupied with theory. A good theory is a conceptual framework that orders the buzzing flow of sensations and experience into a meaningful whole. Thus, we suggest two additional clichés: "Theory is the mother of practice" and "Nothing is as practical as a good theory." Peter Berger (1963) offers a more secular response:

> We would say then that the sociologist . . . is a person intensively, endlessly, shamelessly interested in the doings of men. His natural habitat is all the human gathering places of the world, wherever men come together. The sociologist may be interested in many other things. But his consuming interest remains in the world of men, their institutions, their history, their passions. And since he is interested in men, nothing that men do can be altogether tedious for him. He will naturally be interested in the events that engage men's ultimate beliefs, their moments of tragedy and grandeur and ecstasy. But he will also be fascinated by the commonplace, the everyday. He will know reverence, but this reverence will not prevent him from wanting to see and to understand. He may sometimes feel revulsion or contempt. But this also will not deter him from wanting to have his questions answered. The sociologist, in his quest for understanding, moves through the world of men without respect for the usual lines of demarcation. Nobility and degradation, power and obscurity, intelligence and folly—these are equally interesting to him, however unequal they may be in his personal values or tastes. Thus his questions may lead him to all possible levels of society, the best and the least known places, the most respected and the most despised. And, if he is a good sociologist, he will find himself in all these places because his own questions have so taken possession of him that he has little choice but to seek for answers (pp. 18–19).[3]

POLICY IMPLICATIONS OF SPORT SOCIOLOGY

Although the field of sport sociology is young, we suggest that the research conducted so far by social scientists has implications for sport practitioners—athletes, coaches, athletic directors, physical educators, reporters and sports announcers, and parents. Unfortunately, much of the substance of sport sociology remains

[3]From *Invitation to Sociology* by Peter L. Berger. Copyright © 1963 by Peter L. Berger. Reprinted by permission of Doubleday & Company, Inc.

buried in academic tomes and erudite journals. Somehow this body of information must be diffused to practitioners in the field if it is to have any real-world impact.

Following Schafer (1971a), we also believe that there is a need for a more *applied* sociology of sport. Social scientists writing in the area of sport should increasingly include sport practitioners within the realm of their significant others. While knowledge for its own sake is defensible, the sociology of sport (like the discipline of economics) has an inherent thrust to the real world. If the policy implications of sport sociology are not brought out in the research of social scientists, this burgeoning field will die on the vine of academic trivia. Consequently, we heartily endorse Schafer's appeal to sport sociologists.

> We also need to play an even more direct, active, and useful part in helping create a more inclusive and humane program of sport in the school. In brief, we ought to help design, implement, and evaluate different models of sport and physical education as well as models of training physical education teachers and coaches. For instance, what would be the actual effects on later voluntary exercise habits of giving physical education credit for physical activity carried on outside school hours? What models of training would create the most tolerant and supportive coaches and physical education teachers? What would be the effects of different types of athletic clubs sponsored by the school?
>
> These are samples of the kinds of questions to which applied sociologists of sport could address themselves if they were to leap forth from the academic tower of irrelevance with its entangling and blinding vines of useless theorizing, and pedestrian descriptive studies into the open and fertile fields of practical, applicable research of a policy-related, experimental, or evaluative kind—still employing, to be sure, the best methods and logic available and still drawing upon the best theories of sociology and social psychology as a source of hypotheses and interpretations.
>
> We ought not be talking just with ourselves as we have been for the most part. We ought to be talking with educational and athletic policy-makers and practitioners who badly need the assistance we can provide as social scientists as they re-design old programs and design totally new ones and as they try to assess the impact of these programs on students. In this way, we may well be able to hasten the day when school sports not only contribute to "fitting in" and conformity but to developing aware, independent, self-worthy—in short, mature—young people (pp. 14–15).

CONCLUSION

In this chapter, we have emphasized the significance of sport as an area of social scientific study. Sport has emerged in the last half of the twentieth century to become one of the most pervasive social institutions in contemporary societies. The significance of sport is apparent in the time and money spent on participation and in the viewing of sport events. The symbolism of sport has spilled over into our everyday speech patterns and descriptive metaphors. Furthermore, sport serves the social psychological function of providing a sense of excitement, joy, and diversion to many people. Additionally, the centrality of sport is evident in the play of children, in our public schools, and in institutions of higher education.

The prominence of sports in the mass media is paralleled by increasing rates of active participation in sport on a lifelong leisure basis. The fashion industry is well aware of the trend toward the active life and has produced a wide array of designer clothes for upscale consumers. The increasing popularity of leisure sports is no doubt related to larger societal trends. In particular, the recent spurt in popularity of wilderness-related sports represents an intriguing phenomenon for sociological analysis. One is tempted to theorize that this trend represents a reaction to larger societal trends—increasing bureaucracy, urbanization, isolation from nature, congestion, and environmental deterioration. Wilson (1977) suggests that the interest in wilderness sports (some of these are not true sports as defined in Chapter 2) is a function of these societal trends and not a consequence of marketing and advertising by entrepreneurs for sports equipment and resorts.

> People who are engaged in sports such as backpacking, mountaineering, cross-country skiing, and bicycle touring were motivated by a desire to escape technological urban life and by a desire to attain a greater sense of self-awareness. The increasing participation in wilderness sports between 1965 and 1974 supports Reich's (1970) contention that a segment of American society was moving or had moved to a rejection of America's "immense apparatus of technology and organization." Reich may have overstated the degree to which people had forsaken the arch-typical rat-race life, but by focusing his attention on the "artificiality of work and culture" resulting from rampant technology and urbanization, he correctly identified a source of discontent for a significant number of Americans (pp. 58–59).

These theories represent interesting attempts to impose intellectual order on sport as an institution. Future research could well be directed to systematic tests of these provocative hypotheses. Such theories will be difficult to test, however, because the research design will ideally include time series data for both the societal trends (urbanization, industrialization, bureaucratization, and the like) and the measures of sport involvement. Moreover, most of these theories imply some type of sudden spurt in these societal processes (such as in increasing technology), whereas we tend to experience these large-scale trends as part of a gradual evolutionary process.

In recent years the social scientific study of sport has shed new light on this fascinating area of social life. This new line of research contains the potential not only for exposing some of the myths about the world of sport but also for contributing new insight and understanding of human social behavior. Finally, this insight and understanding can be useful to practitioners as they strive to design and administer wholesome sport programs.

CHAPTER 2
The Nature of Sport

TOWARD A DEFINITION

Everyone seems to know intuitively what sport is, but few attempt to define it. You would find little disagreement that physical activities such as soccer, rugby, golf, racquetball, track and field, handball, and tennis can be classified as sport, but is this also true of sailing, hunting and fishing, mountain climbing, hiking, and cockfighting? Furthermore, how does sport differ from play and games?

It is interesting to note that the term "sport" derives from the Middle English verb *sporten*, to divert (Webster's New Collegiate Dictionary, 1972). Etymologically, then, we see that sport is historically associated with a sense of "turning aside," "distraction"—amusement and giving of pleasure. Although etymology does help us to grasp the historical context of a given concept or term, it does not provide us with a true definition in the sense of genus and species. Some writers conceive of sport as an essentially undefinable process. In this context, Slusher (1967) attempts to define sport by analogy with religion.

> The parallel between religion and sport might not be so far-fetched as one might think. As a result of mystical commitments sport and religion open the way towards the acceptance and actualization of being. A partial answer is now uncovered to our obvious difficulty in *defining* sport. Basically, sport, like religion defies definition. In a manner it goes beyond definitive terminology. Neither has substance which can be identified. In a sense both sport and religion are beyond essence (p. 141).

Slusher's conception of sport is insightful from a phenomenological perspective. However, it does not provide the social scientist with workable analytical handles. Lüschen (1967, 1970, 1972) defines sport in a more operational manner as an institutionalized type of competitive physical activity located on a continuum between play and work. The specification of the activity as physical generally excludes more sedentary activities such as card playing. The competitive motif is another essential component of the definition. The agonistic or struggle aspect of sport is also generally considered as a defining characteristic.

> The concept of the "good strife" is implicit in the word competition, as derives from *cum* and *pedere*—literally, to strive with rather than against. The word contest has similar implications being derived from *con* and *testare*—to testify with another rather than against him (Methany, 1965, p. 40).
>
> A contest is a con-test, a testing or testifying with. This "with" includes and supplements an "against." A contest involves strife, conflict, and an effort to be victorious, but with others who acknowledge the same rules and grant one the right to be treated fairly (Weiss, 1969, p. 151).

Singer (1976) offers a set of definitions of sport, games, play, physical recreation, and physical education from the vantage point of a sport psychologist:

> *Sport* is a human activity that involves specific administrative organization and a historical background of rules which define the objective and limit the pattern of human behavior; it involves competition and/or challenge and a definite outcome primarily determined by physical skill.
>
> *Games* are activities with an agreed-on organization of time, space, and terrain, with rules that define the objective and limit the pattern of human behavior; the outcome, which is to determine a winner and a loser, is achieved by totaling or accumulating objectively scored points or successes.
>
> *Play* is an enjoyable experience deriving from behavior which is self-initiated in accordance with personal goals or expressive impulses; it tolerates all ranges of movement abilities; its rules are spontaneous; it has a temporal sequence but no predetermined ending; it results in no tangible outcome, victory, or reward (p. 40).

To summarize, we define sport as (1) a competitive, (2) human physical activity, (3) governed by institutionalized rules. With this definition in mind, it is clear that some activities can be classified as a sport under some conditions but not under others. For example, sailing is a form of recreation and pleasure that would be considered a sport when carried out as a regatta under competitive conditions and specified rules. Likewise, swimming is a form of play if it is engaged in primarily for exercise and pleasure, but it becomes a sport when it is a competitive activity in which the goal is to defeat an opponent and when it is regulated by specified rules governing a swimming meet. On the other hand, cockfighting and dog racing are competitive activities regulated by rules, but they do not involve human physical activity. Horse racing and auto racing are sports because the jockeys and drivers require considerable physical agility, stamina, and exertion, and because they are competitive activities that occur under conditions determined by institutionalized rules. We would not define games such as bridge and poker as sports because they are not primarily physical in nature, though they are competitive activities regulated by rules. Sports are games in which the physical dimension is primary.

INVOLVEMENT IN SPORT

It is also helpful to consider different types of involvement in sport. For example, athletes are actively and directly involved, while spectators are passively involved. Furthermore, athletic events generally include other individuals who are important in staging the contest (for example, administrators, coaches, officials, and scorekeepers; cf. Loy et al., 1978, pp. 16–18). There can also be additional levels or degrees of involvement, such as assistant and head coaches, and among the players, substitutes, starters, and stars.

In the preceding paragraph we have discussed differing forms of *behavioral involvement*, that is, people are engaged in sport by acting out the norms associated with the various positions embedded in sport contexts. If one is a coach, official, player, cheerleader, groundskeeper, or spectator, he or she is in some way behaviorally engaged in sport. The behavior may include such varied activities as playing, watching, reading, and talking about sport. A second way one may be engaged in sport is by acquiring information about the activity. *Cognitive involvement* refers to the degree of knowledge and facts one has about sport. In modern societies, the media provide a great deal of information about such activities as sport events, players' lives, batting averages, and team standings. While some people will not be aware of an ongoing World Series or Super Bowl Sunday, a sport trivia buff may have committed to memory highly detailed facts about sport events, players, and coaches. A third dimension, *affective involvement*, refers to the feeling, emotions, dispositions, and attitudes one has about sports. We usually expect that affective involvement will be reciprocally reinforced by behavioral and cognitive involvement. However, for purposes of analysis, these forms of involvement need to be differentiated. Thus, as Kenyon (1969) points out, "whether a person is overtly involved in sport at a given point in time is not a necessary condition for harboring certain feeling states or dispositions toward one or more manifestations of sport" (p. 80). Likewise, one need not be actively involved as a participant in sport to be knowledgeable about sport.

This distinction among three dimensions of sport involvement provides greater conceptual clarity and specificity. To appreciate the multidimensionality of the concept, we present the following items used in a research project to measure involvement in sport (Snyder and Spreitzer, 1973):

> *Behavioral involvement* was determined by the frequency of participating in sports, talking about sports, watching sports, reading the sports page, and subscribing to or reading sports magazines.
>
> *Affective involvement* was measured by responses to the following questionnaire items: "Sports are a way for me to relax," "Sports are a waste of time," and "I receive little satisfaction from sports." The last two items are negative indicators.
>
> *Cognitive involvement* was measured on a questionnaire by asking the respondents to match a twelve-item list of sports personalities with their appropriate athletic event.

THE STRUCTURE OF SPORT

Rules constitute the most obvious element of institutionalization in sport. In fact, rules are the sine qua non of games and sport in general. It is interesting to note that even very young children spontaneously generate rules as they make up new games. It is also apparent that the interaction of children's play produces mechanisms of social control in which the participants are obligated to negotiate and align their actions with one another according to the rules of the game (cf. Denzin, 1976). Youngsters are quick to express their anger when a playmate attempts to change the boundaries and framework of the rules to gain an advantage. The concept of fairness imposed by application of the rules equitably is frequently invoked in the tearful context of "Mom, Joey's cheating again!"

Weiss (1969) distinguishes two types of rules in the world of sport: The first type ties together the beginning and end of a particular game in the sense of specifying the conditions of achievement; the second type specifies the ideal norms for evaluation of performance. The players intuitively recognize that rules form the essential framework through which their skills can be expressed. The rules constitute the context within which the challenge is performed. Thus, sport is not spontaneous and open-ended, but shows us what a person can achieve within a standardized (institutionalized) set of constraints. Players' attitudes and stance toward the rules generally change as they become more skilled. If players continue their commitment to a sport, their application of the rules increases; that is, the rules become more formal, impersonal, and more rigidly enforced (Denzin, 1976). The rules represent limitations that facilitate equity, continuity, and the flow of the game, but rules also provide a benchmark against which individual performances can be evaluated and records established.

When a person chooses to participate in a given sport, he or she implicitly accepts the structure of that sport. There is an implicit act of compliance or conformity here that is perennially appealing to the socializing agents of society. The player "accepts the legal tools or objects connected with the sport—specific size of the ball, specific height of the net, etc. Along with the acceptance of the rules and the instruments he is allowed to use, he must accept the boundaries of his own body" (Neal, 1972, p. 107). Sport thus requires individuals to subordinate themselves, that is, submission to something larger in order to experience gratifications that otherwise could not be achieved. This transcendence constitutes a social order that is a prototype of everyday life in matters of authority, seriousness, legitimacy, rules, competition, cooperation, and common values (Denzin, 1976, p. 54).

The structure of rules constitutes a backdrop against which demonstrations of human excellence can be displayed. This manifestation of excellence represents the enduring appeal of sport to both the participants and the spectators.

> It is a great accomplishment to turn a body from a creature of vagrant stimuli, insistent appetites, and poorly focused objectives, into one which is taut and controlled, and directed toward a realizable excellent end. It is a great accomplishment to have made oneself willing to see how to deal well with the obstacles and challenges that one's body, other men, and nature provide. It is a great achievement to make oneself ready and willing to discover the limits beyond which men cannot go in a rule-governed, bodily adventure (Weiss, 1969, p. 84).

This structure of rules within which one tests oneself against others with similar constraints no doubt explains why sport has long been considered good preparation for the larger game of life and why even parents with no manifest interest in sport still encourage their children to participate. In this sense, then, sport is commonly viewed as a microcosm or mirror of the larger society. The assertion that the Battle of Waterloo was won on the playing fields of Eton comes down to us as a verity and not as satire.

INDETERMINACY OF SPORT

The inherent lack of predictability in the outcome of competitive situations constitutes another aspect of the enduring appeal of sport. Coaches and athletes attempt to convert all chance factors into causal variables, but nevertheless a residue of chance or luck always remains. The complexity of sport guarantees that all variables can never by brought completely under control, and this nonrational element represents one of the charms of sport.

> Elusive qualities pop up everywhere that evade reason, and this raises so many questions that may not have an answer, or that may not have an answer that we can pin down because of our ignorance of the human being. Why did Vince Lombardi get more out of his team? Why does sport make some, and break others? Why is it that when an individual feels the best, he sometimes has his worst performance, or vice versa? Why do some players play better under pressure than others? (Neal, 1972, p. 69).

It is the element of chance that offers hope to the participant as well as the spectator. Regardless of the degree of planning, scouting, research, practice, and even spying on the other team's practice, the element of chance remains central to sport. The language of sport contains many clichés to cover the chance dimension—"a game of inches," "when these two teams meet you can throw out the record book," "the ball takes funny bounces," a "toss-up," "whoever makes the fewest errors," "loss of momentum," "they wanted it more than we did," "homecourt advantage," "fan support," and many other explanations.

Elias and Dunning (1970) have noted that the indeterminacy of sport provides the tension and excitement necessary for the survival of a game or sport. Even the rules of games and sports are designed to maintain that tension and excitement by providing some equality between the contestants. If one team has little or no chance of defeating their opponent, there is no contest and boredom soon sets in. Thus in sports we have handicaps in the form of age, height, and weight classifications to maintain some equality and indeterminacy in the outcome of the contest. Rules also are used to reduce the likelihood of unfair tactics and undue advantages by one team over another.

In basketball, for example, with the advent of the "big man" in the 1950s, the widening of the free throw lane and the three-second rule reduced the undue advantage of the team with a tall player, such as Wilt Chamberlain. In baseball, the "spit ball" has been ruled illegal because it presumably gave the pitcher too much advantage over the batters. Furthermore, in any sport when a team is caught using an illegal strategy, they will be penalized in such a way that the offended team is given a temporary advantage and an opportunity to make up the loss they suffered by the illegal tactics. The indeterminacy of sport contests is also an important ingredient in the financial structure of individual professional teams as well as league rules. Thus, institutional arrangements such as player drafts that give priority choices to last place teams in the leagues are partially designed to maintain a competitive parity among the teams in a league (Noll, 1974).

The indeterminacy of sport is a paradox in the sport context in which the primary objective of the participants is to win the contest. Thus, there is frequently an attempt to reduce the chance factor. When all the chance factors cannot be brought under human control, magic and superstition are commonly invoked as coping mechanisms (Gregory and Petrie, 1975). Attempts to cajole Lady Luck are produced by the strong personal involvement of the participants, the high stakes, the climactic nature of sport (sudden turns of events), and the strong aspect of contingency (Weiss, 1969). Thus athletes attempt to reproduce a successful performance by such strategems as eating the same meal, driving the same route to the stadium, wearing the same clothes, and using the same warmup ritual. The greater the uncertainty of a situation, the more likely that players will resort to magic (see Chapter 16).

In sport as well as in everyday life, indeterminacy, uncertainties and ambiguities are manifold; people demonstrate incompetence, or chance factors prevail, and they are unable to meet prescribed standards and goals, that is, to win. In an athletic contest, for every winner there is a loser; yet the generalized expectation by the fan is that their team should win. Under these conditions, social interaction is threatened, and people must jointly interpret and smooth out the discrepancies while developing a new consensus. In this manner, social interaction is repaired, identities that are threatened by the inadequacy are restored, and bridges are built across the gaps between social ideals and actions that fail to achieve these ideals (Scott and Lyman, 1968; Stokes and Hewitt, 1976). Thus, in situations of misalignment in which people recognize that their actions or those of others are "out of line," aligning actions represent attempts to repair these failures and discrepancies and facilitate continued social interaction. In short, aligning actions represent the social process of "patching up" potential or actual ruptures in social relationships.

Two forms of aligning actions are frequently apparent within the sport context—disclaimers and accounts. A *disclaimer* is a verbal device used "in advance of an action that the person thinks may discredit him or her in the eyes of others" (Stokes and Hewitt, 1976, p. 845). Thus a disclaimer is used to discount behavior prior to its enactment and to create an interpretation "of potentially problematic events intended to make them unproblematic when they occur" (Hewitt and Stokes, 1975, p. 2). *Accounts*, on the other hand, are linguistic devices employed after a breach of norms has occurred wherein the perpetrator attempts to account for his or her action. Scott and Lyman (1968) define an account as "a statement made by a social actor to explain unanticipated or untoward behavior—whether that behavior is his own or that of others, and whether the proximate cause for the statement arises from the actor himself or from someone else" (p. 46). There are two types of accounts—excuses and justifications. One or both may be used when behavior fails to meet expectations and is evaluated as undesirable. Excuses are accounts wherein one admits the act in question is bad, wrong, or inappropriate but denies full responsibility. Justifications, on the other hand, are verbal accounts whereby the actor admits responsibility for the act but attempts to justify the behavior by redefining it as positive rather than negative (Scott and Lyman, 1968, pp. 47–51).

It is evident that aligning actions are social in nature; they are verbal attempts to provide new social meanings and redefinitions to behavior that is initially questionable and problematic. It should be emphasized, furthermore, that aligning actions are not always honored by the other party or parties. If disclaimers or accounts are rejected, the social interaction is likely to be broken off; on the other hand, an acceptance of the alignment action will result in a restoration and continuation of the social interchange (Scott and Lyman, 1968, p. 52; Hewitt and Stokes, 1975, p. 6).

When we examine the verbal and written reports in sport we find the disclaimers and accounts presented in a variety of stylized idioms. Table 2-1 provides some well-worn expressions that are examples of aligning actions from the world of sports. Some of these expressions are used both as disclaimers and as accounts.

TABLE 2-1 Frequent Expressions of Aligning Action in Sport Contexts

DISCLAIMERS (BEFORE THE FACT)	ACCOUNTS (AFTER THE FACT)	
	EXCUSES	JUSTIFICATIONS
"We have too many injured players."	"They were lucky."	"We played so well it's a shame we lost."
"We are definitely the underdogs."	"That's the way the ball bounces."	"Even though we lost we demonstrated a lot of character."
"You can't run a zoo without the animals."	"The game was poorly officiated."	"We made a great come-back but just ran out of time."
"We are still a year away from being a good team."	"We were robbed."	"Even though we lost I'm proud of this team."
"This is a rebuilding year."	"I guess we're not living right."	"We showed a lot of heart."
"Our opponents have great talent and they do so many things well."	"They (opponents) got hot."	"They just wore us down."
"We need time to build our program."	"It's a game of inches."	"It's a shame either team had to lose."
"Although we don't promise a lot of victories this year, the fans will see an exciting brand of ball."	"The wind (or other climatic variable) was bothering our passing and kicking game in the fourth quarter."	"This team showed a lot of class."
	"We had an unlucky tournament drawing."	
	"When you are playing with so many freshman and sophomores, you have to pray a lot."	
	"I guess it (winning) just wasn't meant to be."	

Notice that the emphasis of the disclaimers in Table 2-1 is an attempt to provide explanations of why the players will have a difficult time defeating their opponents. Thus, the audience is being prepared for a possible failure. The accounts on the other hand, are an *ex post facto* restructuring of performances. The excuses appeal to the uncontrollable element of the outcome (e.g., luck, the weather, the equipment, the supernatural, or the officials), while justifications demonstrate an attempt to focus on the redeeming qualities of the loss. For example, in spite of the failure to win the players demonstrated courage, high performance, pride, or were playing well when they ran out of time or energy.

The examples cited in Table 2-1 refer to the context of group sports. It should be noted that disclaimers and accounts are also very evident in individual sports, even at the leisure–recreational level. Tennis and golf are particularly fertile areas for aligning mechanisms:

> "I'm just a duffer."
> "Haven't played for five years."
> "These are my wife's clubs."
> "I could use this racquet for a fish net."
> "I just like to play to get outdoors."
> "I don't get hung up on keeping my score."
> "I'm really out of shape."

We noted that a disclaimer or account is not always honored; this fact represents another dimension of indeterminacy in sport. If it is honored by those to whom it was directed (fans, owners, alumni, etc.) an equilibrium is restored to the relationship (Scott and Lyman, 1968, p. 52). These aligning actions may also be thought of as a form of impression management. If the coach or players are not fulfilling their responsibility by their performances, their identities as coaches and/or players are threatened, and thus they might try to integrate the incongruous elements of the situation and save face through some aligning actions. For aligning actions to be honored they must have credibility; the frequent use of excuses and justifications will eventually lose their impact and credibility with continued losses. Although aligning actions are often considered distorted interpretations of reality, they may in fact be accurate and valid explanations (for example, a team may indeed face a difficult game and lose because of a number of serious injuries). Furthermore, coaches and players may openly admit to failures without invoking an alignment mechanism. We suggest that aligning mechanisms are most evident in sports in which the indeterminacy of the outcome is high and there are extreme pressures for a successful performance, for example, major university sports such as football and basketball.

THE DUALISM OF SPORT

In addition to the tension, excitement, and mechanisms for coping with indeterminacy, sport also involves dualisms, paradoxes, and ironies that are sometimes expressed in terms of the agony and the ecstasy, the beauty and the beast, or the angel and the devil. Sport is filled with both violence and tenderness, joy and despair, beauty and repulsiveness, order and disorder. The ecstasy of the peak experience must be accepted with the awareness that sooner or later one will also be the loser. Cheers are inevitably followed by boos, the sweet wine of victory by the gall of defeat.

Sport also includes a strong element of paradox that helps to explain why all social classes are attracted to it. "The hard is made soft and soft appears hard. The athlete is both tough and tender, free and other-directed, fated and free-willed, personally concerned and other-interested" (Slusher, 1967, p. 108). This sense of dualism and paradox is perhaps most evident in hockey in which the aesthetics of graceful skating and play-making are coupled with the violence of the board check. It should be noted in this context that recent outcries against violence in hockey and the cheap shot in football suggest that the balance of this dualism is tilting toward the side of the beast. How much of the current popularity of hockey and football is due to their manifest violence is not easily answered when one also considers that racquet sports are becoming the most popular participatory sports in the United States.

These dualisms of sport are often expressed in irony (Snyder and Spreitzer, 1980). The third edition of *Webster's International Dictionary* (unabridged) defines irony as "a state of affairs or elements that is the reverse of what was or was to be expected." The ironic perspective basically involves a sense that things are not the way they are commonly thought to be. While not necessarily involving a debunking motif, the ironic sense focuses on reality as multilayered and many-splintered. Thus, in sport we often find that irony and paradox prevail where the dualisms result in marked incongruity and seemingly contradictory qualities. The sociologist Lewis Schneider (1975) has suggested the ironic perspective as a means of looking at the latent aspects (that is, unintended consequences) of social behavior that are often contradictory to the manifest forms of social life. For example, in a medical context, drugs used to cure and relieve pain may have the ironic latent and unintended consequence of creating a pathological addiction. The surgical knife ("the healing knife") may, ironically, cut too deep and inadvertently destroy healthy tissues. It is also ironic (and surprising) that our "correctional institutions" may be "corruption institutions" where criminal behavior is learned. In the realm of sport we find irony in the manner in which the emphasis on winning may promote cheating and illegal use of drugs. Similarly, the manifest function of "building character" in sports may be corrupted by practices of illegal recruiting of athletes. The ironic perspective is also evident in a later section of the chapter that focuses on the dualisms of the intrinsic and extrinsic dimensions of sport. A note of ironic pathos is present when we find that the emphasis on developing skill and excellence in athletic performance may reduce the spontaneity, fun, and joy of sport.

Nevertheless, one still frequently hears prominent persons and after-dinner speakers who defend sport against the slings and arrows of its many critics by giving testimony as to how one was born again through sport or at least saved from going astray as a youth. In reverential tones such speakers explain how sport participation insulated them against negative peer influence. No doubt sport serves this function for many; we address this topic in more detail in Chapter 6 as part of an analysis of the consequences of sport participation. In this context, one is reminded of the *bon mot* offered by a proprietor of a bowling alley to a community committee concerned with delinquency: "We need to get our youth off the streets and into the alleys!"

SPORT AS THEATRE

As pointed out by Elias and Dunning (1970), Aristotle's theory of the theatre, formulated about the year 350 B.C., has explanatory value for the sport sociologist. Writing about tragedy as a genre of literature, Aristotle suggested that this form of theatre has a salutary effect on the audience because of the resultant catharsis—a process by which pity and fear effect a purging of the emotions. The fear element involves an impending danger; the component of pity refers to our empathetic identification with the main characters and consequent sense of danger.

Aristotle did not see this process of catharsis as an escapist or opiate experience (Bate, 1952). Tragedy on the stage deliberately excites the human emotions of pity and fear in order to effect a higher order purgation. Whereas Plato had criticized literature for nurturing the emotional juices, Aristotle posited that it was unhealthy to starve the emotions. The catharsis burns off the accumulated turbulence and morbidity with a resulting uplift and purification of the spirit into a harmonious serenity. In this manner, egoism and self-centered subjectivity are purged through a sympathetic identification outward with others. Thus, an enlargement of the spirit through sympathy occurs with feeling united to insight.

Aristotle also noted that tragic theatre appeals to our instinct for harmony in the form of "an ordered and proportioned regularity of structure, interrelated through 'the law of probability and necessity'" (Bate, 1952, p. 18). The audience is transported and incorporated into the development and unravelling of the drama.

> Every tragedy falls into two parts—complication and unravelling or *dénouement*. Incidents extraneous to the action are frequently combined with a portion of the action proper, to form the complication; the rest is the unravelling. By the complication I mean all that extends from the beginning of the action to the part which marks the turning-point to good or bad fortune. The unravelling is that which extends from the beginning of the change to the end (Aristotle in Bate, 1952, p. 30).

Aristotle's line of reasoning concerning the psychology of the theatre helps to explain the appeal of sport. More specifically, within a sports contest the development of tension accompanied by a climax represents a type of denouement or resolution resulting from a definitive outcome which is in marked contrast with the indeterminacy of other domains of human experience. Gregory Stone's (1973) observations concerning the sports page are interesting in this connection:

> We suspect, for example, that the sport pages in the daily newspaper are important for many consumers primarily because they provide some confirmation that there is a continuity in the events and affairs of the larger society. A certain reassurance may be gained from following sporting news that is not possible from following current events, the continuity of which is not readily discernible for many readers. . . . In addition to imposing order upon the vicissitudes of the larger uncertain social scene, the consumption of sports may have the latent function of bringing continuity into the personal lives of many Americans. Team loyalties formed in adolescence and maintained through adulthood may serve to remind one, in a nostalgic way, that there are areas of comfortable stability in life—that some things have permanence amid the harassing interruptions and discontinuous transitions of daily experience (p. 73).

In a similar vein, Elias and Dunning (1970) argue that sport in contemporary life represents a quest for excitement in unexciting societies. Their reasoning is that in urban industrial societies social life requires a large degree of discipline and circumspection, that the range for approved expression of emotion is severely constrained in comparison to preindustrial societies.

> For many people it is not only in their occupational but also in their private lives that one day is the same as another. For many of them, nothing new, nothing stirring ever

> happens. Their tension, their tonus, their vitality, or whatever one might call it is thus lowered. In a simple or a complex form, on a low or high level, leisure time activities provide, for a short while, the upsurge of strong pleasurable feelings which is often lacking in ordinary routines of life. Their function is not simply as is often believed, a liberation from tensions, but the restoration of that measure of tension which is an essential ingredient of mental health. The essential character of their cathartic effect is the restoration of a normal mental "tonus" through a temporary and transient upsurge of a pleasurable excitement (p. 50).

Elias and Dunning note that sports such as football and soccer contain a particularly strong element of the pleasurable excitement that produces a catharsis. They also suggest that this creative tension could be measured across various sporting events by taking physiological measures on the spectators to record changes in pulse rate, heartbeat, and respiration vis à vis the peaks and valleys in the excitement of a contest.

THE INTRINSIC DIMENSION OF SPORT

The pragmatic emphasis within American culture leads one to think of sport in terms of its consequences and benefits for the individual as well as society. This tendency to instrumentalize sport partly accounts for the fact that relatively few adults remain active participants in sport and for the general belief that sport is organically linked with the earlier stages of the life cycle. If sport is primarily a training medium for the larger game of life, then it is clear why most adults cease being active participants.

The preoccupation of the American culture with productivity and performance has caused many to focus on sport as a product rather than as a process. It is interesting to note in this connection that the term *amateur* comes from the Latin word for "lover." Thus, we see that the nonprofessional participant is one who plays for intrinsic rewards, as an end in itself. "I am sure that of the countless millions who compete, only a small percentage are *aware* of the lifeline that one can come into contact with, and that gives one a chance for open and boundless joy. There is no other word to describe it. It is joy in the purest sense . . . the fluidity of movement, the instant reactions under stress, the sense of control over body and wind, the creativeness of *being*" (Neal, 1972, p. 3).

Neal (1972) points out a spiritual element of intrinsic motivation as it emerges in the world of sport:

> Call it a mystical dimension, or a religious experience, or anything you like. But it's *there*. One *explores* the self and the world and its surroundings in a way that cannot be explained or rationalized. One is *aware* of things that one cannot explain. One *understands* things that he cannot describe . . . about himself, about the world. One participates without knowing *why* at times. One plays because one *must*, whether one has the answers or not (p. 57).

Behavior is generally considered to be intrinsically motivated when there are no apparent external rewards. Deci (1975) distinguishes two types of intrinsically motivated behaviors. "The [first] class is behavior that people engage in to seek out optimally challenging situations. These challenges can be thought of as involving an incongruity, or discrepancy, between a stimulus input and some standard of comparison. The second class is behavior that aims to conquer the challenge or reduce the incongruity" (p. 131). The human being is thus continually seeking out and conquering challenges, especially those persons who have reached the later stages of self-actualization.

Psychologists have yet to determine what the optimal level of challenge and incongruity is in terms of facilitating intrinsic motivation. It is clear that there are marked individual differences in the level of tolerance for challenge and incongruity. However, it is generally agreed that the human being needs to receive periodic reinforcement (reward in the form of success) in the realm of sport. Otherwise the response (participation) is likely to be extinguished. This psychological principle has strong implications for parents and the teachers of physical education. One frequently hears people tell how they were turned off to sport by a parent or teacher who was preoccupied with absolute rather than relative level of performance in the sense of tailoring one's expectation to the child's actual skill level.

We emphasize, then, that the core of intrinsic motivation is the person's need to feel competent and self-determining (Deci, 1975). If parental behavior, the curriculum of physical education, and sport do not permit the young person to experience a "taste of honey" within the realm of physical performance, then almost certainly such a youngster will seek other avenues of reinforcement. Here it is relevant to ask whether the ambience of Little League competition militates against intrinsic motivation. It seems clear that the emphasis in Little League competition or other sports on absolute standards of excellence—batting average, goals scored, free throw percentage—is calculated to restrict the joys of success (cf. Yablonsky and Brower, 1979).

In this context, it is relevant to point out that, under certain circumstances, behavior that was originally intrinsically motivated can become less attractive when it receives extrinsic rewards. In other words, if a person who initially engages in an activity as an end in itself begins to receive extrinsic rewards for the same activity, then the original intrinsic motivation tends to decrease (cf. Deci, 1972). This psychological principle also has important implications for parents and teachers. When teaching a skill, the emphasis should be placed on the internal satisfaction from a well-executed movement rather than primarily on praise, criticism, or some external reward.

The following story illustrates how extrinsic rewards can come to displace intrinsic rewards and thus demotivate individuals toward activity that was at one time engaged in just for the fun of it.

> [An] old man lived alone on a street where boys played noisily every afternoon. One day the din became too much, and he called the boys into his house. He told them he liked to listen to them play, but his hearing was failing and he could no longer hear their games. He asked them to come around each day and play noisily in front of his house. If they did, he would give them each a quarter. The youngsters raced back the following day and made a tremendous racket in front of the house. The old man paid them, and asked them to return the next day. Again they made noise, and again the old man paid them for it. But this time he gave each boy only 20 cents, explaining that he was running out of money. On the following day, they got only 15 cents each. Furthermore, the old man told them, he would have to reduce the fee to 5 cents on the

> 4th day. The boys became angry, and told the old man they would not be back. It was not worth the effort, they said, to make a noise for only 5 cents a day (Casady, 1974, p. 5).[1]

The intrinsic dimension of sport might be incorporated with activities that are defined as autotelic (from the Greek: *auto*-self, *telos*-goal). Mihaly Csikszentmihalyi (1975) has reported an interesting study of people seriously involved with autotelic activities. He interviewed people who were involved in such disparate activities that yielded minimum rewards of a conventional nature but had manifold intrinsic satisfaction such as rock climbing, composing, dancing, chess, and college-level hockey and soccer. The interview essentially asked the participants why they had chosen their particular activity and what they received from it.

The study showed that these people devoted large amounts of energy to activities that yielded minimum rewards of a conventional nature but had obvious intrinsic rewards. The research revealed a passionate type of involvement with the activity, a sense of constant challenge, absence of boredom or worry, and relatively immediate feedback concerning performance. Csikszentmihalyi (1975) uses the term "flow" to describe this intense experience of intrinsic enjoyment.

> From here on, we shall refer to this peculiar dynamic state—the holistic sensation that people feel when they act with total involvement—as flow. In the flow state, action follows upon action according to an internal logic that seems to need no conscious intervention by the actor. He experiences it as a unified flowing from one moment to the next, in which he is in control of his actions, and in which there is little distinction between self and environment, between stimulus and response, or between past, present, and future. Flow is what we have been calling "the autotelic experience." . . . Later we shall see that one of the main traits of flow experiences is that they usually are, to a lesser or greater extent, autotelic—that is, people seek flow primarily for itself, not for the incidental extrinsic rewards that may accrue from it. Yet one may experience flow in any activity, even in some activities that seem least designed to give enjoyment—on the battle-front, on a factory assembly line, or in a concentration camp (p. 36).

Many writers have noted the ecstatic element in sport in the root sense of the term—to stand outside of oneself, a sense of rapture.

> That evening, when I shot my free-throws in the finals, I was probably the calmest I had ever been in my life. I didn't even see or hear the crowd. It was only me, the ball, and the basket. The number of baskets I made really had no sense of importance to me at the time. The only thing that really mattered was what I *felt*. But even so, I would have found it hard to miss even if I had wanted to. My motions were beyond my conscious control. . . . The ball and I *had* to react in a certain way. . . . I was carried along by a force of the momentum of *whatever* I was at that time (Neal, 1972, p. 168).

---

[1]Reprinted by permission of *Psychology Today* Magazine. Copyright © 1974 by Ziff-Davis Publishing Company. From "The Tricky Business of Giving Rewards" by Margie Casady.

Slusher (1967) speaks of these peak experiences in sport in a similar vein:

> Sport leads man in a kind of mystical relationship with the forces that compose and challenge him. Like the mountain climber, most men cannot tell you *why* they partake of the experience when "on the ground" but one *does* know once he is on top of the mountain (p. 56).

The integrative psychic function of sport is also frequently noted:

> To be in sport is more than the abstraction of self-fulfillment. In a sense it is release from all earthly holds. It is the exhilarating feeling of knowing that the experience is holistic. It is the complete act (Slusher, 1967, p. 22).

THE EXTRINSIC DIMENSION OF SPORT

It is clear that our discussion of the intrinsic dimension of sport is somewhat poetic and idealistic in tone. No doubt this analysis is applicable to selected amateurs ("lovers") in sport such as long-distance runners, cross-country skiers, and figure skaters. But can we talk about the autotelic nature of sport in the commercialized segment of sport—Ohio State and Michigan, the NCAA finals, the Rose Bowl, Monday Night Football, and other species of mass entertainment?

It is obviously necessary to consider the extrinsic and worklike dimensions of sport if we are talking about the real world. Various writers have used a continuum—gradations between two polar opposites—as a means of conceptualizing sport. Edwards (1973b), for example, analyzes sport as the polar opposite of play. In his conceptualization, play shades off into sport as the following transformations occur:

1. When the physical activity becomes less subject to individual discretion and spontaneity is accordingly decreased.
2. When explicit rules, roles, and regulations become central to the physical activity.
3. When the physical activity is not separated from the routine of daily life.
4. When the individual's accountability for his or her quality of performance in the physical activity is emphasized.
5. When the outcome of the activity (victory) extends beyond the participants in the physical activity.
6. When the motivation for participation becomes more extrinsic and affected by social expectations.
7. When the physical activity comes to consume greater amounts of the individual's time and energy because of the seriousness of the activity—that is, when the participant begins to lose control over the activity's flow.
8. When the physical and mental demands of the activity come to exceed simple leisure and recreational proportions.

Utilizing these dimensions, Edwards defines sport as

> activities having formally recorded histories and traditions, stressing physical exertion through competition within limits set in explicit and formal rules governing role and

> position relationships, and carried out by actors who represent or who are part of formally organized associations having the goal of achieving valued tangibles or intangibles through defeating opposing groups (pp. 57–58).

By contrast, play is the polar opposite of sport and might be characterized as follows:

1. The activity is subject to individual perogative and is spontaneous in terms of starting and finishing.
2. There are usually no formal rules, roles, or hierarchy of positions.
3. The activity is separated from the rigors and pressures of daily life.
4. There is no objective measure of individual liability and responsibilities during the activity.
5. The relevance of the activity outcome is restricted to the boundaries of the activity, exclusive of influences outside the content of the act.
6. The activity goals are intrinsic, autotelic, and nonutilitarian in product.
7. The activity is nonserious and is high in fantasy and make-believe ("let's pretend").
8. The activity is initiated and terminated at will with physical and mental exertion determined only by the intrinsic satisfactions of the act.

Having differentiated play from sport, we focus our attention on play and sport and the range of physical activities that can be distributed along the continuum. Admittedly, play and sport as they have been conceptualized are ideal types. Many activities will not be "pure play" or "pure sport." Consequently, a play–sport continuum is helpful as an analytical tool:

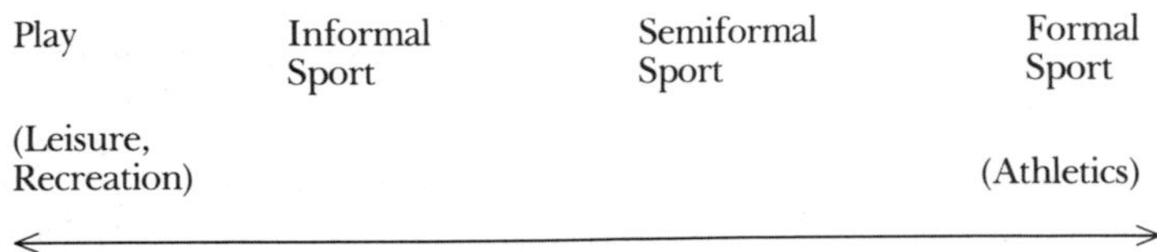

Indeed, many physical activities demonstrate characteristics of both play and sport. For example, in intramural basketball, the performance is not spontaneous because rules, roles, and responsibilities are involved. Yet the formalization of these constraints is more subject to the prerogative of the individual than if one is a member of the school varsity basketball team, and thus it represents an informal sport. Likewise, many adult physical activities are in the nature of informal or semiformal sport. Perhaps, for adults, the term "leisure-sport" would be more appropriate. To play tennis with a friend on Sunday afternoon constitutes a mixture of play (leisure) and sport characteristics in contrast to the varsity tennis player competing in the NCAA championships (formal sport). Eitzen and Sage (1978) use a similar trichotomy for differentiating the levels of sport; they label these levels as informal sport, organized sport, and corporate sport.

It is clear that sport also shades off into a species of work for many participants in big-time collegiate athletics and, of course, for the professional athlete. It is interesting, however, that even in the situation in which athletics become an explicit occupation, the intrinsic and autotelic nature of sport may overlay the extrinsic core. Professional athletes continue to report peak experiences, moments of rapture, and quasi-mystical experiences as part of their work. Perhaps big-time collegiate athletics represent the tipping point on the scale at which the mix between the intrinsic and extrinsic dimensions of sport shifts to the side of the extrinsic. But even this tipping point varies according to the orientation of the individual athlete. Consequently, it is not easy to make generalizations concerning the motivation of athletes. The reader is referred to such popular works as Jim Bouton's *Ball Four* and Dave Meggyssey's *Out of Their League* for colorful descriptions of the mixture of play and work in professional athletics.

The philosopher Michael Novak (1976) argues that the world of sport must be analyzed as an autonomous, immanent sphere of experience, and not as instrumental to extraneous objectives. The Puritan tradition in American culture makes us suspicious of play, and thus we tend to look for ways to rationalize play, games, and leisure—such as restoring our vital energy for the real world of work. In contrast to this pragmatic position, Novak argues that "sports are lovely for their own sake. We should not be naive about how much of their value is transferable to the rest of life" (p. 206).

Novak is also critical of Marxist critics of sport such as Paul Hoch (1972), who reason that sport serves a retrograde function. "Hoch speaks of sports as an opiate. He has it wrong: sports are the real thing. Work is the opiate—work and revolution and politics. Those are the drugs for killing time, making a living, acquiring power, place, and possessions. Sports lie in a different realm altogether, a freer realm, a realm of ends, a point at which time, compressed and self-contained and instantaneous, is transmitted into eternity" (pp. 206–7).

Novak's view of sport is filled with the intrinsic dimension and is near the play end of the continuum. Thus, it is interesting to note that he feels the meaning of sport is violated when one considers it only from an instrumental perspective, as the pause that refreshes or as preparation for the larger game of life:

> Tony Schwartz, author of *The Responsive Chord*, has a piquant phrase that may be used in rebuttal: "Don't should on me!" Play lies outside the realm of *shoulds* and *musts*. Play is an expressive activity. It flows. It reveals outwardly the inner energies of the human being. One doesn't play *because* it is good to play. The natural activity of human beings *is* play. Play is good in itself. The proper category for play is not moral but natural. Play is a pagan part of the human beast, our natural expressiveness. It flows from inner and perennial energies, and needs no justification (p. 219).[2]

CONCLUSION

Sport is primarily a competitive physical activity performed within the structure of prescribed rules. The sport framework provides a backdrop against which skills can be displayed and through which the quality of performance can be evaluated in a relatively objective manner. Participation in sport may take several forms, and

---

[2]From *The Joy of Sports: End Zones, Bases, Baskets, Ball, and the Consecration of the American Spirit* by Michael Novak. © 1976 by Michael Novak. Reprinted by permission of Basic Books, Inc., Publishers, New York.

it can be partitioned into degrees and forms of involvement, for example, the behavioral, affective, and cognitive dimensions. The inherent elements of indeterminacy, dualism, and irony constitute a perennial source of tension, stress, and appeal to participants and spectators. The latent complexity of sport seems to be isomorphic to human nature and the social order, which may account for the universality of play and sport in human societies.

While the structure of sport provides predictability and definitiveness, the informal and autotelic forms of sport behavior appeal to the aesthetic and joyful elements. On the other hand, sport behavior that is more organized and formalized manifests many of the characteristics of work in the sense that it becomes less spontaneous and discretionary and more governed by extrinsic considerations. In subsequent chapters, we analyze the consequences of extrinsic criteria as they function to screen a large proportion of the population out of physical activity as a lifelong form of leisure behavior. As the product motive comes to dominate the process dimensions of sport involvement, more and more individuals are channeled into the role of spectator and fan—that is, into vicarious experience in the world of sport. Yet we are also intrigued by the social and psychological "payoffs" accrued by the skilled and professional athlete; the scientific investigation of sport should proceed on several fronts.

CHAPTER 3
Sport and Social Values

Prologue

In World War II the attacking Japanese troops thought they knew what Americans held most dear. They made their Banzai attacks not only with weapons but with shouted invectives meant to demoralize. One of those cries was, "To hell with Babe Ruth!" So far as I know they did not defame the religions of America, vilify our economic system, or condemn motherhood. Instead, they selected a sports hero as representative of what Americans held in highest esteem.

It is doubtful that the battlefield shout, "To hell with Babe Ruth," created more than mild amusement to the American troops, for in the time of national peril, concern for basic rights and freedom was predominant. But to Japanese intelligence officers, the great amount of sports enthusiasm in the United States had led them to the conviction that this is what Americans loved most.

Not long ago, while on a visit to this nation, a European economist was strangely puzzled. Aware of America's proclamations to the world about the vigor of its commitment to the capitalistic economic system, he searched in vain for a financial section in the local newspapers. An American informant could easily have directed him to it, for in many newspapers it is, in deference to American reading practices, fastened to the end of the horse racing results at the back of the sports section. The priority, so casually accepted by Americans, can be puzzling for visitors (Beisser, 1967, p. 1).

SPORT AS A REFLECTION AND TRANSMITTER OF VALUES

Sport has emerged in modern society as an institution with patterned relationships that disseminate and transmit social values. By values we mean those ideals that are worth striving for (Kneller, 1965, p. 115). Values serve to provide social criteria for assessing what is desirable and are reflected in the normative expectations of a specific situation. Both the social values and the specific norms applicable to the situation are transmitted to individuals through the socialization process within the various social institutions—family, school, church, and sport. Values provide motivation for action.

Although the values of a society tend to persist over a period of time, they are also affected by periods of rapid social change. Furthermore, diverse groups within a society (for example, socioeconomic, ethnic, religious, and sexual) may adhere to different values. Thus, in modern heterogeneous societies, we frequently find dominant or core values that are accepted by most of the members of a society coexisting with alternative or peripheral values accepted by various segments of that society. It should also be noted that social values are occasionally contradictory to each other. Robin Williams (1970, pp. 454–500) lists the following major value orientations as being characteristic of American society.

1. Achievement and success
2. Activity and work
3. Moral orientation
4. Humanitarian mores
5. Efficiency and practicality
6. Progress
7. Material comfort
8. Equality
9. Freedom
10. External conformity
11. Science and secular rationality
12. Nationalism and patriotism
13. Democracy
14. Individual personality
15. Racism and related group-superiority themes

Within these major value themes there are potential contradictions: for example, racism and group-superiority themes versus freedom and humanitarianism, or external conformity versus individual personality.

Sport as a social institution permeates and mirrors many levels of society and "influences such disparate elements as status, race relations, business life, automotive design, clothing styles, the concept of the hero, language, and ethical values" (Boyle, 1963, pp. 3–4). In a similar vein, Voigt (1966, 1974) analyzes the history of early American baseball and shows how, in its growth from an amateur to a corporate sport, it has come to reflect the social and economic changes of this era. Thus we suggest that sport provides a means of expressing some of the dominant values of a society. Indeed, a common justification for sport in schools is that participation in sport serves to transmit the values of the larger society. In other words, the youngster is ostensibly learning not only to play a specific sport but to "play the game of life." Edwards (1973b) aptly summarizes this point by noting that "sport is a social institution which has primary functions in disseminating and reinforcing the values regulating behavior and goal attainment and determining acceptable solutions to problems in the secular sphere of life. . . . This channeling affects not only perspectives on sport, but, it is commonly assumed, affects and aids in regulating perceptions of life in general" (p. 90). Thus we are interested in the various ways in which sport serves to magnify and accentuate the value orientations of the larger society.

One means of analyzing the values attributed to sport is to study the statements that are expressed by people involved in sport. One study classifies the values expressed in sport by an examination of the slogans posted by coaches in athletic dressing rooms (Snyder, 1972b). The slogans represent proverbs, aphorisms, maxims, and adages that are used as part of the coach's strategy to influence the players' performance. While the slogans define the model of athletic behavior with emphasis on the development of physical, psychological, and social characteristics that contribute to winning athletic contests, they also are expressions of social values. This study gathered information regarding the use of dressing-room slogans from basketball players and coaches in 270 high schools throughout Ohio. The slogans were classified according to the primary value that was being expressed. The following provides some appropriate slogans under each of the value themes:

Physical and Mental Fitness

It's easier to stay in shape than to get in shape.
It takes a cool head to win a hot game.
You're as good as you want to be.
The guy who complains about the way the ball bounces usually dropped it.
The mark of a true champion is the one who can conquer the fear of making mistakes.

Basic Skills and Techniques Must Be Painfully Learned

Valuable things in life don't come free, are you willing to pay the price?
The harder I work, the luckier I get.
The will to win is the will to work.
When you're through improving you're through.
No one ever drowned in sweat.
If what you did yesterday still looks big today, then you haven't done much today.
Good, better, best; never rest until your good is better and your better best.
If you can't put out, get out.
Anyone can be ordinary, but it takes guts to excel.
A gentleman winning is getting up one more time.
By failing to prepare yourself, you are preparing to fail.
Winners are made not born.

Aggressiveness and Competitive Spirit

A quitter never wins, a winner never quits.
When the going gets tough, the tough get going.
Winning isn't everything, it's the only thing.
Winning beats anything that comes in second.
It's not the size of the dog in the fight, but the size of the fight in the dog.
To explain a triumph, start with the first syllable.
They ask not how you played the game but whether you won or lost.
When they are drowning, throw them an anchor.

If it doesn't matter if you win or lose, why keep score?
A hungry dog hunts best.
Show me a good loser and I'll show you a loser.
How tall is your hustle?

The Player Must Accept Strict Discipline

Live by the code or get out.
He who flies with the owls at night cannot keep up with the eagles during the day.
The way you live is the way you play.

Subordination of Self to the Success of the Team

There is no I in team.
Who passed the ball to you when you scored?
The best ball players help others to be best players.
Ask not what your team can do for you, but what you can do for your team.
Talent is God-given, conceit is self-given; be careful.
Cooperate—remember the banana; every time it leaves the bunch, it gets skinned.
An ounce of loyalty is worth a pound of cleverness.

The underlying value theme of these slogans is that certain behavior patterns must be adopted in order to excel, succeed, and win. In a manner similar to the analysis of dressing-room slogans just cited, Edwards (1973b) collected value statements from journals, magazines, and newspaper articles dealing with expressed beliefs about the world of sport in America. Based on the content analysis of these sources, Edwards derived what he labels the "American Sports Creed." He concludes that the core value orientation expressed in the American Sports Creed is that of "individual achievement through competition. This orientation gives sport in America a demeanor of practicality and gives cohesion to specific values, activities, and role relationships of the institution" (Edwards, 1973b, p. 334). While it should be noted that sport can also be an agent of change within society, and it is not uncommon for sports personalities to be involved in progressive movements, the world of sport tends to be one of the most conservative sectors of society. The emphasis in sport on achievement and success through competition, hard work, and discipline is isomorphic to the traditional value orientations of the larger society.

Edwards (1973b) identifies seven central themes as constituting the American Sports Creed. In many respects these value themes reflect the dominant value orientations described by Robin Williams.

1. *Character:* general statements pertaining to character development and traits such as clean living, proper grooming, "red-bloodedness," loyalty, and altruism (brotherhood, unselfishness, or self-sacrifice).
2. *Discipline:* statements that relate sport to self-control and social order.
3. *Competition:* statements that relate sport to the development of fortitude and preparation for life in the sense of facilitating subsequent success for the individual.
4. *Physical Fitness:* statements that relate sport to health and physical conditioning.

5. *Mental Fitness:* statements that relate sport to mental alertness and educational achievement.
6. *Religiosity:* statements that relate sport to traditional American Christianity.
7. *Nationalism:* statements that relate sport to patriotism and love of country.

The value orientations that are manifested in the subculture of sport are also illustrated in printed material distributed by athletic organizations. One of these sources of qualitative data is available in the media guides distributed by collegiate (and professional) athletic organizations. In large intercollegiate athletic departments, the revenue sports, primarily football and basketball, are expected to be successful by winning ball games and thus achieving fan support. The head coach is responsible for the team performance; consequently his or her legitimacy as a coach is primarily determined by his or her success as a player and coach. Coaches, like people in other occupational stations, project an image in terms of approved social attributes. This notion was developed by Goffman (1967, p. 5) in his definition of *face* as the "positive social value a person effectively claims for himself by the line others assume he has taken during a particular contact." Thus, we are interested in the attributes associated with, and expected of, coaches; these attributes may be used as an index of the values associated with big time formal sports. To fail in maintaining these attributes will threaten one's coaching position and will be an example of not maintaining "face." According to Goffman, we spend considerable energy in "face work," that is, in managing others' impressions of us so we can maintain a favorable image. The descriptions provided in the press guides represent the attempt, usually by the sports information director of the athletic department, to manage the readers' impressions of the coach and his or her legitimacy for the position (as well as present information about the team). The descriptions of the head coaches and statements by them in the media guides are very revealing in providing further data regarding the attributes of the coaches and, in turn, the values associated with the sport subculture as well as the particular sport. The following are sample statements selected from recent media guides from major university football teams and represent what might be called the *Sports Creed*:

Competition, Fortitude, Success, Win

"The most important traits necessary for a top-notch football player include the willingness to hit, a burning desire to improve each day and the will to prepare and expect to win."

"We must be goal seeking individuals with a hunger to achieve on the field and in the classroom."

"I strongly believe and know that every team wants to win, this is easy, but every team won't prepare to win."

"I don't believe in playing without a scoreboard. I don't feel there is any accomplishment with a tie."

"I honestly think we can have a winning football program here. That's what our staff works around the clock for. I won't sleep until we become a winner."

"Our young men have worked so hard they deserve to be rewarded. I hope we can experience some success early."

"Our success this season depends more on the players than it has in the previous years I've been here. Their attitude and personal desire to improve will be the key factors in determining our final record."

Character

"Teaching our players to perform up to their potential to be the best they can possibly be—and doing it with their best interests in mind—is the right way to get things done. I have always believed if we can work to help a young man to become the best possible person he can be, a better football player will result."

"My coaching philosophy is to win and improve each player everyday. I know that football can play a major role in molding a young man's life. If I can teach him how to win on the field, I know he can win in the game of life. I must get our young athletes to learn to expect to win and learn how to work to win, then we will accomplish our goals."

"All our efforts are aimed at making each individual realize his full potential. It takes a great deal of sacrifice and discipline on the part of each player, but it pays dividends not only now, but in later life."

Discipline

"I believe in discipline and enthusiasm in everything you do in life."

"He is a tough-minded coach."

Basic Skills and Techniques Must Be Achieved by Hard Work

"He believes that a player must play to 100 percent of his ability in practice as well as in games."

"His coaching philosophy is simple: hard work, dedication, and keeping the game fun for players and fans alike."

"Our program should be fun and excitement built around a solid group of young men who possess the desire and attitude for hard work both in the classroom and on the football field."

"There are three kinds of motivation: incentive, punishment, and self-motivation. The only lasting kind is self-motivation."

"How does he do it? He does it with hard work, preparation and enough enthusiasm to fill up the Grand Canyon and overflow into three or four neighboring states."

Subordination of Self to the Success of the Team

"We'll be strictly team oriented, we'll win or lose as a team."

"His teams have a family closeness it takes to succeed."

PUBLIC ATTITUDES TOWARD SPORT

In one research study (Spreitzer and Snyder, 1975), we sought to identify the social definitions of sport in the context of value orientations by asking people what they felt were the functions or consequences of sport. We conducted a survey of over 500 respondents in a large metropolitan area in the midwestern part of the United States, and we found that most people defined sport as having positive functions for both society and the individual participant. For example, nearly 90 percent (both males and females) felt that sport was valuable because it taught self-discipline; 80 percent affirmed that sport was valuable because it promoted the development of fair play; and approximately 70 percent of the respondents noted the value of sport in teaching respect for authority and good citizenship. An examination of the responses in Table 3-1 reveals that the adult men and women in this sample are remarkably similar in the functions they attribute to sport. In general the list of functions in the table reflects the sentiments inherent in the major value orientations of American society and the values expressed in the athletic slogans, media guides, and the Sports Creed.

TABLE 3-1 Distribution of Responses Concerning the Functions of Sport by Sex

	MALES			FEMALES		
	AGREE (%)	NEUTRAL (%)	DISAGREE (%)	AGREE (%)	NEUTRAL (%)	DISAGREE (%)
Sports are not particularly important for the well-being of our society.	20	7	73	16	6	78
If more people were involved in sports, we would not have so much trouble with drugs in our society.	64	18	18	74	15	11
Sports are valuable because they help youngsters to become good citizens.	67	15	18	75	14	11
The emphasis that sport places on competition causes more harm than good.	10	18	72	19	18	63
Sports are valuable because they teach youngsters respect for authority.	69	14	17	75	13	12
Sports are valuable because they contribute to the development of patriotism.	34	29	37	49	31	20
Sports are valuable because they provide an opportunity for individuals to get ahead in the world.	46	23	31	45	29	26
Sports promote the development of fair play.	79	14	7	82	12	6
Sports are valuable because they teach self-discipline.	90	5	5	88	8	4

Source: Adapted from Spreitzer and Snyder, 1975, p. 89.

It is interesting to note that some studies show that males and females have differing views about the personal functions of sport. Kenyon's (1968) cross-national study showed that female adolescents tended to see physical activity as an opportunity for social experience, physical fitness, aesthetic enjoyment, and emotional release, while male adolescents were more interested in the ascetic dimension, physical challenge, the chance factor, and risk-taking. Similarly, Petrie's research (1971) shows that college-age men were more attracted to competition and demonstration of physical skill within physical activities, while their female counterparts associated sport with social experience, fun, and fair play. In short, the different patterns of male–female participation in sport tends to produce different views about the personal functions of sport. However, both sexes manifested similar views regarding the societal functions of sport in reinforcing the basic values depicted in Table 3-1 (cf. Grove and Doder, 1979, for a replication and extension of the Spreitzer–Snyder study). A recent study of 525 undergraduate students attending a liberal arts college and a state university suggests that attitudes toward sport might be changing toward greater sophistication. For example, approximately 95 percent of the students indicated that sport "helps people develop better self-discipline," 87 percent agreed that "athletes tend to enjoy better physical health than nonathletes" 85 percent felt that "sport builds character and makes better citizens," and 81 percent agreed that "participation in organized sport develops leadership qualities." However, contrary to the themes of the Sports Creed, only 23 percent of the students were of the opinion that "in the long run, you learn more about life and success in the sports arena than in the classroom or anywhere else" (sports as a preparation for life), and only 15 percent of the students felt that "athletes tend to be stronger believers in God and country than nonathletes" (Nixon, 1979, p. 148).

SPORT AND THE ROLE OF THE HERO

In the preceeding section we have emphasized the manner in which sport expresses social values. On a personal level, sport likewise is often identified as a medium of socialization whereby socially desirable qualities are taught. Goffman (1967) notes five personal characteristics that are valued as a means of controlling fateful events: courage, gameness, integrity, gallantry, and composure. These qualities have particular relevance to the personal characteristics deemed desirable in the sport milieu, especially because sport contexts are often defined as "fateful events." Such qualities have the effect of defining the moral order of sport and are particularly apropos to identifying desirable attributes of sport heroes (Loy et al., 1978). Thus, persons who are courageous in sport are not intimidated—they stand up under fire, they are not afraid to try, even though they may lose. Gameness is displayed by having pluck, endurance; and an underdog who is greatly "outmanned" should never give up but should display "guts," and a "lot of heart." Integrity in sport should be displayed when participants adhere to the rules even when they might be able to cover up an error, for example, calling a wrist shot on themselves in a handball game or in tennis being honest about a shot that is in court even though they will lose the point. Gallantry is illustrated in sport when athletes recognize the excellence of their competitors or by giving assistance to others even if they may lose as a result, for example, stopping in a race to give aid to another runner. Composure is displayed in sport contexts by being "cool," not getting rattled, showing that you have "ice-water in your veins" when shooting a pressure free-throw, and not clutching up or "choking" in critical situations. These attributes associated within the sport subculture might be manifested within the types of heroes described in the following paragraph.

One manifestation of values is to study individuals who personify cultural ideals. A hero incorporates the major value orientations and symbols that are approved and deemed desirable within a society. Just as values may be contradictory, some heroes may reinforce dominant values while other heroes (antiheroes) can represent contrasting values and symbolize protest and potential social change within a society. Klapp (1962) divides heroes into the following major categories and themes:

Categories	Themes
1. Winners	Getting what you want, beating everyone, being a champ.
2. Splendid performers	Shining before an audience, making a hit.
3. Heroes of social acceptability	Being liked, attractive, good, or otherwise personally acceptable to groups and epitomizing the pleasures of belonging.
4. Independent spirits	Standing alone, making one's way by oneself.
5. Group servants	Helping people, cooperation, self-sacrifice, group service, and solidarity.

Each of these types represents certain value themes and types of achievement worthy of emulation. Although independent spirits may possess some deviant attributes, they receive admiration because their free spirit and independence puts them in an underdog role. Sports heroes can be placed in any of these categories, and some probably fit into more than one category. In essence, the analysis of the sport hero represents another mode of studying the function of sport in reinforcing the major cultural values of a society. Smith (1973) points out that as children grow up they see older "models attending sporting events, watching games on television, and reading about sports in magazines and newspapers. With so much attention devoted to sport the child soon learns that sport is important and worthwhile" (p. 63). The result of this socialization process is a realization of the significance of sport and adulation of the sport hero. Evidence of hero worship in sport is manifested in the seeking of autographs, sports statistics, feature stories, bubble gum cards, publicity events, and athletic halls of fame.

The consideration of the hero within a historical perspective also provides an important means of studying social change. Particularly useful in this respect is the content analysis of fictional and biographical accounts of sports heroes. For example, Lowe and Payne (1974) outline the most prominent values manifested in adolescent sport stories in the early twentieth century. These stories reflect the prevailing social ethos and set a moral code for the young to emulate. The value concepts frequently mentioned include the following: emphasis on winning, sportsmanship, strength, courage, discipline, leadership, determination, and teamwork. One of the most widely known sports heroes of this period was Frank Merriwell, the fictional character produced in the dime novels of Gilbert Patten. The Merriwell series was most popular at the turn of the century when sport was burgeoning in the colleges and high schools of America. Frank Merriwell was first portrayed as a schoolboy at Fardale Academy and later at Yale University as a respected student and leader in university activities, and an outstanding athlete whose fame became world-wide. Frank Merriwell was depicted by Patten as the "idealized image of American youth—gentlemanly, educated, brave, adventurous, athletic, handsome, wealthy, admired, and clean living" (Balchak, 1975, p. 100).

Within an historical context, Rudolf Haerle (1974) presents an interesting content analysis of baseball autobiographies. His research focuses on the changes in success themes represented by baseball heroes and the correlated cultural values. The early years of baseball were represented by the autobiographies of Adrian C. Anson's *A Ball Player's Career* (1900) and *Playing the Game: From Mine Boy to Manager* by Stanley "Bucky" Harris. This period was characterized by an emphasis on the Protestant Ethic, dedication to one's work as a "calling," and the hero as one "who practiced diligently, played the game hard, was not discouraged by adversity, was ambitious and self-disciplined, developed good habits and the like. The belief was strong that hard work would receive the just reward of success" (Haerle, 1974, p. 394). These behavioral expectations clearly approximate those portrayed in the Frank Merriwell novels. By the late 1940s, however, the value orientations had changed; the Protestant Ethic had weakened. The Depression and World War II, two major historical events that were beyond people's control, led to a feeling of uncertainty, along with the sense that one's destiny seemed to be controlled by fate or luck rather than individual responsibility. The baseball autobiography characteristic of this era was Joe DiMaggio's *Lucky to Be a Yankee*. The word "luck" in the title is not entirely coincidental (Haerle, 1974). DiMaggio seemed to represent "being a natural" and the importance of luck as the determinant of one's fate. Finally, the affluence of the 1960s, the civil rights movement, and the Vietnam War seemed to produce another type of cultural hero (perhaps an antihero). Jim Bouton's *Ball Four* (1970) demonstrates another shift in basic values. Bouton's book seems to put aside the traditional emphasis on clean living and dedication and gives way to a "moderated 'selfishness' and desire for individualized 'style of life' " (Haerle, 1974, p. 396). Modern professional athletes tend to be "system questioning," and the corporate structure of the game is only one target of their cynicism.

SPORT SUBCULTURE AND TEAM CULTURE

The social values that are reflected in the subculture of sport are also present in a team context. Yet, the behavior of the team members may not be an exact replica of the sport subculture or the larger society. The research by Fine (1978, 1979) is particularly germane for the understanding of preadolescent socialization within the context of Little League baseball teams. The Little League motto of "character, courage, loyalty" sets the general moral tone that reflects attributes associated not only with Little League but also within sport and the larger sport subculture. Additionally, within the team context Fine (1978) noted four basic value themes.

1. The importance of effort. In sports the objective is to win, and coaches teach their players that hard work will produce success. Thus, "defeat may be *prima facie* evidence of lack of effort or 'hustle' " (p. 85). Failures are often interpreted by coaches as a lack of effort, and therefore a motivational problem that can be corrected rather than a lack of physical ability. Lack of hustle is a common criticism noted by Fine: "Coach to eleven year old utility outfielder: 'Come on, Rich be a hitter. You're not even awake up there' " (p. 86). Some ball players are labeled "hustlers" and "gutsy little ball players" while others are "goof-offs," and both team and individual success are associated with effort. Thus, with a team victory after several defeats the coach links their success with desire when he tells his team, " 'See what hustle can do?'. . .'All you did differently was hustle' " (p. 91).

2. Sportsmanship. This theme is emphasized less frequently than the other themes in the socialization process. In general, the lack of emphasis might be explained because it is rarely seen as an issue. Fine reports that by any standard the players in their study were "well-behaved" in the presence of adults, and the need to stress sportsmanship was seen as an individual rather than a team problem. Likewise, the attention to sportsmanship might be directed more toward providing a model for the actions of parents than for the players.

3. The value of teamwork. Fine reports that whereas effort is defined as personal responsibility, teamwork is considered a social responsibility. Teamwork is determined by coaches as working as a unit, that is, " 'We are a team. We are a family. We got to pull together,' " rather than personal glory. Teamwork is also illustrated by this coach's statement: " 'Isn't it nice to come back and win it. It was a team effort. Everybody played well' " (p. 97).

4. Winning and losing. The final theme stresses the manner of coping with success and failure. In part this incorporates the other three themes and the reconstruction of explanations for wins and losses—for example, "coach to a poor team after a close victory, 'you guys played exactly the way you're capable of playing. . .You're back in the groove' " (p. 99). By contrast consider a comment by a coach after a defeat, "We played five good innings of baseball. The first inning we didn't want to play" (p. 101). In the first quotation victory was defined as playing up to the team's capabilities, and in the second statement the defeat was defined in terms of the deficiencies in one inning. Fine points out that losses are usually not associated with lack of physical ability, rather with a deficiency in motivation of the players and "the coaches believe these are 'moral' rather than technical problems, and thus subject to conscious control" (p. 101). This view is common not only in Little League but also in other segments of life in which the " 'Just World Hypothesis' is applicable. That is, the belief that those who have success—for what ever 'actual' reason—are virtuous; and those who face defeat are liable to charges that their circumstances are attributable to personal culpability" (p. 102). In summary, the four basic themes that are evident in the Little League incorporate the values of effort, sportsmanship, teamwork, and the manner of coping with victories and defeats. In general, these values transmitted by the coach reflect the values of the sport subculture and, in turn, the society in general. However, the degree of overlap in values between the society and sport needs to be spelled out more clearly. Although the overlap in social values and the moral order taught in

Little League baseball is considerable, this association might vary with the type of sport and, furthermore, within a sport there are likely to be variations between teams. One might gain a better understanding of the relationships between these social units by the following Venn diagram.

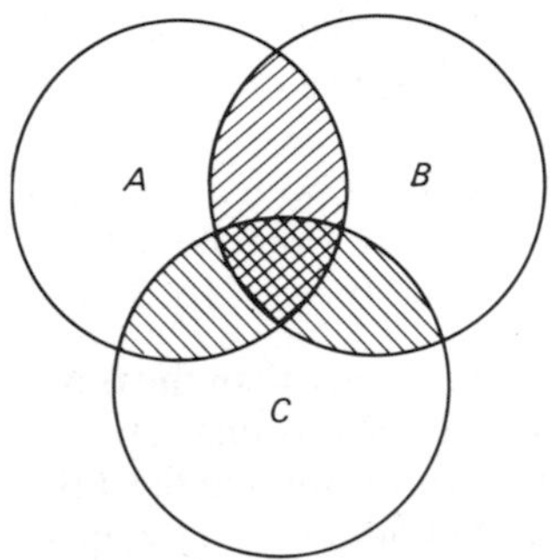

A = Values of the larger culture
B = Values of the sport subculture
C = Values expressed (transmitted) by a specific sport, for example, football, hockey, tennis, golf, baseball, swimming, etc.

It is our assumption that the overlap between *A* and *B* will vary from time to time (thus a measure of social change) and that the overlap among A, *B*, and *C* will vary with the sport, for example, football compared with gymnastics. Additionally, we expect that there are differences in the degree of overlap based on the level of sport (that is, informal, semiformal, or formal participation). As we noted previously, each team as an interacting unit will have developed their own specific culture, an idioculture (idio is derived from the Greek word *idios* meaning *own*) culture, that will include values, beliefs, norms, statuses, customs, and goals. These are constructed out of the face-to-face interaction of the team over a period of time (cf. Fine, 1979). These specific team idiocultures would be visualized as subdivisions of the *C* portion of the diagram; however, in the interest of simplicity we have not included them in the diagram. We can not think of many examples of overlap between *A* and *C* that would not also incorporate *B* (the sport subculture). However, we remember a football player who was running down the sidelines for a touchdown and the officials did not detect him stepping on the sideline during the run. Yet, the coach for the player who scored the touchdown saw the violation and in the interests of honesty (a social value *A* in the diagram) asked that the touchdown be nullified. Although this behavior by the coach is not a value that is associated with football (*B* in the diagram), it was expressed in this game context; yet it was so unusual to the sport subculture (*B* in the diagram) that it made the national news.

CONTRASTING MODELS OF SPORT IN SOCIETY

We noted earlier in this chapter that diverse groups within a society may adhere to different values, and even the dominant or core values of the society may at times be contradictory. From these facts, social scientists have developed two contrasting models of society. These contrasting models represent differing assumptions concerning the nature of people and society and thus have implications for the role of sport within a society. One perspective is generally referred to as an *order* or functional model (Horton, 1966). This view of society stresses the importance of the different institutions and subsystems properly fitting together, with each part fulfilling its function. In this manner, the society is viewed as a harmonious interrelationship of social segments. There is an emphasis on an overall consensus in society and a fear of rapid social change that would disturb the consensus, integration, division of labor, and social equilibrium. Within the order perspective, the socialization process that takes place in the family, school, church, and other institutions (including sport) stresses the internalization of, and adaptation to, the society's dominant values and normative expectations. This perspective tends toward stability and stresses a conservative view of society. Social control mechanisms are considered important to maintain the normative order and integration (law and order).

In contrast, a second perspective of society sees the functioning of society from a very different angle. In sociological theory, this approach is frequently labeled as the *conflict* (or sometimes the Marxian, dialectic, or radical) *perspective.* This model does not see consensus as necessarily desirable. Indeed, social progress frequently is the result of conflicting or contradictory factors—values, ideologies, roles, institutions, or groups (van den Berghe, 1963). Often the conflicts between groups, values, and ideologies are instigated by "consciousness raising"—by making people aware of the internal contradictions and conflicts within society. In this theoretical framework, conflict is not necessarily dysfunctional for the long-term welfare of society. Indeed, dissensus may be viewed as functional because it challenges the existing social order and may thus bring about changes in society and the achievement of a higher level of synthesis. The conflict perspective frequently emphasizes human needs rather than system maintenance (Gruneau, 1976).

Within the world of sport there are elements that adhere strongly to the order model. In general, the sport establishment of coaches, athletic directors, managers, and professional owners embraces this social perspective. This conservative perspective is likely to perceive sport as functional for society because sport can ensure:

1. The transmission of social values and the facilitation of consensus and social integration.
2. The mastery of skill, achievement, ability, mental and physical fitness, and good character.
3. The definition of behavioral problems among athletes in moralistic terms.
4. The facilitation of social order and stability through the teaching of values, the encouragement of social mobility and political solidarity, and the provision of a catharsis for the participants and spectators.

On the other hand, a number of dissenters have strongly advocated changes in sport. This perspective generally posits the following perception of the role of sport in society:

1. Sport tends to be a reflection of a materialistic society; it thus legitimates the existing system. It induces a false consciousness and is an opiate that encourages satisfaction with the *status quo.*
2. Play and informal sport are potentially liberating, but formal sport presently teaches values that are exploitative, inhumane, and pathological because of the inordinate stress on competition.

3. Problems among athletes are seen as the result of alienation from an inhumane, exploitative, and elitist system.
4. Formal sport participation stresses meritocracy and elitism—survival of the fittest—whereas informal sport encourages broad participation by all segments of society.

We have alluded to contradictions in the dominant value system of the American society. Social strains result from the inconsistency between the values of achievement, success, getting ahead, and meritocracy, on the one hand, and the emphasis on humanitarianism, equality, freedom, democracy, and individual worth and respect, on the other. These social strains are also reflected in the order and conflict schemes we have just outlined. One of the leading proponents of the necessity of change within sport is Harry Edwards. He has asserted that discriminatory practices have long been evident in the sport sphere (and society as well). He advocates changes in sport toward greater equalitarian practices that would open up to minority groups the same opportunities in sport that have been available to whites (Edwards, 1970, 1973b). The black revolution within sport derives its ideological roots and tactics from the civil rights movement of the 1960s. The threatened boycott of the XIX Olympiad and the clenched fist demonstration by black sprinters Tommie Smith and John Carlos on the victory stand in Mexico City exemplify their position.

Additionally, humanistic dissent within sport has also occurred under the leadership of Jack Scott (1969, 1971), who has argued that athletics are for athletes, and therefore the emphasis should be on a humanistic rationale for sport (see also Sage, 1980b). The humanistic critique of conventional sport emphasizes that the world of sport should be restructured to encourage altruism and interpersonal responsibility while deemphasizing instrumentalism, inordinate competitiveness, survival of the fittest ("social Darwinism"), and violence. On the administrative level, coaches and athletic directors should strive for maximum feasible participation while phasing out the current elitist and autocratic structure in sports. The humanists argue that sport participation should be open to all—regardless of gender, innate physical capabilities, political philosophy, or life style. Scott (1972) has argued that there is nothing dehumanizing about the agonistic struggle of sport to develop the quest for excellence and accomplishment. However, when competitive sport reflects the emphasis on "winning is the only thing," it tends to become translated into "the end justifies any means," an ethic also in evidence in the political and business spheres. The richness of sport emerges when people are encouraged to develop their potential through the experience of sport but not at the expense of themselves or others.

The most radical critic of the society–sport nexus is Paul Hoch. Hoch (1972) presents a Marxist position toward American society and views sport as a means of socializing players and fans "for production and consumption, for their roles on the assembly line or in the army, and generally, to be docile citizens of a nationalistic, racist, male-dominated and militaristic country" (p. 10). Hoch argues, however, that his criticism is directed toward the society rather than sport per se.

> To "attack" sports would be like the old witch's attacking the mirror that showed her how ugly she is, for sports is nothing else but a mirror, a socializing agent, and an opiate of the society it serves. To "reform" the mirror while leaving the society untouched

> would change nothing at all. We will have humane, creative sports when we have built a humane and creative society—and not until then (p. 10).[1]

Perhaps the most trenchant critique of sport at all levels is found in Thomas Tutko's and William Bruns' *Winning Is Everything and Other American Myths* (1976). The chapter titles alone are revealing of the tone of the book—for example, "Symptoms of a Winning Craze," "Sports Don't Build Character—They Build Characters," "The Destructive Pro Model," "Emotional Child Abuse," and "The Superstar: A Curse or a Blessing." Thomas Tutko is a prominent sport psychologist who has conducted considerable scientific research on sport and who runs a consulting service to large-scale athletic organizations. His writings on sport have become increasingly critical. Tutko's analysis of aberrations on the part of some superstars is particularly trenchant. The implication is that "superjerk" might be a more appropriate appellation in such cases. Tutko and Bruns cite the definition of a superjerk as offered by the Chicago columnist Mike Royko: "the superstar who won't simply kick, hit, throw, or maim someone, and call it a day. The superjerk is not content with earning large sums of money while getting wholesome exercise. He must constantly display his superego, indulge in superwhining, superbragging, superspending, and superpointing" (p. 35). In the same vein, Brower (1979) has concluded from his research of youth sports that there is no valid evidence that sports build character. He notes that the importance of the win ethic often interferes with the enjoyment as well as the skill development of sport. For example, the rational and safe way for getting on base in Little League baseball (where the young pitchers often lack control) is to get a base on balls. This method of getting on base is not, however, as much fun as attempting to get a hit; furthermore, it is contrary to the idea of developing one's skill as a batter. Yet, as Brower points out, a "common practice for coaches who place winning above the child's development or fun in the sport is to have their players keep their bat on their shoulders and get a base on balls" (p. 43).

SPORT AND SOCIALIZATION OF VALUES

Much of the discussion in this chapter has focused on values embedded in sport, but the implications for socialization are clear. Particularly relevant to this topic is a perceptive essay by Walter Schafer (1971) that looks at educational objectives and the function of school athletic programs in achieving these objectives. Schafer sees two polar views regarding the objectives of American education. One viewpoint sees the primary purpose of education to enculturate students with the social values, skills, and knowledge that would guarantee the continuation of the existing political, religious, and economic systems. Emphasis is placed on the development of marketable skills, loyalty to the nation-state, and unquestioning acceptance of the prevailing social values. Learning to play a variety of roles and to accept authority are more important than independent judgment or critical thinking. Indeed, questioning of the social order is discouraged because it might set into mo-

---

[1]From *Rip Off the Big Game* by Paul Hoch. Copyright © 1972 by Paul Hoch. Reprinted by permission of Doubleday & Company, Inc.

tion social change and thus disturb the stability of the existing society. This viewpoint of education coincides with the order perspective of society and the dominant traditional values already discussed.

The second approach toward education outlined by Schafer has the objective of enhancement of student maturity. This position encourages students to develop reflective and questioning attitudes toward themselves and their society. Questions such as the following might be asked and faced.

> Who am I? Why am I here? How am I being shaped? What do I believe? What do I want to become? What is to become of my country and world? Are the values shaping how social problems are approached necessarily the best values? Is technological growth necessarily good, at least beyond a certain point? What is to be my role in the development of a more humane world? (p. 2).

This educational approach, suggests Schafer, will encourage students to evaluate themselves, their society, and, in turn, promote more mature and autonomous persons. This model of socialization approximates the dialectic educational process that is compatible with the conflict perspective of society. It would also be reflected in some of the questions that have been raised concerning the traditional American values.

The central thesis of Schafer's essay is that sport in the American school serves as the enculturation model of education. Athletes "serve first and foremost as a social device for steering young people—participants and spectators alike—into the mainstream of American life through the overt and covert teaching of 'appropriate' attitudes, values, norms and behavior patterns" (p. 6). Furthermore, school athletics are oriented toward instrumental rewards and achievement. There is little opportunity to participate for inherent enjoyment or delight; neither is there very much opportunity for informal or low-key involvement in sport. Additionally, interscholastic and collegiate athletic programs are organized for the benefit of the elite performers. There is little opportunity for students of lesser ability to participate for intrinsic satisfactions or the development of physical fitness. Based on this summary, one might assume that Schafer does not see any desirable qualities in interscholastic and intercollegiate athletics. However, the concluding portion of his paper presents a balanced discussion of the two contrasting views of education and how sport and education might be accommodated.

> In short, I am suggesting that interscholastic athletes, largely covertly, contribute more to fitting young people without raising questions into the mainstream of American life than to fostering careful examination of self and culture, personal autonomy, or unconditional self-worth. This is not to say that education for enculturation is all "bad" and education for maturity is all "good," that they are entirely mutually exclusive of one another, or that school athletics contribute in no way to maturity. But I am contending that the latent and covert enculturation function outweighs in social significance the contribution of school sports to the maturity of the individual student athlete or spectator.
>
> What are the implications of this analysis, then, for educational policy toward interscholastic athletics? Some might argue that it follows that highly competitive sports ought to be banned altogether. I do not come to that conclusion from what I have said. Clearly, some degree of enculturation is needed for social integration, and school sports do have a place in the educational enterprise. Many youth like to compete at a

> high level of quality and intensity, have the talent, and should be given the chance to do so—but not to the exclusion of broad-based opportunities for informed, low-keyed participation for fun, enjoyment, and good health, especially in life-time sports. Schools in the United States are doing far too little in my judgment in encouraging intra-school competition for fun in a variety of carry-over sports. Facilities should be made available for this purpose, clubs should be formed where useful, and as much value ought to be given by teachers, administrators and coaches to this type of engagement in sport as to participation in high levels of competition. Such opportunities should be equally available to boys and girls (pp. 12–14).

Schafer also argues that schools and coaches should not indoctrinate students and suppress individual rights under the guise of athletic discipline. Thus, coaches have no business imposing their own particular moral standards on players, when these are unrelated to athletic training and performance. The main difficulty in building athletic programs that meet Schafer's criteria is that the general public defines athletic success in terms of the win-loss record. Thus, the coaching subculture defines the authoritarian archtypal father-figure as a necessary coaching role for developing winning teams (Massengale, 1974).

This questioning of the worth of high-pressure sport is found also in such staid organs as *The New York Times*. Over a six-day period in March, 1974, this influential newspaper published a series of critical articles on contemporary trends in collegiate sports. This series of articles was expanded into a book-length work by Joseph Durso and *The New York Times* Sport Department (1975) under the title of *The Sports Factory: An Investigation into Collegiate Sports*. The chapter titles—for example, "The Slave Market," "The Hunter and the Hunted," "Big, Big Man on Campus," "The Nouveau Riche," and "The All-American Rip-Off"—are indicative of the tone of the book. Such pessimistic views have been published periodically since the report on the same topic by the Carnegie Commission in the 1920s, yet the juggernaut rolls on. Perhaps the latent functions are becoming more important than the manifest objectives of collegiate sports.

Prominent author James A. Michener has attempted to defend the world of sport from the slings and arrows of its many critics in his recent book entitled *Sports in America* (1976). In almost reverential tone, Michener relates how sport in effect saved his life on two occasions: first, as a youth when sport prevented him from becoming delinquent, and, second, in his mature life when strenuous physical activity helped him to recover from a severe heart attack. And so the debate continues.

CONCLUSION

Sport is a microcosm highlighting and mirroring social values. The values expressed in sport represent the functions of sport in society. We usually think of the sport subculture as a value receptacle for the society. Yet, within sport values and norms may also be generated and negotiated that eventually "flow back" to the larger society.

In this chapter we have identified several ways of examining values within the sport realm. The values are evident in the slogans associated with sport; they are also revealed in printed materials by athletic organizations and through an analysis of sport heroes who are symbolic representations of social values. However, with social change we also find shifts in the value orientations of society. Thus, we can observe this process of social change through the historical analysis of biographical and fictional literature focusing on sport heroes. With the rapid change of the 1960s and 1970s, American society was struck with protests in the areas of race relations, the women's movement, and the antiwar movement. These schisms and ideological strains spilled over into the sports world. In essence, the divisions within sport and society may be analyzed utilizing the theoretical perspectives of social order and conflict. At first glance the two perspectives seem to be contradictory and incompatible, but in a changing society each is a lens that allows us to observe various facets of social reality. Similarly, the transmission of values via the sport subculture has more than one facet. This socialization process has potentially desirable and undesirable consequences. Thus, as was pointed out in Chapter 1, the reality of sport goes beyond the manifest and commonly held assumptions; one function of sociology is to provide the means of dissecting, observing, and understanding the different layers of reality—including sport.

CHAPTER 4
Cultural Variations in Sport

In the last chapter we focused on the relationship between sport and social views. If sport represents a microcosm of society and its values, this might be further elaborated by comparing different cultures, the corresponding variations in values, and the types of sport in the societies. There is, in fact, considerable anthropological data to support this thesis. Using the Human Relations Area Files, Sutton-Smith and associates (1963, 1970) have analyzed ethnographic data to determine the game preferences of children and adults across many cultures. They concluded that cultures that emphasize games of *physical skill* tend to be found in tropical regions. Their economic level is simple and basically one of subsistence. Social stratification and political structures are relatively absent, and child-raising practices are relaxed. Political conflict and war are also relatively absent in cultures that emphasize games of physical skill. Sex roles, however, tend to be strictly differentiated because of a presumed need for masculine self-reliance in areas such as hunting and fishing. Games such as spear throwing and archery bear a clear relationship to the valued skills for males in this type of culture.

Cultures that emphasize games of *chance* tend to be found in higher latitudes where there are marked seasonal changes and cold weather. Consequently, food supplies are more problematic, and shortages are common. The community size is small, and the physical location of the community changes relatively frequently. The divorce rate is high, and child-raising practices tend to be severe. Games of chance are then isomorphic to societal conditions, which are unpredictable and governed by fate.

Cultures that emphasize games of *strategy* tend to be more developed in terms of technology and social organization. The community size is larger and relatively permanent. Social stratification and occupational specialization tend to be highly developed. Child-raising practices tend to be strict. Self-indulgence is sanctioned, while achievement and self-reliance are nurtured in the young. Strategy-type skills are rewarded and salient in the basic social institutions of these cultures, and thus games of strategy represent a logical form of anticipatory socialization.

Cultures that include games of *physical skill, chance,* and *strategy* tend to be found in the most developed of all societies. In modern industrial societies, there is a configuration in games and sports that includes an emphasis on physical skill combined with an overlay of strategy but yet with a residue of chance that produces the intrigue associated with indeterminancy. In complex societies, the larger game of life places a premium on skill, strategy, and decision making. However, the element of chance has still not been eliminated by advanced forms of science and technology.

SOME HISTORICAL EXAMPLES

The Sutton-Smith classification system is useful in considering variations in cultures and the corresponding types of competitive activities. The significance lies in the congruency between the type of culture and the function of games and sports in a particular society. This perspective rests on the assumption that there are specific functions that must be met in societies and that social institutions will be congruent with the cultural values of the society. Thus, we can study sport as an institution and the function it performs. In this section we present several historical examples as case studies to illustrate this point of cultural congruency. In this context, however, one must be cautious in assuming that a particular type of culture or set of values necessarily results in a specific form of sport.

Formal athletic contests on a large scale were introduced by the Greeks. The ancient Olympic games attracted athletes and spectators from the various city states of the Hellenic civilization. With a little imagination we can see that some of the specific athletic feats performed at these contests evolved because the skills had utility for hunting and warfare (e.g., running, throwing, and physical fitness). Moreover, these events had consequences far beyond the physical realm. Prestige and status were obvious rewards from participation in games. In an age lacking modern means of communication, the best way to become well known politically was by participating in the contests or by sponsoring talented athletes; victories brought prestige and glory to the city and the ruler they represented (Strenk, 1979). An important value orientation of the Greek culture is expressed in the concept of *agon* or contest. Glory in athletic competition assured one of a high status approaching god-like immortality. The athletic contests became religious festivals, and the Greek love of anatomy is reflected in sport as well as the arts (Strenk, 1979). Thus, it is apparent that sport served several important functions for the Greek culture. As sport emerged in the Greek city states, it reinforced the values of emphasizing the competitive and physical dimensions of society and it provided mutual support for the military, political, and religious institutions of the society.

Sporting events in the Roman era had a different focus. The Roman tastes were more inclined toward gladiatorial contests and chariot races than footraces and throwing the discus. The Roman believed in physical fitness as preparations for war and entertainment whereas the "Greek principle of a harmonious development of the body, and a striving for bodily beauty and grace was considered effeminate" (Lindsay, 1973, p. 179). Thus, the masses of people in the Roman Empire were entertained by the "bread and circuses" provided by the emperors. These events provided a way for the politicians to increase their prestige with a maximum of pomp and pageantry. It is clear that sport in the Roman era served the function of the political system by providing what later would be labeled as an opiate—that is, to assuage the troubles of the spectators and thus serve as a safety valve for dissent and a means of social control to increase the power and prestige of the government (Strenk, 1979). As time went on the emperors provided the audience with increasingly improbable and unequal encounters to meet the lust for "blood to be spilled" with men fighting animals, and by 90 A.D. the Emperor Domitian titillated the populace with combat of dwarves against women (Guttmann, 1978, p. 29).

In the Middle Ages the jousts and tournaments mirrored the social classes and provided military conditioning for the nobility. The early tournaments were primarily battle-like conflicts; yet in time the tournaments became more regulated and less the image of actual battle. As these contests evolved they became more important as festivals and as an opportunity for the nobility to display their extravagant fashions and lavish accoutrements (Hardy, 1974). Joseph Strutt (1903) summarizes the social function of these contests for the medieval society as follows:

> The tournament and the joust . . . afforded to those who were engaged in them an opportunity of appearing before the ladies to the greatest advantage; they might at once display their taste and opulence by the costliness and elegancy of their apparel, and their prowess as soldiers; therefore these past times became fashionable among the nobility; and it was probably for the same reason that they were prohibited to the commoners (p. 126).

The values of a society can be further illustrated in the orientation toward sport in the Massachusetts Bay Colony. The Puritans of this colony were initially hostile to the frivilous activities of play and sport. Brailsford (1969) reported in his history of sport that "The Puritans saw their mission to erase all sport and play from men's lives" (p. 141). However, Struna (1977) notes that the colonists in Massachusetts Bay accepted some diversions and recreations. For example Governor John Winthrop of that colony wrote that he ". . . findinge it needful to recreate my minde and some outward recreation, I yielded unto it, and by a moderate exercise herein was much refreshed . . ." (Volume I, 1947, pp. 201–2). Because the values of the colony revolved around service to God and the laws of His creation, sport and physical exercise were practiced in moderation that might renew the spirit, refresh mind and body, and therefore be in accordance with God's revealed values (Struna, 1977, p. 39). However, within three generations the value orientations of the colony began to change. This transformation was brought about by an influx of non-Puritans, geographical expansion, and commercial interests. The essential point is that these value changes were likewise reflected in sport. The evolution of the notion of a "calling" was initially to serve God, yet the calling doctrine encouraged each man "to incessantly strive to grow richer, initially for God, but eventually for himself. Gradually the man sought profit for its own sake" (Struna, 1977, p. 43). Indeed, one's success could be interpreted as God's blessing. This transformation established a changing pattern of values that recognized economic success, social position, individual initiative, rationality, and competitive spirit rather than the authority of God. The consequences of this transformation established the climate for sport to become an economic commodity while public opinion became more liberalized toward sport.

If the early Puritans in Massachusetts did not value the joy of sport, the aristocracy of the South was somewhat more liberal, particularly with respect to horseracing. Betts (1974) reports that numerous race tracks were constructed in the State of Virginia, but "in 1696 a complaint was sent to the House of Burgesses against Saturday races since they often led to Sunday morning contests and the 'profanation' of the Sabbath" (p. 6). Nevertheless, organized sports were not played on a regular basis during the first fifty years after Independence. One account notes that "Charles Dickens, who toured the new Republic toward the end of this period, claimed to have witnessed no organized recreation except spitting, 'and that is done in silent fellowship, round the stove, when the meal is done'" (Murphy, 1979, p. 60). Subsequently, with the Civil War, and the decades thereafter, the United States became an industrialized and urbanized nation which involved substantial change in all institutions. While informal recreation had existed in the rural communities, the cities provided a social milieu for organized sport. The concentration of population provided ample spectators for the building of stadia for spectator sports, while the communication systems of the railroad and telegraph provided the technological base for town teams and the beginnings of professional baseball. Thus,

> In many ways, large and small, the growth of sports mirrored growing U.S. affluences, a phenomenon glimpsed by Mark Twain when he described baseball as the 'outward expression of the drive and push and struggle of the raging, tearing, booming 19th Century.' And the growth continued. By 1910, Americans were spending $73 million on sports, not counting capital investment; by the 1920's, even factory workers had enough free time to attend ball games (Murphy, 1979, p. 63).

OTHER EXAMPLES OF SPORT AND CULTURAL CONTEXTS

The diffusion and adaptation of one country's sport by another has been perceptively described by Riesman and Denny (1954) in their account of the origins of American football. They studied the British sport of rugby and delineated how it was changed to football—a sport more suitable to the American culture. Specifically, they noted how the ambiguity of the English scrum or scramble for a free ball changed in American football to a well-defined line of scrimmage with the symmetry of offensive and defensive lines and with a specific point in time when the ball is put into play—when the center snaps the ball. With a line of scrimmage and centering of the ball, the American adaptations resulted in the emergence of a running and passing game rather than a kicking game. Also, to accommodate the American desire for action, the yardage rule was instituted. Thus, a team must move the ball at least ten yards in four downs or give up the ball to the opposing team. The standardization of rules for football was also necessary to adapt the game to the diversity of American collegiate competition and audiences. In short, the sport of football was adapted to the themes of the American cultural milieu. As Riesman and Denny (1954) point out,

> the mid-field dramatization of line against line, the recurrent starting and stopping of field action around the timed snapping of a ball, the trend to a formalized division of labor between backfield and line, above all, perhaps, the increasingly precise synchronization of men in motion—these developments make it seem plausible to suggest that the whole procedural rationalization of the game which we have described was not unwelcome to Americans, and that it fit in with other aspects of their industrial folkways (p. 250).

One of the slogans that depicts the philosophy of sport in the People's Republic of China is "friendship first, competition second." This slogan stands in sharp contrast to many of the slogans associated with American sports. Excellence in the American sports programs is usually measured in terms of having the highest score, speed, or distance and defeating the opponent. In China, on the other hand, the value orientations emphasize the greatest effort or the greatest improvement (Galliher and Hessler, 1979). As part of the collective philosophy (that is, their family, clan, commune) individualism and competition are de-emphasized in China. Galliher and Hessler argue that Chinese values are conducive to greater participation in sport by the masses of people than in a society in which the focus is on competition and excellence. They note that "the most viable sports in the United States are media-supported sports in which active participation is greatly restricted and spectatorship is most prominent. These include football, baseball, and basketball where attendance is booming and games seem ever-present on television" (p. 12). There is some evidence to support the Galliher and Hessler thesis; participation in sport by the general populace in China has increased in the last three decades. Whether this increased participation can be attributed solely to the contrasting orientation toward sport or to the increased governmental emphasis is not clear. The contrasting philosophies toward competitive activities between these two cultures reflect fundamental cultural differences. These differences are aptly illustrated by the outcome of a basketball game between the 1978 touring Chinese men's team and Rutgers University's men's team. When the game ended in an 84–84 tie, the Chinese team went to their dressing room rather than remaining on the floor for the five minute overtime period. The Rutger's coach was perplexed by their response; however, the Chinese coach said, "Why not a tie? This was a friendly visit. Winning or losing was not important. Both sides tie; it is a diplomatic way of ending it." The response of the Rutger's coach was "why did we need a scoreboard?"

More recently the adaptation of soccer to the American society provides another example of the sport-culture nexus. In Europe the strategy of soccer is to score first in home games and then play good defense the rest of the game, whereas on the road the strategy is to try to achieve a zero–zero tie by means of good defense. Such a game is not well-suited to the American desire to reduce the ambiguity of contests to a win or loss; Americans are generally intolerant of ties and prefer offensive tactics to good defense. In 1975 a Brazilian known as an offensive player, Pele, helped soccer promoters in America to develop a more appealing game for Americans; for example, "sudden death" shootout (first goal wins) was added to eliminate tie games. Perhaps the most difficult adaptation of the game was to meet the commercial television interests of the promoters. Soccer needed television to promote its acceptance. Television coverage of soccer is problematic because the game lacks "breaks in the action" to get in the commercials. Faked injuries would be too contrived although the idea was considered; now the producers simply cut to commercials during the game action. In short, the structure of soccer would have to be altered to make it more compatible with American values if it were to become a successful game in terms of television consumption.

VanderZwaag (1977) has suggested that athletic games involving the use of a ball are distinctively popular in complex societies. He argues that the elements of skill, strategy, and chance inherent in ball games are especially compatible with industrial, technological societies. Sports with a ball as the focal object are the prototypical athletic events in the United States as contrasted with other genres of sport such as gymnastics, track, swimming, skiing, and marksmanship. VanderZwaag posits that when a ball is put into play the participants are set into motion in a manner requiring highly developed player coordination within a multiplicity of competitive modes. To illustrate the multiplicity of competing modes in the sport of basketball he notes that players "compete for a basket, total points, a rebound, total rebounds, a loose ball, in the act of dribbling, to draw or prevent a personal foul, in a jump-ball situation, to pass or block the ball, for court position, to screen and to generally outplay an opponent" (p. 66). The ball itself introduces a high degree of uncertainty in the competitive situation. It is probably the most mobile of all objects and its mobility combined with the competitive motif promotes various forms of strategies and requires a high degree of coordination. In short, sports using a ball seem to heighten the challenge for the participant and appeal to the spectator in complex societies. We add in this context, however, that VanderZwaag's theory would not account for the intense popularity of soccer in industrialized Europe and its relatively minor status in the United States.

Allison and Lüschen (1979) have analyzed the differences between two cultures and their orientation toward a single sport in a noncommercial context. Specifically, they compared the content of basketball as played by Navaho Indians and Anglos in the southwestern United States. Several important differences were noted by the researchers in playing the game that reflect the cultural ethos. For example, among Navahos pick-up basketball is less rule-bound than among Anglos. It was observed that Navaho players often travelled with the ball, double dribbled, and stepped out of bounds, but these violations were seldom called or enforced by the participants. In contrast, the Anglo pick-up games were similar to the rule-dominated interscholastic game. Another difference was evident in the contrasting orientations toward domination of one's opponent. The Navaho players competed less against their opponents than against themselves. This point was made by the coaches of Navaho youth when they described them as lacking the "killer instinct" that is needed in the sport (p. 78). Furthermore, in Anglo basketball the reward structure promotes individual achievement and the extrinsic reward of becoming a "star." In the Navaho basketball system, and in their larger culture as well, social sanctions are invoked when one moves toward selfishness. Therefore, status leveling devices are used such as ostracizing the star; "to be highly skilled is one thing, to flaunt that skill and expect public recognition of that skill is another" (p. 78). Finally, Allison and Lüschen point out that the Navaho players know the "correct" way to play the game because in interscholastic competition they adapt to the formalized game format, but when playing pick-up basketball they prefer the format that is more congruent with their culture. In summary, the contrasting value orientations of the two cultures are reflected in the way the games were played, with the Navaho Indians evidencing an orientation toward cooperation rather than competition and being reluctant to excel at the expense of others. This cultural ethos is further illustrated by the anthropologist Ruth Benedict (1934) in her account of the noncompetitiveness in another Pueblo Indian tribe.

> The ideal man . . . is a person of dignity and affability who has never tried to lead, and who has never called forth comment from his neighbors. Any conflict, even though all right is on his side, is held against him. Even in contests of skill like their foot races, if a man wins habitually he is debarred from running. They are interested in a game that a number can play with even chances, and an outstanding runner spoils the game: they will have none of him (p. 95).

BASEBALL IN JAPAN: A CASE STUDY

The case of baseball in Japan represents an interesting example of the way in which cultural differences affect a particular sport. Although the structure of the game is basically the same as in North America, it is clear that the climate and texture of the game are very different in the two cultural settings. An American professor at Tokyo University introduced baseball to his students in 1873. The sport is now immensely popular and draws a crowd at all levels of competition. A national tournament at the high school level lasts ten days and draws about 500,000 spectators in addition to a nationwide television audience (Boersema, 1979, p. 28). At the college level, baseball is televised and draws a following akin to bigtime university rivalries in the United States. The professional baseball leagues attract about 12 million spectators in addition to huge television audiences; several games are broadcast simultaneously on weekend television. Professional baseball in Japan began in 1936 after Babe Ruth and a group of American players toured the country.

Japanese baseball is distinctive in a number of ways that Americans would find quaint. For example, the annual game of musical chairs wherein managers are "replaced" is foreign to Japan. Managers are rarely fired, and when it does take place, a stylized ritual is used to permit the former manager to save face. It is also interesting to note that in Japan baseball games can end in a tie, which is no doubt a reflection of the Japanese emphasis on *process* as well as product. Moreover, the manager and players emphasize the collective goal of winning the pennant even at the expense of individual careers. A manager may call on a star pitcher, therefore, whenever a game is critical. Star pitchers are also used for relief work which commonly results in only two days of rest between starts. Such a heavy use no doubt shortens a career. In a 1958 Japan series, one pitcher worked in six of the seven games, and he once won 42 games in a single season. His career ended at 26 years of age. Nevertheless, a player is unlikely to challenge the system since team loyalty is paramount (Boersema, 1979).

American teams have been playing regularly in Japan since 1951 on an invitational basis. During this period, the teams from America have compiled a record of 163–47–20 (won–lost–tie) against the Japanese teams. The consensus of the visitors is that the Japanese are very competitive in terms of fundamentals and basic skills but lack the strength and power of players from America (Boersema, 1979, p. 31). Two foreign players are allowed on each professional team in Japan. Most of the American players are superannuated veterans of the major leagues. The Japanese recruit the Americans with serious attention paid to personal character and personality traits. The objective is to recruit well-mannered and disciplined players who can adapt to the more structured Japanese system and who can bear the rigorous training schedule that begins in January.

It is relevant to note that sumo wrestling ranks as the second most popular sport in Japan, with baseball first. "Both are very ceremonial sports, both require of the competent spectator very minute and careful observation of the quick move made after rather long pauses for ritual and for mental preparation by the athletes" (Cleaver, 1976, p. 120). To the American observer, Japanese baseball seems authoritarian and highly ritualized; however, a brief discussion of traditional Japanese values will suggest that baseball simply mirrors the larger Japanese society. First of all, it might be noted that individualism and egotism are highly stigmatized personality traits in Japan; the following expressions illustrate the value of selflessness in Japanese society:

> "Have no self."
>
> "Be wrapped in something long."
>
> "The nail that sticks up will be hammered down."
>
> "If one had no selfish motives but only the supreme values, there would be no self."
>
> "If he serves selflessly, he does not know what service is."
>
> "If he knows what service is, he has a self."
>
> "If you think that you work diligently, it is not true service."
>
> "To think of merits and demerits is egotism."
>
> "Because you do not act as you please, things will, conversely, turn out right for you."
> (Minami, 1971, p. 11)

The teamwork that is evident on a Japanese baseball team is paralleled by a remarkable sense of solidarity among industrial workers in Japan (Cleaver, 1976, p. 101). There is a congruity between company policy and worker preferences that precludes alienated labor. Workers consult and advise one another on improved ways of doing a particular piece of work. Although individuals may hold disparate political views off the job, these theoretical differences do not intrude upon team efforts at work. Many leisure activities are organized through the employer as family recreation; this pattern is sometimes referred to as paternalism by Americans. Westerners continually express amazement at the work ethic of industrial workers in Japan. In 1972 an American visitor reported seeing a group of workers assembled one morning outside a factory waiting for the gates to open. While waiting they were singing the company song (Cleaver, 1976, p. 102).

One of the first character traits that Americans note in Japanese is their extreme politeness. The ceremonial and ritual etiquette associated with courtesy in

Japan is expressed in a gradation of honorific language which is reflected in vocabulary as well as in grammar. La Barre's (1962) observations concerning Japanese politeness were originally published in 1945 and are therefore probably less applicable to contemporary Japan; nevertheless, his description of the Japanese character is interesting in terms of its contrast with American individualism.

> By contrast, the Japanese pride themselves on their lack of selfish "individualism" and their willingness to pull together in conformity to the "Yamato spirit." Thus it is often extremely difficult in Japanese social relations . . . to get any clear idea on which side of the fence a given person stands, since everyone pretends there is no fence and since all of them seek the protective cloak of apparent conformity to public opinion. There is so much by-play and face-saving, that in the end the Japanese exasperate occidentals as being *emotionally masked* persons with no honesty of expression whatsoever, "inscrutable" and untrustworthy (p. 335).

Haring (1962, p. 389) interprets Japanese politeness as compliance with a code of behavior that specifies correct behavior vis à vis others as a means of maintaining face and one's own self-esteem. The operative question is, "Have I acted correctly?"

The Japanese concepts of self-discipline and self-sacrifice are linked with implicit assumptions concerning skill, competency, and expertness. Self-pity is a foreign concept, as is individual frustration. "In Japan one disciplines oneself to be a good player, and the Japanese attitude is that one undergoes the training with no more consciousness of sacrifice than a man who plays bridge. Of course the training is strict, but that is inherent in the nature of things" (Benedict, 1946, p. 233). Interestingly, competency drives out self-consciousness; thus when one is living on the plane of expertness, Japanese say that he or she is "living as one already dead." Through self-discipline an inherently difficult activity can be made to appear easy. This stress on "competent self-discipline" has some desirable consequences.

> They pay much closer attention to behaving competently and they allow themselves fewer alibis than Americans. They do not so often project their dissatisfactions with life upon scapegoats, and they do not so often indulge in self-pity because they have somehow or other not got what Americans call average happiness. They have been trained to pay much closer attention to the 'rust of the body' than is common among Americans. (Benedict, 1946, p. 235)

The highly explicit codes of behavior in Japan account for the structured nature of the individual's response; behavior has the quality of being thoroughly planned. Spontaneous behavior is not admired. Tha mature individual is assumed to anticipate all emergencies and to be able to meet them calmly. Display of emotion is discouraged (Haring, 1962, p. 389). Similarly, a person who is touchy or easily affronted evidences an insecure ego. In child raising the parents make it clear that claims of the individual ego are to be systematically suppressed. In order to preserve face, "there must therefore be not only a constant checking and correcting of behavior, but also an anxious concern lest any lapse be publicly noted" (LaBarre, 1962, p. 341).

This description of Japanese personality traits and cultural values explains why baseball is so different in the two countries—sport is a value receptacle for society. A respect for authority, devotion to the collectivity, and self-discipline would understandably be conducive to team harmony. In Japanese baseball, doing your own thing is strongly stigmatized—salary disputes, asking for individual exemptions from team policies, temper tantrums, moodiness, complaining, clubhouse lawyers, attacking the umpire, criticizing the manager, mouthing-off to the media, bad-mouthing teammates, violation of training rules, fist fights, and *ad nauseam.* American players in Japan who have behaved in a selfish manner have experienced prompt and strong sanctions (Objski, 1975; Whiting, 1979).

Shenanigans of this type would lead to strong ostracism in a shame culture such as Japan. "Shame is a reaction to other people's criticism. A man is shamed by being openly ridiculed and rejected or by fantasying to himself that he has been ridiculous. In either case it is a potent sanction" (Benedict, 1946, p. 223). In brief, the Japanese place a premium on the quality of the athlete's character; sport performance alone is not sufficient. Thus, the "superbrat" (the columnist Mike Royko's term) is persona non grata in Japanese baseball.

GEOGRAPHICAL ASPECTS OF SPORT

Thus far we have provided historical and contemporary accounts of social values and the corresponding institutional arrangement of sport. Similarly, sport may reflect different subcultures or regions within a society. In the following account Axthelm (1970) has perceptively noted how sports mirror different elements of the American culture.

> Every American sport directs itself in a general way toward certain segments of American life. Baseball is basically a slow, pastoral experience, offering a tableau of athletes against a green background, providing moments of action amid longer periods allowed for contemplation of the spectacle. In its relaxed, unhurried way, it is exactly what it claims to be—the national "pasttime" rather than an intense, sustained game crammed with action. Born in a rural age, its appeal still lies largely in its offer of an untroubled island where, for a few hours, a pitcher tugging at his pants leg can seem to be the most important thing in a fan's life.
>
> Football's attraction is more contemporary. Its violence is in tune with the times, and its well-mapped strategic war games invite fans to become generals, plotting and second-guessing along with their warriors on the fields. With its action compressed in a fairly small area and its formations and patterns relatively easy to interpret, football is the ideal television spectacle: it belongs mostly to that loyal Sunday-afternoon viewer. Other sports have similar, if smaller, primary audiences. Golf and tennis belong first to country club members, horse racing to an enduring breed of gamblers, auto racing to throngs of Middle Americans who thrive on its violent roaring machines and death-defying vicarious risks. And basketball belongs to the cities.
>
> The game is simple, an act of one man challenging another, twisting, feinting, then perhaps breaking free to leap upward, directing a ball toward a target, a metal hoop ten feet above the ground. But its simple motions swirl into intricate patterns, its variations become almost endless, its brief soaring moments merge into a fascinating dance. To the uninitiated, the patterns may seem fleeting, elusive, even confusing; but on a city playground, a classic play is frozen in the minds of those who see it—a moment of order and achievement in a turbulent, frustrating existence. And a one-on-one challenge takes on wider meaning, defining identity and manhood in an urban society that breeds invisibility.

> Basketball is more than a sport or diversion in the cities. It is a part, often a major part, of the fabric of life. Kids in small towns—particularly in the Midwest—often become superb basketball players. But they do so by developing accurate shots and precise skills; in the cities, kids simply develop "moves." Other young athletes may learn basketball, but city kids live it. (pp. *ix-x*)[1]

An interesting aspect of the connection between sport and culture is found in the spatial distribution of sport. The sport geographer John Rooney (1974, 1975) has conducted extensive studies on the distribution of sports in the United States in terms of the recruitment of players from one region of the country to another. It is difficult to explain why a particular sport has an affinity for a given region. In some cases the geographical and climatic conditions provide a partial explanation; for example, ice hockey is more likely to be popular in a cold climate. Basketball is popular in the cities where a small space between buildings may be sufficient only for a basketball court. Moreover, an ethnic variable may provide an explanation; for example, inner-city blacks play basketball. Perhaps there is an ethnic affinity between the second and third generation eastern Europeans who settled in eastern Ohio and western Pennsylvania which accounts for a uniqueness to the sport of football. However, football flourishes in the southwestern United States, particularly in Texas, under quite different socioeconomic conditions. Rooney (1975) points out that while it is difficult to provide definitive explanations for the existence of various types of sports in different regions, the explanation may rest with distinctive combinations of demographic, economic, ethnic, religious, educational, and political variables. Furthermore, once a sport becomes established in a locality, it is likely to become a part of the subculture of the region, a source of pride, with feelings of communal spirit becoming associated with the sport. In some regions and communities where the emphasis on sport is particularly strong, junior high school boys may be held back a year to allow for greater physical development that would be desirable for his participation in high school sports. This practice imposes additional education expense on the school system and may or may not contribute to the emotional and educational development of the student.

Figures 4-1 and 4-2 depict the state of origin of major university football and basketball players based on 1971–72 samples. The states of Texas, Arkansas, Louisiana, Mississippi, Idaho, Montana, and North Dakota provide the greatest per capita production of *football* players. Similarly, a greater than average number of college *basketball* players come from the states of Indiana, Kentucky, Ohio, Illinois, Pennsylvania, Utah, Idaho and the Dakotas (Rooney, 1975, pp. 76–79).

By the middle 1970s Rooney (1981) noted some significant regional shifts in the production of football players (perhaps changes will also be evidenced with more data on basketball players). For example, the northern region of Ohio and Pennsylvania declined in relative importance and Texas, Louisiana, Mississippi, Georgia, and Florida increased as sources of major college football players. These changes are displayed in Figure 4-3. The shift toward the South is also illustrated

---

[1]From "Introduction" (as it appeared in *Harper's Magazine*, October 1970) to *The City Game* by Pete Axthelm. Copyright © 1970 by Pete Axthelm. By permission of Harper & Row Publishers, Inc.

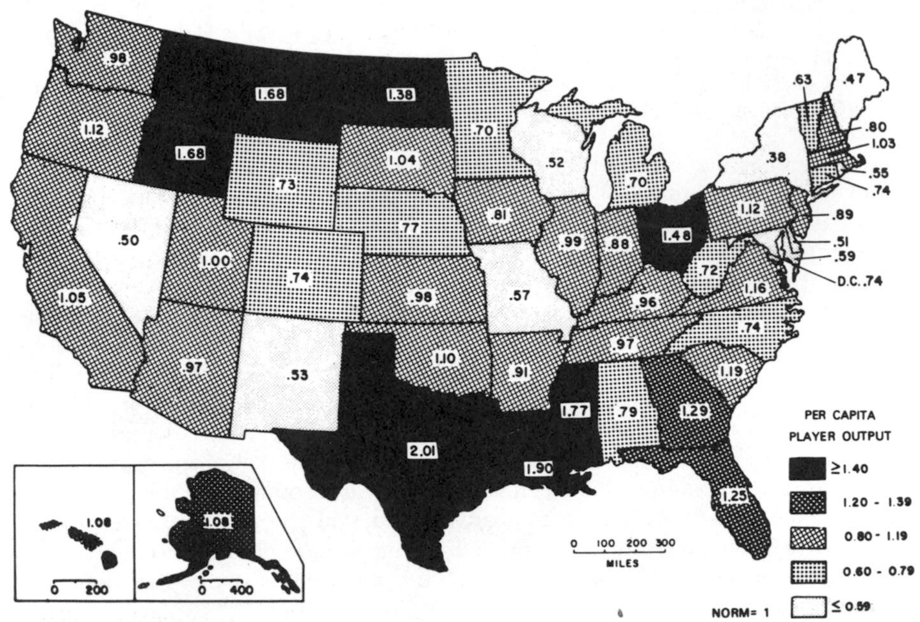

FIGURE 4–1 Per capita origin of major college football players: 1971–1972 (*Source:* Rooney, 1975, p. 78).

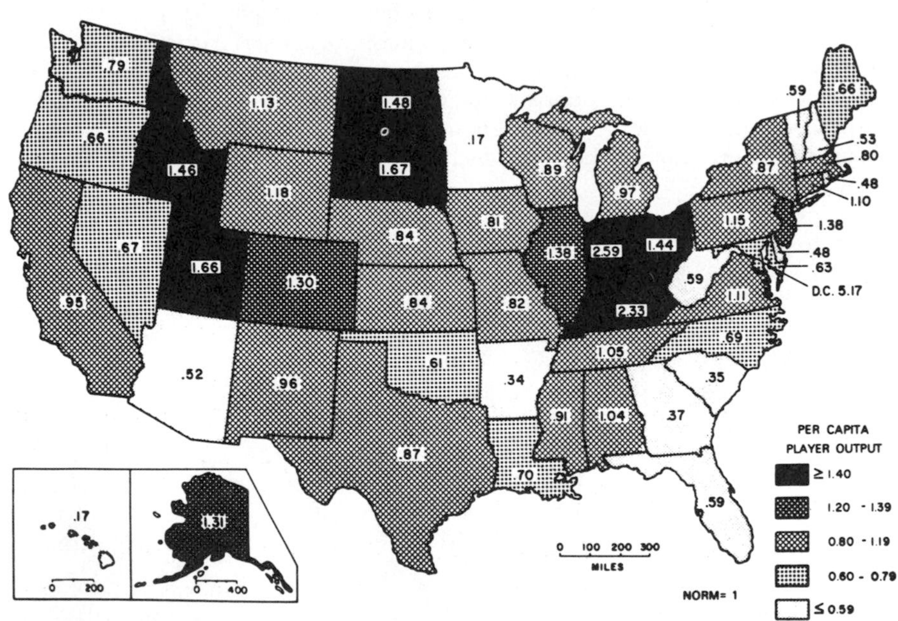

FIGURE 4–2 Per capita origin of major college basketball players: 1971–1972 (*Source:* Rooney, 1975, p. 79).

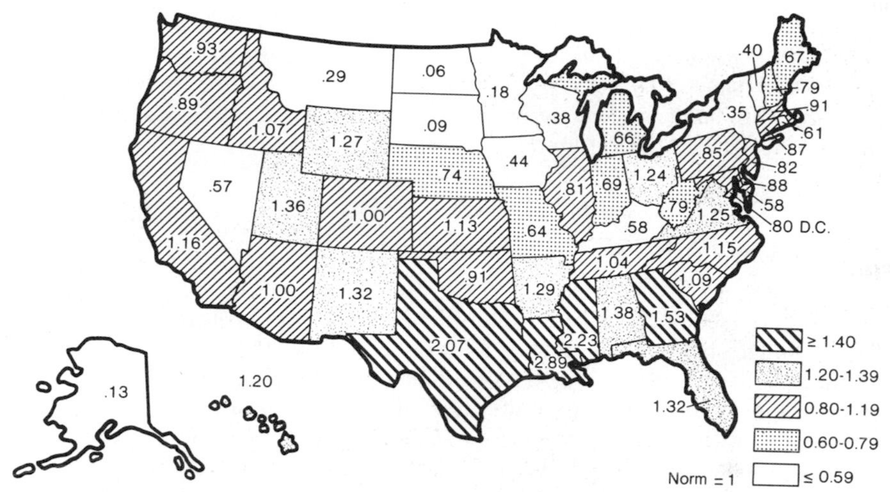

FIGURE 4–3 Per capita origin of major college football players: 1973–1976 (*Source:* Rooney, 1981, p. 153).

in the following 10 leading football counties (i.e., production of major college players) from a per capita standpoint between 1958–66 and 1973–76 (Rooney, 1981: 154–155):

1958–66	1973–76
Jefferson, Ohio	Ouchita, Louisiana
Beaver, Pennsylvania	Calcasieu, Louisiana
Potter, Texas	East Baton Rouge, Louisiana
Harrison, Mississippi	Jefferson, Texas
Galveston, Texas	Caddo, Louisiana
Westmoreland, Pennsylvania	Hinds, Mississippi
Washington, Pennsylvania	Montgomery, Alabama
Fayette, Pennsylvania	Trumbull, Ohio
Lucas, Ohio	Galveston, Texas
Trumbull, Ohio	Dekalb, Georgia

Note that there are no Pennsylvania counties and only one Ohio county in the top ten in the 1973–76 period. Rooney elaborates on several of the possible explanations cited previously for the importance of football in the culture of the South and Southwest (Rooney, 1981: 157-158):

1. There is an emphasis on rugged individualism which finds expression in football.
2. There is an emphasis on militarism which is reflected in the attraction for games that emphasize discipline.
3. The state-related "nationalism" finds expression at the local community level through the prestige of the football team.

4. The long autumn provides time for a long season and "play off" games.
5. There is an absence of other opportunities in small towns in the South and Southwest; football simply offers something to do and a focus for community activities.
6. There are numerous local opportunities to play major college football for the most outstanding high school players.

FROM RITUAL TO RECORD

One way to understand the relationship between sport and contrasting cultures is to differentiate between the format of sport as well as the contrasts in culture. Guttmann (1978) provides a model of modern sport that can be contrasted with primitive sport. This model is a useful heuristic device for distinguishing the gradations in sport across historical eras and between different cultures today. He uses seven characteristics to distinguish modern sport: secularism, equality of opportunity to compete and the conditions of competition, specialization of roles, rationalization, bureaucratic organization, quantification, and the quest for records (p. 16). While sport in most primitive societies is closer to our definition of play than sport (see Chapter 2), the elementary forms of sport come into being when their playful physical activities begin to be governed by rules. The contrasts between primitive and modern forms of sport are evident when examined in light of these seven criteria.

1. Primitive sport was usually embedded in religious festivals and ceremonies. They were sacred, spiritual, and religious in nature. Modern sport is secularized and pursued for secular ends—victories, economic rewards, and prestige. The secularity of both sport and religion is now exemplified in sport as a form of "civil religion."
2. In the premodern era sport tended to be ascriptive and usually limited to males, aristocrats, and the leisure class. Indeed, a legacy of this notion remains in the Modern Olympic Games with the pretense of amateurism. Modern sport emphasizes the equity principle, including an increasing proportion of participation by women and minority groups. The equity principle also applies to standardization of rules and conditions of competition.
3. Very early in the evolution of sports a trend toward specialization and "professionalization" emerges. Guttmann notes that, "It did not take the Greeks long to discover that some men were physically equipped to run and others to wrestle or throw the discus" (p. 36). The Middle Ages with their folk games were probably less specialized than the Greeks and Romans. For example, medieval football was village against village with a lack of specialization; even the distinction between player and spectator was not clear. Modern sport is characterized by a high degree of specialization as exemplified by American football. To achieve a high level of performance, increasing specialization is necessary, and specialization when coupled with an emphasis on performance promotes professionalization in sport. Professionalization in this sense is defined by Guttmann not in terms of money but time—"how much of a person's life is dedicated to the achievement of athletic excellence? In other words, to what degree does a person specialize in excellence?" (p. 39).

4. Primitive sports were limited and regulated by taboos and traditions. Modern sports are regulated by prescribed rules; rules regulate the competition. However, the difference between the primitive and modern rules is that modern sports are rationalized rather than prescribed by tradition (Guttmann, 1978). By this we mean that there is a logical connection between ends and means. Primitive hunters are trained in their youth; as adults they do not practice. They hit or miss based on what they perceive to be "the will of the gods" and the forces of magic. On the other hand, the "Greeks did more than practice. They trained. The distinction is important. Training implies a rationalization of the whole enterprise, a willingness to experiment, a constant testing of results achieved" (p. 43). Rationality encourages calculability, that is, the use of logical means to achieve a desired goal; this process is illustrated in the scientific study of physiology, psychology of performance, and scientific training schedules that are used to produce greater achievements in athletic competition.
5. An additional characteristic of modern sport is bureaucratization. Primitive societies are not bureaucratized. Sport bureaucracy began with the Greeks and continued with the Roman affinity for administration. Today most sports are governed by a sports organization (for example, National Collegiate Athletic Association, International Olympic Committee, National Football Association, Marylebone Cricket Club, Office of the General Supervisor for the Physical Development of the Peoples of Russia). Bureaucratization promotes universalism, standardization of rules and regulations, and efficiency.
6. Modern sports, according to Guttmann, are distinguished "by the almost inevitable tendency to transform *every* athletic feat into one that can be quantified and measured" (p. 47; italics in the original). Thus one sees the emergence of the stop watch, electronic timers and innumerable statistics on batting averages, earned run averages, number of times at bat, shooting percentages, number of passes completed, goals scored, number of shots on goal, number of aces and double faults, *ad infinitum.* Although modern baseball is considered a slow game, it is amenable to modern sport and the media because it provides ample opportunity for the commentators to provide "color," including the statistics of every conceivable combination and permutation of the game, past and present.
7. Finally, Guttmann notes that records emerge from the combination of quantification with the desire to excel (p. 51). A record is an abstraction that allows athletes to compete with each other across time and space. Present day milers can challenge Roger Bannister's 1954 record of a four-minute mile. Henry Aaron surpassed Babe Ruth's record of 714 home runs. We have even been able to quantify the aesthetic–athletic performances of gymnastics, diving and figure skating. On an interval scale from 0–10, Nadia Comaneci achieved "perfection" (a 10) seven times at the Montreal Olympics. This was a record. Her record surpassed Nelli Kim's attainment of "perfection," and her total score of 79.275 was better than Ludmilla Tourescheva's 77.025 (pp. 52–53). Note the use of even three decimal places!

These seven characteristics of modern sports are presented in Table 4-1 in conjunction with historical periods. The extent to which these characteristics were present in different cultural eras can also be extended to the degree of sport modernity in various nations. For example, Eastern Europe is today considered the epitome of rationalization in sport—East Germany in swimming, Romania in gymnastics, and the Soviet Union in most all Olympic sports.

TABLE 4-1 The Characteristics of Sports in Various Ages

	PRIMITIVE SPORTS	GREEK SPORTS	ROMAN SPORTS	MEDIEVAL SPORTS	MODERN SPORTS
Secularism	Yes and No	Yes and No	Yes and No	Yes and No	Yes
Equality	No	Yes and No	Yes and No	No	Yes
Specialization	No	Yes	Yes	No	Yes
Rationalization	No	Yes	Yes	No	Yes
Bureaucracy	No	Yes and No	Yes	No	Yes
Quantification	No	No	Yes and No	No	Yes
Records	No	No	No	No	Yes

Source: Guttmann, 1978, p. 54

CONCLUSION

In this chapter we have focused on the general relationship between culture and sport. Although we cannot draw one-to-one relationships about the culture type and the specific form of sport, we generally find that the structure of sport is isomorphic with the culture in which it exists. Based on the values and institutional structure of a society, we can observe variations in sport in terms of such dimensions as skill level, strategy, chance, formalization, aggression, and technology. Modern sports have increasingly developed characteristics that promote the achievement of excellence, high levels of performance, and the establishment of new records. In general, this trend toward records parallels the social change from a sacred to secular form of society that results from the processes of industrialization and urbanization. Although it is evident that play and/or sport exist in all human societies, a cross-cultural analysis demonstrates that the particular format that is "natural" to the people in one society is, in fact, a cultural rather than a biological fact. This point is illustrated by the variations in the degree of aggressiveness and competitiveness that are present in the sports of different cultures.

In the modern world the adaptability of sport to a culture is determined not only by the value configuration but also by the overall institutional structure—particularly the economic, technological, and political structures. For example, formally organized sports in the United States are most likely to become popular if they are compatible with the commercial interests of the mass media. Additionally, sports are now becoming important tools in international politics. Basketball is a traditional sport of the United States, yet it has been adopted by many nations, including the Soviet Union, as a means of gaining prestige in international competition. We devote attention to some of the political ramifications of international sport in a later chapter.

CHAPTER 5
Socialization into Sport

It is often said that someone is a "natural athlete." This expression can be misleading if it is understood to mean that a given person did not have to learn the cluster of ideas, attitudes, and movements associated with a given sport. The notion of a natural athlete no doubt applies primarily to people who are born with physical attributes such as coordination, agility, speed, power, and stamina. However, the refinement of these attributes, skills, and techniques as well as the psychological and social aspects of play and eventually sport have to be acquired.

In the broadest area, learning to be an athlete is incorporated in the process of socialization. The socialization process refers to the assimilation and development of the skills, knowledge, values, dispositions, and self-perceptions necessary to perform present or anticipated roles in society or particular groups within society (Brim, 1966; Clausen, 1968). Psychologically, this process involves the development and molding of the individual within society and its subgroups. Viewed sociologically, socialization includes teaching the individual to behave in a manner that is consistent with social expectations and thus maintains social order, continuity, and predictability. Socialization also results in a set of constraints in the sense that it leaves a social imprint, limits the range of acceptable behavior, and thus induces conformity.

Fundamental to the model of socialization we wish to present is the premise that the process begins with the biological organism and, through a series of interpersonal relationships, continues throughout the person's life. Thus, in "the life of every person, there are a number of people directly involved in socialization who have great influence because of their frequency of contact, their primacy, and their control over rewards and punishment" (Brim, 1966, p. 8). Significant others continue to influence behavior, values, and dispositions throughout the life cycle, although the salience of specific persons will change as new significant others are added and older ones displaced.

Generally, social interaction reflects the use of rewards and punishments to produce socially acceptable behavior. Social interaction is not unidirectional. Even though the child is being molded by the rewards and punishments of significant others, the child is also responding in a way that shapes the behavior of the socialization agents. The child soon learns, consciously or unconsciously, the norm of reciprocity, that is, reciprocity with another person (a smile, kiss, or hug) that will result in a positive response (e.g., a compliment, hug, food, and security). In short, the socialization process is a two-way interaction and does not result in a one-way internalization or total congruence between the person and society. Rather, individuals are never perfectly compliant; to assume otherwise is, according to Dennis Wrong (1961), an "oversocialized view" of humanity and an "overintegrated view" of society. Indeed, Wrong points out, if people were completely socialized, how is it "that violence, conflict, revolution, and the individual's sense of coercion by society manage to exist at all . . .?" (p. 186).

In complex societies, values and norms are often pluralistic, which can lead to conflicts in behavior and attitudes. Potential contradictions in value orientations have been noted in Chapter 3; for example, the emphasis on individual achievement versus subverting oneself to the team effort, or the importance of competition (being "number one") versus qualities of humanism and equality. In a pluralistic context, values and norms cease to be absolute and come to be applied on the basis of situations, persons, and times (Ingham and Loy, 1974). It is within this generalized perspective that we focus on socialization into the sport role, on how one learns to be an athlete. We need to remember, however, that each person brings different attributes and potentials to the socialization situation. Each will experience the process somewhat differently and will be playing and learning other roles in addition to the athletic role. In short, the degree of involvement or psychological distance between the person and the athlete role will differ from individual to individual.

Sport socialization has been analyzed from two perspectives. The first focuses on *socialization into sport*—that is, the agents or agencies that have been influential in attracting children and youth into sport involvement. This includes the acquisition of social, psychological, and physical skills requisite for participation in sport. This process is the topic of the present chapter. The second focus relates to *socialization through sport*. Here the interest is on the probable consequences or outcomes of sport participation (Sage, 1980a). Our attention will be given to socialization through sport in subsequent chapters. These two aspects of sport socialization are illustrated in the following diagram.

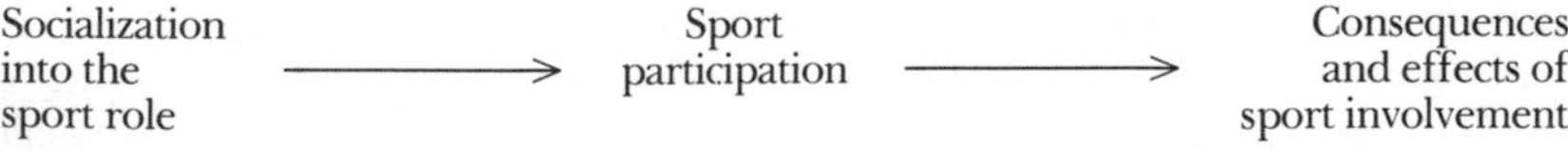

This socialization process into sport and through sport begins in childhood and adolescence, but is intertwined with continued sport involvement across all stages of the life cycle.

INITIAL SOCIALIZATION INTO SPORT

A number of classical and contemporary theorists have studied socialization as a reflection of the interactional process that occurs in childhood play and game situations (Piaget, 1962; Stone, 1965; Sutton-Smith, 1975). In essence, play is unstructured, spontaneous, and fantasylike. It involves simple and specific role playing. In play, small children play the roles of specific persons—mother, father, policeman, football player—as they spontaneously improvise and assume separate identities. This "play stage" is an important developmental step for the child in learning the behavior and attitudes of adults and is a prelude to participation in games.

Games are rule-bound and involve competition with another player or players. This activity requires adherence to rules and multiple role taking at the same time. As Mead (1934) has pointed out, to participate in a game (as opposed to play) requires a more sophisticated level of socialization that permits the players to "take the role" of all the other players and to adjust their behavior to the related positions and roles of the other team members within the framework of the game rules. When a child has successfully participated in games, he or she can be considered mature enough to be socialized into sport.

Childhood socialization occurs within the social milieu that is likely to include agents and agencies as the family, school, church, peers, and mass media; additionally, the child may be affiliated with organizations such as 4H, scouts, community sports groups, and other interest groups in areas of music, art, dance, dramatics, and so on. The overall shape and configuration of these social systems, degree of involvement, and their socialization impact will vary with the child. Figure 5-1 illustrates this array of social systems in the child's environment. These social systems will provide the child with values, norms, and expectations to be followed within each role sphere. However, socialization into sport will usually be carried out by several of these agencies and significant others associated with childhood and adolescence. The child's self-perception will reflect the degree of involvement in the several role spheres.

The introduction to sport is most likely to occur in the family if the child has parents or older siblings who participate and are interested in sport activities. Later in this chapter we present empirical data demonstrating the impact of familial interest in sport on participation in athletics by high school students. Peer influence within the neighborhood is likewise an early socialization experience into sport participation. The opportunity to learn athletic skills and to evaluate one's perception of ability is likely to occur in early childhood among neighborhood friends. In the elementary and junior high school years, children continue to refine their perceptions of themselves as "one of the fastest runners in my class," "I'm about average," "I'm one of the best basketball players in my gym class." If this self-evaluation indicates less ability than most of the children in the class, and the reward structure of the school places a great importance on this ability, the child is likely to turn to other activities of interest that provide more positive feedback. The self-evaluation of physical ability will be further reinforced by the formal evaluations given by teachers and coaches.

Community agencies, where they exist, also present opportunities to become involved in sport through Little League, Ban Johnson, Babe Ruth, American Le-

FIGURE 5–1 Social systems having an impact on the child's self-perceptions (*Source:* Adapted from B. McPherson, "The Child in Competitive Sport," in R. Magill, *Children in Sport,* © 1978. Reprinted by permission of Human Kinetics Publishers).

gion baseball, Pop Warner football, youth hockey leagues, and the like. The mass media also provide a constant opportunity for youngsters to become acquainted with sports, and the media provide sport heroes as role models for behavioral emulation (see Kenyon and McPherson, 1973; Loy and Ingham, 1973; and Sage, 1974a, for a detailed discussion of these socialization experiences).

Several empirical studies shed light on the factors that contribute to an interest in sports either as spectator or participant. For example, Kenyon (1970) investigated the social and psychological correlates of watching major league baseball games and the Olympic Games in Mexico City among college students. He identified the following school-related variables as being associated with watching these athletic events:

Encouragement in sport by physical education teachers
General interest in sport during high school
Attendance at sport events during high school
Secondary involvement in sport during college

Additionally, Kenyon noted the importance of familial and peer influences and perceived athletic ability as correlates of these forms of athletic involvement. McPherson (1972) surveyed students from three metropolitan high schools to determine the socialization process that explained their involvement in sport as spectators. He found that involvement in sport for both males and females was promoted by the collective influence of the family, peers, school, and community systems.

Susan Greendorfer (1976) conducted two investigations of why college women enter into athletic participation. Her research was based on a sample of 585 college women in Wisconsin and 86 women at the University of New Mexico. In both groups the females' peers served as the most significant agents of socialization into sport participation from childhood through adulthood. Greendorfer reported that "teachers-coaches become a factor only during the adolescent stage, which casts them more as reinforcing agents of socialization rather than initiating the process" (p. 7).

Greendorfer's research also calls attention to possible social class and geographical differences in athletic involvement, including the particular type of sport. For example, in the Wisconsin sample, the team sports of volleyball and basketball were preferred by students from a lower class background, while students from the higher social classes were more likely to participate in individual and dual sports such as gymnastics, swimming, cross-country running, badminton, and tennis. In the New Mexico sample, no such relationships were found, but Greendorfer noted that this sample may have had unique cultural characteristics and that caution should be exercised in making generalizations from this finding. Most previous research on sport involvement focused on male participation because, in essence, sport has traditionally been defined as a male world. Fortunately, current social change is bringing about a redefinition of the athletic behavior appropriate for females.

Another study of factors associated with high school girls' participation in sport has been reported by Snyder and Spreitzer (1976b). Data in this study were collected from a representative sample of high school girls in Ohio who were participating in interscholastic gymnastics, basketball, and track. A control group of nonathletes was also selected for purposes of comparison. An examination of Table 5-1 indicates that the parents of the athletes were only slightly more interested in sports than the parents of the nonathletes. However, the striking difference among the childhood factors is that the athletes started their participation early in life. One stereotype of the female athlete is that she is a "tomboy." Presumably this means that her behavior is more masculine than that of most girls. The basketball players in the study were more likely to have been considered tomboys than the other athletes or nonathletes. Perhaps the girls who participated in basketball (a game that involves body contact, hard running, and rebounding) were not considered "ladylike." It will be interesting to see if research continues to show such stereotypes of females who participate in the traditionally "less feminine" sports.

Table 5-1 also shows that the female athletes were much more likely to receive familial encouragement than the nonathletes. Parental encouragement was most evident for the gymnasts. This, no doubt, indicates that the parents perceive gymnastics as an appropriate sport for their daughters. It is also interesting to note that the mothers were less likely to provide encouragement for their daughters to participate in basketball than either gymnastics or track. This pattern suggests that basketball had less social acceptability than the other sports. Data in Table 5-1 show that female athletes received considerable encouragement from their peers, teachers, and particularly coaches, with their girlfriends providing more support than boyfriends. The data were gathered on high school youth. Similar data gathered by Nicholson (1978, pp. 66–67) indicate that junior high school girls are also far more likely to have parents, siblings, and friends who are participating in sports than a comparison group of nonathletes.

TABLE 5-1 Type of Female Adolescent Sport Participation by Background Characteristics

CORRELATIVE FACTORS	GYMNASTS (*N* = 137) (%)	BASKETBALL PLAYERS (*N* = 97) (%)	TRACK (*N* = 88) (%)	NO SPORT PARTICIPATION (*N* = 234) (%)
Childhood Factors				
Father was very interested in sports	45	39	38	35
Mother was very interested in sports	18	20	18	13
Participated in organized sports as a child	48	33	33	14
I was often called a Tomboy	20	50	24	21
Familial Encouragement to Participate in Sports				
Much encouragement by father	43	33	38	11
Much encouragement by mother	48	25	38	14
Much encouragement by brother(s)	22	22	28	8
Much encouragement by sister(s)	28	24	24	8
Much encouragement by relatives	23	16	12	6
Peers, Teachers, and Coaches' Encouragement to Participate in Sports				
Much encouragement by girl friends	39	41	33	14
Much encouragement by boy friends	34	21	27	9
Much encouragement by teachers	26	24	20	5
Much encouragement by coaches	67	57	52	11

Source: Snyder and Spreitzer, 1976b, p. 806.

The process of socialization into sport is similar to socialization leading to involvement in other social activities. For example, there are a number of similarities between participation in sport and music activities. Both activities are comparable in the sense that they can require extensive training, practicing, coaching-teaching, discipline, performances, and are likely to be important in one's identity. They also represent major areas of school resource allocation and are sources of prestige among adolescents. Table 5-2 provides parallels for comparison among approximately 500 high school girls who were participating in sport only, music only, both sport and music, or neither of these extracurricular activities (Snyder and Spreitzer, 1978). The explanatory variable in this analysis is the parents' encouragement to their daughters to participate in either of these activities. The assumption was that the greater positive support by the parent for the activity, the greater likelihood the daughter would engage in the activity. Because there might be differences in the encouragement based on the parental education, this factor was used as a control variable. Table 5-2 shows that the fathers' encouragement for their daughters' participation in sport tended to be stronger than their support for their daughters' involvement in music. Moreover, the maternal encouragement for participation in sport was almost as strong as the degree of maternal encouragement for their daughters' involvement in music. These findings are interesting because some studies have suggested that participation in music might be more acceptable for girls than involvement in sport (see Chapter 9 for an elaboration of this thesis). However, the data in Table 5-2 clearly show that parental encouragement is positively associated with both activities; on the other hand, the girls who

TABLE 5-2 Type of Extracurricular Involvement by Perceived Parental Encouragement for Sports and Music

	LOWER EDUCATION LEVEL				HIGHER EDUCATION LEVEL			
ADOLESCENT REPORTS OF PARENTAL ENCOURAGEMENT FOR SPORTS AND MUSIC	SPORT ONLY ($N = 426$) (%)	MUSIC ONLY ($N = 60$) (%)	SPORT AND MUSIC ($N = 168$) (%)	NEITHER ($N = 222$) (%)	SPORT ONLY ($N = 155$) (%)	MUSIC ONLY ($N = 22$) (%)	SPORT AND MUSIC ($N = 40$) (%)	NEITHER ($N = 42$) (%)
Much encouragement by father for sport	38	3	33	14	46	0	48	7
Much encouragement by mother for sport	40	6	36	12	43	4	35	9
Much encouragement by father for music	12	19	21	13	22	36	48	16
Much encouragement by mother for music	20	45	46	23	36	50	60	44

Source: Snyder and Spreitzer, 1978, p. 346.

TABLE 5-3 **Mean Rating of Socializing Agents on Encouragement to Participate before High School, during High School, and during College (Scale Values 1-5)**

SOCIALIZING AGENTS	BEFORE HIGH SCHOOL *N*	BEFORE HIGH SCHOOL $\overline{X}$	HIGH SCHOOL *N*	HIGH SCHOOL $\overline{X}$	COLLEGE *N*	COLLEGE $\overline{X}$
Father	57	4.05	69	4.26	85	4.24
Mother	57	3.96	70	4.07	87	4.14
Brother	49	3.92	63	4.06	76	4.10
Sister	44	3.39	55	3.53	68	3.74
Other relative	46	3.59	58	3.91	72	3.90
Male friend	57	4.28	70	4.38	87	4.20
Female friend	50	3.32	69	3.77	84	3.88
Classroom teacher	55	3.40	69	3.75	71	3.41
School coach	49	4.08	69	4.65	85	4.60
School counselor	39	3.28	64	3.59	60	3.33
Nonschool personnel	40	4.05	47	4.15	51	3.84
Other	26	3.81	32	4.00	44	3.86

Source: Kenyon and McPherson, 1973, p. 321.

were participating in neither sport nor music received little parental encouragement for either extracurricular activity. In general, parents with a higher educational level were more supportive of both sport and music than parents with less education.

The influence of significant others is also evident in the research by Kenyon and Grogg (cited in Kenyon and McPherson, 1973, p. 321), who studied elite male college athletes at the University of Wisconsin to determine the factors that contributed to their participation in sport. Table 5-3 shows the relative encouragement of socializing agents. The data suggest that the influence of the parents was more evident at the higher educational levels.

The studies cited focus on antecedent variables associated with participation of high school and college students in sport. Another method of studying this process is to take a retrospective view from the vantage point of adult involvement in sport. Survey research (Spreitzer and Snyder, 1976a) indicates that adult sports participation for both males and females can be traced back to childhood rein-

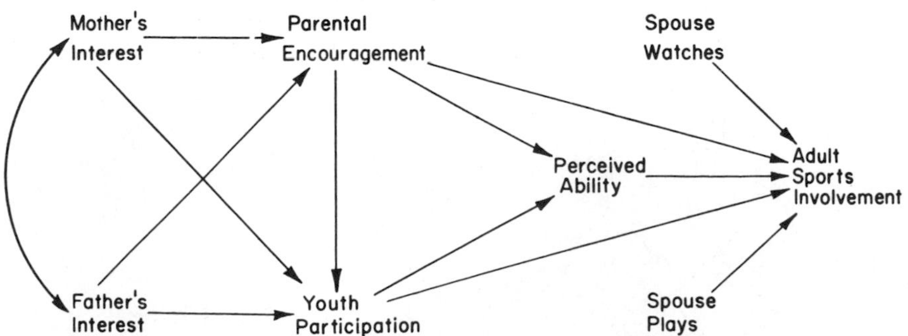

FIGURE 5–2 A theoretical model of socialization into sport (*Source:* Spreitzer and Snyder, 1976, p. 243).

forcement. Findings from a community sample revealed that the following factors were associated with adult involvement in sport: parental interest in sport, parental encouragement to participate in sport, participation in formally organized (at school, for example) athletic programs as a youth, self-perception of athletic ability, and involvement in sport by one's spouse. These factors are interrelated in the form of a causal model in Figure 5-2.

The arrows in Figure 5-2 suggest causal relationships that flow from early childhood to adulthood. This model does not include, however, other variables that would be helpful in explaining adult participation in sport. This sociological model would, no doubt, be amplified by the addition of physiological and psychological variables, particularly with respect to personality characteristics.

In summary, the causal linkage of variables associated with involvement in sport seems to be as follows:

Parental interest in sport → Parental encouragement for sport → Offspring's participation in sports → Offspring's perceived ability in sports → Adult participation in sports

This chain of variables reflects the underlying influence of the family and the socialization process that results in sport participation among youth and eventually as an adult. This socialization process operates for both males and females (Kenyon and McPherson, 1974; Snyder and Spreitzer, 1973; Snyder and Spreitzer, 1978; Spreitzer and Snyder, 1976).

In another study of 435 college students, we analyzed the degree of encouragement that the students received from their parents when they were in high school to participate in sports as related to their degree of participation. Participation on an interscholastic varsity team requires a greater degree of involvement and commitment than being a member of an intramural team; thus, if parental encouragement is an important factor in determining youth participation in sport, we would expect that the degree of encouragement would be associated with the degree of involvement.

Figure 5-3 summarizes correlations between the three variables analyzed in this study (i.e., parental encouragement, high school participation in intramurals or varsity sports, and perceived athletic ability; correlations for females are indicated in the parentheses; see Chapter 6 for a discussion of correlations).

It is evident from these findings that parental encouragement is strongest among students who were varsity athletes; there was clearly less parental encouragement for sport participation at the intramural level of involvement. It is in-

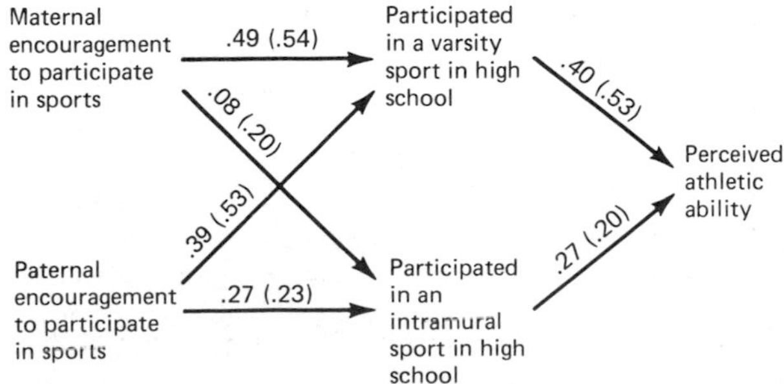

FIGURE 5–3
Parental encouragement and participation in high school sports.

teresting to note that these results provide further verification for the socialization model noted previously because explicit parental encouragement is directly related to the level of sport participation; these findings are apparent for both male and female students. Parenthetically, within the high school social structure, participation in varsity sports is more prestigious than intramural sports. In most high schools intramurals generally serve as a channel of sport participation for "less athletic" students; accordingly, students report less parental encouragement for this "lower level" of athletic involvement. The correlation analysis further indicates that the level of athletic participation is a good predictor of perceived athletic ability. Apparently, self-definitions of athletic ability develop through skill testing in adolescent athletic participation via self–others evaluation of ability (the "others" include parents and coaches). The higher levels of athletic involvement contribute to the prominence of athletic ability as part of one's identity. Thus, we suggest that the degree of parental encouragement is directly related to the level of athletic participation; moreover, for some students, intramural sports serve a "cooling out" function (Goffman, 1952). That is, for the student who lacks the skill to participate on a varsity level of competition, intramurals serve to soften the disappointment associated with his limitation. This vicarious participation in adolescent sports is likewise accompanied by modest parental encouragement and a reduced self-perception of athletic ability for the marginal player (cf. Ball, 1976). Probably both the socialization and "cooling out" explanations operate for most adolescents.

Kenyon and McPherson (1973) provide a model that summarizes the overall process of socialization into sport. Their model takes into account the influence that family, school, peer group, and community have in introducing youngsters to the world of sport. Their model is not exclusively sociological in nature in that it also focuses on sport role aptitude, for example, on the importance of physical aptitudes in the form of coordination, strength, and speed. The Kenyon and McPherson model, as treated in the original source, deals separately with the childhood and adolescent periods and also distinguishes active involvement from spectatorship. Figure 5-4 summarizes the Kenyon and McPherson model of socialization into sport. The multiplicity of relationships in the model indicates the complexity of social scientific research in this area and the need for multicausal explanations (p. 309).

The process of socialization into sport can be further explicated by an examination of demographic and social variables that are associated with an opportunity to engage in athletics. For example, in the previous chapter we noted the influence of the geographical region as a factor affecting the type of sport that is practiced. Thus, whether one lives in a rural or urban environment, whether there are unique climatic conditions, or whether a particular sport is popular in a geographical region are factors that have an impact on the opportunity to learn a sport. We have already noted the importance of gender and family variables in the opportunity for socialization into sport. In the past, females have generally had less exposure to sport than males. In recent years, the opportunity for female athletes has increased markedly due to Title IX legislation sponsored by the federal government (see Chapter 10); yet a legacy of differential opportunity remains in the value structure of the American society. Several variables that are linked with family background may affect socialization into sport. For example, such factors as social class and race may determine the type of sport that is available to a youngster. It is evident that members of the lower class are less likely to afford the financial expense required to participate in the club and lessons usually associated with

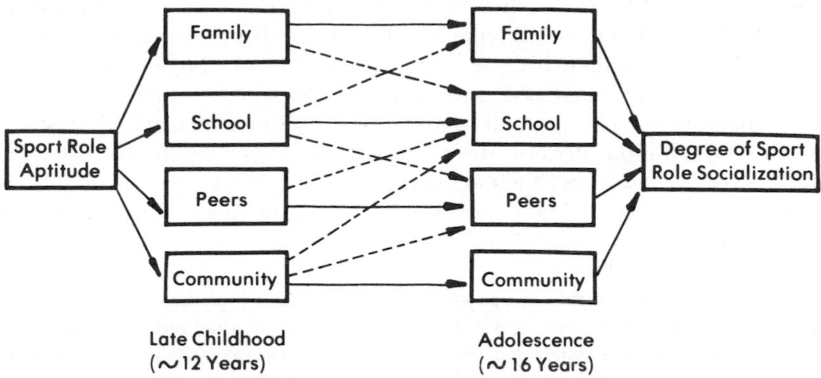

FIGURE 5–4 Kenyon and McPherson's model of socialization into sport.

sports such as tennis, ice skating, golf, swimming, and gymnastics; furthermore, in some cases the differential opportunities in sports have been affected by overt or covert discrimination against members of a class, race, religious, ethnic group, or age group. Specific studies focusing on these variables are presented later in this book.

Although the importance of the family in sport socialization has usually focused on the parental influence, recent studies also indicate the influence of siblings because brothers and sisters are likely to learn to participate in sports from each other. Furthermore, the ordinal position of the child in the family may influence the opportunity to learn to play a particular sport. For example, Nisbett (1968) noted that first borns are less likely to play a dangerous sport than later borns, and Landers (1979) suggests that parental attitudes vary toward first born and late-born children participating in dangerous and high risk sports (e.g., football, hockey, and wrestling). In summary, interaction in the family is particularly important for sport socialization because it tends to be linked with other variables such as social class, race and ethnicity, religion, and the influence of siblings.

It might be noted in this context that sport socialization is not always a unilateral process flowing from the older generation to the younger. Although the empirical literature documents that parental involvement and interest in sport are good predictors of a child's degree of participation, nevertheless the literature also shows that sport socialization occurs through peers, coaches, community athletic programs, and athletic programs in the schools. Consequently, a form of reverse sport socialization also occurs between parent and child. Quite commonly, for example, a parent may develop an interest and knowledge about sport through a son or daughter's participation. It is not clear, however, whether such a parent's interest in sport is merely idiosyncratic or whether it continues once the child leaves the home. In any event, we suggest that this process of reverse socialization in the sphere of sports is worthy of systematic research.

AVERSIVE SOCIALIZATION

In the initial portion of this chapter the discussion has focused on the manner in which most children, adolescents, and adults have been socialized into sport through favorable opportunity and encouragement to learn the skills, values, and attitudes associated with sport. Yet, explaining how individuals become involved with the world of sport is not very helpful in understanding why a substantial proportion of the population is indifferent, or even antagonistic, to sport in its many forms. At some point in their lives, usually during childhood, many persons become turned off by sport. For social scientists, educators, parents, and concerned citizens, it is probably more important to understand negative socialization in sport than positive socialization, because the aversive consequences can have lifelong consequences for one's self-concept and overall life style. The following vignette of aversive socialization conveys the double-edged nature of sport as a medium for self-development.

> Can you remember a spring day in your thirteenth year? A seductive breeze, a few white clouds sketched by a careless artist, the sun striking maddening smells from the moist earth and encouraging unaccustomed pulses in various parts of your body. It was on such a day in 1972, on a late-morning walk in a small Virginia town, that I came across a group of some thirty-five or forty thirteen-year-olds sitting on a grassy bank. I was on a lecture tour, summoned from my motel room by the sight and smell of April blossoms. Standing in front of the boys and girls was a taut-muscled young man with gym shoes, gym pants, a white T-shirt, a crew cut, a whistle, and a clipboard. Next to the young man, like a guillotine in the sunlight, was a chinning bar. I stopped to observe the scene.
>
> The man looked at his clipboard. "Babcock," he called.
>
> There was a stir among the boys and girls. One of them rose and made his way to the chinning bar: Babcock, the classic fat boy.
>
> Shoulders slumped, he stood beneath the bar. "I can't," he said.
>
> "You can try," the man with the clipboard said.
>
> Babcock reached up with both hands, touched the bar limply—just that—and walked away, his eyes downcast, as all the boys and girls watched, seeming to share his shame.
>
> I also walked on, flushed with anger. Beneath the anger, I sensed something tentative and hurt. The incident seemed to touch an area of my past that I had conveniently forgotten. The day was so lovely—no time to explore painful areas. I started thinking about other things.
>
> But Babcock was not to let me off easily. The vignette kept replaying itself in my mind. I was fascinated by the way the fat boy walked to the chinning bar, waddling slightly but moving fast as if eager to have it done with; his condemned stance beneath the bar; the minimal, symbolic touch of his hands on the metal; his utter resignation as he walked away, his head bobbing from side to side. Again and again Babcock rose, walked to the bar, stood there, touched the bar, walked off. The scene took on the quality of Greek drama. The man with the clipboard became the stern-visaged god who devises tests for us then sends us on without mercy to our respective fates. The boys and girls took the part of the chorus, by their silence condemning the unworthy, and yet, by the same silence, expressing their own uneasiness and shame (Leonard, 1975, pp. 4–5).[1]

In the jargon of the sociologist, Babcock was being socialized from the world of sport—obviously, his experience was not likely to dispose him to a lifelong appreciation of physical activity. In the terms of Harold Garfinkel (1956), Babcock was experiencing a "degradation ceremony." In a sense, Babcock was being drummed out of respectability. "Since failure involves the demonstration of a

[1]From *The Ultimate Athlete* by George Leonard. Copyright © 1974, 1975 by George Leonard. Reprinted by permission of The Viking Press, Inc.

moral lack, to be failed is to be deemed not-to-be-normal, to be adjudged as not 'fitting in' " (Ball, 1976, p. 727).

Gary Shaw's (1972) description of a degradation ceremony used as part of big-time collegiate football is most poignant.

> Here Royal was not lacking in imagination. He had all injured players (if below the first four teams) wear a jersey with a big red cross stenciled on both sides. And if at all able to walk, the injured were to continually jog around the practice field the complete workout. The red crosses were to be signs of humiliation. And throughout the spring, Royal would refer to the guys that would do anything to get out of workout and "couldn't take it." It may sound silly, but it was really an embarassing stigma to be standing out there on the practice field with a big red cross on your jersey. I only missed eight spring training workouts the entire four years—all coming that first spring. But those eight I missed, I wore the jersey and red cross. Any time a player on one of the first two teams came near me, I would suddenly be occupied—ducking my head and hoping they wouldn't notice. It was never explained to us why only those injured below a certain team were "fake injuries." There were always several members of the first few teams who were injured, yet they wore only solid jerseys (p. 166).

Dave Meggysey (1971) comments on the more subtle modes of degradation in his autobiography, entitled *Out of Their League*.

> One of the worst things that can happen to a player, especially a rookie or younger man, is to get a serious injury in training. A guy who gets hurt falls behind everybody else in learning and practicing the various offenses and defenses, and is immediately ostracized by the coaching staff. Healthy ball players don't like to fraternize with an injured man either. It's like some voodoo in which the injured player becomes a sort of leper. Most coaches believe in mind over matter where injuries are concerned. They constantly ask, "How's the leg?" or "How's the ankle?" with great sarcasm, then pat the player and say, "well, get well soon, you're missing a lot out there" (pp. 152-153).

Ball (1976) has suggested there are two basic processes through which one is screened out of the athletic stream: to be degraded and thus preclude one's identity as an athlete and to be "cooled out" by removing the participant to a lower step in the ladder of success. Thus, they gradually redefine their identity as an athlete (see also Harris and Eitzen, 1978). Both processes represent aversive forms of socialization that are applicable to athletic participation at any level from childhood through professional ranks.

It is clear that many persons are turned away from sport for a lifetime as a result of experiencing aversive socialization during their childhood or youth. Tutko and Bruns (1976) ask, "How many million youngsters are we sacrificing along the way so that ten players can entertain us in a pro basketball game? How many people are we eliminating who love sports but who never make the team because they're not going to be a 'winner'—they're too short or too slow or too weak" (p. *ix*). A child's initial exposure to the world of sport should be a positive one. Children learn early in life, through the media and adult conversation, that sport is an important area of activity and interest. People who do well in sport are lionized, even by children in elementary school. Consequently, the consciousness of children, especially males, is gradually shaped by the salience of sport. Therefore, if children's initial attempts at sport are unsuccessful, they may freeze sport out of their consciousness for later life. In this context, Orlick and Botterill (1975) suggest

> the most important thing you can do to insure that the child gets the right start is to see that the child's participation is fun and enjoyable above everything else. The simple fact is that if children are not receiving some sort of positive rewards from their participation, they will not continue. Having fun, playing, and being a part of the action can be extremely rewarding for kids. In fact, interviews with young kids who played organized sports revealed that "fun" and "action" were the things they liked best about sports. A typical response from an eight-year-old when asked why he wants to play sports is "I like it. It's fun!" (p. 7).

It is clear that children become more negative about sport as the fun dimension is gradually replaced by the performance criterion. Studies have shown that as children move into more organized forms of athletic competition, the attitudes of coaches and parents become professionalized in the sense that skill and success become the dominant criteria. Systematic research also shows, as would be expected, that children who participate in more formally organized sports express more professionalized attitudes than children who are involved in sandlot-type activities (Albinson, 1973; Maloney and Petrie, 1972; Mantel and Vander Velden, 1971).

Larson, Spreitzer, and Snyder (1975) surveyed parents' perceptions of the objectives of a hockey league for preadolescents to shed light on the discrepancy between the ideal and real goals of such organized athletics for children. Their questionnaire asked the parents to indicate both the objectives that *should be* emphasized as well as the objectives that actually *were* emphasized. The findings (Table 5-4) revealed considerable discrepancy between the manifest purpose of the league and its actual operation. For example, *none* of the parents thought that the importance of winning should be emphasized, but 25 percent of the same parents thought that winning was heavily emphasized within the league's operation. Moreover, 43 percent of the parents affirmed that the development of basic skills should be emphasized, but only 21 percent believed that skill development was actually stressed during the daily functioning of the league.

The Pygmalion effect also operates in the world of sport. Research shows the operation of a self-fulfilling prophecy in teaching children. "Kids sometimes become what we prophecy for them. If a coach has the expectation that a child will

TABLE 5-4 Parents' Perceptions of the Ideal and Real Objectives of a Youth Hockey League (*N* = 58)

OBJECTIVES	SHOULD BE EMPHASIZED (%)	IS ACTUALLY EMPHASIZED (%)
Developing skills	43	21
Having fun	19	7
Learning sportsmanship	15	2
Learning to compete	7	21
Learning discipline	4	4
Learning teamwork	0	7
Importance of winning	0	25

Source: Adapted from Larson, Spreitzer, and Snyder, 1975.

not be a good athlete or that he is immoral (and irrevocably so), the child may sense his coach's expectation and act to fulfill it" (Martens, 1976, p. 107). Youngsters such as Babcock come to internalize the definitions of adults concerning their potential, and this image can become a lifelong part of their self-concept. "The process, of course, may function in reverse. Coaches' positive expectations may help motivate kids to achieve what they otherwise thought could not be attained. What coaches must remember is that expectations can reinforce both positive and negative behavior and that these expectations are communicated not only knowingly but often unknowingly" (Martens, 1976, p. 107).

In this context, the behavior of the coach and parents toward less able youngsters is critical for later development. The treatment accorded to the little guy on the bench, the substitute, has lifelong implications. Such a status can reinforce a youngster's sense of being inferior. This badge of second-class citizenship can spill over into a child's school work and social relations.

> There are several important ways in which parents can help their child effectively handle the role of substitute. It is vital that they let their child know that they are not judging him as a person based on his playing ability, and that they love him because of the kind of person he is. Unfortunately, many parents respond as if it were a personal insult that their child is a substitute, no matter how uncoordinated he might be. This simply compounds the child's guilt and misery (Tutko and Bruns, 1976, pp. 85–86).

Given these emotional factors for youngsters, the coach must be particularly solicitous for the less able.

> Many coaches have a motto that the test of their team—and their coaching—is whether the last substitute has good morale. If he has, it means everybody has. Yet how does the coach maintain this motivation among the players who seldom get to play? . . . He makes it clear that he cares about each of his athletes, no matter what position they play and how far down the bench they might be. Even the lowliest scrub on the team will feel that the coach is concerned about how he is progressing toward his potential, not about whether he is winning or contributing directly to a victory. The coach will try to make practice fun for everybody and will never use the benchwarmers as fodder for the team, nor identify the scrubs as a separate and basically useless wing of the team (Tutko and Bruns, 1976, pp. 184–85).

Novak suggests that a negative experience with sports as a youth can have lifelong consequences.

> Since sports are so much of boyhood, boys who turn away from sports frequently seem crippled in humanity, poisoned against their peers, driven to competitiveness in intellect or lost in the acquisition of power and wealth, never graced by the liberty of play. . . . They seek revenge in later life for the supposed injustices they suffered at the hands of fate for their earlier athletic inabilities. While they won the lavish praise of parents and teachers, and basked in the successes of the classroom, they had to accept some humane measure of humiliation on the ball field and could not bear it. Others who felt panic when the teacher asked questions they could not understand, whose tongues were tied in knots, whose necks reddened at the implicit accusations of stupidity they felt in the superior glances of so many girls, redeemed their self-respect in sports. Sometimes in life—in the army, perhaps—the athlete gained revenge upon the unathletic. But, mostly in later life, the nonathletic, nursing childhood injuries to their self-esteem, get even with the athletes, becoming their bosses, managers, paymasters, commanders, civilizers, preachers, and instructors (Novak, 1976, pp. 44–45 and 80–81).

ALTERNATIVE MODELS

As an alternative to miniaturized big leagues, a new spirit is spreading in physical education that insists every child be a winner. This more humanistic posture emerged out of a new approach to physical education that has come to be termed "movement education." Movement education is an individualized approach to teaching children that emphasizes the child's natural inclination toward free physical expression (Singer, 1976). A physical education class in this context is markedly different from the traditional winners-and-losers model. For one accustomed to the games-and-relays approach, a large room full of young children doing movement education makes a striking picture. In a class devoted to ball play, every child has a ball and every child is moving. "See if you can put the ball in the air without using your hands," the teacher says. The children use their feet, knees, forearms, wrists, elbows, and chins to handle the ball. "Now roll the balls to each other and see how many body parts you can use to stop them." More activity and experimentation. "Now, stand and move slowly around the room. Throw the balls to each other while you are moving. Throw gently." The air is filled with balls. Surprisingly, very few are dropped. Later, the children are asked to make up their own games with the balls. Everybody is involved. There are no losers (Leonard, 1975, p. 144).

As an antidote to aversive socialization experiences, other efforts are being made to substitute cooperation for competition as the motif of sport-type play. Orlick (1975), for example, has devised a series of games that make it "necessary for children to interact in a cooperative way in order to meet the challenge of the game or to achieve the specified goals. In short, the rewards within the game were made contingent upon cooperative social interaction" (p. 9).

Orlick's research on restructured games shows that such play can be stimulating and fun while also promoting desirable social and psychological outcomes. Orlick has noted

> Cooperation is essential for the survival of the individual, and fun is an essential rejuvenation of the spirit, adding meaning and joy to life. In games and sport the value of cooperating with others and the significance of fun become increasingly important as our society becomes increasingly competitive and technological in makeup. Where else can a child become so immersed in something so joyous and yet learn something so valuable about himself and others. Opportunities for cooperative social interaction, self acceptance, and sheer fun must be nurtured rather than destroyed in the games children play. Those of us concerned with overall quality of life, and more specifically, with children's mental health, must work together so that confident, cooperative, carefree, jubilant children do not become an endangered species (pp. 19–20).

Physical educators report that cooperative games are readily accepted by both boys and girls; competition is not the exclusive mode of physical expression. Youngsters participating in cooperative games are heard to express sentiments such as "I'm making someone happy," "scores are higher," "nobody wins and nobody loses," "you are just playing to have fun," "you work as a team," "you teach each other to play fair" (Orlick, 1978, p. 179).

COMMITMENT TO SPORT

Thus far we have argued that socialization into sport involves the teaching of skills, knowledge, values, and attitudes of sport by parents, peers, coaches, and others who are significant to the individual. This socialization begins in early childhood, continues into adolescence, and to some extent into adulthood. Furthermore, this socialization process is dependent upon an opportunity structure that permits the learning to take place. As we have described this process, the individual receives positive and negative reinforcements that affect the continued participation in sport. In other words, the person comes to develop a degree of commitment to sport; by commitment we mean the person evidences continued motivation to participate in sport activities even in face of other activity spheres. Thus, the person who is committed to sport decrees it to be of sufficient importance to engage in it even when not required to do so. This predisposition to sport may be in terms of the behavioral, affective, and cognitive dimensions of sport that were discussed in Chapter 2. In the following discussion we take the analysis one step further and describe how the socialization process results in a commitment (or lack of commitment) to sport.

We suggest that there are several rewards or gratifications that accumulate through sport participation that serve to reinforce the commitment to the activity (this process applies to other activities as well, such as music, art, dramatics, or customizing cars). Becker (1960) refers to such concomitants as "side bets," meaning that they are extra inducements that incline one to a particular activity such as sport participation. Of course, one will also be developing commitments with the associated gratifications and rewards to other spheres of activity. Therefore, the degree of commitment to one activity will, in part, be dependent on the commitments to other activities or roles. In fact, the commitments may conflict (in time, money, energy) with each other, for example, playing a musical instrument versus participation in sports. It may be impossible to place a high commitment on both activities, and thus it is necessary to strike a compromise by "scaling down" the commitment to both activities, or more likely by reducing the commitment to one of the activities. It should be noted, however, participating in several activities with a modicum of commitment to each might result in a greater accumulation of extrinsic rewards than a deep commitment to one activity. Of course the pattern of commitments across the several activity spheres will vary with the individual and at different stages of their life.

We suggest that the following rewards and valuables or gratifications serve to enhance and maintain a commitment to sport and physical activities.

1. **Intrinsic enjoyment, pleasure, fun, and pure joy that is received from physical movement.** This satisfaction approximates the concept of "flow," the spontaneous enjoyment experienced when one is performing a task that is challenging yet within one's capacities (see Chapter 2). Unfortunately, because of the instrumental orientation in most forms of sport and the desire for external rewards, the intrinsic enjoyment is often de-emphasized. Nevertheless, much of sport is satisfying to people for the simple reason "that it is fun." This affective dimension of sport is hopefully internalized in the sport socialization process. The development of cooperative games and human movement activities may be helpful in this regard.

2. **The anticipation of extrinsic rewards such as prestige, recognition, trophies, victories, pride, health, and money that are associated with sport.** These extrinsic rewards are most likely to be internalized by the skilled athletes with peak performances within their age and sex categories.
3. **Satisfaction flowing from approval by significant others.** The sentiments, loyalty, companionship, and mutual esteem that emerge from sport participation serve to reinforce the sociability aspects of participation. This affective dimension tends to be reciprocal—both to the participant and to parents, peers, teachers, coaches, and others who receive satisfaction from being closely associated with the athlete. Additionally, many people are involved in sport because of the pleasant relationships that are associated with participation and because others want them to participate in sport; here we note the examples of curling, social tennis, golf, and racquetball.
4. **The avoidance of negative sanctions in the form of loss of status, subjective failure, stigma, and embarrassment that threaten one's identity.** Commitment to sport for some individuals is based on the feeling that they would receive negative sanctions if they did not participate in sport. Conversely, for others, commitment can be diminished because they fear a loss of status, failure, and embarassment. We have already noted the way that degradation and "cooling out" mechanisms are used in sport as a screening process and come to decrease one's commitment to sport. In such cases equilibrium results from a disengagement from sport with a corresponding reduction of commitment.
5. **The individual may be committed to sport because of an identity that is anchored in the sport world.** This element of commitment may incorporate one or several of the other reasons for commitment noted previously. An identity involving a heavy dose of the sport role develops through the social interaction with other people; it usually includes success in sport and the rewards resulting from an involvement in sport (intrinsic as well as extrinsic). One who developed a sport identity wants to maintain the requisite athletic skill to sustain the identity.

Each of these elements of commitment (and perhaps others) represents a possible reward that enhances one's commitment to a sphere of activity such as sport involvement. On the other hand, there are costs associated with sport that can result in a reduction of commitment. Thus, if one is a skilled athlete and there are social pressures for participation, the desire to avoid the negative sanctions may induce participation in sport. However, if one's sport skill is perceived as inadequate, a fear of embarassment may reinforce a weak commitment with subsequent withdrawal from sport contexts ("I'm an awful volleyball player and too self-conscious to play"). Similarly, continued failure or the fear of failure is likely to produce a lack of commitment to competitive situations. Few care to continue participating in an activity if they are not competitive and have no reasonable opportunity to succeed. These elements of commitment are important for understanding involvement in sport as well as other spheres of activity at any age, and they have particular value in understanding the development of a commitment to sport. This commitment process usually begins in childhood, and by junior high school or high school many youngsters have developed a strong commitment to sport. A graphic summary of this discussion on commitment to sport is presented in the following diagram (Figure 5-5).

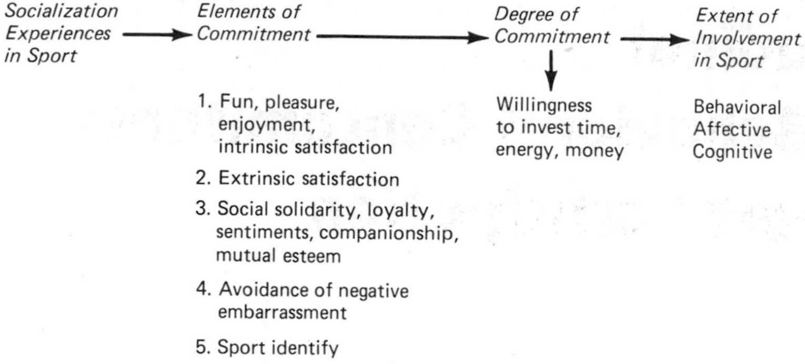

FIGURE 5–5 The process of commitment to sport.

CONCLUSION

Learning to be an athlete must be approached in the same manner as learning skills in music, art, automobile mechanics, dramatics, academic subjects, or any other area of special expertise. The development of such skills and knowledge also includes the internalization of the appropriate values, attitudes, dispositions, and self-image. Persons and agencies which are significant in both positive and negative learning of the athletic role include four social systems vital to the overall socialization process for children and adolescents—family, peers, school, and community. Negative socialization includes mechanisms of screening out, "cooling out," and degradation in sport contexts. As an alternative to competitive sports and games, cooperative physical activities contain the potential for learning and enjoying physical movement without the fear of failure. However, because sports, like schools, serve as a sorting and screening process, some people might argue that there is a value in learning how to fail. There are many youngsters who learn that they are not talented at many of the things their parents, coaches, and teachers value. Socialization into sport results in the development of a commitment to sport. Commitment is based on the following reinforcements associated with sport: intrinsic and extrinsic rewards, sociability, loyalty, avoidance of negative sanctions, and sport identity. The degree of commitment to sport determines the amount of time, energy, and money one is willing to invest in sport. In the next chapter we investigate some of the social and psychological concomitants of sport involvement. That is, we turn to an analysis of how sport participation may be a cause rather than an effect.

CHAPTER 6
Attitudinal and Behavioral Concomitants of Sport Participation

To the Kid on the End of the Bench

Champions once sat where you're sitting, kid.

The Football Hall of Fame (and every other Hall of Fame) is filled with names of people who sat, week after week, without getting a spot of mud on their well-laundered uniforms.

Generals, senators, surgeons, prize-winning novelists, professors, business executives started on the end of a bench, too.

Don't sit and study your shoe tops.

Keep your eye on the game.

Watch for defense lapses.

Look for offensive opportunities.

If you don't think you're in a great spot, wait until you see how many would like to take it away from you at next spring practice.

What you do from the bench this season could put you on the field next season, as a player, or back in the grandstand as a spectator.

(A United Technologies message)

In the previous chapter we discussed the process whereby people become socialized into sport. In this chapter we discuss some of the social and psychological concomitants of athletic involvement. Presumably, if one has participated in sport, the experiences associated with this activity have an effect on the individual. These consequences may include increased physical fitness, and this is an important consideration; however, we also want to consider social and psychological factors that may be associated with athletic participation. It is logical to expect that the intensity of the sport experience might spill over into other areas of an athlete's life. In fact, such transfer effects are frequently cited as the justification for sports—"Sound mind and sound body," "The Battle of Waterloo was won on the playing fields of Eton," and so on.

METHODOLOGICAL ASPECTS

The scientific literature concerning the concomitants of athletic participation contains a certain degree of indeterminancy because almost all this research is based on cross-sectional, correlational designs.[1] More specifically, it is very difficult to establish the temporal sequence between sport involvement and psychological characteristics. It is logical to expect that the differential experience of athletes will produce some social and psychological changes within the individual. However, it is also possible that any characteristics that are found to differentiate athletes from nonathletes could also be due to selectivity in the sense that certain types of persons are attracted (or recruited) into athletics. For example, if we find that in a study of adolescent boys, the athletes tend to be more conventional and law-abiding, these characteristics may have been present prior to the athletic experience—that is, conventional individuals might find athletics more attractive. Moreover, nonconventional adolescents may have been selected out of the athletic subculture through eligibility rules, decisions by coaches, and so forth.

Figure 6-1 illustrates the athletic and nonathletic "tracks" that are found in most school systems in the United States. Informal sport, often evident in the late elementary school years, merges in high school into the semiformal and formal

---

[1]This chapter focuses on social and psychological concomitants of participation in sports. As a matter of shorthand, scientists commonly refer to the "correlates" of a particular phenomenon such as factors associated with delinquency. In all areas of science it is helpful to be able to measure the degree to which two or more variables are related—that is, the extent to which changes in one variable are associated with changes in the other. Thus, a researcher might be interested in the relationship between job satisfaction and participation in leisure sports such as softball.

A number of techniques have been developed to measure the degree of relationship between variables; these techniques are generally referred to as measures of association. The numerical values that are produced as part of the techniques are called correlation coefficients and typically range in value from −1.00 to +1.00 on a continuum. A coefficient of −1.00 refers to a perfect negative relationship between two variables; that is, one variable *increases* to the extent that the other variable *decreases*, and all the variability in one variable can be explained in terms of changes in the other variable. Similarly, a coefficient of +1.00 refers to a perfect positive relationship between two variables; that is, one variable increases in direct proportion to increases in the other variable. A coefficient of .00 indicates no relationship between two variables; they are completely independent. In social scientific research a perfect correlation is virtually nonexistent; consequently, a researcher typically reports coefficients falling between −1.00 and +1.00 such as −.42 or +.63.

A measure of association can be calculated for both quantitative (age, height, speed) and qualitative variables (race, gender, type of car ownership). Regardless of the strength of a relationship, a correlation in itself does not necessarily indicate a *causal* relationship. For example, it has been suggested that the academic quality of a college or university is directly proportional to the number of tennis courts on a given campus. We know, however, that a causal interpretation of this relationship (if it exists) would be spurious. Playing tennis does not cause one to be an intelligent student; rather, young persons from privileged backgrounds are more likely to learn to play tennis for basically the same reasons that youth from poor backgrounds are more likely to be exposed to the sport of boxing. Thus, youth who come from advantaged backgrounds are exposed to the class-linked sport of tennis and are also more able to afford the high cost of enrolling in an elite private university.

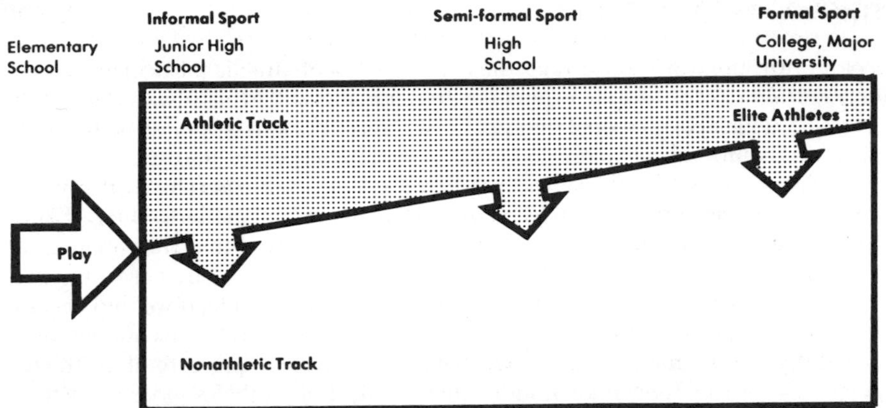

FIGURE 6–1 Athletic and nonathletic tracks within educational levels.

sport participation that reaches its zenith in the big-time, bureaucratized sport structures of the major universities. The diagonal demarcation line between the athletic and nonathletic tracks is not impermeable in the informal sport stage, and in some cases a student may begin participating in sport for the first time in senior high school when sport has already become somewhat formalized. However, the sport track becomes increasingly narrow, and athletes must demonstrate a high degree of competence to continue participation in the higher educational levels. The selection process out of the athletic track is illustrated by the diagonal arrows. This process may be voluntary—"I quit the football team"—or involuntary—"I didn't make the team." By the junior high and high school years, this weeding-out process brings together coaches and players who have selected each other (a "goodness of fit"), and thus the athletic setting is conducive for continued socialization. Both processes—selectivity and socialization—tend to have a reciprocal relationship.

In summary, the behavioral and attitudinal differences cited in this chapter may be attributed to an interaction of the socialization process (that is, the opportunity to learn skills, values, and develop attributes) within sport where specific characteristics associated with sport are emphasized: the selectivity process at the entry into the athletic/nonathletic tracks as well as the screening out of the athletic stream as it becomes increasingly elitist. Thus, it is not surprising that we find differences between athletes and nonathletes, but we must be cautious about assuming a direct cause-and-effect relationship between athletic participation and the various behavioral and attitudinal differences under consideration.

ATTITUDINAL AND BEHAVIORAL CORRELATES OF SPORT PARTICIPATION

Studies generally indicate that involvement in physical activities lead to a positive image toward one's body and in turn a positive self-concept (Berscheid, Walster, and Bohrnsted, 1973; Rohrbacher, 1973). In short, for many people, sport affords an opportunity for a sense of physical exhilaration, goal attainment, group identification, and ego gratification that are not often available in everyday life. There is, however, another aspect of the characteristics of athletes we should consider. In Chapter 3 we discussed some of the value orientations associated with the sport subculture; thus, we should find that the characteristics of persons exposed to this subculture will more likely reflect these values than persons who have not had these experiences.

One study that is relevant for the consideration of personal characteristics of athletes has been conducted by Jones and Williamson (1979). These researchers developed an athletic profile inventory that focused on three factors:

Traditional achievement orientation—An emphasis on hard work and effort in pursuit of a goal.

Power—This factor emphasizes the importance of success, that is, winning. "It reflects competition in its purest form as a zero-sum contest with one winner and one loser" (p. 169).

Antiestablishment—This factor is a rejection of the notions that success comes from submitting to the established values of hard work, training, sacrifice, and selflessness.

The researchers suggest that the first two factors are attitudes the coach would instill in an athlete. On the other hand, the third factor (anti-establishment) represents an attitude that would likely result in conflict between the coach and athlete. These three factors were incorporated into a profile gradient from "coach's dream" to "athlete dropout," with an intermediate category classified as "moderates." Based on the assumption that sport consists of a way of life, a set of values, philosophies, and expected behaviors (a sport role), Jones and Williamson asked a number of questions that would have a bearing on these issues. Table 6-1 provides a summary of the responses that were cross-tabulated by the three sports-attitude groups. The 444 respondents included high school and college athletes, males and females, and some blacks; however, 78 percent of the respondents were male and 83 percent were white.

Several of the indices are particularly interesting in profiling the athlete. By examining the column of dropouts and moving across to coach's dream, we can see that the respondents who are profiled as coach's dream began organized sports earlier, spent more time practicing between the ages of 10 and 15, and spend more time practicing now. Furthermore, respondents were asked if their social status in school was enhanced as a result of their participation in sport, the overall effect of sports on their lives, if their families attended their sport events, if there was sport talk at meals, positive influence of sport on the family, what percentage of their friends were also athletes, and what were their interests other than sports. It is interesting to note the consistent linearity of responses from dropouts to coach's dream on each of the indices. The athletes who more readily embraced the values of sport (the sports creed) with emphasis on hard work, effort, winning, training, sacrifice, and selflessness were also likely to be deeply involved in sport presently and in the past. This involvement in sport is perceived as having affected personal training, enhancement of status via sport, overall influence in life, and social relationships with family and friends. We would conclude from this research that sport participation and competitive physical activity do have an impact on personality characteristics and attitudes. Additional research is needed to determine whether

TABLE 6-1 Socio-Behavioral Relationships among Sports-Attitude Types

SOCIO-BEHAVIORAL INDICES	SPORTS-ATTITUDE GROUP		
	DROPOUTS	MODERATES	COACH'S DREAM
Height (in.)	69.50	70.94	70.58
Weight (lb.)	156.33	167.00	170.00
Age (organized sports)	9.94	9.45	9.24
Time practice (10-15)	1.27	1.62	1.68
Practice now	1.24	1.21	1.55
Status enhanced	1.27	1.46	1.60
Effect on life	2.52	2.63	2.83
Family attend	2.87	3.21	3.52
Sport talk at meals	2.91	3.18	3.52
Effect on family	2.98	3.41	3.92
Percent athletic friends	51.4	56.2	67.2
Outside interests	3.51	2.86	2.82

Source: Adapted from Jones and Williamson, 1979, p. 178.

these value orientations are primarily anchored to sport contexts or whether they also transfer to areas of life outside sport.

If the value orientations and lifestyle of high school and college athletes differ from nonathletes, it would be interesting to know whether they also differ in their self-perceptions. One study gathered data from 384 college freshmen through a questionnaire that included a measure of self-described personality characteristics. The operational definition of athlete in this study was based on whether or not the respondent had participated in varsity sports during high school. Furthermore, the research included a measure of the respondents' orientation toward sport; that is, whether they were primarily concerned with high performance and winning as contrasted with having fun and playing fairly (an intrinsic orientation). We would expect the athletes and persons with an extrinsic orientation toward sport to express values and self-descriptions associated with the athletic subculture. Table 6-2 presents cross-tabulations between athletic status and a series of self-described personality characteristics. As might be expected, the data indicate that athletes are more likely than nonathletes to describe themselves as "athletic." It also is interesting to note that the "activistic" personality characteristics of aggressive, competitive, and perfectionist are more evident among athletes with an extrinsic orientation than among athletes with an intrinsic orientation. The males in general were slightly more likely than the females to describe themselves as "relaxed," while the females were more likely than the males to rate themselves as "gentle." No clear associations were evident in the data between athletic status and life satisfaction, regardless of gender or orientation toward sport (Snyder and Spreitzer, 1979a).

The associations evident in Table 6-2 should be interpreted with caution because, as we emphasized in the initial portion of this chapter, it is not clear whether such patterns are due to self-selection into athletic participation, the coach's selection process, or the socialization effects via sport (see Stevenson, 1975). In any event, the findings do reveal differences among undergraduate students in terms of orientation toward sport, and these orientations are associated with degree of

TABLE 6-2 Self-Described Personality Characteristics by Athletic Status, Orientation Toward Sport, and Gender

SELF-PERCEIVED CHARACTERISTICS	INTRINSIC ORIENTATION		EXTRINSIC ORIENTATION	
	ATHLETES (%)	NONATHLETES (%)	ATHLETES (%)	NONATHLETES (%)
Males				
Athletic	92	44	94	45
Aggressive	61	48	78	40
Competitive	87	75	98	80
Restless	65	60	75	65
Perfectionist	67	54	79	65
Relaxed	73	72	59	65
Gentle	79	84	81	90
Generally in good spirits	87	88	84	90
Satisfied with life	80	80	78	80
Females				
Athletic	81	28	94	39
Aggressive	47	49	65	54
Competitive	75	51	90	59
Restless	67	53	65	60
Perfectionist	56	56	63	69
Relaxed	69	64	66	56
Gentle	93	86	78	88
Generally in good spirits	100	90	86	93
Satisfied with life	94	89	88	93

Source: Adapted from Snyder and Spreitzer, 1979a, p. 174.

athletic involvement, gender, and self-described personality characteristics. Because most studies have utilized samples of high school and college students, it is difficult to determine when these differences emerge. Nicholson (1979) investigated 502 junior high school girls in five Michigan schools with father's occupation as a control variable. Table 6-3 indicates that the junior high female athletes were more likely to describe themselves as ambitious, and in two of the three comparisons the athletes were more competitive. The girls who participated in athletics were more likely to perceive themselves as "strong" and "fast" in comparison to their nonathletic counterparts. Finally, the athletes were somewhat more likely to describe themselves as happy than the nonathletes. This study suggests that some of the characteristics associated with athletic participation among high school and college students are already evident by early adolescence.

One of the values frequently attributed to sport is that it promotes sportsmanship and fair play. The popular literature, however, is replete with examples suggesting that the dominant motif of organized athletics is victory at all cost. Thus, we are interested in the attitudinal dimensions of fair play and victory. In a seminal paper, Webb (1969a) asked over 1200 students in grades 3, 6, 7, 10, and 12 to rank what was most important: (1) to beat your opponent (to win), (2) to play

TABLE 6-3 Self-Described Personality Characteristics of Junior High School Female Athletes and Nonathletes by Father's Occupational Status

SELF-PERCEIVED CHARACTERISTICS	PROFESSIONAL		SEMI-PROFESSIONAL		BLUE-COLLAR	
	ATHLETES (%)	NON-ATHLETES (%)	ATHLETES (%)	NON-ATHLETES (%)	ATHLETES (%)	NON-ATHLETES (%)
Very ambitious	63	32	40	29	49	37
Very competitive	50	40	26	38	40	20
Very strong	24	15	18	12	29	17
Very fast	27	13	27	14	22	14
Very happy	66	46	64	55	66	59

Source: Adapted from Nicholson, 1979, p. 664

as well as you can (skill), and (3) to play the game fairly (fairness). Webb concluded that, as students progress to the higher grade levels, their attitudes toward playing a game became more professionalized and achievement-oriented; that is, skill and the importance of victory become more important than fun and fair play. These conclusions were further substantiated by Maloney and Petrie's (1972) study of Canadian youth in grades 8–12. Their findings showed that males were more likely than females to endorse the achievement dimension of sports (skill and victory). Moreover, they found that the attitudes of the boys became progressively more professionalized as they moved through high school. Maloney and Petrie also found that the youths who were more actively involved in organized athletics tended to be more professional in their orientation (as shown by an emphasis on skill and victory) toward sport as compared to nonparticipants, which suggests the influence of organized youth sports as a socialization agent.

Whereas the Webb and Maloney and Petrie research analyzed student orientations toward play and games across several age levels, Mantel and Vander Velden (1971) focused their study on a comparison of 10- and 11-year-old participants and nonparticipants in organized sport. Their findings corroborated the finding by Maloney and Petrie that participation in organized sports tends to result in an orientation that emphasizes skill and victory as the central ingredients of sport. The preadolescents in their sample who were not participants in formal sport settings, on the other hand, were more likely to emphasize fairness as the most important factor in sport. These findings have important implications for life-long involvement in physical activity in the sense that the *product* motif of organized youth sport seems antithetical to a more intrinsic *process* conception of sport that is conducive to continued participation by a wide segment of the population.

Additional research reported by Albinson (1976) and Vaz (1974) conducted on minor league Canadian hockey coaches further indicates that professional and achievement orientations rather than fair play are associated with athletic participation in the preadolescent and adolescent ages. Furthermore, among college students, Richardson (1962) found that nonathletes demonstrated a higher level of sportsmanship than athletes, and students who received athletic grants-in-aid ranked lower in sportsmanship than those who were not awarded athletic grants.

In a study of 236 British soccer players, Heinila (1974) obtained similar results. He reported that among professional players, 70 percent agreed with the statement that "an opponent who is in an obvious position must be brought down unmercifully," whereas 54 percent of the amateurs agreed with this statement. Likewise, 69 percent of the professionals and 42 percent of the amateurs affirmed that "In a match a player may attempt anything provided he is not caught" (Pilz, 1979, p. 11). In conclusion, the preponderance of research does not support the assumption that sport promotes attitudes of sportsmanship and fair play.

Kidd and Woodman (1975) reported a modification of the Webb scale by substituting the item "to have fun" for "to play fairly." This modified scale format involves an important distinction because "to have fun" represents the intrinsic, autotelic, or expressive facet of sport rather than conformity to norms ("to play fairly"). On the other hand, the scale item "to beat your opponent" represents a measure of extrinsic motivation, that is, victory. Table 6-4 presents data collected from a study of 384 college students; athletic status was based on participation or nonparticipation in interscholastic athletics during their high school years (Snyder and Spreitzer, 1979). The findings replicate previous research in showing that nonathletes (both male and female) are more likely than athletes to manifest an intrinsic orientation toward sport. Among males, 55 percent of the nonathletes ranked "to have fun" as the most important criterion compared to 27 percent of the athletes; the parallel figures for the females were 47 percent for the nonathletes and 24 percent for the athletes.

These findings differ from previous research, however, in showing that when athletic status is held constant, the males were slightly more intrinsically oriented ("To have fun") than the females. Interestingly, the modal choice among athletes of both sexes was the skill dimension ("To play well"), whereas the modal choice among the nonathletes of both sexes was the normative dimension ("To play fairly"). Surprisingly, the female nonathletes were slightly more win-oriented than the female athletes.

In summary, it might be helpful to outline in tabular form the four orientations toward sport and their modal locations as observed in this study.

Orientation	Location
process (have fun)	nonathletes of both sexes
process (play fair)	nonathletes of both sexes
process (play well)	athletes of both sexes
product (win)	male athletes

Most of the previous correlational studies of athletic participation have been based on samples of secondary school and college students. A study by Snyder and Baber (1979) provides a follow-up of college graduates that includes subsamples of former varsity athletes and nonathletes. This type of analysis has the advantage of focusing on the linkage between college athletic involvement and adult behavior. Although this study does not deal with the probability of selectivity into and away from sport during the years of sport participation, it does shed some light on athletic participation in college and its behavioral and attitudinal correlates in a later stage of the life cycle. The analysis in this study was based on samples of former male college athletes and a comparison sample of nonathletes who

TABLE 6-4 Orientations Toward Sport According to Athletic Status and Gender

	NONATHLETES (%)	ATHLETES (%)
	Males	
(Kidd/Woodman format)		
To have fun	55*	27
To play well	41	56
To win	4	17
(Webb format)		
To play fair	63	26
To play well	35	61
To win	2	13
N	(46)	(91)
	Females	
(Kidd/Woodman format)		
To have fun	47	24
To play well	48	71
To win	5	4
(Webb format)		
To play fair	59	44
To play well	37	54
To win	4	2
N	(162)	(70)

*The cell values reported in this table indicate the percentage of respondents who ranked the various dimensions of sport participation as the most important criterion.

Source: Snyder and Spreitzer, 1979, p. 174.

were graduates of a middle-sized state university during the years of 1965–1975. Table 6-5 shows that the subsamples of alumni are similar in their current satisfaction with different aspects of their life. However, it is interesting to note that former athletes were more likely to be satisfied with their health and physical condition than the nonathletes.

Table 6-6 provides a breakdown of leisure activities that are engaged in by the two subgroups. It is evident from the responses that the athletes have not completely disengaged from their sport role; they are more likely to continue to participate at an informal or semiformal level. This continued participation in sport may account for the more positive response of the athletes toward their health and physical condition in Table 6-5. The former varsity athletes also spend more time watching and attending sport events than their nonathletic counterparts. The data suggest that while the athletes are more likely to attribute the characteristic of sociability to themselves as measured by the item "Entertain friends in your home," the nonathletes spend more of their time reading books. Perhaps for many of the ex-athletes the time spent watching television, watching and participating in sports, and entertaining friends absorbs time that otherwise would be used for reading books. Additional data presented in this study indicated that the two samples were similar in their attitudes and orientations toward their occupational and work role.

TABLE 6-5 Satisfaction with Aspects of Life by Former Athletes and Nonathletes

HIGHLY SATISFIED WITH THE FOLLOWING ASPECTS OF LIFE	ATHLETES (N = 299)* (%)	NONATHLETES (N = 184) (%)
Marriage	85	89
Health and physical condition	85	76
General life style	81	79
Friendships	78	78
City or place you live	68	69
Work activities	65	65
Financial situation	50	50

*The number of respondents varied slightly for each question; the maximum N is given in the parentheses.
Source: Adapted from Snyder and Baber, 1979, p. 217.

Because of the similarities of the two samples we might speculate that although the athletic role is particularly important for the individual in high school and especially in college, it begins to diminish in adulthood, and it is reduced to the leisure sphere within the overall constellation of roles.

Kroll (1970) has reviewed the extensive literature dealing with sport, physical activity, and personality and has concluded that the picture remains unsettled. He notes, especially, the difficulties in measuring personality characteristics. For example, personality inventories may be measuring variation in the behavioral expectations of a particular social situation as much as they are measuring the respondents' actual personal characteristics. Further questions remain regarding

TABLE 6-6 Type of Leisure Activities by Former Athletes and Nonathletes

OFTEN ENGAGE IN THE FOLLOWING LEISURE TIME ACTIVITIES	ATHLETES (N = 233)* (%)	NONATHLETES (N = 190) (%)
Watch sports on television	80	59
Play competitive sports	80	38
Watch television	72	62
Attend sports events	63	38
Entertain friends in your home	59	46
Travel	53	50
Hobbies and crafts	51	46
Visit relatives	48	54
Read a book	38	53
Go to the movies	31	29
Play games such as cards and chess	26	26
Attend church activities	21	29
Attend musical concerts or operas	12	12
Attend stage plays	8	13

*The number of respondents varied slightly for each activity; the maximum N is given in the parentheses.
Source: Adapted from Snyder and Baber, 1979, p. 215.

the structure of personality—particularly the validity of the trait theory of personality that underlies many of the personality inventories utilized by many of the research studies in this area. Layman (1968, 1972) has conducted an extensive review of the literature that focuses on emotional development as a consequence of sport and motor development. She concludes that physical fitness does have a positive influence on emotional well-being. However, she cautiously cites the following points that should be kept in mind when interpreting the data.

1. Different sports as well as different positions played in team sports are by no means uniform in the extent to which they contribute toward the development of physical fitness. This points to the importance of an overall conditioning program for all sports participants.
2. The causes of poor emotional health are many, and even an individual with a sound physique can become emotionally ill if one or more of these other factors is operative.
3. The picture is confused by the fact that different criteria are used to assess physical fitness. Sometimes strength tests are used, sometimes cardiovascular tests, and sometimes tests of motor skill. Again, in some studies physical fitness is judged on the basis of the individual's having participated in a physical conditioning program, with tests of emotional health being given on a before-and-after basis.
4. Many studies assessing the relation between physical status and emotional health have been done in connection with programs in which a therapist or clinician has had a relationship with students or patients in a program designed to improve fitness. This, of course, makes it impossible to say to what extent improved emotional health is the result of improved fitness and to what extent it stems from the teacher–student or therapist–patient relationship (Layman, 1968).

More recently, Folkins and Sime (1981) reviewed a number of research studies that related physical training to mental health. In general, the studies suggest that physical fitness training leads to an improved self-concept as well as other measures of mental health. Several additional studies have been guided by the theoretical assumption of an affinity between athletics and personal characteristics. Cooper (1969) noted research findings that described athletes as more outgoing, socially confident, dominant, and more emotionally stable. Similarly, Merriman (1960) studied over 800 high school boys and found that athletic ability was related to personality traits. For example, boys with greater innate athletic ability tended to score higher than boys with less ability on measures of social poise, leadership, self-confidence, intellectuality, and breadth of interest. Merriman's analysis suggests that motor ability per se, and not simply participation in athletics, is a significant factor in the development of positive personality traits. Cofer and Johnson (1960), Morgan (1973, 1974), Singer (1969), and Straub and Davis (1971) have identified differences between levels and types of athletic competition, physical activities, and personality characteristics. However, the pattern of these differences is not consistent from one study to another. In fact, sport psychologists are no longer enthusiastic about the psychological trait approach in research comparing athletes and nonathletes.

CONVENTIONALITY AND SPORT PARTICIPATION

One of the commonly held assumptions regarding athletic participation is that it serves to "keep kids out of trouble," presumably because through sport they are taught conventionality, traditional social values, and are kept busy. Eitzen and Sage (1978) argue that the "world of sports generates a fundamental acceptance of the established norms and values" (p. 314). Moreover, several athletic dressing room slogans suggest there is a process of socialization toward conventionality within athletics: "Stay out for sports and stay out of courts," "Live by the code or get out," "He who flys with the owls at night cannot keep up with the eagles during the day," "Profanity is an ignorant mind expressing itself," and "Garbage tends to collect garbage."

In 1976, a survey sponsored by a national magazine included a number of variables that focused on social conventionality and athletic participation. The magazine had an independent research organization commissioned to conduct a college student survey at twenty randomly selected colleges and universities in the United States. The student survey pulled a random sampling of students from school directories. In all, 3,700 students responded to the study. This sample checked out as representative of the sex, age, class level, family income, and grade-point average of students across the country. We were able to acquire the data set from the research organization for purposes of secondary analysis. Our analysis of the data from the survey is reported in Tables 6-7 and 6-8.

In reviewing the findings from the survey, it should be kept in mind that the survey's definition of athletic participation is nominal in nature because the purpose of the original survey did not include athletics as a topic of central interest. More specifically, the measure of sport participation is dichotomous in nature and includes no scaling of degrees of participation. The questionnaire item that we used in this context simply asked the respondent to "please state whether you belong (1) or do not belong (2) to any of the following types of campus organizations:

Fraternity or sorority
Political organization
Ethnic social or cultural society
Athletic team
Campus press or broadcasting
Intellectual organization
Vocational society
Professional association"

Table 6-7 presents a summary of academic orientation and social conventionality as associated with sport participation at the collegiate and university level. The data in this table provide no support for the "dumb jock" stereotype. Athletes were not more likely to have lower academic grade averages; nor were they more likely to be enrolled in "cushy" curricula. Moreover, the data show that athletes were slightly more likely to belong to campus organizations that are vocationally oriented. However, athletes were slightly less likely to endorse the intellectual value that "knowledge is important as an end itself."

On other dimensions of conventionality, athletes did not tend to rate themselves higher than nonathletes on religiosity, nor was there a clear pattern for athletes to rate themselves as political conservatives relative to nonathletes. The male athletes were slightly more likely (22 percent versus 18 percent) to rate themselves "as more interested in making a living than reforming society," and "as feeling optimistic about the future of the United States." The pragmatic strain among the athletes also shows up in the finding that they were less likely to cite reading as a favorite leisure activity.

With respect to what might loosely be termed "social conventionality," Table 6-7 lends some credence to the stereotype that athletes are more "conformist" in nature than nonathletes. For instance, athletes were much more likely to be members of fraternities and sororities, to agree that it is important to have a good

TABLE 6-7 Academic Orientation and Social Conventionality as Related to Athletic Participation at the Collegiate Level

	MALES		FEMALES	
CHARACTERISTICS	ATHLETES (*N* = 483) (%)	NONATHLETES (*N* = 1459) (%)	ATHLETES (*N* = 291) (%)	NONATHLETES (*N* = 1373) (%)
Academic Orientation				
Grade average of "C" or lower	20	19	17	18
Major area of study				
humanities	8	14	21	24
social sciences	27	26	27	30
physical sciences	27	19	21	13
business/engineering	35	38	13	16
education	3	4	17	17
Belong to campus organization that is occupationally oriented	11	7	14	9
Believe that knowledge is important as an end in itself	52	59	64	66
Conventionality				
Member of fraternity/sorority	35	15	28	11
Agree that it is important to have a good time socially at college	34	21	34	26
Cites parties as favorite leisure activity	24	15	17	13
Cites sporting events as favorite leisure activity	11	4	10	3
Cites reading as favorite leisure activity	31	36	32	37
Rates self as religiously devout	23	22	28	28
Rates self as political conservative	13	13	12	9
Rates self as more interested in making a living than reforming society	22	18	11	14
Rates self as very optimistic about the future of United States	22	18	13	12

time socially at college, and to cite parties and sporting events as favorite leisure-time activities.

Table 6-8 compares athletes and nonathletes at the collegiate/university level in terms of sexual behavior and the use of alcohol and drugs. The data show that both the male and female athletes were slightly less likely than nonathletes to be living with a person of the opposite sex. Although male athletes had a lower contact rate with prostitutes than their nonathletic peers, they tended toward a slightly higher frequency of sexual intercourse and agreed more with the subjective statement that "I am sexually more active than other students." The female athletes, on the other hand, were less active than nonathletes in terms of sexual intercourse and were less likely to say that they were sexually more active than other students.

It is also interesting to note in Table 6-8 that both male and female athletes were less favorably disposed than comparable nonathletes toward homosexual practices. This finding contrasts with a recent spate of reports in the mass media noting that male homosexuals constitute a disproportionately large proportion of the athletic population. The findings from the survey are consistent with a recent report on homosexuality among male athletes in *Human Behavior* (1977) that stated:

> Using the most stringent criteria, only about 8 percent of the athletes seemed exclusively homosexual. The others who admitted gay activities had engaged in heterosexual activities as well, and, of course, the majority of the athletes were exclusively heterosexual, even on the rumored teams. But the researchers contented themselves that no juggling of the data could remove the rates of homosexuality that are at least as high as those found in studies of the population at large. (p. 38)

TABLE 6-8 Sexual Behavior and Alcohol/Drug Use as Related to Athletic Participation at the Collegiate Level

	MALES		FEMALES	
	ATHLETES (*N* = 483) (%)	NONATHLETES (*N* = 1,459) (%)	ATHLETES (*N* = 291) (%)	NONATHLETES (*N* = 1,373) (%)
Sexual Behavior				
Presently "living with" another person of the opposite sex	5	7	6	9
Did not have sexual intercourse during past month (asked only of nonvirgins)	21	24	37	27
Never have, and would not like to engage in homosexual activity	87	77	81	80
Ever been to a prostitute	13	17	—	—
Agree that "I am sexually more active than other students"	50	45	36	37
Alcohol and Drugs				
Do not drink alcohol at all	11	17	20	24
Never used marijuana	25	22	27	31
Never used amphetamines	72	67	72	73
Never used barbiturates	81	77	80	82
Never used LSD	75	68	84	81

The findings from the survey concerning alcohol and drug use showed that both male and female athletes were more likely to be nondrinkers than their peers who were not athletic participants. Similarly, the male athletes consistently reported less use of marijuana, amphetamines, barbiturates, and LSD. The pattern of drug use among female athletes was not clearly different from the nonathletic females. In sum, the magazine survey showed more similarity than dissimilarity between athletes and nonathletes at the collegiate/university level. Perhaps the only clear difference shows up in rate of membership in fraternities and sororities and the associated propensity for athletes to place a higher value than nonathletes on socializing as a component of college life.

ATHLETIC PARTICIPATION AND DELINQUENCY

Several investigations have focused on participation in sport as a deterrent to delinquency. Furthermore, various sociological theories of delinquency can be used to interpret these studies. Because these theories serve as explanations for both deviant and conforming behavior, the general hypothesis predicts a negative relationship between athletic participation and delinquency. These theories provide explanations of individual deviance rather than organizational deviance; the latter form of deviance within athletic organizations is considered in the next chapter.

A theory of delinquency formulated by Edwin H. Sutherland (1939) focuses on patterns of differential association; it emphasizes that one learns deviant behavior from other people within a cultural setting. Socialization into delinquent and criminal behavior occurs in much the same way that one learns to be a conformist or any other social behavior. From this theory it follows that youth who live in a neighborhood or attend school where there is a high frequency of delinquency are more likely to learn delinquent behavior. Within this theoretical framework, if the coach exerts an influence on his or her players' behavior off the field in the form of training rules and regulations that are contrary to the delinquent subculture, the delinquent associations will probably be discontinued. Moreover, if the athlete internalizes these conventional standards and forms friendships with other athletes and members of the "leading crowd" in the school, than he or she is less likely to be drawn into delinquent behavior. In short, the differential association theory provides an explanation whereby athletic participation leads to a circle of relationships that promote conventional behavior.

Closely related to the differential association theory is the subcultural theory of deviance (Cohen, 1955). This perspective emphasizes the negativism and anti-establishment values, norms, and behaviors inherent in the delinquent subculture. One of the values of the delinquent subculture is an emphasis on masculinity. Moreover, this deviant group is not likely to see a connection between the school norms and their occupational aspirations. Thus, delinquent behavior can represent a rebellion that flows from their perception of a lack of payoff from the school and their resentment of punitive sanctions (Stinchcombe, 1964; Schafer, 1969). For the athlete, integration into the athletic subculture is "establishment oriented" and is consistent with the values of the larger culture. Thus, participation in sport is usually a source of social rewards in the form of positive public recognition and self-satisfaction; consequently, athletes are likely to embrace the dominant culture or they will be weeded out of the athletic stream. Furthermore, athletic competition provides an institutionalized means of displaying force, skill, strength, and competitiveness—masculine qualities—in a socially acceptable way (Schafer, 1969).

Another sociological approach to delinquency is labeling theory. Frequently deviant behavior has been studied by focusing on the individual; deviance was thought to be "in" the person. However, labeling theory holds that deviance is not inherent in the person but is socially determined and applied by social control agents. Thus, Becker (1963) states that:

> Social groups create deviance by making the rules whose infraction constitutes deviance, and by applying those rules to particular people and labeling them as outsiders. From this point of view, deviance is not a quality of the act the person commits, but rather a consequence of the application by others of rules and sanctions to an "offender." The deviant is one to whom that label has successfully been applied; deviant behavior is behavior that people so label. (p. 9)

This approach to delinquency depends not only on the act but on who is applying the label to the deviant; central to the theory is the fact that the label may not be applied uniformly. Thus, behavior by the poor and minority groups is more likely to be defined as deviant than the same behavior by middle class groups. Furthermore, the deviant label is likely to result in negative sanctions and self-definitions that become fulfilled through additional deviant acts. When this theory is applied to the behavior of athletes, they may be defined (labeled) as "good kids" and the delinquent acts they commit may be considered merely mischievous pranks. Moreover, youthful athletes may be protected by school officials and the police such that their delinquent acts do not turn up on the official records. Sometimes athletes who commit acts that would be defined as delinquent will be referred to the coach who will discipline the athletes informally rather than through the courts and law enforcement officials. Athletes who perform delinquent acts, being athletes, may get preferential treatment and are not looked upon as being delinquent. One study gives special attention to the possibility that preferential treatment for athletes is a factor in reducing the frequency of deviancy (Snyder and Spreitzer, 1979b). We studied 384 college students from over 200 high schools and classified the schools according to the importance of sport in the school. We expected that in those schools where sport is highly valued by the students, teachers, and administration the athletes might be the recipients of gratuitous treatment by faculty and staff based on their athletic visibility. Indeed, findings from the investigation indicated that the schools varied according to the amount of preferential treatment given to athletes (i.e., special counseling, graded easier, and considered more important than other students by school officials). Nevertheless, the *perceptions* of the general student body was that high school athletes were less likely to be involved in the three forms of deviance outlined in Table 6-9. Furthermore, even where sport is very important in the school, the level of perceived deviancy approximates the percentages in the schools where sport is less important. In this regard the data provide some support for the selectivity factor as an explanation of athletic conventionality; in any event, the perceived conventionality of athletes is present regardless of the value climate of the school.

TABLE 6-9 Perceptions of Conventionality among Male and Female Athletes by School Value Climate

PERCEPTIONS OF STUDENT BODY CONCERNING ATHLETES AS COMPARED TO NONATHLETES	SCHOOL VALUE CLIMATE FOR MALES			SCHOOL VALUE CLIMATE FOR FEMALES		
	SPORT VERY IMPORTANT (*N* = 237) (%)	SPORT OF SOME IMPORTANCE (*N* = 94) (%)	SPORT OF LITTLE IMPORTANCE (*N* = 21) (%)	SPORT VERY IMPORTANT (*N* = 39) (%)	SPORT OF SOME IMPORTANCE (*N* = 142) (%)	SPORT OF LITTLE IMPORTANCE (*N* = 164) (%)
Disciplinary Problems Outside the School						
Athletes are overrepresented	12	5	5	5	4	1
Athletes are proportionally represented	39	49	48	53	49	56
Athletes are underrepresented	49	46	47	42	47	43
School Disciplinary Problems						
Athletes are overrepresented	8	7	0	0	4	0
Athletes are proportionally represented	36	45	48	42	40	50
Athletes are underrepresented	56	48	52	58	56	50
Smoke Marijuana						
Athletes are overrepresented	18	10	10	5	6	2
Athletes are proportionally represented	52	61	65	45	49	50
Athletes are underrepresented	30	29	25	50	45	48

Source: Adapted from Snyder and Spreitzer, 1979b, p. 465.

Two additional explanations have been offered by sociologists for understanding delinquency. One theory holds that delinquency may be the result of weak social controls from parents, school officials, or other authorities. If this is true, the external control provided by coaches and training rules can serve as insulation against delinquent acts that would not be available to nonathletes (Segrave and Chu, 1978, p. 8). Additionally, some writers contend that delinquency is the result of the desire to escape sheer boredom. Schafer (1969, pp. 72–73) suggests that slashing tires, stealing, beating up drunks, and smoking pot are simply ways of getting one's kicks. Clearly, athletes are less likely to be bored and thereby be more immune to delinquency than comparable nonathletes, because sports are likely to provide excitement as well as take up much after-school and weekend time.

Each of the theoretical approaches supports the hypothesis that participation in sport is expected to be negatively associated with delinquent behavior. Furthermore, we might suppose that among lower-class youth with which delinquent behavior is more prevalent, the effect of athletic participation is apt to have the greatest influence.

Perhaps the first major study of athletic participation and delinquency was by Schafer (1969), who collected data from 585 high school boys. This study lends some support for the assumption that participation in sport "keeps kids out of trouble." However, when social class background and grade point average were used as control variables, the relationship remained only for the disadvantaged boys. An examination of Table 6-10 reveals small differences in the percentages, except for boys in the subpopulation in which delinquency rates are the highest. The research of the Schafer study was later replicated by Segrave and Chu (1978) with similar results. Their study of high school and college males concluded that male athletes were less delinquent than nonathletes; however, this relationship was evident primarily among lower class athletes rather than middle or upper class athletes.

TABLE 6-10 Delinquency Rates for Athletes and Nonathletes, Controlling for Father's Occupation and Grade-point Average

	DELINQUENT (%)	NONDELINQUENT (%)	TOTAL *N*
White-Collar			
High grade-point average			
Athlete	4	96	(74)
Nonathlete	8	92	(113)
Low grade-point average			
Athlete	11	89	(27)
Nonathlete	5	95	(94)
Blue-Collar			
High grade-point average			
Athlete	8	92	(36)
Nonathlete	11	89	(57)
Low grade-point average			
Athlete	10	90	(20)
Nonathlete	23	77	(126)

Source: Adapted from Schafer, 1969, p. 77.

A study of Buhrmann (1977) of 857 girls from seven different rural and small town high schools in Iowa provide additional support for the hypothesis that sport participation serves as a deterrent to delinquent behavior. Table 6-11 summarizes the correlation between degree of athletic participation and incidence of deviant behavior among girls at four grade levels of high school. The pattern is consistent; athletes are less likely to engage in all five of the deviant behaviors enumerated in the study. Moreover, this pattern is slightly stronger among seniors as compared to students in the previous three years of high school. The findings are particularly strong relevant to smoking and the use of alcoholic beverages.

TABLE 6-11 Relationship between Athletic Participation and Deviant Behavior among Female Students in Grades 9–12

DEVIANT BEHAVIOR	GRADES			
	9	10	11	12
Smoking	−.70	−.84	−.25	−.84
Drinking alcoholic beverages	−.49	−.62	−.04	−.55
Breaking school rules and regulations	−.06	−.07	−.05	−.11
Cheating on tests and examinations	−.00	−.30	−.15	−.29
Trouble with police and the law	−.00	−.26	−.07	−.68

Source: Adapted from Buhrmann, 1977, p. 21.

In another study, Landers and Landers (1978) studied 521 high school males who were classified according to their participation in extracurricular activities in the years 1959–1972. The study focused on delinquency as measured by court records. The findings indicated that extracurricular participation generally resulted in less likelihood of showing up as delinquent on the court records. The analysis showed that 8 percent of the students not participating in extracurricular activities were identified as delinquent; 3 percent of the students who participated only in school service organizations were so classified, while 4 percent of the students who were participating only in athletics were delinquent, and only 2 percent of the students participating in both school service clubs and athletics were on the court records as delinquents. Although Peek, Picou, and Curry (1979) have raised some questions about the methodology of the Landers and Landers' investigation, the results are consistent with the previous studies cited. Furthermore, the Landers and Landers study suggests that the apparent negative relationship between sport and delinquency is not unique; it is also applicable to participation in other extracurricular activities. Moreover, the theories of deviant behavior discussed previously are applicable to other forms of extracurricular involvement. These studies generally report a modest negative correlation between athletics and deviancy; however, the findings must be interpreted with caution. Considerable selectivity takes place; those who are less prone toward delinquency may be drawn to school extracurricular activities. Furthermore, as we have previously discussed, participation in extracurricular activities (including athletics) is likely to result in some bias against being labeled a delinquent.

Most of the studies on conventionality cited in this chapter have focused on interscholastic sports. Few scientific studies are available on the topic for collegiate and professional athletes. Information that is available at the collegiate and professional levels is primarily in the form of news reports. There is considerable evidence to suggest that the extreme emphasis on high performances at the elite levels of sport has resulted in some use of drugs to achieve this end. Sometimes drugs such as cortisone and novocain have been used to reduce pain and allow the player to continue playing, even when this could cause further physical damage. Athletes in football and track have also been under pressure to use anabolic steroids to increase body muscle mass; the long term effects of these drugs remain uncertain. Moreover, some collegiate and professional athletes report that they have been encouraged to use amphetamines (pep) pills to achieve additional energy and aggressiveness in game situations. Because the athletes' livelihood at the professional level depends on continued high achievement, some athletes will no doubt use almost any means available to improve or maintain their performance.

In the summer of 1980, news accounts surfaced that suggested an extensive use of cocaine among players in the National Basketball League. These reports imply that the use of cocaine is a reflection of the increased use of drugs in the society generally, as well as the need for social relaxation by the players who have high pressure schedules and boring road trips. The newspapers published unconfirmed reports of 40 to 75 percent of the NBA players using cocaine (*Toledo Blade*, August 21, 1980). These variations in conventionality at different levels of sport participation suggest that explanations for the relationship between sport and behavior are based primarily on the social context surrounding sport rather than internalized character traits of athletes.

ARE SPORTS DYSFUNCTIONAL?

So far, we have noted some of the frequently cited positive aspects of sports—the development of emotional well-being, conventionality, and less delinquency. A closer examination, however, reveals that each of these advantages requires some qualification. In short, the school sports environment cannot be categorically defined as positive or negative. The socialization process associated with sport may in some respect build character, but Ogilvie and Tutko (1971) felt justified in publishing an article entitled, "If You Want to Build Character, Try Something Else." The emphasis in formalized sport on victory may, in fact, promote deviant behavior and poor sportsmanship. In this context Orlick (1974) notes

> For every positive psychological or social outcome in sports, there are possible negative outcomes. For example, sports can offer a child group membership or group exclusion, acceptance or rejection, positive feedback or negative feedback, a sense of accomplishment or a sense of failure, evidence of self-worth or a lack of evidence of self-worth. Likewise, sports can develop cooperation and a concern for others, but they can also develop intense rivalry and a complete lack of concern for others. (p. 2)

In the same vein, Schafer (1971a) has argued that our educational institutions are primarily concerned with the teaching of "correct attitudes" and transmitting the existing, and basically conservative, values that are functional in our present society. Such educational goals may result in inordinate conformity and may encourage the blind following of orders rather than a critical and questioning attitude. Schafer feels that organized school sports contribute to this conservative influence and serve to transmit values in favor of the status quo by emphasizing the importance of external rewards, teaching the passive acceptance of orders, and generally developing bureaucratic personalities. Research by Malmisur and Schmitt (1975) substantiates Schafer's conclusions with findings showing that male athletes in college tended to be highly conformist, to obey rules just because they were rules, and to base their interpersonal relations primarily on prestige and status.

The big-time collegiate sports establishments are not primarily concerned with building character. Rather, they are highly bureaucratized business organizations that sometimes resort to unethical practices to achieve the goals of winning and the resultant gate receipts. Indeed this professionalized and hard-nosed approach to sport begins long before the college level. The competitiveness of sport is an important ingredient in its appeal. But, when school sports become primarily a test of performance skills, the subsequent stages of sorting and selecting leaves fewer and fewer participants remaining as the conveyor belt moves through high school and college. Although most youngsters develop an admiration of the skills and strategies of sport, the successive tests of competence leave many by the wayside. Consequently, their orientation toward sport becomes that of vicarious participation through spectatorship. In short, the emphasis of formal programs on performance promotes self-attitudes that are often antithetical to participation in sport activities.

On a more subjective level, sport in the American society performs a socialization function that provides a life script for males in general that is a blueprint for acting, feeling, and thinking. This scripted message, according to Schafer (1975), emphasizes that boys are taught to "be successful," "be strong," and "be objective and unemotional." The script is played out by an emphasis on dominance, emotional toughness, and lack of sentiment. A "real man" does not show weakness, helplessness, or sentimentality; he takes charge, shows he can take it, doesn't show pain, he comes out on top, and he is a winner! This message, promoted by sport, may have dysfunctional consequences that lead to the difficulty of men to express sentiments, to be in touch with their own feelings, as well as in transmitting affectionate and feeling-level communications with others. Schafer argues that most of the "emotions encouraged in high competitive sport are those related to maximizing achievement (e.g., anger, nonacceptance of self, tension) or to celebrating victory (e.g., elation, excitement). Other feelings such as doubt, sadness, fear, love might well be either ignored or scorned" (p. 53). Needless to say, this scenario is not easily assimilated by females who are attracted to athletic participation. We discuss the ambiguity of the role of athletics for females in Chapter 10.

Another dysfunction of sport that has been noted by several researchers is the potential addictive nature of exercise. William Glasser (1976) has argued that extensive running can lead to a "positive addiction" with desirable psychological consequences in the form of ego strength, euphoria, and an altered mental state that he described as trancelike and "spinning free." Conversely, when the individual fails to continue the running regimen, there is the feeling of misery, irritability, pain, and similar withdrawal symptoms. One piece of research by Carmack and Martens (1979) on 315 runners has provided some support for Glasser's theory. For example, they found that "altered states of consciousness" and a psychological "spin out" were associated with runs of 40 minutes or longer.

Since the publication of Glasser's theory of positive addiction, sport psychologist William Morgan (1979) has offered a cautionary note about the effects of long distance running. He has argued that exercise addicts must continue to increase their dosage of running to receive the same level of euphoria; furthermore, the "feeling good" becomes more important than anything else. Thus, the exercise addict has passed from the self-enhancement stage of exercise to a destructive stage where he or she is concerned more with self-gratification and less with work, family, and physical disabilities that have resulted from running. Robbins and Joseph's (1980) study of 315 runners who had varying degrees of commitment to running provide some support for the Morgan thesis. For example, the full-time runners (at least 40 miles a week) report more complaints from spouses for neglect than the part-time, occasional runners. Also, neglect of work responsibilities, a characteristic of negative addition, is somewhat more frequent among the more serious runners. However, these relationships are not easy to interpret; perhaps for some people running is a form of compensation for a marital relationship or a work orientation that has already turned sour. Furthermore, Robbins and Joseph argue that the reordering of priorities between running and work may not be at the expense of work performance as suggested by Morgan; rather, the running is an added source of gratification they receive from the leisure sphere of their lives. In fact, the authors suggest that running may contribute to a greater productivity at work. This tentative conclusion is offered because the majority of the runners in their study considered running to be beneficial to their work. It is evident that the research on the addictive aspects of physical exercise is still tentative; however, we would suggest that the potential benefits of physical activity might be subverted if carried to the extreme levels of involvement.

CONCLUSION

Throughout this chapter we have focused on the social and psychological concomitants of sport participation. It is evident that the physical activity of sport (e.g., catching a baseball, dribbling a basketball, or throwing a discus) not only have physiological consequences but also social consequences; that is, because of the social values, definitions, and expectations attached to these physical activities, sport involvement has social and psychological effects on the participants. One of the difficulties in analyzing the consequences of sport involvement is in isolating the probable effects of *selectivity* into and out of the sport stream from the *socialization* that occurs within sport. Thus far, sophisticated longitudinal studies of athletes and nonathletes are not available to untangle the interacting effects of these two processes. Evidence suggests that both processes operate to bring about the differences that are observed between athletes and nonathletes. The results flowing from the selectivity factor should not, therefore, be attributed to the socialization that might occur as a result of sport participation. This process of selectivity should be kept in mind when interpreting research that reports a lower rate of delinquency among athletes as compared to nonathletes. As noted above, athletes are likely to be given preferential treatment by social control agents. Moreover, nonconformist youth are likely to be screened out of organized athletics by eligibility requirements and by coaches who tend to be conservative.

A number of studies have focused on aspects of social and emotional adjustment as a consequence of sport and physical activity. Theoretically, we should expect to find that a healthy body promotes mental health, and many studies provide evidence of the validity of this thesis. Consequently, the role of active physical participation needs further research in the context of whole health, preventive medicine, and rehabilitation (e.g., alcoholism). A recent article on the therapeutic value of running as part of a rehabilitation program is interesting in this respect in terms of its implication for both physical and mental well-being. The author (Schlenoff, 1980) suggests that the "self-devaluation that so frequently accompanies a disabling condition may be combatted through the use of jogging as a treatment modality. A more positive sort of body-image is likely to develop, along with a greater awareness of one's physiological responses to stress" (p. 76).

There are, however, some ambiguous findings on the benefits of participation in highly structured formal sport. Attempts to assess behavioral and attitudinal consequences have produced mixed results. The norms of conventionality that are evident in the sport world seem to be present to some degree among players. However, this characterization may be a reflection of the social structure associated with the level of sport (i.e., high school, college, or professional level) rather than a "trait" of the players. Moreover, the emphasis in sport on conventionality and conservativism can lead to an *uncritical* acceptance of the status quo. This characteristic is hardly functional in a democratic society. Likewise, the emphasis on "masculinity" and a "macho" image among male athletes may be dysfunctional in relating to other people on a more expressive affective level (cf. Sabo and Runfola, 1980). Additionally, the stress in sport on achievement and winning contain the potential for a conflict with the norms of fair play, sportsmanship, and intrinsic enjoyment of physical expression in sport. Furthermore, although the healthful benefits of exercise are often touted, dysfunctional consequences may also develop in the form of a negative addiction.

CHAPTER 7
Sport within Educational Institutions

"I would like to build a university of which the football team can be proud"—G. Cross

In the United States much of sport takes place within the context of educational institutions. In European countries, on the other hand, sport is more closely linked to the community within a nexus of clubs. In communist countries, sport tends to be closely linked with governmental and political units. The peculiarly close relationship between sport and educational institutions in the United States represents a sociologically intriguing connection that has important implications for both athletes and the society at large.

A social institution can be defined as a structure that evolves to regulate and channel the behavior of people in order to achieve collectively shared goals. Every society has the perennial need to control certain areas of social life—for example, to regulate the procreation and education of children, the production and distribution of goods and services, the system of government, and the relationship of people to the supernatural. Each institution contains values and norms that prescribe acceptable modes of behavior in a given sphere of social life. The educational institution specifies, for example, the way in which attitudes, knowledge, and skills are transmitted to each new generation. Similarly, the world of sport is an institution in the sense that values and norms are specified concerning the expression of physical activities in the form of athletics. The institution of sport includes definitions of the meaning and value of physical activity as well as specifications concerning the ways in which sport is socially organized in a given society.

Anthropological research shows that play is present in every society in one form or another and is thus a cultural universal in the same sense as the family and religion. Because play is always with us historically and geographically, it can be argued that play is isomorphic with human nature and represents the natural expression of physical needs in a manner analogous to the way that art expresses the aesthetic needs of human beings. When play becomes formalized and competitive, we find the incipient stages of sport.

Sport is one of the most pervasive institutions in modern societies. It permeates society from the societal level down to the consciousness of the individual. Education is also a major social institution and plays a primary role in socializing each generation to become productive members of their society. The school in industrial societies is an agency of education that is of major importance from early childhood to early adulthood, whereas the family serves the main educational function in preindustrial societies.

Both of these institutional structures overlap within the framework of school sports. For most youth the school athletic program provides the primary institutional arrangement for formalized participation in sport. From an educational perspective, school sports may either support or subvert formal academic goals. School athletic programs are also important in maintaining the link between the school and community. In fact, school athletic programs represent an important means of community recreation and social integration. Furthermore, school athletic programs are major suppliers of professional sports as well as an important source of adult involvement and continued interest in sport. Thus, the relationship between education and sport represents an interesting topic for sociological analysis.

It is in light of this discussion that we focus our attention on the subject of sport within schools. This topic incorporates the sociology of both education and sport. The main thrust of our discussion centers on an effort to relate sport to the context of formal education, focusing on the secondary and higher educational levels. When we describe and explain the nature and function of sport within schools, we also need to consider aspects of the social context and institutional configuration within which each is embedded. Thus, our objective is to analyze the social organization of formal education as a means of delineating the relationship between sport and education in the larger society.

SPORT AT THE COLLEGIATE LEVEL

One of the important changes in college and university life between 1860 and 1890 was the emergence and steady growth of student interest and participation in athletic competition between schools (Betts, 1974). In spite of the hostility or indifference of college administrators to this movement, baseball, rowing, football, and track and field sports rapidly emerged in the leading universities of the East and Midwest. The growth of intercollegiate sports is at least partially attributed to the expanding railroad service that permitted the transportation of teams and their supporters. It is reported that a baseball game between Williams and Amherst in 1859 was the inauguration of intercollegiate athletic competition, at least in the East. The first intercollegiate football game was played at Rutgers against Princeton on November 6, 1869.

By the turn of the century, intercollegiate athletic competition was a well-established part of higher education. Stadia were built, and the increase in gate receipts soon established commercialism as a primary characteristic of collegiate athletics. In 1914, it is reported that 150 colleges spent more than $2,000,000 annually on athletics. Alumni served as pressure groups to promote and recruit prospective players for their teams, and the press served to popularize coaches such as Amos Alonzo Stagg, Glenn (Pop) Warner, Percy Naughton, and Fielding (Hurry Up) Yost, while Walter Camp's "All-American" selections attracted national attention to the outstanding players of the period.

Critics as well as proponents of collegiate sport emerged very early in this era. Betts cites the *Popular Science Monthly* (March, 1880) as reporting "a positive serious evil of athleticism in that it tends to become a power in the schools, rivaling the constituted authorities." In 1904, President William Faunce of Brown University lamented that "we are living in a time when college athletics are honeycombed with falsehood, and when the professions of amateurism are usually hypocrisy. No college team ever meets another today with actual faith in the other's eligibility" (Betts, 1974, p. 216).

One of the most perceptive critics of the American university in that period was Thorstein Veblen. In his opinion, one of the "drawbacks to the cause of learning" was the increase in the "accessories" of college life, including extracurricular activities such as sports.

> These accessories of college life have been strongly on the increase since the business regime has come in. They are held to be indispensable, or unavoidable; not for scholarly work, of course, but chiefly to encourage the attendance of that decorative contingent who take more kindly to sports, invidious intrigue and social amenities than to scholarly pursuits. Notoriously, this contingent is, on the whole, a serious drawback to the cause of learning, but it adds appreciably, and adds a highly valued contribution, to the number enrolled; and it gives also a certain, highly appreciated, loud tone ("college spirit") to the student body; and so it is felt to benefit the corporation of learning by drawing public attention. Corporate means, expended in provision for these academic accessories—"side shows," as certain ill disposed critics have sometimes called them—are commonly felt to be well spent. Persons who are not intimately familiar with American college life have little appreciation of the grave solicitude given to these matters (Veblen, 1918, p. 87).

On the other hand, the athletic movement had its proponents who cited the benefits of competition in the development of character, reduction of rowdiness, and the development of physical and mental health.

> Friends of organized athletics were valiant in defense, stressing the improvement in student health, the decline of illness and absences, the remarkable increase of strong men in college classes of the eighties, and the diminishing problem of tobacco and alcohol. Some noted the decided moral uplift derived from athletic interest, the disappearance of riots and rowdiness, the increasing respect for college property, and the danger of turning students to temptations of the theater and saloon if sports were barred by the authorities. Already sport was said to provide a "safety-valve for the superabundant physical effervescence of the young men" in our colleges. As the possibilities of applying athletics in education became manifest, appeals were made to the teacher to appreciate and to direct games, since an effective teacher must keep in touch with his students (Betts, 1974, p. 213).[1]

---

[1]Betts, *America's Sporting Heritage, 1850–1950* © 1974. Addison-Wesley, Reading, Mass. Reprinted with permission.

While collegiate sport originated as an informal student movement, by the 1920s the commercialization of sport in major universities was well established, particularly King Football. Issues that in the 1970s continue to be hotly debated—the lowering of scholastic standards for athletes, safety of players, overemphasis on sport, excessive competition, and professionalism of college players—were likewise controversial topics in college athletics in the 1920s (Betts, 1974). The economic collapse of 1929 resulted in a temporary decline of intercollegiate athletic spectacles. However, by 1935, football was again burgeoning in the South and Far West. Since World War II, the growth of big-time sports has continued to become an even more permanent fixture of university life, particularly with the inception of television contracts that are available to major teams with national recognition. The financial significance of television is so obtrusive that the natural flow of the game is often sacrificed to provide time for commercials.

Page (1973) has provided an excellent sociological analysis of this change in the social organization of sport. He uses a bureaucratic model as the mode of analysis. Sport (especially large university athletic departments), like other big business concerns, has become more bureaucratic—that is, a formalized, hierarchical, rule-laden, and efficiency-seeking type of social organization (see also Nixon, 1976b; Voigt, 1974). In a historical perspective this represents a transition from player-controlled games to big-time corporate sport (Page, 1973, p. 32). Furthermore, it should be emphasized that in the big business/bureaucratic model of social organization, success is determined by the output or product. In sport this means winning teams must be produced so that the athletic department can in turn compete successfully for the entertainment dollar.

In a recent study of 115 large, public-university athletic departments with NCAA affiliation, Young (1975) identified four criteria for a successful operating program.

1. Financial solvency of the total program
2. Success based on the win–loss record
3. The total number of sports in the program
4. The total number of participants

Although Young recognized the desirability of an athletic department to measure educational outcomes, these criteria are generally most important in defining a successful athletic department. To be economically sound requires winning teams, prestigious coaches, and a heavy recruitment budget. In short, athletic programs must compete for the entertainment dollars of the public. The product that is being sold is sport. Revenues are increased through concessions, selling programs, banners, parking, and renting athletic facilities to the public.

This social context is helpful in explaining unethical athletic practices such as illegal recruiting of high school athletes, exploitation of players, "under the table" subsidies, manipulation of eligibility standards, and other abuses that have emerged with big-time sport. Thus the ultimate product of sport—winning—becomes the justification for the questionable methods that are sometimes used to achieve it.

Figure 7-1 provides a diagram of the social and cultural context, the organizational characteristics, and the usual goals or outputs of most athletic depart-

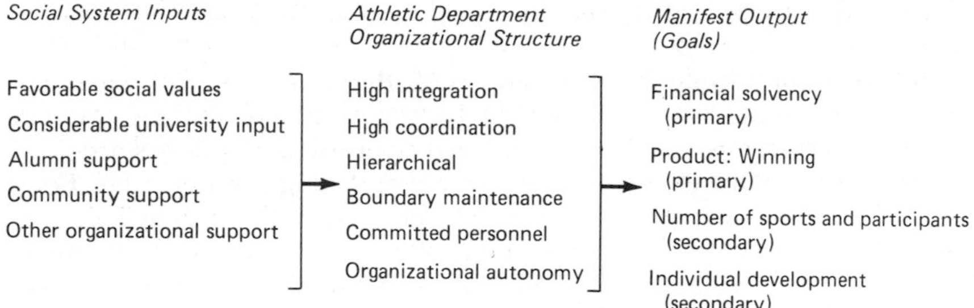

FIGURE 7–1 Organizational characteristics of the sport subsystem within the university.

ments. In general, athletic departments receive support for their organization from the university, alumni, community, and the social values of the surrounding society. From an organization standpoint, the athletic department usually manifests many of the same characteristics as other bureaucratic organizations, for example, integration, coordination, and a hierarchical structure that promote efficiency. Furthermore, athletic departments within the broader university often have some separate financial support provided by the income-producing sports and alumni contributions. Thus, the athletic department is often able to maintain a partial insulation from intrusions of the other segments of the university organization, that is, boundary maintenance and functional autonomy. Finally, the primary goals are product oriented to maintain financial solvency and win games. Secondary goals include the extent and range of participation and the personal development of the athletes. The product orientation of major university athletic departments provides the context for the consideration of organizational deviance (Snyder and Spreitzer, 1976c).

THE ATHLETIC DEPARTMENT, ORGANIZATIONAL DEVIANCE, AND RELATED PROBLEMS

In the previous chapter we discussed several correlational studies of athletic participation and deviance. These reports dealt with individual forms of deviance such as violations of school regulations and laws. In the last decade we have seen a number of reports, for example the Watergate investigation, of improper actions by large-scale organizations. Associated with the increased awareness of these improper actions by organizations is the recognition that this form of deviance is not individualistic but is committed by individuals "who act for and in the name of the corporation" (McCaghy, 1976, p. 204). Thus, organizational deviance "refers to action attributed to an organization which is labeled deviant because it violates the normative expectations surrounding the organization" (Ermann and Lundman, 1978, p. 58). This form of deviance is supported by the norms of a unit within an organization; in a sense, the deviance is encouraged or ignored. Organizational deviance includes such violations as medical frauds, fraudulent business practices, price fixing, political corruption, providing illegal goods and services, and racketeering. However, the admitted and alleged improprieties and violations of the law and NCAA rules by athletic departments also represent a form of organizational deviance.

The major universities, where the impact of athletic violations is greatest, are under the control of the National Collegiate Athletic Association (NCAA). Most of the university infractions that have been acted upon by the NCAA since 1952 (when penalties were first imposed) have involved recruiting violations. The Committee on infractions has processed a total of 1,042 cases; in 452 of these cases, violations were not established. In the remaining 590 cases, 465 resulted in punitive action by the NCAA, 97 of these involved both recruiting violations and improper payments to athletes, an additional 128 involved only recruiting regulations, 32 involved improper payments only to athletes, and 86 were violations of rules related to playing and practice sessions or postseason games. The remaining 122 cases do not fit any particular category or pattern of regulations set forth in the NCAA manual (Berst, 1979, personal communication).

Beginning in late 1979, a spate of major universities have come under investigation by the NCAA and in some cases by the FBI. Most of the investigations involve the practice of keeping athletes eligible through the use of fraudulent transcripts that include course credits extension courses offered by several small colleges and community colleges. In most cases the scandals have involved athletes who have been enrolled for courses for which they received credit but which they never attended. The investigations indicate that some athletic advisors in several universities in the western United States were using the extension courses as a means of securing bogus credits for their athletes. Investigations of the transcripts and credits of athletes have been conducted at Arizona State University, San Jose State, New Mexico University, the University of Utah, Oregon State, Oregon University, California Polytechnic at Pomona, and Purdue University. Furthermore, President John Zumberge of the University of Southern California has called for an investigation of athletes who were enrolled in a speech class at USC for which they were to receive credit while doing little or no work. Additionally, USC, like many other schools, has admitted athletes under an affirmative action or minority access program designed to provide an opportunity for disadvantaged youth to enter college who would not otherwise meet the admission requirements. However, some universities have apparently abused the spirit of these affirmative action programs to get the wholesale admission of athletes who would otherwise not be admitted. President Zumberge of USC noted that the admission of the academically marginal athletes was "based chiefly on athletic prowess as judged by the athletic department," and "it was a system gone awry" (*Toledo Blade*, October 14, 1980, p. 21). As a result of these investigations, including irregularities in admissions and credits, five member schools in the Pacific-10 Conference (USC, UCLA, Arizona State, Oregon, and Oregon State) were disqualified from the 1980 football championship and the 1981 Rose Bowl. These investigations have an ironic twist when viewed in the context of remarks made by the preceding President of USC, Dr. John Hubbard, who retired in 1980:

> A good athletic program is indispensible as a kind of glue that holds the university and community together. It keeps the alumni and our other friends interested in the university. . . . College football is more than a game—it's an event. It comes under the rubric of tradition: The pregame parties, the band marching over to the Coliseum,

> the song girls, the card stunts, the horse. On a Saturday during the football season, as many as 10 different support (fund-raising) groups will gather on campus for brunch. The fiscal well-being of the university is tied up with these people—and their appearance on campus is tied up with the spectacle that is a Saturday afternoon football game. The catalyst is the game (*Toledo Blade*, March 8, 1980, p. 2).

The victims in this form of organizational deviance include the student-athletes who receive an inadequate education, though under the pressures of athletic and classroom activities they are likely to accept the easy credits and other favors. Given the fact that the most talented athletes are highly recruited by many universities, the temptation is to "sell" one's athletic ability to the highest bidder. Although the prestige of a university and economic advantages are forthcoming with athletic fame, the use of *any* means to achieve these ends in the long run threatens the academic integrity and credibility of the university system. One of the difficulties in controlling this form of deviance is that it has considerable social acceptance. Many alumni, students, and university publics are not particularly concerned with the ethics of an athletic program as long as it wins and does not get caught. Nevertheless, bogus credits threaten the validity of an academic community in the same way counterfeit money threatens a monetary system. In this context, one might note that although the competition for athletes has led to abuses, the competition for other students, including in some instances graduate students, has also had the effect of lowering academic standards. Any degree from an accredited university or academic branch is sufficient to meet some state certification requirements and to secure pay increases or a promotion in a school, business, or government agency (Ashworth, 1980). One school superintendent "who wanted a program brought to his school district said, 'Our teachers don't meet the state requirements, and I need some quickie courses in here during the spring break to get us up to snuff in the state' " (Ashworth, 1980). Moreover, these low quality programs generate state subsidy and tuition fees. In short, academic credibility is threatened not only by the expediencies of the desire for athletic success and gate receipts, but also in other segments of the university by the need to attract student enrollments in various undergraduate and graduate degree programs.

The plethora of problems involved with contemporary athletics in higher education prompted officials of American universities to undertake an inquiry into these issues through a Commission on Collegiate Athletics under the auspices of the American Council on Education. The findings from the two-year study were summarized in the Fall 1979 issue of the *Educational Record* (Nyquist, 1979). These issues have been much discussed in the United States since the 1920s. The intensity of the debate has been heightened by economic pressures and the legal requirement to provide athletic opportunities for women as well as men. The problems associated with athletics in higher education are peculiar to the United States since formal athletics in other countries are anchored to noneducational institutions—trade unions, clubs, community associations, the military, and other governmental structures. The future of big-time sports in higher education today becomes even more problematic as budgetary pressures increase. It is clear that the educational functions of these athletic programs will have to become more clearly documented; otherwise, officials of universities and colleges will be forced to reallocate their scarce resources away from interuniversity athletics.

SPORT: A COLLECTIVE REPRESENTATION

In the previous section we cited President Emeritus Hubbard of the University of Southern California who credited the university's increase in resources to its athletic success. Some empirical support for this position is provided by the research of Ullrich (1971). This study analyzed a sample of fifty state universities that granted doctoral degrees during the years of 1948–1968. The focus of this research was on the possible relationship between athletic success and academic productivity as defined by the number of doctorates produced by each university. Additionally, the research considered the correlation between athletic success and federal allocations in the form of grants and contracts received by each of the universities. Athletic success was defined in terms of football performance—games won, participation in bowl games, victories in bowl games, rankings by the Associated Press and United Press International, recipients of the Heisman Trophy, and Coach of the Year awards. The Ullrich study reported a positive correlation between football success and the production of doctorates and the receipt of federal funding during the 1948–1968 period. However, these relationships were qualified because they were particularly strong for emerging multiuniversities that engage in intense interstate rivalry, for example, UCLA, Michigan State University, and Florida State University. The relationships were insignificant for long established universities such as the University of California at Berkeley, Michigan, and Wisconsin; however, athletic success may have been important in their emergence at an earlier period in their history. Ullrich is careful to point out that his study is exploratory and that the correlations do not necessarily indicate causation. Nevertheless, the football success of a university may serve to increase its prestige, bring pride to the state, and promote legislative and alumni support that in turn promote the growth of the academic side of the institution.

This feeling of identification with an athletic team is further documented in a study by Cialdini et al. (1976), who observed that successful athletic programs increase the degree to which students identify with a university. This inclination to "bask in the reflected glory" was evident in a greater tendency for university students to wear school identifying apparel (e.g., jackets, sweaters, and tee shirts) on days after their universities had won football games. Furthermore, their research demonstrated that students were more likely to use the pronoun "we" ("we won") when describing a football victory as compared to a defeat ("they lost"). Presumably the tendency to identify publicly with a successful athletic team represents an attempt to enhance both one's own self-image and institutional public image.

In brief, an athletic program can serve as a collective representation of a university, region, or a state and thus mobilize community sentiments, pride, loyalty, and identification with the institution. For many people, "brief concise symbols such as the Golden Gate Bridge or Fisherman's Wharf in San Francisco, the French Quarter in New Orleans, and Beacon Hill or Boston Commons in Boston serve through collective representation to help symbolically incorporate some residents in social and cultural systems of the city" (Anderson and Stone, 1980, p. 5). Similarly, references to such universities as Notre Dame, Texas, Alabama, Oklahoma, UCLA, Michigan, Pennsylvania State, Ohio State, and Kentucky bring to mind their athletic achievements. Furthermore, these achievements may promote a social solidarity, a feeling of community, and a common basis for integration. We suggest that the emergence of pregame, postgame, and tailgate parties associated with football may serve to further a collective consciousness.

The former president of the University of Oklahoma, George Cross, has explicitly stated that as president his leadership helped create a football team that gave the university prestige and pride to the people of Oklahoma (Cross, 1977). President Cross did raise the question whether "athletic extravaganzas are relevant to the overall mission of the university," but he concluded that "a university should be a place where a student has the opportunity to develop to the fullest extent any potential—mental, physical, or both—that he or she may possess" (Cross, 1977, p. 274). Furthermore, he is reported to have used the success of the Oklahoma football team in a budgetary presentation to the state legislature. It is in this context that he remarked, "I would like to build a university of which the football team can be proud" (Cross, 1977, p. 145). Whether the university was improved academically via football success is debatable, but Cross' argument that the team has done a great deal for the state of Oklahoma is self evident.

If sport is one form of collective representation, then the game is a type of integrative ritual. In this regard, a local athletic team is a means by which the community expresses itself to other communities. From the standpoint of the team, the social support from the local community may have an effect on performance (Schwartz and Barsky, 1977). An investigation by Schwartz and Barsky is based on the theoretical work of Emile Durkheim, who was particularly concerned with the influence of social supports on human behavior. Specifically, this study considered the effect of the home advantage, that is, the social support of the home audience in several different sports and the game outcome. The influence of fan support on performance is related to the social psychological concept of social facilitation, that is, how the behavior of an individual is influenced by the presence of others (Zajonc, 1965; Martens, 1969; Landers, 1975). The research findings of Schwartz and Barsky confirm the existence of a home advantage, which was shown to be as important a determinant in team performance as team quality. Home advantage was most evident in hockey and basketball, less in football, and least in baseball. The variations between sports are attributed to the indoor settings of those sports, which tend to focus the social (fan) support in closer proximity to the playing area. Interestingly, the research found that the home advantage is almost totally independent of a visiting team being fatigued or a lack of familiarity with the playing area. In summary, sport frequently serves as a symbolic representation of larger social groups, and this process serves as a means of collective identification, loyalty, and pride, or conversely, of shame and in the embarrassment by members of the school or region represented by the team. Furthermore, the team performance is likely to be influenced by the degree of external social support. These interrelationships between sport and higher education begin in the lower levels of the educational ladder. In the remainder of the chapter we discuss the relationship between education and sport at the precollegiate levels.

SPORT AT THE SECONDARY LEVEL

With the emergence of sports at the collegiate level, diffusion to the high schools soon followed. Betts (1974) reports that the New York Public Schools Athletic League was founded in 1903 and was soon copied in other major metropolitan areas throughout the country. In 1909 a study of the seventy-five largest Nebraska high schools revealed that 95 percent of the schools were participating in interscholastic athletic competition (Betts, 1974, p. 180). Additional information on the growth of interscholastic sport reported by Betts shows that in 1904–1905 a study of 555 American cities found that 432 had football, 360 had baseball, 213 had basketball, and 161 had track teams.

The sport of basketball seems to have followed a different pattern of diffusion. Dr. James Naismith originated the game in 1892 as a wintertime substitute for gymnastics exercises for men at Springfield College and at the Springfield YMCA. However, Dr. Naismith (1941) wrote that "basketball was accepted by the high schools before the colleges took it up as an organized sport. I believe that the younger boys who played in the YMCA gymnasia took the game with them into the high school. It was only after these boys graduated from high school and entered college that basketball really began to take hold in that institution" (p. 105).

At the collegiate level, the most prominent feature of sport was the development of sport along the lines of the big business–bureaucratic model discussed earlier. At the high school level, the prevalence of sport is best characterized by its influence in the everyday life of students. A number of studies over a forty-year period attest to the continued salience of sport in the value structure of the adolescent subculture. The growth in the importance and pervasiveness of high school sports in the 1920s was cogently described by the Lynds in their classic analysis of Middletown (1929). As an index of the increasing importance of high school athletics, they compared the school annuals of the 1890s with those of the 1920s. They noted the following contrasts.

> Next in importance to the pictures of the senior class and other class data in the earlier book, as measured by the percentage of space occupied, were pages devoted to the faculty and the courses taught by them, while in the current book athletics shares the position of honor with the class data, and a faculty twelve times as large occupies relatively only half as much space. . . .
>
> This whole spontaneous life of the intermediate generation that clusters about the formal nucleus of school studies becomes focused and articulate, and even rendered important in the eyes of adults through the medium of the school athletic teams—the "Bearcats" (Lynd and Lynd, 1929, p. 212).

The centrality of sport in Middletown High School is further suggested by the fact that "the highest honor a senior boy can have is captaincy of the football or basketball team" (p. 214). Furthermore, the sport teams in Middletown were frequently a source of civic pride and loyalty.

The salience of sport within the high schools in the 1930s was also pointed up in the classic study by Waller (1932). With reference to the culture of the school, he noted:

> Of all activities athletics is the chief and the most satisfactory. It is the most flourishing and the most revered culture pattern. It has been elaborated in more detail than any other culture pattern. Competitive athletics has many forms. At the head of the list stands football. . . . Then come basketball, baseball, track, lightweight football, lightweight basketball, girl's basketball, girl's track, etc. Each of these activities has importance because the particular school and its rivals are immersed in a culture stream of which competitive athletics is an important part (pp. 112–113).

Waller cited as the functions of sport in the school system its serving as a catharsis and as a means of focusing the attention of students on a unifying and morale-building activity. He also viewed sports as a means of learning fair play and the important "lessons of life." In general, Waller considered the effects of athletics as desirable. However, he felt too much pressure was exerted on players by coaches to win games. He noted the tendency for the coach to train "his men (aged sixteen) a bit too hard, or he uses his star athletes in too many events, or he schedules too many hard games; all this he does from a . . . desire to gain a better position or raise in salary . . . but he often fails to consider the possible effects upon the physical well-being of the rising generation" (1932, pp. 144, 155).

In the 1940s, Hollingshead (1949) studied the youth of a midwestern community with a particular focus on the importance of the extracurricular activities of the local high school. In Elmtown High School the prestigious activities were those athletics, musical performances, and dramatics which had spectator appeal and served to entertain students, parents, and the community. However, greater public support and school interest were centered on the football and basketball teams than on all the other extracurricular activities combined (pp. 192–93). The school athletic program served as a collective representation of the school and community. The superintendent of schools was publicly judged by the performance of the school's teams, and Hollingshead noted that the school board "pays the maximum salary to the coach, and it expects him 'to deliver the goods.' A coach knows his 'success' is determined wholly by the number of games he wins—particularly in basketball and football" (p. 193).

A decade later, the importance of athletics for social status within the high school was analyzed by Coleman (1961). He studied the adolescent attitudes and value orientations in eleven midwestern public and private high schools. As one component of his research, Coleman (1961, p. 28) sought to measure student attitudes and values by the following question, which required the respondent to make a forced choice among three roles within the school system.

> If you could be remembered here at school for one of the three things below, which one would you want to be?
>
> Boys: ______ Brilliant student
> ______ Athletic star
> ______ Most popular
>
> Girls: ______ Brilliant student
> ______ Leader in activities
> ______ Most popular

For boys, not only was the athletic star's image more attractive at the beginning of the school year, but the boys moved even slightly further in that direction—at the expense of the popularity image—over the period of the school year.

The girls showed somewhat similar choices. At the beginning of the school year, the activities leader and most popular were about equally attractive images, and both were mentioned more often than the brilliant student. By spring, the activities leader image had gained slightly in attractiveness, at the expense of both the brilliant student and the most popular.

When the high school students in Coleman's sample were asked about their parents' preferences, more students thought their parents would be more proud of them if they made the basketball team or cheerleading squad than if they were selected as an assistant by a science teacher. Coleman concluded that "even the rewards a child gains from his parents may help reinforce the values of the adolescent culture—not because his parents hold these same values but because parents want their children to be successful and esteemed by their peers" (p. 34). Research by Gordon (1957) and Turner (1964) likewise supports the notion of an adolescent subculture with participation in school-sponsored extracurricular activities, including athletic teams, as an important means of achieving esteem within the high school.

Since these studies of the adolescent subculture in the 1960s, significant social changes have occurred in American society—increased racial unrest in schools, the emergence of a drug subculture, student protests, and a tendency for students to question authority figures. One might expect that because of these changes, athletes might no longer be granted the high social status they previously received. Eitzen (1976) addressed himself to this issue by replicating some of Coleman's (1961) research.

Eitzen used questionnaire items from the Coleman study including a ranking of various criteria necessary for status among boys and an item that ranked the girls' criteria for what "makes a guy popular with the girls around here." These comparisons are presented in Table 7-1. Although Eitzen noted important variations between respondents depending on the type of community and size of school, he concluded that sport participation remained an important dimension for status among adolescent males.

TABLE 7-1 Ranking of Criteria Boys and Girls Use to Rate the Popularity of Boys

CRITERIA FOR STATUS	EITZEN (1976)	COLEMAN (1961)
Boys' Ranking of Criteria to Be Popular with Boys		
Be an athlete	2.2	2.2
Be in leading crowd	2.15	2.6
Leader in activities	2.77	2.9
High grades, honor roll	3.66	3.5
Come from right family	3.93	4.5
Girls' Ranking of Criteria for Boys to Be Popular with Girls		
Be in leading crowd	2.17	
Be an athlete	2.38	
Have a nice car	3.03	
Come from right family	3.32	
High grades, honor roll	3.80	

Source: Adapted from Eitzen 1976, p. 152.

Now that athletics are more readily available for girls in high school, an important consideration is the value of sport participation in the school status system for girls. A study by Feltz (1979) of 258 girls in three high schools concluded that athletics has become an important way for girls to spend their extra time in school. Moreover, the ranking of criteria for popularity among the girls was as follows (Feltz, 1979, p. 115):

In the leading crowd
Leader in activities
A cheerleader
Clothes
An athlete
Right family background
High grades, honor roll

In short, sport participation has become an important criteria for status evaluation among girls at the high school level. With the increased opportunity for participation in sports and the greater emphasis on the distaff sports in the society and the mass media, we expect that it will become more important in the school status structure in the future.

SPORT AND THE PRIMARY GRADES

The role of sport among preadolescents has not received the scholarly attention that is evident at the high school and collegiate levels. One of the reasons for this relative and unfortunate neglect is the fact that most sport activity for children is organized outside the context of the elementary school. Sports activities for children should be serious topic for scientific study because the organizers of such community activities are largely untrained volunteers who organize and coach the activities. The impact of the formal physical education curriculum in the elementary school is substantially less potent than the energy surrounding Little League, Pop Warner teams, and community hockey leagues. Furthermore, although participation in sport affects people of all ages and educational levels, its influence is likely to be greatest on younger, more impressionable people.

Organized sports for children have grown substantially in the past two decades. Perhaps the best-known program is Little League baseball, which involves over 2.5 million youngsters, although hockey is the fastest-growing organized sport for children. By 1973 there were 781 hockey teams in the United States for children under age 9, 2,054 teams in the 9–10 age bracket, and 2,384 teams for the 11- and 12-year-olds (Amateur Hockey Association, 1973, p. 5).

Much of the writing on organized sport for children points to overzealous coaches and parents as the principle problem. Organized sports in their extreme form may represent a type of child abuse. When an inordinate amount of pressure is put on youngsters to demonstrate the attitudes and skills of the "big time," they are likely to become frustrated and fail to acquire skills when under pressure. Excessive competition, the star system, screaming parents, and berating 8- and 10-year-old children for having "no guts" and "choking" is not conducive to the development of healthy attitudes toward sport participation.

Tutko and Bruns (1976) write sharply concerning emotional child abuse by parents of child athletes.

> Parents would never think of binding a child's legs so they wouldn't grow. Yet they will straitjacket their child's emotional growth without even realizing the damage they are doing. Emotional abuse can occur in several ways.

> It can occur when, directly or indirectly, a child is coerced into athletics without volunteering and before he is ready physically or psychologically. His parents may want him to do the things they always wanted to do but were unable to do. Now that the opportunities are available, they don't want their child to miss out. To carry out the parents' hopes and expectations is a tremendous burden even for the most gifted and ambitious child (p. 96).[2]

We have heard reports that parents in youth hockey leagues travel 200 miles to bring their children to practice. Hockey players only 5- and 10-years-old often practice at 5:00 A.M.—the only period when ice-time is available—and may play as many as seventy games a year against teams that may be 500 miles away. Year-round hockey practice is now rather common, as are summer camps. Moreover, youth hockey league play-off games in some localities are televised (Larson, Spreitzer, and Snyder, 1975).

An obvious concern is the impact such intense participation has on the child participants (not to mention the family). Dowell's (1971) review of the literature summarized the reasons for favoring organized sports for children: contribution to physical fitness, emotional development, social adjustment, development of competitive attitude, and insulation against delinquency. Similarly, Dowell summarized the deleterious aspects: overemphasis on winning, physical harm, emotional strain, psychological unreadiness of the children, premature athletic specialization, dominance by adults, and elitism, leading to narrowing of participation to the relatively gifted.

Although the literature has yet to show definitely the physical and psychological consequences of sport for children, it is clear that certain patterns of current youth athletic competition have strong implications for an individual's adult involvement with the world of sport. It is evident that much of the spontaneous fun associated with childhood sports is eliminated in overly organized athletic leagues for children. Many writers have commented on the lack of authenticity in such leagues.

> The other day I had an opportunity to view a Pop Warner League football game. These children were approximately ninety to one hundred pounds and probably in the sixth grade of their schooling. My attention was first drawn to the linebackers, they were *kind of* "jitterbugging." I say *kind of* because, unlike their college or professional counterparts, there seemed to be no reason besides *imitation* for their action. It was almost like watching a bad theatrical production. One could watch a child's play and not expect high level performance. In fact because of the "childish nature" of these productions they became "cute." But one does not think an imitation is cute. It is simply ridiculous. . . . Unlike most theatrical performers, these youngsters did not know why they were acting. They fool themselves into believing they are *something* they are not. *Something* rather than *someone*, because in this act they *use themselves* as instruments and lose their personhood (Slusher, 1967, p. 176).

In a similar view, Tutko and Bruns (1976) comment on the lack of authentic spontaneity in organized athletics for children.

---

[2]Reprinted with permission of Macmillan Publishing Co. from *Winning Is Everything* by Thomas Tutko and William Bruns. Copyright © 1976 by Thomas Tutko and William Bruns.

> We need parents and other interested adults to be involved in youth leagues in order to help things run smoothly, and to offer technical advice so that youngsters will improve their skills. The problem is that adults feel they have to organize and run *everything*, from determining the starting line-ups to calling the plays in football, and eventually they can strangle much of the fun by imposing all their rules, traditions, and grandstand pressures. Instead, when the game begins they should think about withdrawing as coaches and overzealous spectators and let the kids learn to rule their own affairs, with their own self-imposed pressure to play well. (p. 56)

Edward Devereux (1976) has written very perceptively concerning the contrast between spontaneous games and organized sport among children. Looking back to his childhood fifty years ago, he recalls games that were played regularly: puss in the corner, red rover, capture the flag, one-o-cat, statues, stealing sticks, blind man's buff, croquet, leap frog, duck on the rock, prisoner's base, and others. "No doubt some of these are still around, in vestigial form; but my impression is that I rarely see these, or other games like them being spontaneously played by children. Those which are played seem to be adult-instigated and supervised" (pp. 38–39).

James Riordan (1977, pp. 325–26) reports that in the Soviet Union a high degree of coordination exists at the governmental level among educational systems, health programs, and community recreation. A national Sports Committee oversees the entire physical education system to insure uniformity across the nation. The links in the system include a monitoring of physical education of preschool children in the home, nurseries, and children's homes as well as careful supervision of the physical education curriculum for children in the 7 to 17 age range. Standards of achievement are defined by the government in the syllabus as age norms. For example, 11-year-olds are expected to be able to perform basic gymnastic routines—mounts and dismounts, balancing exercises on the beam, and vaults. A child can be held back if he or she fails the physical education test at the end of the year.

In addition to this emphasis on sports within the school curriculum, trade unions and army sport societies sponsor many sport programs that youngsters attend in the Soviet Union after school and on weekends. This intense programming in sports for children as young as age 6 represents a sophisticated feeder system for the Olympics, particularly in sports with an emphasis on early specialization—gymnastics, swimming, and track and field. The system in East Germany is believed to be even more intense than the Soviet program for children.

GRADATIONS IN SPORT

It is clear that sport takes on different meanings and modes of organization in moving from the elementary grades to the secondary level and on into the collegiate context. In analyzing this unfolding of the world of sport through the age cycle, the earlier years are of particular importance because basic attitudes and modes of participation are crystallized. Thus one's posture toward sport is formed early in life and is usually sustained through the adult years. Consequently, physical education classes, intramurals, community-based athletic programs, and interscholastic athletic programs should be viewed as molding the general life style of children and adolescents with a strong carryover into the adult years.

When we consider educational levels in progressing from elementary school to higher education, it is evident that play is more characteristic at the lower educational levels, while formally organized sport is dominant in higher education. It is also true, however, that there are mixtures of play and formal sport at the different educational levels. It is not uncommon for an athlete on a major university football team to express the sentiment that "the last time I really had fun playing football was in high school." This attitude reflects the highly competitive and work-like ("professional") climate that the varsity experiences. However, this does not mean that athletes never experience some aspects of play even in that context. Moreover, we can see among high school varsity teams many of these same professional characteristics, although the activity has a greater mixture of play with sport than in major university varsity teams. Figure 7-2 sketches some physical activities that range from play to formally organized sport. Obviously the calibration of this scale is not very precise, and we would expect to find variations depending on the school, sport, and community. For heuristic purposes we have also suggested the approximate location of community recreational activities that are not directly administered by the schools (see Chapter 2 for an elaboration of the characteristics of play and sport).

The contrasts between play and sport have been aptly drawn by Devereux (1976) in an essay titled, "Backyard versus Little League Baseball: The Impoverishment of Children's Games."

> Maybe we didn't learn to be expert baseball players, but we did have a lot of fun. Moreover, in an indirect and incidental way, we learned a lot of other kinds of things which are probably more important for children between the ages of eight and twelve. Precisely because there was no official rule book and no adult or even other child designated as rule enforcer, we somehow had to improvise the whole thing; this entailed endless hassles about whether a ball was fair or foul, whether a runner was safe or out, or more generally, simply about what was fair. We gradually learned to understand the invisible boundary conditions of our relationships to each other. Don't be a poor sport or the other kids won't want you to play with them. Don't push your point so hard that the kid with the only catcher's mitt will quit the game. Pitch a bit more gently to the littler kids so they can have some fun, too; besides, you realize that you must keep them in the game because numbers are important. Learn how to get a game started and somehow keep it going, as long as the fun lasts (pp. 47–49).

Note that the objective of the play experience is to keep the game going and to have fun. There is a considerable amount of rule improvision, negotiation, and adaptations to keep the action flowing. For example, among children the more inept players might be given four strikes in a baseball game, or if a sufficient number of players is lacking the children might invoke a rule of "no hitting to right field" or use a "shadow man" as a baserunner. Similarly, a player who is too skilled might be forced to bat from the side opposite to the accustomed side. The climate in this informal sport context is to equalize the competition, allow maximum participation, cater to individual proclivities, and most of all to keep the action flowing. By contrast, the Little League context is characterized by a strict adherence to rules, an emphasis on team victory, and less concern for the unskilled performer.

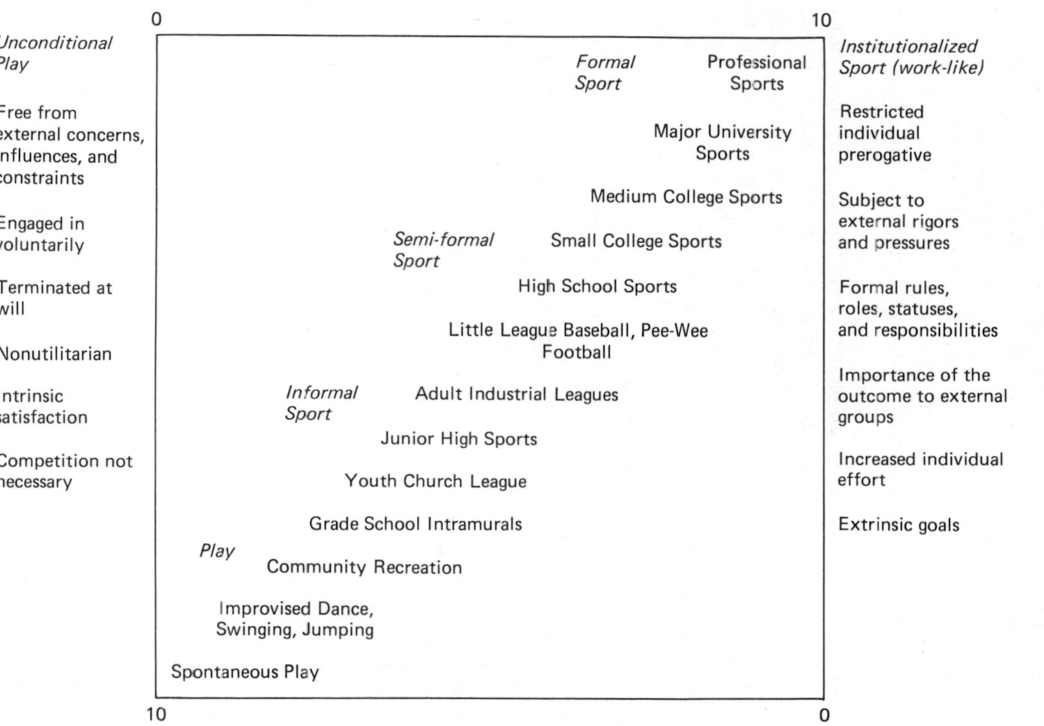

FIGURE 7–2 Summary of physical activities from play to formal sport.

CONCLUSION

We have discussed the ways in which athletics have become a prominent part of modern educational institutions. In higher education, sport has become a big business with the characteristics of bureaucracy that are present in large organizations. In major universities, the athletic teams provide publicity and prestige; however, the desire to achieve athletic fame has led to improprieties and recruiting violations that represent a form of organizational deviance. It is clear that the emphasis on athletic success is fueled by the tendency for teams to become symbolic representations of larger social groups—the student body, alumni, and citizens in the region.

The salience of sport at the university level has also diffused downward to the high schools. Athletic participation and its associated activities are sources of prestige in the adolescent subculture. The importance of sport in the status structure for boys has existed since the early twentieth century; moreover, the recent growth of female sports indicates that athletic participation is now an important facet of status at the junior and senior high school levels for girls. Much of the "professionalization" of college-level athletics has been adopted by athletic directors and coaches at the high school level.

Similarly, the same process is evident in community-based athletic programs for preadolescents. Youth leagues in baseball, football, hockey, and basketball have assimilated more and more of the trappings of big-time athletics. Thus, at all levels of education, sport has become progressively more detached from physical education, intramurals, and play. In fact, the term "player" is becoming an anachronism as heavily organized athletic programs move closer to the world of work.

CHAPTER 8
Sport Participation and Academic Orientation

It is widely believed that sport participation is an avenue of social mobility in either a direct sense, as an athletic career, or through the inculcation of achievement-related qualities such as deferred gratification, self-discipline, and leadership that lead to academic success. The rags to riches stories of such sports heroes as Babe Ruth, Joe Louis, Stan Musial, Althea Gibson, and Mohammed Ali lend credibility to this belief. The fact that some athletes go on to second careers as a movie star, restaurateur, executive, or politician also helps to sustain this notion of sport as a social escalator. We will consider aspects of sport as a direct avenue of mobility in the next chapter. In this chapter we want to consider the indirect form of mobility, that is, does sport participation lead to an achievement orientation that in turn provides an opportunity for higher occupational status? Again, as in Chapter 6 in which we discussed other concomitants, we will need to be cautious of assuming that correlations are equated with causation. In most of the research studies we are not able to determine a direct causal relationship between sport participation and academic performance, although there are some logical reasons why such a relationship might exist. On the other hand, there is also the stereotype of the "dumb jock," which is a negative perception of athletics as an avenue for academic success. Although James Coleman (1961) does not explicitly support this notion, he does argue that if an individual or school expends energy and other resources on extracurricular activities and athletics, these resources are not available to be invested in academic pursuits. The purpose of this chapter is to review the scientific literature in an attempt to sort out some of the positive and negative consequences that sport can have on academic success.

One other preliminary point should be made; we are focusing our attention on the dependent variable of academic orientation. In the research studies, this variable is often conceptualized as academic performance, educational aspirations, educational plans, and educational achievement. These concepts are related in the sense that they represent aspects of an academic orientation. Yet, they do not have exactly the same meaning (for example, one's educational plans are not the same as educational achievement), and we need to recognize that these different conceptualizations may manifest somewhat different relationships with the independent variable of athletic participation.

SPORT AND ACADEMIC ROLES

When we analyze a student's participation in the athletic and academic spheres, we are concerned with two roles within the more generalized role of student. Some sociologists have viewed the study of several roles that a person plays in terms of how they may conflict with each other, that is, role conflict or role strain (Goode, 1960). Coser (1974) emphasizes that people typically participate in a variety of social circles or roles with different loyalties to each. "People are expected to play many roles on many stages, thus parceling out their available energies so they can play many games" (p. 3). This conceptualization of multiple roles might be understood in terms of a plumbing metaphor in which energy and effort that are channelled into one role will be drained away and are not available for another use. Thus, the James Coleman (1961) theory would be consistent with this imagery; that is, energy, time, and effort that are spent on the sport role will not be available for the academic role. Therefore, the two roles would seem to conflict with each other, and we would then expect the research findings to show a negative relationship between athletic participation and academic orientation.

There is, however, another conceptualization of the relationship between roles that is critical of the "spend and drain" theory. Energy is not a finite substance but rather is abundant, expandable, and may be available for several roles in which the individual is committed. Consequently, "abundant energy is 'found' for anything to which we are highly committed, and we often feel more energetic after having done it; also, we tend to 'find' little energy for anything to which we are uncommitted, and doing these things leaves us feeling spent, drained, or exhausted" (Marks, 1977, p. 927). In short, if one is committed to both athletic involvement and academic orientation, they need not conflict with each other. Therefore, the association between the two role spheres would either be neutral, or conceivably one role might actually enhance the other role through an additive effect which produces a greater feeling of ego gratification and satisfaction than either of the roles alone. In summary, contrary to the Coleman thesis, there is some theoretical support for the notion that the sport and academic roles might have little effect on each other, or they might be mutually supporting.

One of the first studies to measure the relationship between sport and academic orientation was Schafer and Armer's (1968) research involving 585 boys from two high schools in the Midwest. First of all, they found that the athletes tended to have a higher grade average than the nonathletes, even when controlling for factors such as intelligence, type of curriculum, and the social class background of the parents. Because athletic prowess alone may not be sufficient to secure admission to college, students whose educational aspirations are higher might be motivated to work harder for the necessary grades. Schafer and Armer found that the athletes did have higher educational expectations—82 percent of the athletes planned to complete at least two years of college as compared to 75 percent of the nonathletes. The athletes were also more likely to expect to complete four years of college (62 versus 45 percent).

A study by Rehberg and Schafer (1968) reports that the association between athletic participation and higher educational expectations was evident among high school boys from less advantaged backgrounds. It appears that athletics did not have a similar impact on boys from more privileged backgrounds toward higher education. An examination of Table 8-1 indicates the 95 percent of the athletes of high social status who received parental encouragement to attend college and had high academic performance were planning to attend college for at least four years. Similarly, 96 percent of the nonathletes with the same background characteristics were planning to attend for the four or more years. On the other hand, 68 percent of the athletes with the same background characteristics but low academic performance planned at least four years of college as compared to 49 percent of the nonathletes with the same background characteristics. In summary, the findings in Table 8-1 indicate that educational plans are positively related to athletic participation among adolescents who are not otherwise predisposed toward college in terms of social background characteristics.

TABLE 8-1 Percentage of High School Boys Planning on Four or More Years of College According to Athletic Participation

DISPOSITION VARIABLES			ATHLETIC PARTICIPATION			
			YES		NO	
SOCIAL STATUS	PARENTAL ENCOURAGEMENT	ACADEMIC PERFORMANCE	(%)	(*N*)	(%)	(*N*)
High	High	High	95	40	96	57
		Low	68	31	49	45
	Low	High	75	8	75	16
		Low	67	6	11	18
Low	High	High	85	52	84	73
		Low	45	82	25	121
	Low	High	69	13	50	46
		Low	26	38	7	82

Source: Adapted from Rehberg and Schafer, 1968, p. 738.

Using a more complex research design, Buhrmann (1972) studied a group of adolescent boys over the period 1959 to 1965. His research also shows that athletic participation is more strongly linked with educational success among boys from poorer socioeconomic backgrounds. Buhrmann concludes that "athletes may be the most important means for these lower socioeconomic status students to gain social recognition and acceptance, and through it, gain academic aspirations and higher scholarship" (p. 127).

Findings from a study by Picou and Curry (1974) provide further elaboration of the relationship between sport participation and educational aspirations among high school boys. Their research indicates that participation in high school athletics has a moderately positive effect on educational aspirations. Furthermore, they also reported that "nondisposed" athletes from lower socioeconomic backgrounds who received little parental encouragement to attend college had higher scholastic aspirations than similarly situated boys who were not participating in interscholastic athletics. Moreover, this pattern was particularly evident among boys from rural backgrounds. Note that the Rehberg and Schafer, Buhrmann, and Picou and Curry studies all indicate that athletic participation is positively associated with an educational orientation when the background characteristics are otherwise not favorable for educational plans or achievement.

Research by Spady (1970) illustrates the importance of the high school peer group as a source of educational goals; furthermore, participation in extracurricular activities, especially athletics, was an important determinant of these goals. Apparently, the recognition the student receives in the peer group through extracurricular activities stimulates the desire for the continued status and recognition that are associated with these activities beyond high school. Spady noted that this system may backfire by stimulating inflated educational expectations without developing the requisite scholastic skills. Consequently, high school students were less likely to complete college if their educational goals were solely a function of athletic participation, and if college was perceived simply as a means of extending one's athletic career.

A study by Spreitzer and Pugh (1973) sheds further light on the relationship between athletic participation and educational aspirations. By controlling for possible variations in climate of student values between high schools, they found that the unrealistic and inflated educational expectations of athletes described by Spady may be limited to high schools in which athletics, rather than scholarship, is the primary source of peer status and heightened educational aspirations. Data shown in Table 8-2 support the hypothesis that the positive relationship between sport participation and expectations is highest in those high schools where the athletic specialist is accorded a great deal of prestige. The relationship is diminished in schools where the primary means of status is based on scholarship.

In the consideration of these correlational data, we note two important points. First, the relationship between involvement in sport and academic pursuits is not uniform for all participants. The relationship is most evident among boys not otherwise disposed toward education and at schools that emphasize athletics. Second, the correlations are not necessarily indicative of a causal relationship between sport participation and academic pursuit. For example, students with a nonacademic orientation may not enter sport, or they may be cut out of the athletic stream. Indeed, research by Lueptow and Kayser (1973–1974) and Houser and Lueptow (1978) shows that, in a comparative analysis of athletes and nonathletes, the athletes in their sample did not show as much improvement in grades during their high school years as the nonathletes. They conclude that a causal interpretation should not be made of the association between athletic involvement and academic achievement. It is clear, however, that these studies dealing with academic achievement and sport participation do not support the thesis that involvement in sport (and extracurricular activities) has negative consequences for

TABLE 8-2 Educational Expectations by Athletic Participation, Controlling for School Value Climate

EDUCATIONAL EXPECTATIONS	ATHLETES (%)	NONATHLETES (%)
Athletic Specialist Value Climate		
16 or more years	80	57
13–15 years	7	13
12 years	13	30
(3 schools)	(*N* = 85)	(*N* = 107)
All-Around Boy Value Climate		
16 or more years	59	43
13–15 years	23	20
12 years	18	37
(2 schools)	(*N* = 24)	(*N* = 60)
Scholar Specialist Value Climate		
16 or more years	52	53
13–15 years	23	23
12 years	25	24
(2 schools)	(*N* = 31)	(*N* = 53)
Mixed-Type, Indeterminate Climate		
16 or more years	58	49
13–15 years	19	17
12 years	23	34
(6 schools)	(*N* = 130)	(*N* = 214)

Source: Adapted from Spreitzer and Pugh, 1973, p. 179.

scholarly pursuit. In another study, Rehberg and Cohen (1975) analyzed the characteristics of 936 male high school seniors in seven urban, suburban, public, and parochial schools in New York State. The students were identified as athletes and scholars as determined by their participation in interscholastic sports and/or in academic honor societies and clubs during their senior year. Of the 936 subjects, 43 percent were athletes and 25 percent were scholars. Boys who were both athletes and scholars, called athlete-scholars, made up 17 percent of the students. Pure athletes (athletes who were not scholars) constituted 24 percent, and scholars who were not athletes comprised 7 percent of the seniors. To summarize, the following diagram may be helpful in identifying the categories presented in Table 8-3.

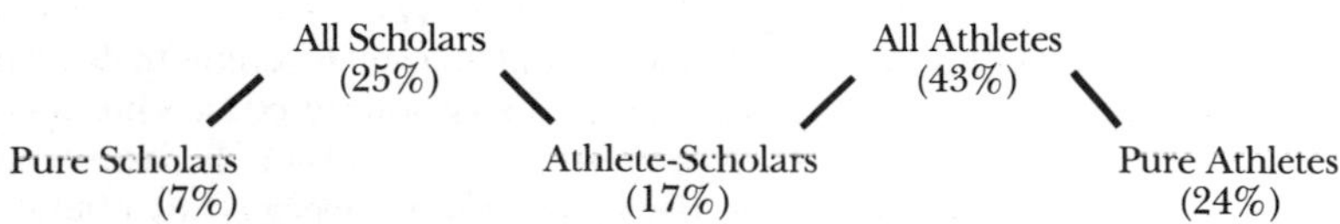

TABLE 8-3 Summary of Cross-Tabulations between Athlete-Scholar Typology and Selected Background Characteristics

VARIABLE AND LEVELS	PURE SCHOLARS (%)	ALL SCHOLARS (%)	ATHLETE SCHOLARS (%)	PURE ATHLETES (%)	ALL ATHLETES (%)	ALL MALES (%)
Socioeconomic status						
Upper-middle	31	30	28	23	25	23
Lower-middle	29	29	30	34	32	30
Total	60	59	58	57	57	53
Measured intelligence						
Highest quarter	53	47	44	24	33	31
Next highest quarter	29	26	25	24	24	24
Total	82	73	69	48	57	55
Importance of being good student						
Very important	50	57	55	31	41	39
How good a student want to be						
One of the best	48	49	48	16	29	25
Above the middle	43	42	43	53	49	47
Total	91	91	91	69	78	72
Comparative subjective IQ						
Among the brightest	35	28	24	09	15	13
Above average	42	44	45	29	36	32
Total	72	72	69	38	51	45
Educational expectations senior						
Grad or professional school	40	41	41	12	24	20
Four years of college	49	48	47	41	44	38
Total	89	89	88	53	68	58
Time spent on homework						
At least 1½ hrs. per day	31	34	35	18	24	24
Reputation with teacher for school work						
Very good	39	31	28	05	15	12
Good	46	42	40	46	43	44
Total	85	73	68	51	58	56
Reputation with teacher for deportment						
Very good	35	32	30	15	21	21
Good	48	50	51	57	55	53
Total	83	82	81	72	76	74
Frequency of skipping school						
At least three days	18	17	17	22	19	24

Source: Rehberg and Cohen, 1975, p. 96

The "all males" column in Table 8-3 includes all 936 senior males (that is, these categories plus those who were neither scholars nor athletes). The categories employed in Table 8-3 are interesting in terms of our earlier discussion of role conflict and energy expenditure. The data from the Rehberg and Cohen (1975) study show that the student who is both an athlete and a scholar scores higher on most of the academic variables than the athletic specialists or the scholar specialists. Although these findings may have been influenced by the social class backgrounds of the students in the sample, nevertheless it is clear that some of these youths found no conflict between the scholar and athletic roles. Although this chapter focuses on athletic participation and aspects of academic orientation, Table 8-3 presents other characteristics because they are logically related to academic orientation. In general, the athletes, particularly the "pure athletes," scored lower on academic qualities such as desire to be a good student, educational expectations, and time spent on homework. However, some of these findings might have been affected by lower socioeconomic status of these students. Also, it is evident that the type of student who was both an athlete and scholar was able to play both roles successfully.

Few studies are available that focus on correlates of involvement in sport by females. However, data on high school athletes and nonathletes provide some information in this regard (Snyder and Spreitzer, 1977). Because participation in music activities is comparable to sport in the sense that it requires intensive training, discipline, and coaching, comparisons were made between sport and music as related to educational expectations. The data in Table 8-4 include the following comparison groups: high school girls who were participants in both sport and music, sport only, music only, and nonparticipants in either activity. The analysis compares the four criterion groups in terms of educational performance, aspirations, and background variables. The data show that grades and educational expectations are higher for female students who participated in both sport and music as compared to those who participated only in sport. When students involved solely in music were compared with those involved only in sport, the students in music had higher grades, but the participants in sport had higher educational expectations. Of particular interest is the fact that the students who had the lowest grades and educational expectations were not participating in *either* of these extracurricular activities. We interpret these findings to mean that athletic participation for high school girls, as for boys, does not have undesirable academic consequences. Indeed, the data suggest positive effects.

Hanks and Eckland's (1976) research concerning athletic participation and educational attainment is the most sophisticated study yet reported on this topic. Their longitudinal research design included males and females at both the high school and college levels and focused on actual completed years of education as an adult rather than on educational plans. They found that athletic participation by itself was correlated only slightly with educational attainment; however, extracurricular participation in general was a good predictor of ultimate educational achievement. Hanks and Eckland concluded:

> Athletics appears neither to depress nor to especially enhance the academic performance of its participants. This is not to say that some athletes may be only nominally interested in learning, that sports may be an avenue for upward mobility for some, and that it has an exaggerated status on many school and college campuses. It nevertheless appears that the institution of sports has been largely *compartmentalized* in America. While perhaps a source of community or campus solidarity and even of alumni support, for the vast majority it has little relevance to the primary functions of the educational institutions which support it (p. 292).

TABLE 8-4 Selected Educationally Related Variables According to Participation in Sport and Music

	SPORT AND MUSIC (*N* = 193) $\overline{X}$	SPORT ONLY (*N* = 523) $\overline{X}$	MUSIC ONLY (*N* = 75) $\overline{X}$	NEITHER (*N* = 252) $\overline{X}$
Educational Expectations	15.3	15.0	14.9	14.5
Grade Average*	6.2	6.0	6.2	5.9
Mother's Educational Encouragement	3.9	3.8	3.9	3.7
Father's Educational Encouragement	3.6	3.6	3.6	3.5
Teacher's Educational Encouragement	3.4	3.3	3.0	3.2
Mother's Education	12.8	12.9	12.8	12.2
Father's Education	13.0	13.5	13.7	12.5
Peer Plans for College	3.4	3.4	3.3	3.2

*Grade average was measured on an eight-point scale ranging from A to D−.

Source: Adapted from Snyder and Spreitzer, 1977, p. 51.

A fifteen-year longitudinal study by Otto and Alwin (1977) provides further information on the effect of athletics on educational aspirations and attainments. Specifically, they found support for the hypothesis that athletic participation among high school boys has a salutary effect on educational aspirations and later educational attainment. These relationships prevailed when controlling for variables usually associated with an educational orientation: socioeconomic status, mental ability, academic performance, and significant others' influence. The Otto and Alwin study emphasizes the importance of extracurricular involvement in school for long-term behavior. They suggest that athletic participation is used by parents and friends (significant others) to teach appropriate definitions and expectations for the athlete's educational and occupational aspirations and goals.

Additional explorations of the relationship between athletic achievement and educational aspiration were carried out by Picou (1978) among black and white high school boys. Picou's research findings indicate that athletic participation for white youth leads to increased contact with achievement-oriented peers, teachers, coaches, and family members who have positive effects on adolescents' educational ambition. Thus, involvement in sport for white males has an indirect effect (via peers, teachers, etc.) on academic aspirations. However, for black males the findings revealed a modest but direct relationship between sport and educational ambitions. Picou suggests that explanations for the sport–academic nexus are probably different among white and black youth. Additional research by Hanks (1979) using a nation-wide sample of males and females of both races showed that athletic participation has a significant impact on students' educational orientation and attainment among males and females regardless of race. This relationship is indirect because athletic participation apparently increases parental educational encouragement and friendships with college-oriented peers. A listing of these studies is provided in Table 8-5 with the generalized relationship between the

TABLE 8-5 Research Studies Focusing on the Relationship between Sport Participation in Schools and Academic Pursuits

RESEARCH STUDIES	SAMPLE	RELATIONSHIP BETWEEN SPORT PARTICIPATION AND ACADEMIC PURSUITS
Schafer and Armer (1968)	Male high school students	Positive relationship.
Rehberg and Schafer (1968)	Male high school students	Qualified relationship—positive relationship for boys of less advantaged backgrounds; no relationship for boys already disposed toward college.
Spady (1970)	Male high school students	Negative relationship if sport is the primary means of status.
Buhrmann (1972)	Male junior high school students	Qualified positive relationship—primarily for boys of less advantaged backgrounds.
Spreitzer and Pugh (1973)	Male high school students	Qualified positive relationship—primarily for boys from schools with an athletic value climate.
Lueptow and Kayser (1973–1974); Houser and Lueptow (1978)	Male high school students	No relationship; athletes showed less improvement in grades than nonathletes.
Picou and Curry (1974)	Male high school students	Qualified positive relationship—primarily for boys of rural, less advantaged backgrounds.
Rehberg and Cohen (1975)	Male high school students	Negative relationship for "pure" athletes.
Hanks and Eckland (1976)	Male and female high school students	Qualified positive relationship—weak positive effects for males and females.
Otto and Alwin (1977)	Male high school students	Positive relationship.
Snyder and Spreitzer (1977)	Female high school students	Positive relationship for females.
Picou (1978)	Male high school students	Qualified positive relationship—for males, different effects for whites than blacks.
Hanks (1979)	Male and female high school students	Positive relationship for males and females, regardless of race.

independent and dependent variables. In general, the tenor of these studies indicates a qualified positive relationship between athletic participation and an academic orientation. The degree of relationship varies with the social class, rural–urban setting, sex, race, and other variables associated with a predisposition to academic performance.

If we find differences between athletes and nonathletes in academic orientation, as in fact we have, will we continue to find variations based on the *degree* of involvement within the sport roles? The likelihood is that substitute players are not likely to be as deeply involved in the athletic subculture and its norms, values, rewards, and sanctions as more highly visible players. During practice sessions and game situations, the role of substitute is different from that of the regular performers. For example, the physical spatial arrangement of players during time-out periods is indicative of psychological distances between players and coaches. This role differentiation and the concomitant social expectations carry over into relationships with peers, teachers, coaches, and other adults. The data in Table 8-6 provide some support for the thesis that the degree of involvement within sport is a significant variable. Note that the players' college expectations, influence of the coach, and the advice he gives to the players about their future college plans increase from substitute to the star athletic roles.

TABLE 8-6 College Plans, Coach's Advice, and Perceived Influence According to Degree of Athletic Success among High School Senior Boys (Basketball Players)

	SUBSTITUTES (N = 69) (%)	STARTERS (N = 89) (%)	STARS (N = 41) (%)
Probably will attend college	80	91	95
Coaches often gave advice whether to attend college	26	48	75
Players perceive their coaches to be a great influence	31	51	79

Source: Adapted from Snyder, 1975, p. 197.

How can one explain these academic differences between athletes and nonathletes? Some might argue that the athletes are physically and mentally superior to the nonathletes. We do not deny that there are genetic variations in physical and mental ability, but we prefer to take a social behavioral approach in tracing the linkages between sport participation and academic achievement. We offer the following as possible explanations (Buhrmann, 1972; Schafer and Armer, 1968).

1. Some athletes attend college who would not otherwise do so because they received an athletic grant-in-aid to college.
2. Some athletes attend college primarily so they can continue their athletic careers beyond high school.
3. Because of the prestige and visibility associated with sport, the athlete is given support by parents, teachers, coaches and is a member of the "leading crowd" which is influential in shaping educational plans and expectations beyond high school (Coleman, 1961; Duncan, Haller and Portes, 1968; McDill and Coleman, 1965; Rehberg and Schafer, 1968).
4. By becoming a member of the peer elite through the prestige of sport, the athlete develops a positive self-evaluation that is translated into academic achievement. Researchers have noted a positive relationship between one's self-image and school achievement (Brookover, Thomas, and Paterson, 1964).
5. Exposure to the athletic subculture with respect to interpersonal skills, hard work, persistence, discipline and achievement transfers to nonathletic activities such as school work.

6. Because of their prestige, athletes are graded leniently and receive extra encouragement from teachers and counselors.
7. Athletes benefit from academic assistance and encouragement. High school coaches frequently encourage their best athletes to attend college. "Brain coaches" and tutors are frequently available at major universities to provide special academic assistance for their athletes.
8. Athletes make more efficient and effective use of their limited time and energies.
9. The superior physical condition of athletes improves their mental performance (Cooper, 1969; Layman, 1972).
10. Some athletes strive to get good grades to be eligible for athletic participation. In fact, eligibility requirements would ordinarily preclude failing students from participation; this fact in itself makes academic comparisons between athletes and nonathletes suspect.

These explanations vary in credibility. Research provides support for some of them, but these processes are difficult to isolate for an adequately controlled analysis. Several of these explanations may be applicable to outstanding high school athletes who are recruited by major universities. Certainly there are strong pressures on them to attend a university, primarily to participate in athletics.

SPORT PARTICIPATION AND ACADEMIC ACHIEVEMENT AT THE COLLEGIATE LEVEL

There are few scientific studies available of athletic participation and academic pursuit at the postsecondary level. Relatively few high school athletes participate in intercollegiate teams; drastic selectivity for college participation makes causal inferences problematic. Valid comparisons between collegiate athletes and nonathletes are difficult because of variations in institutional quality, degree programs, type of sport, and other potentially contaminating factors.

Exploratory research conducted at the University of Minnesota for the graduating classes of 1966 and 1967 found that the academic grade-point average for athletes was 2.42 as compared to 2.40 for nonathletes (Pilapil, Stecklein, and Liu, 1970). Additional comparisons between the athletes and nonathletes indicate that 50 percent of the athletes as compared with 41 percent of the nonathletes earned a four-year degree within five years after entering college. Data from the Minnesota study also show that athletes in the classes of 1966 and 1967 had a higher percentage of the original group in attendance quarter by quarter than the nonathletes. For example, at the end of the twelfth quarter, the percentage of athletes remaining was 75, as compared with 47 of the nonathletes. In summary, the University of Minnesota study does not show that athletic participation is negatively correlated with academic pursuits.

At Michigan State University, research conducted by Harry Webb (1969b) provides a somewhat different picture. Data on athletes at Michigan State University between 1958 and 1963 were analyzed five years after their classes had graduated to determine whether the percentage of athletes who graduated was equivalent to the percentage for the entire class. The graduation rate for the athletes was 49 percent for team athletes and 60 percent for individual athletes—considerably lower than the 70 percent graduation rate for the entire class. Webb concedes that these data may not be precise because some students who dropped out of Michigan State University eventually graduated elsewhere.

A follow-up study by Dubois (1978) of university senior male athletes and nonathletes in the San Francisco Bay area indicated no significant relationship between athletic status and grades of academic achievement. The findings showed identical grade point averages between the two comparison groups and similar educational levels attained by both groups. However, another follow-up study of Notre Dame football players who graduated between 1946 and 1965 shows a different picture (Sack and Thiel, 1979). For example, the former football players were less likely to earn a graduate or professional degree after graduation than the regular students regardless of their fathers' educational background. More specifically, of the regular students whose fathers had less than a high school degree, 44 percent earned advanced degrees, whereas this was true of only 29 percent of the ballplayers from similar origins (Sack and Thiel, 1979, p. 63). This negative relationship between athletics and postgraduate education was also evident when controlling for social class background.

Participation in athletics in large universities limits the time and energy that might otherwise be devoted to studying. Thus, the relationship between athletic participation and academic performance in the collegiate context may be different from their relationship at the high school level (Nixon, 1976a). Reports from athletes at major universities suggest that, while coaches publicly proclaim that "winning football players are winning students," this is often not the case. Anecdotal evidence indicates that "brain coaches" and tutors are not primarily interested in the education of the players (though they might hope for this); rather, their primary concern is to keep them eligible. This may include scheduling courses that are not particularly beneficial to the "scholar-athlete" other than providing an easy grade. "Free grade" courses, getting copies of examinations, and hiring graduate students to take exams or write term papers for them are other techniques (Meggyesy, 1971; Shaw, 1972).

Meggyesy (1971) reports:

> Syracuse recruited top football players regardless of their academic ability, and the athletic department's biggest jobs were to get football players admitted and then to keep them eligible. I remember one citizenship course which all Syracuse freshmen, including football players in the remedial program, were required to take. I knew most of the other players hadn't been going to class or done any studying and I couldn't figure out how they were going to pass the exam. Then, just before midterms, we had a squad meeting with one of the tutors hired by the athletic department. The tutor didn't exactly give us the test questions but he did give us a lot of important information. He told us cryptically that if we copied down what he said we would do all right on the exam. He wasn't joking: when I took the exam I discovered he had given us the answers to the test questions. When the general tutoring session broke up, the tutor asked about ten ball players to stay. These were the guys who were really out of it and made no pretense about being students. They had neither the ability nor the interest to do college work. I don't know exactly what kind of help they got after we left, but I do know it was this kind of tutoring that kept them eligible for four years.
>
> There were even less ethical techniques than these. For example, my brother, Dennis, who also came up to Syracuse on a football scholarship, flunked his freshman

year. He was told he would have to get six units of "A" during summer school to get back to school and be eligible for football. After registering for summer school, Dennis immediately drove back to Ohio, where he spent the summer working for a Cleveland construction company. He returned to Syracuse in September with six units of "A" for courses he had never attended.

By the time I graduated, I knew it was next to impossible to be a legitimate student and a football player too. There is a clear conflict and it is always resolved on the side of the athletic program (pp. 43–44).

Such reports indicate that while the athletic department is very interested in keeping athletes eligible, they may not be as concerned about whether they graduate after their eligibility is completed. Nevertheless, there is considerable variation among universities in the academic treatment of athletes. Accounts of intercollegiate athletic participation and academic achievement provide a conflicting and ambiguous picture. Such descriptions probably reflect the variability in athletic emphasis and academic excellence within and between institutions of higher education. A study of intercollegiate athletics conducted for the American Council on Education provides an excellent summary of the academic performance of college students.

Although no definitive studies were reviewed or conducted in the course of the inquiry, the impression gained from the reports of research that has been done on individual campuses and from the observations of those close to the scene is that college athletes as a group tend on the average to beat their academic predictions and to have a higher persistence rate than students not engaged in intercollegiate sports. Research at the secondary level has demonstrated that individuals playing on interscholastic teams get higher grades than would be expected from their standardized test scores and that they do better regardless of the subgroup of students chosen—poor, wealthy, bright, slow, black, white. It is generally admitted that in the big-time, scholar-athletes on the average have lower school records, test scores and academic predictions than other students at the time of admission—in effect, that they do indeed get preferential treatment because of their athletic ability. That they tend thereafter to outperform other students comes as no surprise to careful observers of the scene. They point to the incentive which the athletes have for continued development and demonstration of their talents and to the special academic care and feeding which they receive.

At the same time, there is the apparently contradictory observation noted in other connections on this report that only the very brightest athletes are able to carry a full academic load, an observation given credence by the existence of the NCAA's five-year rule (which allows an athlete four years of eligibility within a five-year period). This allowance, however, is but one manifestation of the special care and feeding which is given. Supporters of intercollegiate sports then point to the outstanding records of exceptional athletes—All-Americans who become Rhodes Scholars, for instance—as further evidence that big-time sports don't get in the way of academic achievement. Such cases, however, appear to be exceptional and one student of the problem, the academic counselor at a major athletic power, notes that athletes tend generally to earn Bs and Cs regardless of their initial predictions—the higher predictors drawn back to the middle of the scale by the demands of their participation in sports and the lower predictors brought up toward the average by the special efforts of "brain coaches" like himself (Hanford, 1974, pp. 131–32).

Figure 8-1 attempts to unravel the various factors that might intervene between athletic participation and academic achievement. The complexity of this model is due to the multiplicity of factors that have been cited in the literature as possible causal factors. The interrelationship of variables is also indicative of the complexity of social and psychological research and suggests why behavioral scientists have yet to provide definitive explanations of the phenomena addressed in this book.

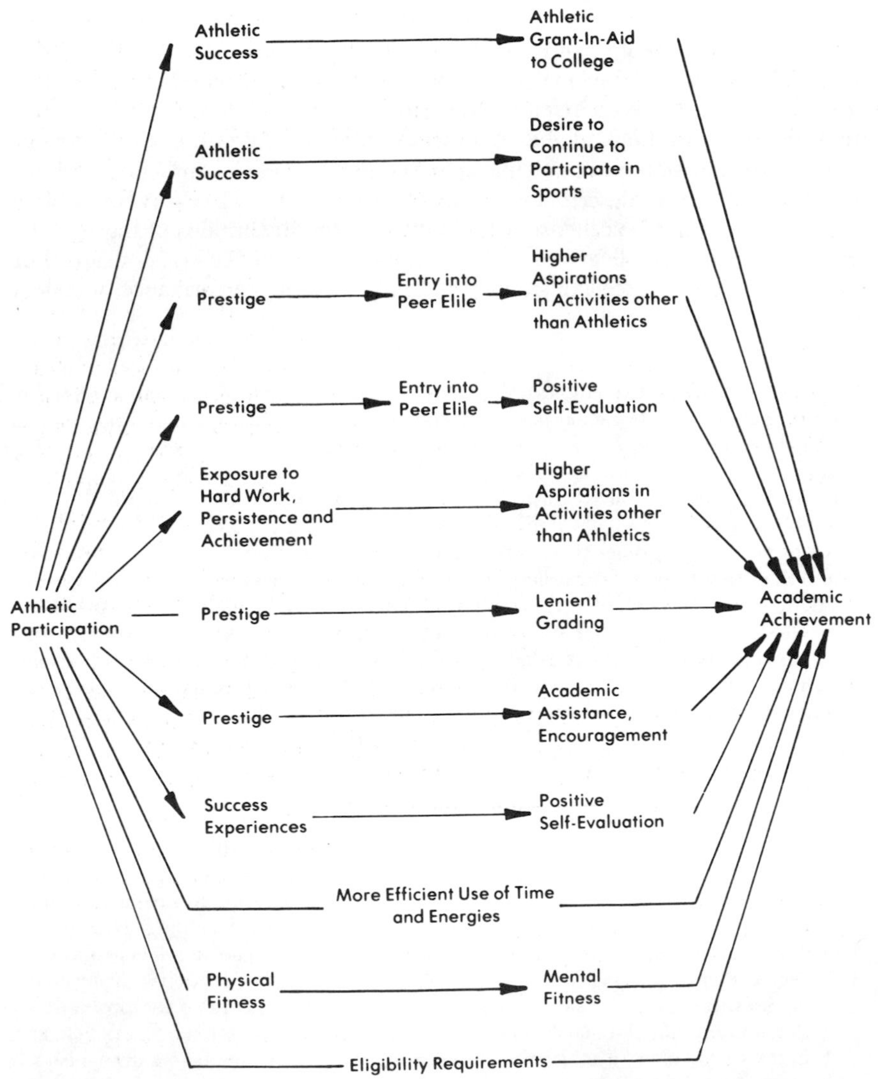

FIGURE 8–1 Causal model illustrating the intervening variables between athletic participation and academic achievement (*Source:* Adapted from Buhrmann, 1972, p. 128).

CONCLUSION

Two contradictory themes are evident in people's attitudes toward sport: (1) sport is an escalator for social mobility, and (2) sport is a deterrent to academic achievement. Research studies cited in this chapter do not support this latter assumption, that is, that athletic participation necessarily drains away energy from the academic role. Indeed, some of the findings provide moderate support for a positive relationship, particularly among students who are otherwise not disposed toward academic achievement. In this respect, success in the athletic realm may enhance one's academic performance and aspirations. This relationship would not be immediate in the sense that dribbling a basketball will directly influence one's grades in American history. Yet, if dribbling a basketball gives one visibility, recognition, status and self-esteem, and if these in turn provide social support from parents, peers, teachers, and coaches, then the athletic skill may indirectly lead to a positive academic performance. Thus, sport may serve an integrative function and as a stimulus toward academic achievement that would not otherwise be present.

For other students, the sport and academic spheres may not be interrelated, particularly for those students who are high academic achievers. In a sense, the two roles remain independent and compartmentalized; yet, each activity may provide a sense of ego support and social satisfaction. We would hesitate to say that sport must contribute to academic success to be worthwhile. In fact, most youth do not go out for sports with the view that grades will necessarily improve or that educational aspirations will be raised. Furthermore, their parents probably do not expect that this will necessarily result. Rather, the assumption is held that participating in sport is intrinsically worthwhile and gratifying, as is also the assumption for other extracurricular activities. On the other hand, one important finding that emerges from the Spady (1970) study is that students are not likely to experience educational success if their educational identity is based primarily on an inflated role as an athlete.

At the college level, the relationship between sport and academic achievement is more ambiguous. Because university athletic departments have a considerable investment in the individual athletes, they often go to great lengths (sometimes through illegal means) to see that the athlete remains eligible for competition. Autobiographical and ancedotal evidence indicates that academic standards are sometimes, perhaps often, compromised in this process.

CHAPTER 9
Social Stratification and Sport

In all societies, people differ in terms of social and biological characteristics such as age, sex, physical strength, size, race, ethnicity, and skill. When these characteristics are differentially valued and ranked within the society, we have social inequality and a system of social stratification. In effect, the individual differences are ranked or evaluated according to social values; the resulting hierarchy is based on the degrees of prestige, honor, importance, material possessions, and other rewards that accrue from these characteristics. Although social stratification systems exist in all societies, except perhaps very small and primitive tribal societies, the criteria that are used to rank people and the nature of the stratification system vary with the society. In fact, in a complex society several social stratification structures are present. For example, people may be ranked on age, sex, race, and ethnic affiliation. Other rankings are based on economic factors (usually defined as social class), prestige, honor, and power. Although these characteristics are closely related, it should be noted that a person might have wealth but not be accorded prestige, and one may have power but lack honor. For purposes of our discussion, we are primarily interested in social stratification based on economic factors, that is, social class, and the consequences of economic position for behavior associated with sport.

THEORIES OF SOCIAL STRATIFICATION

In Chapter 3 we outlined two contrasting perspectives for viewing society—the functionalist and conflict (Marxian) models. Each of these perspectives incorporates a theoretical explanation or interpretation of social stratification. The functionalist perspective contends that social stratification is universal and is therefore functionally necessary for society; indeed, the stratification structure is an expression of the social values and thus facilitates stability and social integration within society. As we noted in Chapter 3, sport is often associated with the functionalist position because it generally reinforces the existing social values and societal institutions. Furthermore, differential rewards are viewed as a useful way of motivating people to fill necessary positions in society (Davis and Moore, 1945). According to this theory, the higher positions in society are functionally more important, and therefore they must be made attractive to people of talent and motivation by rewards such as prestige and wealth. The functional perspective also assumes that the opportunity for social mobility is relatively open and that individuals generally achieve their appropriate rung on the social ladder based on their abilities and effort. Sport can be viewed as isomorphic with these functionalist assumptions in the following ways (see Gruneau, 1975, p. 142; Loy et al., 1978, p. 341; Lüschen, 1967).

1. Sport reflects the social values and serves an integrative and maintenance function in society.
2. Sport functions to reinforce the social stratification structure of a society. The reward system in sport as in society stresses the "need" for a hierarchy of rewards to assure positions will be filled. For example, the role of quarterback is functionally more important than defensive backs or kickers. Consequently, the monetary rewards and prestige are usually greater for the quarterback position. Similarly, pitchers who are twenty-game winners with low earned run averages, and hitters with high batting averages, runs batted in, and home runs can demand high salaries when contracts are signed or when they become free agents. "Status is usually gained by a variety of means, including possessions and performance, both of which may be readily reflected in sport involvement. These reflections operate at two levels. Performance in sport may be a means of generating status at one level, but at another level, participation in sport, or in a specific sport, may function as a display of status" (Gruneau, 1975, p. 142).
3. Participation in sport is a means of achieving social mobility. "High performance in sport may allow entrance into positions based on more durable criteria such as the possession of valuable material goods and the control of nonmaterial values" (Gruneau, 1975, p. 142).

The conflict perspective views social stratification as reinforcing inequalities that are unjust and inhumane. Within society there are laws as well as informal control mechanisms that use power and coercion to maintain the inequalities that are embedded in the structures of domination and discrimination. Additionally, the bureaucratic nature of contemporary society contributes to the alienation and exploitation of the workers. Within this perspective, a conflict theorist sees the necessity of the oppressed to exert pressure on the ruling class to effect a redistribution of power. Furthermore, this critical perspective does not consider the mechanisms of social mobility to be as open; rather, status is viewed as ascriptive, with the existing power structures being used to limit the opportunities for upward mobility. Critics view sport as a tool of the capitalists, as exploitive, and as a means of maintaining the status quo. Furthermore, sport serves as an opiate and results in a form of "false consciousness" by providing entertainment to the masses. Brohm (1978, pp. 28–29) expresses the sentiment of these critics by pointing out that the vocabulary of the machine dominates sport as if the human body were a finely-tuned piece of equipment to be used in achieving the goal of efficiency and production. Thus, the slang of sport uses the metaphors of automation such as "he's revving up," "she's burning up the track," "he's working well—producing the goods," "he has wheels," a runner may be a "well oiled machine," or conversely she "ran out of steam." The exploitive nature of sport is evident in this mechanistic imagery. Similar imagery suggests that players are merely "meat on the hoof" to be "used" and then discarded as tax write-offs or traded away. Also, critics of professional sports as hockey and football have argued that some of the violence associated with these sports might be tacitly encouraged to promote gate receipts at the expense of the player's physical and mental well-being. Moreover, Guttmann (1978) maintains that the advent of specialization and quantification in sport has a way of reducing the romance of sport to an abstract number (the record). Thus, "there is no time left for considerations of grace, no room for fair play, no chance to respond to the kinesthetic sense of physical exuberance. The phenomenon of alienation, by which the worker disappears into the fetish of the commodities he produces, can be seen most clearly when the individual athlete vanishes into the abstraction and becomes the ten-second man or the .300 hitter" (pp. 67–68). (It should be pointed out that the alienating effects of bureaucratized sports are probably most prominent in Eastern European socialist countries.) The analysis of sport from the conflict perspective includes the following points (see Gruneau, 1975, pp. 136–137; and Loy, McPherson, and Kenyon, 1978, p. 340):

1. Sport represents a manifestation of the economic infrastructure of society and inculcates a bourgeois mentality.
2. Sport reflects and reinforces the inequitable distribution of wealth and power in the larger society.
3. Sport views the instrumental, bureaucratic, and meritocratic aspects of a technocratic culture. The record and product reign supreme over subjective satisfactions.
4. Sport participation therefore represents a form of alienated labor wherein the human person is imprisoned in false consciousness.

In some respects both the functional and conflict models are correct. Society could not exist without some integrative functions. Furthermore, the reward structure provides motivation for some talented members of society to strive for important positions. Nevertheless, the importance of a task to society does not always mesh with the rewards. Additionally, professional and business interests are often able to wield economic and political power to maintain their favored status in society (tax shelters for the rich, but not welfare for the poor). Within sport, players with the most talent are usually rewarded with prestige and high salaries; however, there is some evidence of discrimination against minority group players that limits their opportunities (such as in coaching). Also, within the last two decades professional and collegiate sport has been increasingly controlled by the economic dictates of television. On the other hand, many participants enjoy leisure sports within the nonalienative context of fun and sociability. In short, society contains elements of both functionalism and conflict; social reality requires a synthesis of both perspectives to provide a broader understanding of the way that social stratification operates. In the next section we present data that illustrate the relationship of sport and social class and the manner in which sport enables one to display his or her social status.

SOCIAL CLASS AND SPORT

We are all familiar with stereotypes surrounding various types of leisure. For example, the blue collar worker is commonly viewed as tinkering with his snowmobile, outboard motor, or motorcycle on Saturdays, and as settling into his lazy-boy chair on Sunday afternoon and Monday night with a six-pack of beer to watch football on television. Similarly, golf carries the connotation of the salesman hot on the chase of another account via the comaraderie of the links and some refreshments at the "19th hole." In a like manner, tennis conjures the image of a refined participation by the more advantaged members of society; here there is an aura of gentility, *haute couture*—"whites" in tennis or cricket and maintenance of a privileged life style. All of these images imply that there is a correlation between background characteristics and the use of leisure time.

Sociologists have noted that leisure life styles are an important component of the social class system. Many movies and novels are based on the realization that each social class has a distinctive life style, and that conflict can occur when persons from different social class backgrounds attempt to interact as friends or as prospective marriage partners. Life style differences emerge and continue basically from the fact that individuals tend to interact with other persons from a similar social background. As is usually the case, some of these stereotypes are painted with broad strokes that result in oversimplification. In some respects sport cuts across all social groupings. This common denominator pattern makes sport a particularly interesting institution for scholarly analysis. Yet, the specific form and the meaning of sport is likely to reflect the leisure dimension of differences in social status.

Although much research has been conducted concerning the rates and correlates of sport participation, relatively little has focused on the *meaning* of sport. That is, it is important to know how people define sport and the degree to which sport is salient in the consciousness of persons during the course of everyday life; in other words, to what extent is sport integrated with mundane experience as contrasted with a segmented and compartmentalized experience outside the realm of the "real world?" This type of phenomenological analysis is not easily conducted within the context of questionnaires in survey research.

Gregory Stone's (1969) article, "Some Meanings of American Sport: An Extended View," represents an early attempt to analyze the role of sports in the life space of the individual person. Data in this study were based on a 1960 interview of 562 metropolitan residents from a broad range of social backgrounds. In 1975, another 397 metropolitan residents were asked identical questions concerning the meanings of sport in their lives (Anderson and Stone, 1979). One portion of the interview focused on the person's favorite sport and whether this sport was mostly as a spectator or as a participant. Table 9-1 shows the social class differences are apparent in both 1960 and 1975. The upper and lower classes show an increase for the frequency of mentioning a spectator sport as a favorite, while the middle class percentages are almost identical for the two studies. However, the upper class in both studies manifests a greater tendency toward a participant sport than a spectator sport. Conversely, the middle and lower classes are more likely to select a spectator sport. We speculate that the trend toward spectatorship may reflect the impact of sports on television across all social classes. However, the continued tendency for the upper class to select a participant sport may be explained by their financial ability to purchase memberships in club sports.

TABLE 9-1 Social Class Differences in the Designation of Spectator or Participant Sport as Favorites in 1960 and 1975

FAVORITE SPORT	UPPER CLASS		MIDDLE CLASS		LOWER CLASS	
	1960 (%)	1975 (%)	1960 (%)	1975 (%)	1960 (%)	1975 (%)
Spectator	36	44	57	58	55	65
Participant	64	56	43	42	45	35

Source: Adapted from Anderson and Stone, 1979, p. 174.

The Anderson and Stone research also provides an analysis of the saliency of sport in terms of its currency in everyday conversation for the time periods of 1960 and 1975. Sport is a meaningful activity that motivates people to act. One such activity is the way conversation on sport topics circulates throughout a society. Anderson and Stone (1979) suggests that "a conversational knowledge of sport gives strangers access to one another even in the presumed anonymity of the mass urban milieu. Because of the salient nature of sport in our society, one can gain easy access to total strangers in public places such as cabs, trains, planes, buses and bars by discussing sports" (p. 176). Sport is even better as a topic of conversation than the weather because it leads to cues for self-disclosure and knowledge of others. When comparing the frequency of conversations on sport in Table 9-2 over the fifteen-year period, it is evident that the social class differences have decreased. The 1960 findings indicated that 32 percent of the respondents in the lower social stratum rarely or never talked about sports as compared to only 11 percent in the upper stratum. Stone (1969) interpreted this finding as another indication of the general insulation of the lower class from the larger society. The 1975 data show a shift in the proportion of the lower stratum respondents from the "rarely or almost never category" to the "occasionally" category. Anderson and Stone (1975) interpret this shift as an increase in the "democratization" of sport in the metropolitan environment (p. 179).

TABLE 9-2 Social Class Differences in the Frequency of Sport Conversations in 1960 and 1975

FREQUENCY OF SPORT CONVERSATION	UPPER CLASS		MIDDLE CLASS		LOWER CLASS	
	1960 (%)	1975 (%)	1960 (%)	1975 (%)	1960 (%)	1975 (%)
Rarely or never	11	17	18	19	32	23
Occasionally	33	32	33	30	21	32
Frequently	32	27	27	27	24	21
Very frequently	24	24	22	24	23	24

Source: Adapted from Anderson and Stone, 1979, p. 177.

The Anderson and Stone research not only analyzed favorite sports and frequency of conversations about sport but also the degree of participation in sport. They found that social status was related to sport participation in 1960, and these differences were also evident in the 1975 data. In both 1960 and 1975, the data clearly show active sports participation is associated with a more privileged social background (see Table 9-3). These data provide additional support of the notion that the lower class tends to be insulated from the larger society. It might also be noted that the occupational demands of the lower class require a greater expenditure of physical energy than in the upper and middle classes; therefore, the leisure activity of the working class tends to be less physical than in the upper strata. Moreover, as we noted in our discussion of the data in Table 9-1, the participation of the upper strata is often in a club context that requires membership fees.

TABLE 9-3 Social Class Differences in the Degree of Active Sports Participation for the Time Periods of 1960 and 1975

NUMBER OF SPORTS PARTICIPATED IN	UPPER CLASS		MIDDLE CLASS		LOWER CLASS	
	1960 (%)	1975 (%)	1960 (%)	1975 (%)	1960 (%)	1975 (%)
0	9	11	20	22	31	31
1	15	20	18	15	26	22
2	25	24	23	27	21	22
3	20	19	23	15	13	13
4 or more	31	26	16	21	10	12

Source: Adapted from Anderson and Stone, 1979, p. 180.

The findings by Anderson and Stone showing that sport is less salient with the lower class have been corroborated in another study involving 510 urban residents. Spreitzer and Snyder (1975) studied the meaning of sport among these residents via a questionnaire survey which elicited opinions concerning the social function of sport in our society. Sample statements included: "Sports are valuable because they help youngsters to become good citizens." "Sports are valuable because they contribute to the development of patriotism," and "Sports are valuable because they teach youngsters respect for authority." Among the respondents with less than a high school degree (a rough measure of the lower status), only 25 percent felt that sport had a high social value. On the other hand, among the respondents with a college education, 61 percent felt that sport had a high social value.

In general, several studies have reported a relatively impoverished style of leisure among the poor. In 1973, Noe and Elifson found that the poor tend to engage in a narrow band of leisure activities and frequently on a solo basis. "The leisure life style of the poor can best be characterized by their response to an open-ended question probing what they do in their free time. Many responded by saying that they did 'nothing' or just 'sat relaxed,' a response perhaps symptomatic of deeper ills that reflect a general subsistence level of existence" (p. 6). On the other hand, we need to be cautious about imposing a middle class bias against the leisure style of the working class. It may be that the values of the work ethic are so ingrained with the upper strata that one can approach leisure as if it is a form of work. Thus, the emphasis on recreational forms of sport are loaded with the importance of participation, doing well, achievement, and demonstrating improvement. Furthermore, we need to be cautious of assuming that these relationships apply to all minority groups.

Social stratification is also evident in the world of sport because sports are class-linked. Loy's (1969) study of 1,097 former athletes at UCLA provides some interesting data on the social background of these athletes. Table 9-4 shows the percentage of athletes in various sports who came from homes in which the father was engaged in a blue-collar occupation. Nearly half of the wrestlers and about one third of the baseball, football, and track athletes came from blue-collar homes, while less than one fifth of the basketball, swimming, tennis, and crew athletes came from similar backgrounds. We suspect that more recent data would show that basketball players now typically would come from lower status backgrounds than was the case in the 1969 report. It is also worth pointing out that two of the three sports with the highest percentage of athletes from blue-collar homes are body contact sports—wrestling and football. This correlation between type of sport and social class has also been reported by Lüschen (1969) as evident in Germany. Among German soccer players, 53 percent came from the lower class, 29 percent from the lower-middle class, 12 percent from the upper-middle class, and only 5 percent were from the higher class background. In addition to soccer, wrestling, weight-lifting, and field handball were associated with the lower class and lower-middle class backgrounds. Conversely, tennis, field hockey, skiing, and rowing were identified with the middle and upper-middle classes.

TABLE 9-4 Percent of Fathers in Blue-Collar Occupations According to Sport

SPORT	*N*	BLUE-COLLAR (%)
Wrestling	(27)	48.1
Baseball	(90)	36.5
Football	(192)	34.6
Track	(119)	30.5
Soccer	(32)	26.3
Gymnastics	(33)	26.3
Basketball	(91)	16.4
Swimming	(81)	13.3
Tennis	(50)	13.3
Crew	(64)	10.4

Source: Adapted from Loy, 1969, p. 114.

PROLE SPORTS

In our discussion of the meaning and types of sports as related to social class, we have noted that some sports obviously are exclusive because of the economic requirements, for example, private golf clubs. Yet there are sporting (and sport-like) events that seem especially attractive to the lower class. These *prole* sports—referring to proletariat or working class—have several characteristics that make them "grand spectacles": (1) speed and power rather than agility, grace, or finesse; (2) artifacts that are derived from the prole culture such as motorcycles; (3) identification with the "players" or participants; and, (4) the fact that the spectators often become "participants" (Lewis, 1972, pp. 43–44). Prole sports would include demolition derbies, stock car racing, motocrossing, roller derbies, and professional wrestling; some of these activities would not technically be defined as sports because the violence, power, and outcome are partially contrived. One writer has suggested that the appeal of prole sports has a legacy in the Roman Era.

> The nature of their appeal is clear enough. Since the onset of the Christian era, i.e., since about 500 A.D., no game has come along to fill the gap left by the abolition of the purest of all sports, gladiatorial combat. As late as 300 A.D. these bloody duals, usually between women and dwarfs, were enormously popular not only in Rome but throughout the Roman Empire. (Wolfe, 1972, pp. 39–40)

Demolition derby is a typical prole sport. Its primary objective is the destruction of the opponents' cars. In prole sports, speed, physical and mechanical power, strength, and violence are paramount. These characteristics are also evident in the blue-collar world of machismo, muscles, automobiles, cycles, machines, tools, and equipment. Thus the emphasis is on artifacts that are consistent with, and derived from, the working class subculture.

Furthermore, as Eitzen and Sage (1978) note, in prole sports "the actors are easy to identify with—some emphasize their ethnic or racial background; some are fat, while others are musclemen; some are heroes, while others are villains. Unlike other sports, these activities (especially roller derby) give equal billing to female athletes, allowing women the possibility of someone with whom they can identify" (p. 215). Also, although most spectator sports make a distinction between the activity of players and the passivity of the spectators, prole spectators are frequently part of the action. Because the spectators identify with the actors (players) in this arena, the fans react in emotional and physical ways. For example, they cheer their heroes, boo the villains, throw objects, argue and fight with other fans, and occasionally attack officials and players. Their behavior is a sharp contrast to the genteel demeanor of golf and tennis (Eitzen and Sage, 1978, p. 215). In sum, prole sports serve some of the same functions of the "circuses" of the Roman Era for the less advantaged citizens.

We have suggested that the close association of prole sports with the lower class can be partially explained by the derivation of the sport artifacts from the lower class culture. Martin and Berry (1973) provide a more generalized explanation based on the consequences of broader societal trends, especially in the realm of the world of work. In particular, they attempt to explain the recent popularity of prole sports such as motocrossing (motorcycle racing over a course of sharp turns, jumps, and obstacles) as a result of deprivations on the job. Historically, work for males has provided an opportunity to express such characteristics as rivalry, competition, tests of skill, pride in work, and comaraderie. These are basic to the identity of the working class and were reaffirmed in their trade and provided a sense of self-respect and identity. Likewise, the socialization of males continues to instill the values of "rugged individualism," "aggressive activism," "competition," "achievement," and "success." Martin and Berry (1973) note that

> At our present stage of post-industrial development, the world of work for working class males has become so corporatized, specialized, automated, assembly lined, and in other ways so altered and changed, as to depreciate and constrict opportunity structures for the expression and exercise of these basic values (rugged individualism, aggressive activism, competition, and achievement) in their traditional form. In simple

> terms, technological and industrial growth has, in the last couple of decades, transformed the working man's world of work into a psychological wasteland.
>
> Hence, as a consequence, a segment of working class American males increasingly estranged and alienated from the world of work as an opportunity structure or setting in which core values may be expressed and realized, turn to competitive forms of sport and recreation (in this case, motocrossing) as an effective alternative or functional substitute (p. 12).

In brief, prole sports such as motocrossing provide an opportunity for the working class to express the characteristics of individualism, achievement, success, and aggressiveness that may not be available to them in their work. Thus, for many cycle riders "the only time they 'really live' is at the Sunday races: the rest of the week is viewed with detachment as they play out the other roles demanded of them by circumstance and society" (Martin and Berry, 1973, p. 7).

The consideration of prole sports introduces a related dimension of social stratification—namely, the interrelationship between work and leisure. For example, while one's work may be psychologically unsatisfying and merely a means of making a living, one's leisure may serve a compensatory function and thus be the area of life that is most satisfying and expressive of one's identity. Indeed, people are likely to be evaluated and ranked by different criteria in their work and leisure spheres. In essence, these different spheres represent alternative stratification systems (it is Weber who is recognized for viewing the presence of multiple stratification systems—classes, status groups, and parties). Thus, in multiple stratification systems, working class persons may be accorded low social status in their work and low income; however, in another sphere, such as a commitment to leisure, individuals may achieve proficiency, recognition, self-respect, and status. In this context, Aventi (1976) studied autocrossing, a form of auto racing, as a leisure activity containing a hierarchy of respect within the sport. He found that the respect individuals had for each other was not primarily a function of their occupation, education, and income. Rather, proficiency in the leisure pursuit of autocrossing provided an alternative system of social stratification. Aventi points out that status gained in leisure activities that are independent of occupationally-related attributes can also have significance for middle- and upper-class persons. While such individuals "are often afforded respect during their day-to-day routines on the basis of well-established status symbols, such as title, clothing, and style of speech, participation in leisure pursuits can provide the opportunity for new and independent bases of being evaluated and respected" (p. 63). Furthermore, the leisure sphere provides an opportunity for social interaction of peoplc from different social classes, that is, a melting pot.

SPORT PARTICIPATION AND SOCIAL MOBILITY

One common assumption about sport is that it is a means (some might even suppose an easy means) of climbing the social ladder. One writer, noting the value of college athletics as a social escalator, pointed out that "football would enable a whole generation of young men in the coal fields of Pennsylvania to turn their backs on the mines that had employed their fathers" (Rudolph, 1962, p. 378). The clustering of prominent ethnic football players from the mining regions of

Pennsylvania—such as George Blanda, Joe Namath, and John Unitas—illustrates this social escalation function in a manner similar to the stream of prominent black basketball players from large cities. Nevertheless, *most* coal miners' children and ghetto youth have not found sport to be a means of escape. For every Joe Willie Namath, there are thousands who have been left behind. For example, there are approximately 200,000 high school senior boys in the United States playing basketball in the 22,000 public and private secondary schools. The following statistics indicate the odds of becoming a professional basketball player (Durso, 1975, p. 76).[1]

High school senior players	200,000
College senior players	5,700
Drafted by the pros	211
Signed by the pros	55

It has been estimated that in 1968 over 900,000 athletes were participating in football at the high school level, yet less than 30,000 were participating in intercollegiate football. Because only about half of the college football players received athletic grants-in-aid, it is evident that less than 2 percent of the high school football players will eventually receive financial aid to play college football (Scott, 1971). In 1980 it was reported that close to a million high school boys played football, 41,551 played football on a National Collegiate Athletic Association varsity team (others played for schools within the National Association for Intercollegiate Athletics, an athletic organization for small colleges), but only 330 football players survived the player draft and reported to NFL teams, and about 150 made the final teams (*Toledo Blade*, November 30, 1980, p. 42).

The situation is similar in professional baseball. A newsletter from the U.S. Department of Labor reports that "about 400,000 young men played on high school baseball teams in 1970, another 25,000 were on college teams, and about 3,000 were in the minor leagues. However, only about 100 rookies made the 24 squads in the major leagues that year" (Department of Labor, June 21, 1973). It is noteworthy that the odds of making it into the grand circle of elite performers in professional sports are rarely reported, while gigantic salary figures for a relatively few star performers are routinely reported in the mass media.

Rosco C. Brown, Director of New York University's Institute for Afro-American Affairs, has been particularly concerned about black youth being seduced by sport as an avenue to success. Brown argues that "what we need is balance. . . . We need more education. Black youngsters pour too much time and energy into sports. They're deluded and seduced by the athletic flesh peddlers, they're used for public amusement—and discarded. . . . Most of them are left without the skills needed for servicing or enriching the community" (quoted in Durso, 1975, p. 76).

Arthur Ashe (1977), U.S. Open and Wimbledon tennis champion, echoes Roscoe Brown's sentiments in his article entitled "An Open Letter to Black Parents: Send Your Children to the Libraries." Ashe argues that the black subculture overemphasizes the dubious glory of black heroes in the world of sport. This glorification of the black athlete is shared by black parents, friends, relatives,

[1]From *The Sports Factory* by Joseph Durso. Copyright © 1975 by Joseph Durso. Reprinted by permission of Quadrangle/The New York Times Book Co.

teachers, books, movies, newspapers, ministers, and especially television. As an antidote to this adulation, Ashe raises some penetrating questions.

> There must be some way to assure that the 999 who try but don't make it to pro sports don't wind up on the street corners or in the unemployment lines. Unfortunately, our most widely recognized role models are athletes and entertainers—"runnin' " and "jumpin' " and "singin' " and "dancin.' " While we are 60 percent of the National Basketball Association, we are less than 4 percent of the doctors and lawyers. While we are about 35 percent of major league baseball we are less than 2 percent of the engineers. While we are about 40 percent of the National Football League, we are less than 11 percent of construction workers such as carpenters and bricklayers.
>
> Our greatest heroes of the century have been athletes—Jack Johnson, Joe Louis and Muhammad Ali. Racial and economic discrimination forced us to channel our energies into athletics and entertainment. These were the ways out of the ghetto, the ways to get that Cadillac, those alligator shoes, that cashmere sport coat.
>
> Somehow, parents must instill a desire for learning alongside the desire to be Walt Frazier. Why not start by sending black professional athletes into high schools to explain the facts of life.
>
> I have often addressed high school audiences and my message is always the same. For every hour you spend on the athletic field, spend two in the library. Even if you make it as a pro athlete, your career will be over by the time you are 35. So you will need that diploma. . . .
>
> I'll never forget how proud my grandmother was when I graduated from U.C.L.A. in 1966. Never mind the Davis Cup in 1968, 1969 and 1970. Never mind the Wimbledon title, Forest Hills, etc. To this day, she still doesn't know what those names mean.
>
> What mattered to her was that of her more than 30 children and grandchildren, I was the first to be graduated from college, and a famous college at that. Somehow, that made up for all those floors she scrubbed all those years (p. 2).[2]

Walt Frazier (1977), star basketball player with the New York Knickerbockers, was moved by Arthur Ashe's comments to submit his own perceptions concerning the possible deleterious impact of athletics on black youngsters. Frazier has been much publicized by the media for his flashy life style and conspicuous consumption. Nevertheless, Frazier strongly reinforces academic preparation as a more likely source of mobility for disadvantaged youngsters than the risky world of professional sports: ". . . when I talk to kids, I tell them that they might not have the talent to become a pro athlete. But they have other talents. They should make the most of what they have. And school is the best place to develop those talents" (p. 2).[3]

It should also be noted that active athletic involvement at any level is necessarily short-lived. It is difficult to speak of playing sports as a career. Many (cf. Hill and Lowe, 1974) have commented on the identity crisis that can occur at the end of one's playing days. Page (1969) points out some of the difficulties associated with this transitional process from one career to another.

---

[2]Arthur Ashe, "An Open Letter to Black Parents: Send Your Children to the Libraries," *The New York Times*, February 6, 1977. © 1977 by The New York Times Company. Reprinted by permission.

[3]Walt Frazier, "Talk About Doctors Instead of Athletes," *The New York Times*, May 1, 1977. © 1977 by The New York Times Company. Reprinted by permission.

I have met, in the last twenty-five years or so, at least six or eight ex-great athletes from the Ivy League schools, Princeton, Harvard, and particularly Yale (I don't know why) who didn't make it, in their terms. They came from upper middle-class families, were great football stars, didn't become distinguished attorneys, physicians, businessmen, bankers and faced terrific crises in their lives (this is often portrayed in fiction) about the age of 35 or 40—they can no longer cash in, psychologically speaking, on the hero role they once had. In other words I'm suggesting that this sort of thing happens not only to kids coming out of working-class families, but is a much more widely spread pattern (p. 200).

Wayne Embry, the former general manager of the Milwaukee Bucks professional basketball team, has also commented on the identity crisis associated with a short-lived athletic career.

I see that every year—the guys who have gone to school and never thought of having a vocation to fall back on. You tell them they have been cut and they can't believe you. Somebody should have told them a long time ago that their chances of success in pro basketball are small, almost minute (quoted in Hannen, 1976, p. 3).

Cratty (1974) has pointed out that the identity crisis associated with the termination of one's athletic career can occur across a wide age spectrum.

The loss of a way of expressing one's aggressions as the season or career terminates may result in severe adjustment problem; the loss of status and self-respect felt by high school and college athletes, as their talents do not permit them to ascend to the next higher level of competition, may similarly cause them to need professional help in the realizement of values, energies and general outlook upon life. Career's end may come following the finish of a Little League career when the boy or girl finds he or she cannot make the high school team, when the high school star finds that his talents are not desired by college or university coaches, when the professional athlete finds himself with a crippling injury, or when the symptoms of aging prove debilitating (p. 154).

Mihovilovic (1968) conducted an empirical study concerning the adjustment problems of former athletes. His research focused on the career of professional-type soccer players in Yugoslavia. The findings from this study show that the players fought to stay on the team as long as possible, rather than disengaging gradually, with consequent harmful results from a sudden termination. Mihovilovic also found that termination of the soccer career was a particularly painful experience for the players who had no other occupational skills. Moreover, the circle of friends diminishes upon termination of one's athletic career with concomitant feelings of social isolation. Further research concerning the disengagement process of athletes terminating their careers, such as the Mihovilovic study, is needed to round out our knowledge in this area because much of our information on this topic is only anecdotal in nature.

The following autobiographical account by Jerry Kramer (1969), former lineman for the Green Bay Packers football team, illustrates the agonizing psychological disengagement process as well as the manner in which he used his athletic fame to develop business interests.

My other business interests also kept me busy. A major oil company made a bid to buy out the off-shore diving company I had helped found in Louisiana. If the deal went through, the oil company wanted me to keep working with them. At the same time, I was getting deeper into the restaurant business, with pieces of four restaurants in Colorado and Illinois, and deeper into the real estate business in Oklahoma. The more I moved around, the more people I met, and the more people wanted to help me and advise me. At least half a dozen companies implied that I could go to work for them. I got so much attention that I figured somebody must have got me mixed up with a quarterback.

My head was swimming from all the possibilities, and slowly—slowly, because I wanted it to be slowly—I began to realize that I couldn't play football in 1969, that I simply couldn't afford to put another year into football. It was a terribly agonizing realization. Sooner or later, of course, everyone who plays football must quit. For the player, rare these days, who has no outside business interests, the decision is relatively simple. He keeps playing until his coaches or his doctors tell him that he is no longer able to meet the demands of the game. For the more typical player, who is thinking about coaching or selling insurance or stocks full time, the key to his decision is timing. He has to make certain that he does not get out too soon or too late, that he takes maximum advantage of opportunities on and off the field. I was in a fairly unusual position, a strong position. I had no financial worries about getting out of football. I knew that I could make a living a dozen other ways. This should have made my decision easy. It didn't (pp. 6–7).

While Kramer was agonizing over whether to leave professional football, he clearly had business opportunities open to him. In an empirical study, Haerle (1975a, 1975b) found some evidence that fame was a lever to open doors to business opportunities and thus improve occupational achievement. However, while the fame of being a major league baseball player was likely to assist in securing the initial nonplaying job, later occupational attainment depended on the more traditional criteria, primarily education and socioeconomic status. Thus, the former players who attended college eventually attained higher postbaseball jobs than the nonattenders. Furthermore, Haerle found that the players who had attended college without athletic grants-in-aid generally attained a higher occupational rank than the college attenders with athletic assistance. The three groups of former professional baseball players had the following occupational rankings.

College players without athletic grants
College players with athletic grants
Players who did not attend college

In fact, those who attended college with athletic financial aid were somewhat closer to the occupational level of the noncollege group.

Although fame is a factor in social mobility, the relative impact of education is greater in the long run for occupational achievement. Haerle speculated that athletes who attended college had more options open to them that they can exploit after their athletic careers. Additionally, the athletes who attended college on an athletic grant may have been stimulated to attend primarily to play baseball. Thus, as we noted in the last chapter, athletic participation by itself can result in inflated expectations without developing the necessary academic and social skills for education and occupational advancement.

A coaching career is an obvious channel of mobility for former athletes. In an interesting study, Loy and Sage (1972) analyzed the family backgrounds of over 600 college football and basketball coaches. Table 9-5 summarizes some of their findings. It is clear that the college basketball and football coaches come from generally more modest family backgrounds than other professionals. For example, only 24 percent of the coaches had fathers who attended college as compared to 57 percent of physicians and 39 percent of the engineers. Table 9-5 also indicates that college coaches in football and basketball experienced more intergenerational mobility than college faculty in other fields. For example, only 23 percent of the faculty in the biological sciences had fathers with manual occupations as compared to about 50 percent of the college-level coaches.

TABLE 9-5 A Comparison of Social Background of College Coaches with Other Faculty by Field

ACADEMIC DISCIPLINE (OR PROFESSION)	FATHER'S EDUCATION (% ATTENDING COLLEGE)	FATHER'S OCCUPATION (% MANUAL WORKERS)
Medicine	57	10
Law	50	14
Anthropology	53	16
Political science	48	22
Humanities	43	21
Economics	43	18
Biological sciences	42	23
Physical sciences	41	25
Psychology	41	22
All fields	40	23
Engineering	39	26
Sociology	34	25
Social work	34	26
Business	32	27
Education	30	32
Agriculture	25	21
Athletics	23	51
Basketball	22	51
Football	24	52

Source: Adapted from Loy and Sage, 1972, p. 21, and Lipset and Ladd, 1972, p. 89, and from "An Occupational Analysis of the College Coach" in D. W. Ball and J. W. Loy (eds.), *Sport and Social Order: Contributions to the Sociology of Sport* © 1975. Addison-Wesley, Reading, Mass. Reprinted with permission.

We suggest that the career pathway for coaches begins with athletic participation in high school and college athletics. Because only a very small minority of collegiate athletes have an opportunity to become professional athletes, a logical alternative is a coaching career. This may be particularly true for athletes who have invested heavily in their athletic roles and who have not developed alternative career possibilities. This description may be more apropos for athletes from the lower class who are more likely to see their own coaches as a career model. Some empirical support for this thesis is provided in the data presented in Table 9-6. In this study, the high school coaches who come from less-privileged backgrounds (based on their father's education and occupational status) were more likely to rank their own coaches as the most important influence in their educational and occupational plans. On the other hand, the coaches who come from more advantaged backgrounds tended to name their own fathers and mothers as the primary influence in their educational and occupational plans.

TABLE 9-6 Sources of Career Influence as Cited by High School Basketball Coaches

SOCIAL STATUS BACKGROUND	RANKING OF SOURCES OF INFLUENCE IN EDUCATIONAL/OCCUPATIONAL PLANS		
Education of Father	**First**	**Second**	**Third**
Less than high school	Coach	Mother	Father
High school	Coach	Father	Mother
Some college or more	Father	Mother	Coach
Occupation of Father			
Semiskilled, unskilled	Coach	Mother	Father
Clerical, sales, skilled, farm	Coach	Father	Mother
Professional, executive, proprietor	Father	Mother	Coach

Source: Adapted from Snyder, 1972a, p. 318.

We do not know the proportion of parents who believe that the athletic path will lead to occupational well-being and who therefore encourage their children to concentrate on athletic skills. Although some parents place great emphasis on their child's athletic performance, and spend a considerable amount of money providing lessons and opportunities for competition (especially in such club sports as tennis, swimming, gymnastics, and golf), we do not know how many parents believe that their offspring will make their living as professional athletes. We have already cited statistics that show the remote probability of becoming a professional athlete. Nevertheless, one might argue that participation in sport will lead to subsequent occupational attainment in a nonathletic context. The argument for this relationship might rest on the assumption that a collegiate athlete is a visible person who possesses a "name" as well as personal traits desired by employers. The research on this topic is ambiguous. We have already cited the Haerle (1975a, 1975b) research showing that the initial nonplaying job might be secured on the basis of one's athletic visibility; however, their long-term occupational status was influenced more by their educational achievement. On the other hand, Otto and Alwin (1977) studied 340 former high school youth over a fifteen-year period and concluded that athletics have a positive effect on occupational aspirations, attainment, and income. This association remained when "controlling on variables usually associated with the status attainment process, namely, academic performance, significant-others' influence, aspirations and attainments" (pp. 111–12). In another study, Dubois (1978, 1979) compared college male athletes and a group of nonathletes; his findings showed that athletic status had no significant effect on occupational prestige and earnings; however, his research did show slight variation by type of sport.

If there is a likelihood of variation in mobility based on type of sport, we might also find other athletic background variables worth consideration. One particularly relevant study examined the social origins and career mobility of football players who graduated from Notre Dame University between 1946 and 1965 (Sack and Thiel, 1979). The significance of this research is enhanced by the fact that Notre Dame University probably has the strongest tradition in football of any American university (going back to the 1920s and the coaching of Knute Rockne). Thus, we would expect that former football players at Notre Dame would be in a particularly advantageous position for occupational mobility. In terms of social mobility, the Sack and Thiel study showed that both the former football players and a comparison sample of nonathletes have moved well beyond their parental social status, but the Notre Dame players generally came from lower social origins than the other students. For example, only 23 percent of the football players came from upper-class homes, while 53 percent of the other students came from upper-class backgrounds. On the other hand, 51 percent of the football players, as compared to 21 percent of the students, came from lower-class origins. These data reveal that football was the mechanism whereby the lower class players were able to attend the University. Comparisons of the two groups after graduation show that the nonathletes were more likely to have earned advanced degrees than the athletes regardless of their fathers' educational background. Concerning the level of income earned, there was very little difference when the nonathletic students were compared with the ballplayers as a group. However, the prominence of the athletes in the senior year had a bearing on their present income. Whereas 41 percent of the first team players are now earning $50,000 a year or more, only 30 percent of the second teamers and 13 percent of the reserves are earning this amount (Sack and Thiel, 1979, p. 63). Additionally, the first team players who were engaged in business were overrepresented as top ranking executives in their companies. Several additional questions are raised by the Sack and Thiel study. First, this is a very select group of athletes; we would be interested in similar studies at a variety of colleges and universities. Second, while this research focuses on alumni, we would like to know how the athletes fare who do not graduate from college? Finally, what are the explanations for the variations in income and business success of the first team, second team, and marginal players? Is the success based on a celebrity status, or on the interpersonal skills or other characteristics that allow them to thrive in highly competitive situations?

CONCLUSION

In this chapter we have reviewed the functionalist and conflict perspectives of society and how these are reflected in the theories of social stratification. Because social position affects many aspects of one's life style, it is evident that sport is also interrelated with social stratification. Thus, the functionalists emphasize the ways in which sport is a mechanism of social integration and an avenue of social mobility. Conversely, the conflict theorists argue that the bureaucratic nature of organized sport reflects the widespread differences in wealth and power in society and the exploitation of workers (players). Furthermore, according to this perspective, sport serves the privileged class by providing an opiate that dissipates the demands for humane social reforms that would redistribute wealth and power.

Research studies cited in this chapter support the assumption that the meaning of sport differs by social class; likewise, the type of sport involvement is class-linked. In general, the working class is less involved in sport than the middle and upper classes; however, this conclusion may vary by ethnic or racial groups. This fact may be partially explained by the general insulation of the lower class from the institutions of society and the economic costs of sport participation. However, some of the leisure sports most attractive to the working class—prole sports—are not regularly reported in the traditional sport media. These prole sports incorporate behavior often associated with the working class, that is, speed, power, strength, daring, and violence, and may serve as an alternative avenue for social recognition and prestige that is not provided in the world sphere.

The relationship between sport and vertical mobility is ambiguous. One important finding in the research by Haerle (1975a, 1975b) is that students are not likely to experience occupational success if their educational identity is based primarily on an inflated athletic role. Athletic prominence per se is usually not sufficient for climbing up the social ladder. An adequate educational base is necessary for long-term occupational achievement, although a distinguished athletic career may provide an initial impetus in this direction. The single occupation most available and attractive to former athletes is a continuation of their association with sport as a coach. Social background data on coaches indicate that they often have come from less advantaged backgrounds, they have been influenced by their own coaches, and their athletic proficiency has led eventually to a middle-class status as a coach (educator) in an educational institution.

CHAPTER 10
The Female Athlete

Sex roles in most societies are specific and well defined. However, the cultural prescriptions associated with gender will vary from group to group and from time to time. In Western society, the attitudes and ideals regarding the woman's role in the family and other social institutions, including sport, that emerged during the Victorian era in the late 1800s were consistent and distinctive. The ideal

> was of an ethereal person, on a pedestal, somewhere above the realities of life. . . . To defy [the ideal] was to be unwomanly. Thus passiveness, obedience to husband, circumspectness of behavior, and most of all, attractiveness were necessary to maintain the Victorian image of womanhood (Gerber, 1974, pp. 9–10).

For girls and women to participate in sport was contrary to the Victorian ideal. Sport would take a woman out of the home to engage in vigorous activity. It would place a woman in a situation where modesty might be compromised, where emotional control might be jeopardized, and where overall propriety could be endangered. It was also feared that attracting a mate and childbearing could be hindered or prevented by injuries to the face and reproductive organs resulting from sport accidents.

The Victorian ideals were vividly expressed in the views of Pierre de Coubertin, founder of the modern Olympics.

> Respect of individual liberty requires that one should not interfere in private acts . . . but in public competitions, [women's] participation must be absolutely prohibited. It is indecent that the spectators should be exposed to the risk of seeing the body of a woman being smashed before their eyes. Besides, no matter how toughened a sportswoman may be, her organism is not cut out to sustain certain shocks. Her nerves rule her muscles, nature wanted it that way. Finally, the egalitarian discipline that is brought

> to bear on the male contenders for the good order and good appearance of the meeting risks being affected and rendered inapplicable by female participation. For all these practical reasons as well as sentimental ones, it is extremely desirable that a drastic rule be established very soon (cited in Gerber, 1974, p. 137).[1]

In spite of his strong opinions on the matter, Pierre de Coubertin was overruled, and women were included in the Olympics as early as 1900. Yet social definitions still prescribe and limit the range of athletic participation for girls and women. The "appropriateness" of the type of sport continues to reflect the tenets of the Victorian ideal of femininity. Metheny (1965) has provided the following analysis of how the appropriateness of a sport for women continues to reflect those historical ideals.

Categorically unacceptable are sports such as wrestling, judo, boxing, weightlifting, hammer throw, pole vault, longer foot races, high hurdles, and many forms of team sports. These sports are unacceptable because they involve attempts to physically subdue the opponent by bodily contact, direct application of bodily force to some heavy object, projection of the body through space over long distances, and cooperative face-to-face opposition in situations in which some body contact may occur.

Generally not acceptable (except possibly for minority groups) are sports such as shot put, discus, javelin throw, shorter foot races, low hurdles, and long jump. These sports require direct application of bodily force to a moderately heavy object, the projection of the body through space over moderate distances, and a display of strength in controlling bodily movements.

Generally acceptable forms of competition include swimming, diving, skiing, figure skating, gymnastics, golf, archery, fencing, badminton, squash, tennis, volleyball, and bowling. These sports are acceptable because they involve projection of the body through space in aesthetically pleasing patterns, utilization of a manufactured device to facilitate bodily movement, application of force through a light implement, overcoming the resistance of a light object, and maintenance of a spatial barrier that prevents body contact with the opponent.

For most women, then, engaging in sport invokes two contradictory role expectations: the expectations associated with being a woman, and the expectations of being an athlete. The traits often cited for being a successful athlete—aggressiveness, tough-mindedness, dominance, self-confidence, and risk taking—are usually associated with males rather than females (Harris, 1971, p. 1). In contrast, mentally healthy females are likely to be described as dependent, emotional, intuitive, passive, and submissive (Broverman et al., 1970). Hart (1971) points out that "the woman who wishes to participate in sports and remain 'womanly' faces great stress. By choosing sport she places herself outside the social mainstream" (p. 64). Dorothy Harris (1973) elaborates on this conflict.

> When a female chooses to participate in vigorous competitive activity she may be risking a great deal. She is laying on the line everything she may represent as a female in much the same way as the girl who first smoked in public risked her image, or the female who first appeared in public wearing pants. The female who has the courage of

---

[1]Gerber et al., *The American Woman in Sport* © 1974. Addison-Wesley, Reading, Mass.

> her convictions and the security of her feminine concept is still taking a risk when she wins a tennis match from her male opponent or outperforms any male whether it be in sports, business, or a profession dominated by the male. Competitive sports are still primarily the prerogative of the male in this society (p. 193).

In essence these traditional prescriptions against female participation in vigorous physical activity represent a type of social inequality and a form of discrimination or sexism. In this case the stratification is based on the ascribed characteristic of gender rather than some other characteristics such as income, power, or prestige. In recent years the gender roles have been liberalized, yet only one out of every five women today (as opposed to 30 percent of the men) reports that she is an active participant in some form of exercise; about 42 percent of the women in 1980 claim to be moderately active, while 38 percent say they are not very active at all (Roper Organization, Inc., 1980). Moreover, the data of Table 10-1 indicate that the extent of female participation in physical activity is associated with age and educational status. The least active are women 50 years of age and over; women with college degrees tend to be more active than women with less education.

Because the traditional gender roles have been changing, one might ask whether sport involvement for females still carries a stigma. Table 10-2 summar-

TABLE 10-1 Female Participation in Physical Activity by Age and Educational Level

	TOTAL WOMEN (%)
Very active	20
Moderately active	42
Not very active	38
Don't know/no answer	*

	AGE			
	18–19 (%)	30–39 (%)	40–49 (%)	50 AND OVER (%)
Very active	26	24	20	13
Moderately active	50	42	42	36
Not very active	24	34	38	50
Don't know/no answer	*	*	—	1

	EDUCATIONAL		
	NON-HIGH SCHOOL GRADUATES (%)	HIGH SCHOOL GRADUATES (%)	COLLEGE (%)
Very active	19	18	22
Moderately active	28	45	49
Not very active	52	36	29
Don't know/no answer	1	*	*

*Less than .05%

—No response

Source: Roper Organization, Inc., 1980, p. 84.

izes data collected from a cross-section of over 500 adults from the general population. It is clear from the rank ordering of sports that the general population continues to perceive differences in the appropriateness of certain sports for females. In terms of desirability, swimming leads the list, followed by tennis, gymnastics, softball, basketball, and track. It is interesting to note in the bottom panel of Table 10-2 that 30 percent of the adult sample feel that participation in track is stigmatizing for females, as compared to only a 2 percent stigma rate for tennis and swimming.

TABLE 10-2 Perceptions of the General Population Concerning the Effects of Athletic Participation on Female Characteristics

QUESTIONNAIRE ITEM	PERCENT RESPONDING "YES"
In your opinion, would participation in any of the following sports enhance a girl s/woman's feminine qualities?	
Swimming	67
Tennis	57
Gymnastics	54
Softball	14
Basketball	14
Track	13
In your opinion, would participation in any of the following sports detract from a girl's/woman's feminine qualities?	
Track	30
Basketball	21
Softball	20
Gymnastics	6
Tennis	2
Swimming	2

Source: Snyder, Kivlin, and Spreitzer, 1975, p. 167.

Additional research on athletic involvement and the female role has been derived from an analysis of data from college students. The data in Table 10-3 were gathered from surveys of female athletes who were competing in the national intercollegiate championships (in basketball, track and field, gymnastics, and swimming and diving); data were also collected from a comparison sample of college women nonathletes. The findings showed a similar rank ordering of the sports. It is interesting to note, however, that college women who were participating actively in sports were much more favorable in their perceptions of sport as appropriate for females than was the control group of nonathletes. College women who were not participating in athletics were quite traditional in their perceptions, 65 percent of them expressing the feeling that athletes tended to detract from a woman's feminine qualities (Snyder, Kivlin, and Spreitzer, 1975).

TABLE 10-3 Perceptions of College Women Concerning Female Participation in Athletics According to Type of Sport Participation

QUESTIONNAIRE ITEM	PERCENT RESPONDING "YES"
Do you feel there is a stigma attached to women who participate in the sport you specialize in?	
Female Athletes:	
Basketball players	56
Track and field participants	50
Swimming and diving participants	40
Gymnasts	31
Female Nonathletes*	65

*The questionnaire item for the sample of female nonathletes was worded as follows: "Do you feel there is a stigma attached to women's participation in sports?"

Source: Snyder, Kivlin, and Spreitzer 1975, p. 168.

It is evident from the data presented in Tables 10-1, 10-2, and 10-3 that a residue of the Victorian ideals of femininity remains within our culture. These ideals manifest themselves in the continued stigma and social sanctions imposed on the serious female athlete. Further, remnants of the Victorian era remain in the variation in frequency of participation that are evident between males and females as well as the "appropriateness" that is attached to the type of sport.

Research by Snyder and Kivlin (1975) on college women—athletes as well as nonathletes—revealed that athletic competition for females ranges from complete acceptance to complete rejection. The following excerpts from these studies convey the attitudes of athletes concerning female participation in sport.

> "Sports help to develop graceful bodies; sports add to grace of body movements; people think that this sport is graceful or enhances one's grace."
>
> "Society accepts the superior person regardless of activity; a superior athlete is appreciated by society. Society approves of skill and success in any activity."
>
> "Acceptance depends on the individual not the sport. I am accepted by others. I feel that I am accepted as a person not as an athlete only. People accept you for what you are, not what you do. A woman can be accepted as feminine regardless of her participation if she is willing to act feminine."
>
> "Some sports are more 'masculine,' others are more 'feminine'. Some sports are more suited for women than are others; some sports are not as rough as others."
>
> "Those who participate in the more feminine sports are better accepted than those who compete in the more masculine sports. Women competing in individual sports are better accepted than those competing in team sports. Women competing in sports that require less strength and physical activity are better accepted than those competing in the rougher and more active sports; sports which require grace and skill are better accepted than those which depend on strength."
>
> "People feel that participation in this sport produces unattractive muscles. Sports detract from body appearance by producing unattractive muscles. This sport tends to make one look masculine."

> "Sports are too competitive; the competitive nature of sports detracts from femininity. Too much competition is not conducive to personal and mental development."
>
> "People hold unfavorable stereotypes of women who participate in athletics. People stereotype all female athletes as masculine and muscular. People think that all women who participate in sports must be 'lesbians' or 'odd.' "

It is interesting to note that some of these beliefs are also shared by outstanding female athletes. In the 1976 Olympics, the U.S. women's swimming team won only one gold medal, compared to eleven gold medals for the East German swimmers. The response of many Americans was that the East Germans' success was attributed to the use of steroids to create muscular *superfrauen*. More serious analysts attributed the success of the East Germans to superior training regimens and state support for living expenses.

Controversy concerning the femininity of female athletes has existed for a number of years. Often the problem revolved around sex tests and whether the athletes, especially in track and field, were really men disguised as women. This dispute over sexuality also received considerable media coverage when Renee Richards, a transsexual tennis player had sexual surgery. After the operation Miss Richards had difficulty being accepted on the Women's Tennis Association tour and her entry in major national and European tournaments has often been questioned. More recently, female athletes have had to undergo tests to determine whether they are using steroids, which help build muscles and improve strength performances.

On the other hand, in gymnastics the small and slim physique is desirable for executing routines and to receive high scores from judges. Consequently, the trend is to impose strict diets and sometimes drugs on young gymnasts that restrict their growth.

One traditional argument against female participation in competitive sport is that it promotes the development of masculine characteristics. This may be a kind of "guilt by association," because sports have been a male domain and females who become associated with it are therefore suspect. One of the stereotypes of female athletes that reflects this stigma is the "female jock" who is an Amazon in terms of physical size. Snyder and Kivlin (1975) analyzed the height and weight of 328 athletes who were competing in the Women's National Intercollegiate Championships against the height and weight of a comparison group of nonathletes. The differences were not statistically significant. The average height and weight for the athletes was 5 feet, 6 inches, and 129 pounds as compared with 5 feet, 5 inches, and 126 pounds for the nonathletes. These data replicate the height and weight studies presented by Wyrick (1974). Women competing in certain sports are consistently larger than athletes in other sports, but these differences simply reflect the physical skills necessary to compete in those particular sports. Gross generalizations leading to conclusions of the sportswoman's being an Amazon are simply not supported by the data.

Furthermore, Snyder, Kivlin, and Spreitzer (1975) compared the perceived femininity of collegiate women athletes and nonathletes. There were few differences between the samples based on their self-ratings of femininity. Snyder and Spreitzer (1976a) likewise analyzed the femininity scores of female athletes and nonathletes in high school. Relative to the other girls, 70 percent of the gymnasts perceived themselves as being "very feminine." In contrast, only 44 percent of the basketball players perceived themselves as "very feminine," while the participants in track and the nonathletes had percentages of 56 and 58, respectively. These findings suggest that basketball's being a less socially accepted sport may be reflected in the participants' viewing of themselves as less feminine. Admittedly the findings of this study are tentative, and the variability among female athletes is a fact that must be recognized. Nevertheless, social scientific research provides no evidence for the assumption that less "feminine" girls are attracted to sport.

PSYCHOLOGICAL DIMENSIONS

Given the fact that a substantial proportion of the population views athletic participation as incongruent with femininity, one might suppose that a woman's participation in sport would produce role conflicts and psychological strain between her social self-image and her athletic self-image. If an individual has internalized two contradictory role prescriptions, we would anticipate behavioral and psychological ambiguity, confusion, and a lack of psychological integration. Is there any research to suggest that women's participation in sport has such dysfunctional effects on self-identity and psychological well-being?

One pertinent study involved a sample of 268 female varsity athletes representing thirteen colleges and universities (Sage and Loudermilk, 1979). These athletes had an extensive background in sports because over 90 percent had reported that between the ages of 14 and 17 they considered themselves to be above average or well above average in sports activities when compared to other girls their age, and 92 percent had participated on varsity teams in high school. One portion of the research dealt specifically with a measure of role conflict (a sample item: "Because American society traditionally places little value on girls' participation in sports, the female athlete receives little recognition for her skills and accomplishments"). Although many of the respondents did not experience conflict between their feminine and athletic roles, 20 percent of respondents reported that they experience substantial role conflict. When those who experience conflict were analyzed by dividing the athletes into two groups, that is, the socially approved "feminine" sports (tennis, golf, swimming, and gymnastics) and the stigmatized "masculine" sports (softball, basketball, volleyball, field hockey, track and field), the athletes in the "nonfeminine sports" experienced significantly more role conflict (see Table 10-4). That is, 46 percent of the athletes in the stigmatized sports experienced role conflict as compared to 34 percent of the females in the socially approved sports.

TABLE 10-4 Role Conflict Among Female Athletes According to Type of Athletic Participation

	DEGREE OF ROLE CONFLICT				
TYPE OF SPORT	NONE (%)	SOME (%)	MODERATE (%)	MUCH (%)	VERY MUCH (%)
"Masculine"	30	23	24	14	8
"Feminine"	38	27	18	10	6

Source: Adapted from Sage and Loudermilk, 1979, p. 93.

Although the Sage and Loudermilk study indicates that some female athletes experience role conflict, it does not indicate any negative psychological consequences. One relevant study focuses specifically on aspects of the psychological well-being of female athletes (Snyder and Kivlin, 1975). Data for this study were gathered from a sample of athletes who were participating in the 1972 Women's National Intercollegiate Championships for gymnastics, basketball, track and field, and swimming and diving. Table 10-5 provides data on these female athletes and a comparison sample of collegiate women who were nonathletes. The findings indicate that the athletes demonstrated higher scores on the three dimensions of psychological well-being than the nonathletes. These data tend to refute the assumption that athletic participation has a negative impact on females. The athletes in this study appear to be remarkably pleased with themselves and their lot in life. Furthermore, when this research was replicated with samples of female student athletes and nonathletes in Australia and India, those cross-national data provided additional support for the positive relationship between athletic involvement and psychological well-being (Snyder and Kivlin, 1975). In short, data from these research studies offer little evidence of psychological stress on the part of college-age female athletes.

TABLE 10-5 Comparison of Female College Athletes and Nonathletes on Psychological Well-Being

	ATHLETES (%)	NONATHLETES (%)
"Generally feel in good spirits"		
Most of the time	70.6	51.5
Much of the time	26.3	42.0
Some/seldom	3.1	6.6
"Very satisfied with life"		
Most of the time	63.4	47.4
Much of the time	31.4	41.2
Some/seldom	5.2	11.3
"Find much happiness in life"		
Most of the time	74.0	59.5
Much of the time	22.0	32.8
Some/seldom	3.5	7.6

Source: Snyder and Kivlin 1975, p. 195.

Another dimension of interest concerning the female athlete is the analysis of their self-image. One common measure of self-image is to determine an individual's feelings toward his or her body. Studies of body image show positive correlations with self-esteem and self-concept and negative correlations with anxiety and insecurity, particularly for women (Berschied, Walster, and Bohrnstedt, 1973; Secord and Jourard, 1953; Zion, 1965). Furthermore, research generally supports the thesis of positive feedback between physical activity and body image (Harris, 1973). This research tradition formed the backdrop for further data analysis by Snyder and Kivlin (1975) on collegiate female athletes and nonathletes. Table 10-6 measures attitudes toward various aspects of one's body; the findings show that female athletes have more positive feelings toward their bodies than do nonathletes. An extension of this research to Australian and Indian samples of athletes and nonathletes demonstrated a similar positive relationship between feelings toward one's body and participation in sport (Snyder and Kivlin, 1975).

These studies have focused on samples of collegiate female athletes and nonathletes. But the elite athlete who is participating in national intercollegiate competition is likely to be deeply involved in the athletic role. Would we find different results with younger and less involved athletes? Snyder and Spreitzer (1976a) addressed themselves to this question. They surveyed high school female athletes and nonathletes in Ohio. The athletes participated in three sports: gymnastics, basketball, and track. Theoretically, because gymnastics is usually considered an "appropriate" sport for girls, one might expect to find differences between the participants in this sport vis à vis those in sports such as basketball or track. However, this assumption was not borne out by findings of this study. The results, which are shown in Table 10-7, indicate that, in general, the high school female athletes expressed a body image that was at least as favorable as a comparison sample of nonparticipants.

These studies of the psychological well-being and self-perception are not conclusive because of methodological limitations. Nevertheless, they provide no evidence for the belief that participation in athletics is psychologically stressful for females. Perhaps, as studies on male samples have indicated, increased physical activity and fitness tend to promote mental well-being. Likewise, even though female participation in sport has an aura of stigma, many participants receive positive feedback in the form of recognition and rewards from parents and friends.

TABLE 10-6 Comparison of Female College Athletes and Nonathletes on Body Image

	POSITIVE IMAGE	
	ATHLETES (*N* = 328) (%)	NONATHLETES (*N* = 275) (%)
Health	97	81
Energy	91	56
Body build	72	47
Face	71	51
Posture	69	43
Legs	67	47
Waist	56	44
Weight	54	39
Profile	53	34
Hips	51	29
Bust	51	35

Source: Adapted from Snyder and Kivlin, 1975, p. 196.

It is also probable that through participation in sport females as well as males are able to gain an increased awareness of themselves, their bodies, their capacities, and an appreciation of motor ability and skill learning. These studies provide support and optimism for the continued expansion of sport and physical activities for females in schools.

TABLE 10-7 Perceived Body Image of High School Girls According to Type of Athletic Participation

PERCEIVED BODY IMAGE	GYMNASTS (*N* = 293) (%)	BASKETBALL PLAYERS (*N* = 189) (%)	TRACK PARTICIPANTS (*N* = 196) (%)	NO SPORT PARTICIPATION (*N* = 495) (%)
"Consider myself fortunate"				
Energy level	83	80	89	52
Build	60	50	59	41
Waist	54	38	48	41
Bust	40	52	38	40
Profile	39	33	40	35

Source: Adapted from Snyder and Spreitzer, 1976a, p. 807.

The research of Ogilvie and Tutko (1971) showed that female athletes tended to be more independent, creative, and autonomous than male athletes. Perhaps as the female athlete strives to overcome the social barriers, she develops increased self-confidence and security. In short, either more psychologically secure females enter sport or they develop this ego-strength through participation. Furthermore, with the liberalizing and broadening of the sex roles in the last decade, the social and psychological costs of participation are probably disappearing with a concomitant increase in rewards and recognition.

Earlier research has documented that sport participation for males can have positive academic consequences. Snyder and Spreitzer (1977) replicated this research to determine whether the same pattern holds for females. Table 10-8 reports findings from their study concerning the relationship between athletic participation and academic orientation among a sample of high school girls in Ohio. The findings show that the female athletes tended to have higher grade averages and educational goals than their nonathletic counterparts. The data in Table 10-8 also permit a comparison between the girls who were involved in athletics and those who were seriously involved in music. Athletics and music are parallel socialization experiences in the sense that they both require self-discipline, commitment, coaching, and performance. The findings show that the girls who were involved in both sport and music had higher grade averages and educational goals than the girls who were involved only in athletics or music. When comparing those girls who were involved solely in music with those involved solely in athletics, the athletes tended to report slightly higher educational goals but had slightly lower grade averages. Thus, as with male athletes, female participation in athletics need not have a deleterious effect on academic performance.

TABLE 10-8 Summary of Means for Educational Expectations and Grade Averages According to Extracurricular Participation of High School Girls

	SPORT AND MUSIC	SPORT ONLY	MUSIC ONLY	NEITHER
Educational expectations	15.3	15.0	14.9	14.5
Grade average	6.2	6.0	6.2	5.9

Source: Adapted from Snyder and Spreitzer, 1977, p. 51; grade average was measured by an eight point scale ranging from "A" to "D−."

THE FEMALE ATHLETE AND GENDER ROLE SOCIALIZATION

As we noted earlier in this chapter, the traditional orientations toward female involvement in physical activities may be viewed as a form of sexism. This type of discrimination is transmitted via the socialization process. That is, the expected behavior associated with one's gender is learned as a part of the culture, and thus it feels appropriate and normal. One particularly interesting study relevant to this topic focuses on the informal learning that occurs in play activities of children. Janet Lever (1978) has highlighted the levels of complexity in children's play activities with particular attention to the way in which play contributes to the learning of attributes such as division of labor, differentiation, heterogeneity, and rationalization. Her basic premise is that the play activities of boys are more complex than those of girls and thus there is differential access to the social skills and attributes that are requisite in work roles later in life, especially at the executive and professional level. A summary of some sex differences in the play activities of children are displayed in Table 10-9. It is evident that there is greater complexity in the boys' activities on all six dimensions. Lever suggests that a significant aspect involves the explicitness of the goals in play and games. Interestingly, 65 percent of the boys' activities were competitive games as compared to only 37 percent of the girls' activities; in "other words, *girls played more* while *boys gamed more*" (p. 476).

TABLE 10-9 Sex Differentiation on Six Dimensions of Complexity in Play and Games

DIMENSIONS OF COMPLEXITY	GIRLS (%)	BOYS (%)
1. Number of roles (three or more roles)	18	32
2. Interdependence of players (high interdependence)	46	57
3. Size of play group (four or more persons)	35	45
4. Explicitness of goals (game structure)	37	65
5. Number of rules (many rules)	19	45
6. Team formation (teams required)	12	31

Source: Adapted from Lever, 1978, p. 476.

The Lever study substantiates the notion presented in Chapter 6 ("Attitudinal and Behavioral Concomitants of Sport Participation") that sport participation is a means of developing attitudes, skills, and values. In this respect, the differential participation in complex games and sports gives males an advantage in acquiring these characteristics. Though we do not suggest that sport is the only activity in which these qualities can be learned, males have traditionally grown up with more opportunity to engage in competitive games and sports than females. Perhaps this pattern is part of the more general tendency for males to engage in risk-taking and adventure-seeking activities than females (Zuckerman et al., 1978). Those attributes are probably not biologically determined; rather, they are engrained in the cultural expectations prescribed for gender. In short, males in most societies are more likely than females to grow up with the physical and mental risks of athletic competition. They are familiar with the immediate feedback in the form of success and failure. In our society, they learn that even the best batters can only hit a baseball about one time out of three. Perhaps the fear of failure is less traumatic, and one is ready to risk failure with the corresponding possibility of a high "pay off." The person who has struck out or double-faulted thousands of times has also experienced the satisfaction of a crucial hit or serving an ace at match point.

In Chapter 3 we outlined the values associated with the institution of sport and the manner in which these values are expressed in athletic slogans. Sage (1980c) listed several common slogans that reflect an emphasis on winning in sports and studied the responses of collegiate male and female athletes' responses to these slogans. Table 10-10 indicates that the male athletes were more likely to stress the importance of winning than the female athletes. For example, in the first slogan, 48 percent of the male athletes agreed that "winning isn't everything, it's the only thing"; whereas, only 16 percent of the female athletes agreed with this statement. In general, even the males do not take an extreme view toward the winning orientation; however, within the athletic subculture, the variations between the sexes suggest that the socialization process for males is more "professionalized," serious, and competitive than for the females.

TABLE 10-10 Orientation Toward Sport by Male and Female Collegiate Athletes

		STRONGLY AGREE (%)	AGREE (%)	DISAGREE (%)	STRONGLY DISAGREE (%)
Winning isn't everything, it's the only thing.	Males*	10	38	42	10
	Females	2	14	49	36
Show me a good loser and I'll show you a loser.	Males	11	23	44	22
	Females	5	10	38	47
Defeat is worse than death because you have to live with defeat.	Males	2	15	54	29
	Females	0	7	38	55
It isn't in the winning but in the taking part in sport which is most important.	Males	30	41	24	4
	Females	52	36	10	1
It isn't whether you won or lost, but how you played the game.	Males	21	52	24	3
	Females	45	47	6	2

*N = 497 male athletes and 268 female athletes; the number of responses differ for each item due to missing values.

Source: Adapted from Sage, 1980c, p. 359.

From a sociological perspective, the physically active female violates the traditional gender role expectations. We might view the female athlete as a liberationist because she has freed herself from the traditional gender role insofar as she has become involved in sport. Indeed, the mass media have often portrayed the professional female athlete—Billie Jean King, for example—as the prototype of the women's liberation movement. A number of reasons are frequently cited as the rationale for the continued prohibition of female participation in sport. Most of these reasons are of questionable validity, and in some cases they are outright falsehoods.

Dr. Dorothy Harris, a prominent physical educator who has researched the biological and cultural factors of sport performances, has pointed out several myths regarding women's athletic performances (cited in Wexler, 1979).

Size and Weight Factors

Females respond and adapt to exercise and physical training in much the same manner as males, in spite of being on the average five inches shorter, 30 to 40 pounds lighter, and ten percent fatter than males. The differences that have been observed between men's and women's athletic performances, says Harris, are influenced more by non-biological factors than by biological ones. When physical fitness levels are equalized, there are more differences in athletic ability within *one* sex than between the sexes.

In most sports, larger, faster, and stronger individuals win out over smaller, slower, and weaker ones. That there is much overlapping of the sexes somewhere around the middle between the two extremes of these characteristics is factual and should not necessarily be surprising. It has too long been assumed that the female who is large and powerful and who is successful in putting the shot got to be large and powerful as a *result* of putting the shot, rather than because she was genetically endowed with the physical characteristics necessary for success in that event. If participation in sport does alter one's physical characteristics, says Harris, then all those who wish to be taller should play basketball. (All basketball players are tall; therefore playing basketball must make one grow taller, goes the fallacy.) This and similar types of flawed logic, maintains Harris, have contributed a storehouse of myths and ignorance about female athletes, including the belief that women athletes are more "masculine" than "feminine."

Effects of Body Fat

The average untrained college male has 15 percent body fat; his female counterpart has 25 percent body fat. Of 78 female distance runners, 12 were found to have less than ten percent body fat, while 32 had less than 15 percent. Though Harris concedes that genetics may play a part in an individual's having low body fat, she believes that high intensity, endurance-type exercise enables females to approach the relative fat values of males.

The female's body fat gives her advantages in some activities. A woman swimmer is more buoyant in water and has better insulation against cold. This combination has made it possible for women to better world records in long-distance open-water swimming. Cynthia Nicholas, the 19-year-old Canadian woman who swam the English Channel round trip in 1977, knocked ten hours off the male's record. Joan Ullyot, a medical doctor and marathoner, believes that women "run off their fat," giving them an extra source of energy. While the biochemical mechanics have not been isolated, there may be a difference in the way males and females adapt to strenuous endurance-type exercise.

Strength Differences

Dr. Jack Wilmore of the University of Arizona, a sports medicine expert, has found that though the average male has greater shoulder and trunk strength, leg strength is nearly identical for both sexes. Women gain strength with training in much the same manner as men, although women do not gain as much in visible muscle bulk. In 1977, a 114-pound female broke the males' lift record in that weight class by lifting 225 pounds.

Menstruation and Athletic Stress

Any kind of stress, including athletic competition, may produce a decrease, or occasionally cessation, of menstruation. Under stress of athletic competition, males, too, have hormonal changes that decrease their fertility. Thus there may be a relationship between athletic stress and infertility in both males and females.

It is no longer believed that during menstruation women lose hemoglobin, the substance in the blood that combines with and makes oxygen usable by the body. The fact is that women have made and improved upon their own top performances during all phases of the menstrual cycle.

Exercise and Bone Maintenance

Why is osteoporosis (decreased bone density resulting in easy fracture) more prevalent among women? During the years when bones are developing and growing, Harris explains, girls are not generally socialized to participate in vigorous exercise. If they exercised as strenuously as boys, and continued to exercise regularly throughout adult life, such athletic stress would result in stronger, denser bones as they mature and grow old.

Sweat Rates of Males and Females

Studies show that males sweat sooner and more profusely than females in response to increased body temperatures. But this apparent advantage of the male in dissipating heat is balanced by the female's ability to adjust her sweat rate more efficiently; that is, she can compensate for the observed differences. Both males and females acclimatize to work or exercise in heat, but females are able to do so without increasing their sweat rates. Before a female begins to sweat, her body temperature must be two to three degrees higher than a male's sweat point temperature. And because the female generally has more active sweat glands than the male, her sweat is distributed more evenly over the body for maximal cooling by evaporation, compensating for her smaller body surface.

Predisposition to Injury

When training and conditioning are equal, male and female athletes appear to be about equally disposed to injury. Statistics suggest that females are more vulnerable to leg and knee injuries. But again, the level of physical conditioning and fitness is more critical than gender in predisposition to injury. As increasing emphasis is placed on early conditioning of female athletes, the injury statistics correlate more closely with the type of sport played than with gender. In short, individuals who play the same sport—say basketball—will experience similar types and rates of injuries, regardless of whether they're male or female (pp. 38–39).

The refutations to these stereotypical statements further illustrate attempts by women to free themselves from the social controls of traditional role prescriptions and thereby redefine and broaden the range of behavior that is available and acceptable for them. Because the female athlete is breaking with traditional norms, we might wonder about the extent to which this nontraditional posture spills over into other aspects of the gender role—for example, in the realms of family, work, and male-female relationships. More specifically, do female athletes tend to be traditional or modern in these areas? By "traditional" we mean the role of the woman that carries with it the notion of remaining in the home and fulfilling nurturant and subordinate functions to her husband and children. In contrast, the "modern" orientation may be described as a broader and less dependent role behavior that incorporates employment outside the home for material gain, personal achievement, and self-satisfaction. Snyder and Kivlin (1977) studied the responses of collegiate athletes and nonathletes to a set of questionnaire items designed to measure orientations toward the female role in the family and employment outside the home.

Table 10-11 indicates the relationship between athletic participation and gender role orientation. One would expect that women who assume a liberated stance in sport would also assume a similar position in other areas of life. Such a finding was not supported by the Snyder and Kivlin (1977) study. On all eight items, the female athletes registered more traditional responses than the comparison group of nonathletes. This pattern is surprising because participation in highly competitive athletics by females is often considered deviant and contrary to the traditional gender role. Apparently the nontraditional role of the woman in athletics does not spill over into all aspects of the gender role. In short, the "traditional/modern" gender role orientation seems to be situationally specific. We emphasize, however, that more research is needed to develop conclusive explanations of these processes and their behavioral consequences. In the meantime, we should be cautious in accepting assumptions concerning the female athlete as an archetypal women's liberationist.

TABLE 10-11 Perceptions of Female College Athletes and Nonathletes Toward Aspects of the Female Sex Role

	PERCENTAGE WHO AGREE	
ASPECTS OF THE FEMALE SEX ROLE	ATHLETES	NONATHLETES
The major responsibility of a wife is to keep her husband and children happy.	70	56
Women who want to remove "obey" from the marriage service don't understand what it means to be a wife.	27	19
I believe that a woman's personal ambitions should be subordinated to her family.	50	33
One of the most important things a mother can do for her daughters is prepare them for the duties of being a wife.	39	34
Successful careers and successful homes are not likely to work out for most women.	19	16
It goes against nature to place women in positions of authority over men.	26	21
Women should not compete on an equal basis with men for all jobs.	43	25
A woman loving another woman cannot be as fulfilling a relationship as with a man.	90	80

Source: Adapted from Snyder and Kivlin 1977, p. 26.

FROM PLAY DAYS TO TITLE IX

During the nineteenth century, Victorian ideals created a dilemma for collegiate women. Physical exercise was often deemed necessary by the administrators of colleges and universities in order to develop the stamina of female students so they could withstand the rigors of college life. For example, the first president of Smith College pointed out in 1875 that

> we admit it would be an insuperable objection to the higher education of women, if it seriously endangered their health. . . . We understand that they need special safeguards. . . . With gymnastic training wisely adapted to their peculiar organization, we see no reason why young ladies cannot pursue study as safely as they do their ordinary employments (cited in Gerber, 1974, pp. 49–50).

By the beginning of the twentieth century, sport had become a central part of the physical education curriculum for women. However, most female physical educators were strongly opposed to intercollegiate athletic competition.

One of the popular means of providing participation in sport without the feared consequences of varsity athletics was the development of "play days." During play days, women from several colleges would meet for sport and recreational activities, but the participants would be mixed so that the teams did not represent a particular school. By the middle 1930s, about 70 percent of the colleges participated in play days for women. During the 1930s a modification of the play day, the "sports day," developed (Gerber, 1974).

The sports day allowed competition between the teams representing their respective institutions. However, various strategems were employed to soften the competitive thrust. For example, only "pickup" games were allowed in which the players did not know beforehand in which sport they would participate. Also, winners were sometimes not announced, and scores were occasionally not recorded. Game rules were also altered to make the contest "more feminine." Nevertheless, the sports day represented a big change from the play day in that opportunity was provided for the expression of physical skills.

Intercollegiate varsity sport was opposed by the majority of female physical educators, and this was reflected in their professional organizations. In 1923 the Women's Division of the National Amateur Athletic Federation was formed, and they soon adopted a creed that expressed the philosophy of maximum feasible participation for college women to the end of fostering health, physical conditioning, and good citizenship (Schoedler, 1924; cited in Gerber, 1974). This creed explicitly criticized an elitist approach to intercollegiate sports among women as well as any exploitation of female athletes for purposes of spectator enjoyment. The repudiation of the corporate organization of sport is very contemporary in tone and reminiscent of the position expressed by current humanistic proponents of sport for sport's sake.

The policy expressed in the 1923 statement by the Women's Division of the National Amateur Athletic Federation was reaffirmed in 1957 by the Division for Girls' and Women's Sports of the American Alliance for Health, Physical Education, and Recreation. The 1957 statement reiterated the goal of broad-scale participation in sports for the maximum number of collegiate women. The need for extramural sport programs for women was also affirmed. Subsequent statements from the same professional association have reiterated the objective of intrinsically motivated sport participation among collegiate women and expressed a continued fear concerning the possibility of intercollegiate sport programs for women evolving into the corporate model characteristic of men's programs. It is interesting to observe that the humanistic approach to sport is still central in the official statements of associations involved with physical education and athletic programs for women. Some observers believe, however, that recent equal opportunity legislation might have an unanticipated consequence of subverting the humanistic posture because of the new resources that are becoming available to women and that represent a temptation to move toward the corporate model.

Equal Opportunity Legislation: Title IX

The primary impetus for change in school sports for girls and women has come from Title IX of the Education Amendments Act of 1972 which provides: "No person in the United States shall, on the basis of sex, be excluded from participation in, be denied the benefits of, or be subjected to discrimination under any education program or activity receiving Federal financial assistance." Further, the Education Amendment of 1974 instructed the Secretary of Health, Education, and Welfare to prepare and publish "proposed regulations implementing the provisions of Title IX of the Education Amendments of 1972 relating to sex discrimination in federally assisted education programs which shall include with respect to intercollegiate athletic activities reasonable provisions considering the nature of particular sports."

Prior to Title IX the opportunities for females in school-sponsored sports were extremely limited. Whereas skilled male athletes in high schools and colleges had a range of opportunities for participation, few were available for females. Girls' and women's teams were often denied access to athletic facilities because the practice sessions for male varsity sports were considered more important. At the collegiate level, women's sports were usually inadequately financed as club sports out of intramural or physical education budgets. The women athletes were often required to provide their own uniforms, use discarded varsity uniforms and equipment, pay their own way to athletic events, and raise money by bake sales and other promotionals. The primary problem and source of conflict in most schools is money, but the whole approach to female sports reflected remnants of the Victorian ideal of women.

The final Policy Interpretation of 1979 provides the guidelines on "equal opportunity" in intercollegiate athletics that is to be followed by the government in determining whether an institution is in compliance with the law. The Policy Interpretation is divided into the following three sections (Fields, 1979, p. 13):

1. Compliance in financial assistance (scholarships based on athletic ability): Pursuant to the regulation, the governing principle in this area is that all such assistance should be available on a substantially proportional basis to the number of male and female participants in the institution's athletic program.
2. Compliance in other program areas (equipment and supplies; games and practice times; travel and per diem, coaching and academic tutoring; assignment and compensation of coaches and tutors; locker rooms, and practice and competitive facilities; medical and training facilities; housing and dining facilities; publicity; recruitment; and support services): Pursuant to the regulation, the governing principle is that male and female athletes should receive equivalent treatment, benefits, and opportunities.
3. Compliance in meeting the interests and abilities of male and female students: Pursuant to the regulation, the governing principle in this area is that the athletic interests and abilities of male and female students must be equally effectively accommodated.

These guidelines do not necessarily require a college or university to spend an equal (i.e., per capita) amount of money on sports programs for men and women, nor do they require grants-in-aid be equal for men and women. For example, the financial aid given to a women's basketball team does not have to equal the aid given to the men's team. Furthermore, a school does not need to develop or upgrade an intercollegiate team if there is not a reasonable expectation of intercollegiate competition for that team. Compliance with these guidelines does not require a school to provide identical rooms and coaching staffs, but the crucial point is that the athletic programs provide equality of opportunity for each sex to participate in intercollegiate competition.

Equal opportunity legislation is forcing secondary schools and colleges to modify sports programs that were once reserved for males. Additional funds are being sought to expand athletic programs to comply with Title IX regulations. This has created new problems in higher education at a time when projected student enrollments are expected to level off, legislative support is limited, and the inflationary spiral is continuing upward. Faced with growing deficits partially created by the cost of complying with the federal regulations barring sex discrimination, some colleges and universities are being forced to eliminate varsity sports. Examples include the following (Paul, 1980, p. 1):

1. The University of Colorado dropped six sports: men's baseball, swimming, wrestling, and gymnastics, and women's swimming and gymnastics.
2. Yale University dropped men's volleyball, gymnastics, and water polo, and women's volleyball.
3. Colorado State University dropped men's swimming and gymnastics, and women's gymnastics.
4. The University of California at Berkeley dropped men's wrestling, volleyball, and golf.

Some schools are eliminating athletic grants-in-aid for nonrevenue sports and restricting travel. In spite of these reports of athletic programs being cut back, an NCAA report found that, since the academic year of 1978–1979, the number of men and women's collegiate sports have actually increased (*Chronicle of Higher Education*, November 3, 1980, p. 2). Regardless of the long term consequences, these new federal guidelines can be seen as a long overdue opportunity to alleviate discriminatory practices. If sports meet desirable educational goals for males, similar opportunities should be available for females. Utilizing the perspective of the conflict theorist, if the redistribution of resources threatens the favored position of male sports, this is a natural result of societal trends. What will be the ultimate consequence? It is likely that litigation and social adjustments will continue for some time. Questions of equality often come from unexpected quarters. One such case involves possible discrimination against high school girls in areas of the country where "girls' rules" are still used in basketball. In girls' rules there are six players on a team, and each player can only dribble twice before passing or shooting the ball. Furthermore, the girls generally play on one side of the center line or the other. These rules were instituted because at one time the regular rules that applied to basketball were deemed too strenuous for girls. How can one say there is discrimination with girls' rules? Suppose an outstanding high school female basketball player seeks an athletic grant-in-aid at a university; her ability to compete for this aid may be reduced because she has not had the opportunity to play basketball under the rules of intercollegiate basketball. This inequality of opportunity is highlighted by the probability that she will not have developed "an all around game" under the girls' rules, that is, dribbling, offensive, and defensive skills. The irony is that in Iowa, one of the states where this issue has arisen, the sport of basketball for girls has a long and glorious history, generally rivaling the boys' game in popularity. In a societal context, these issues of equal opportunity for females may turn out to be more revolutionary than mere redistribution of power and resources within athletic programs of educational institutions. The ultimate consequence might be a transformation of the overall female role. Comes the revolution! "*Vive la difference*" might now be interpreted as sexism.

CONCLUSION

This chapter discussed research on the female athlete. The data indicate some continuation of the Victorian ideal that defines sport as an inappropriate activity for females. Given this role conflict, one might expect that female athletes would experience psychological stress; however, the research findings reveal no deleterious effect. In fact, the female athletes in these studies are basically secure and adjusted in terms of their femininity, psychological well-being, self-image, and academic orientation. Perhaps a selectivity factor operates whereby the girls who are the most secure with their own identities can handle the traditional stigma of female athletics. Also, even though female athletes have experienced some discouragement, their participation has apparently been sufficiently rewarding to counter the social costs of participation. Furthermore, with the broadening of sex roles, alternative roles are increasingly available; women who have developed a sense of autonomy and self-esteem may be better able to select their roles with more freedom of choice.

As the old myths are dispelled and the traditional expectations crumble, the liberation of females for participation in sports has become more evident. For example, in 1970–1971 about 62,211 high school girls participated in track and field; in 1978–1979 the number was 430,266. Likewise, in 1970–1971 approximately 294,000 high school girls participated in all interscholastic sports; in 1976–1977 the number had increased to 1,600,000. These figures are symbolic of the changes that have also occurred at the collegiate level, where under the impact of Title IX educational institutions have opened up opportunities for females to engage in athletics. Similar increases in female participation in leisure sports such as running in road races and marathons have been evident in recent years. Perhaps social change has already advanced to the stage at which the symmetry of sex roles requires a social redefinition of the consequences of athletic participation for women.

CHAPTER 11
The Black Athlete

In the preceding chapters we have discussed several aspects of social stratification and sport—including gender. Race is another criterion used for social evaluation and for the determination of social status and prestige. Thus, race is important to the social scientist because of how it is socially interpreted (it is a social construct) rather than for its biological characteristics. A commonly held assumption is that sport represents the one segment of society in which members of minority groups have an equal opportunity. For example, although the proportion of blacks in the United States population is approximately 12 percent, in the last 20 years they have become heavily overrepresented in such sports as basketball, football, baseball, track, and boxing. Nevertheless, anecdotal as well as empirical data suggest that subtle forms of discrimination still occur in the world of sport. Discrimination within the larger society inevitably spills over into sport. For example, Pearman (1978) analyzed the content of the sports pages of a local newspaper and the coverage given to two local colleges, one predominantly white and one predominantly black. Press coverage of the sport events at the two schools was uneven, and particularly evident was the lack of photographs of black athletes and the unfavorable placement of articles on sports at the black school. Is this a form of discrimination against the students at the black school? Are black children in the community being deprived of photographs that would provide role models in the form of prominent black athletes? Apparently the unequal news coverage is explainable in terms of the interests of the majority of the readers. The majority group wants news about white athletic events. Another example comes from an analysis of what announcers say about white and black players on televised National Football League games (Rainville and McCormick, 1977). Based on a content analysis of sports broadcasting, the announcers showed a greater tendency to mention negative, off-the-field behaviors on the part of black players as compared to white athletes.

Furthermore, the on-the-field actions of the black players were more likely to be described in unfavorable terms than the actions of whites. According to the researchers, these descriptions were explained as a convenient form of stereotypical thinking and prejudicial attitudes. These subtle forms of discrimination in the media suggest the need to examine further the theoretical relationship between race and sport.

REPRESENTATION OF BLACKS IN SPORTS

The large numbers of black athletes relative to their percentage in the general population and the prominence of black superstars support the image of sport as the "land of equal opportunity" and as an avenue of mobility from the ghetto; however, the racial proportions vary by sport. Figure 11-1 displays selected sports and the approximate ratio of white and black athletes (see Kanter, 1977, and Yetman, 1980, for a similar typology). If we extrapolate from aggregate data, some teams are "uniform groups" (the proportion would be 100:0) or have only token minority members (a proportion of perhaps 85:15). The sports of gymnastics,

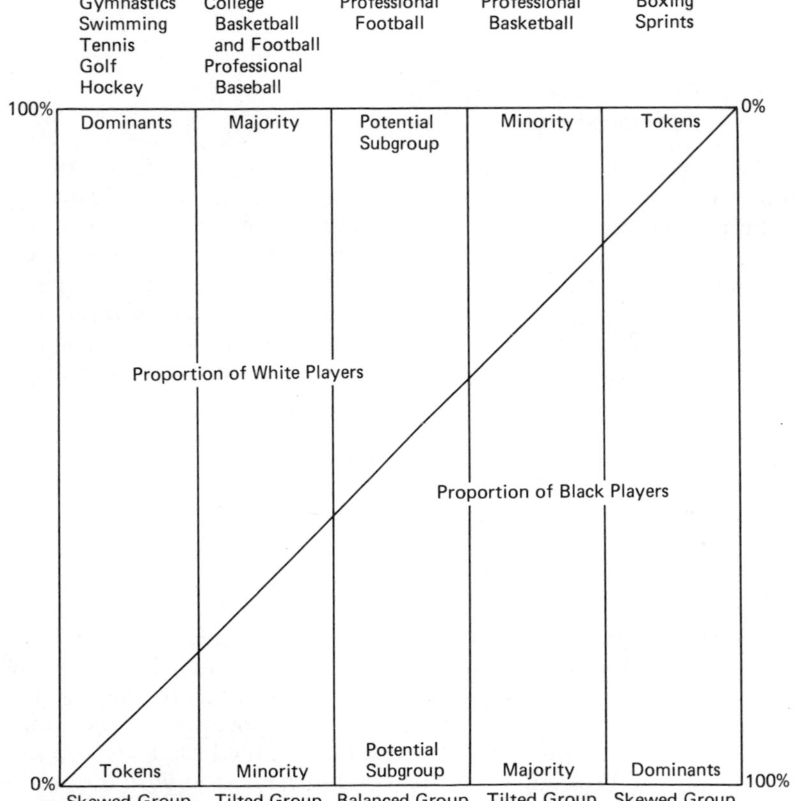

FIGURE 11–1 Proportional racial representation in selected sports.

swimming, tennis, golf, and ice hockey are uniformly white or contain only a token number of blacks. A "tilted group" has a ratio of about 65:35 and include sports such as college basketball and football; approximately 35 percent of the players in these sports are black. Professional football teams represent "balanced groups" where approximately 45 to 50 percent of the players are black, and professional basketball teams represent "tilted groups" where about 65 percent of the players are black. On the other hand, boxing represents a sport where whites represent a small minority. These percentages are approximations, and the proportion of blacks and whites will vary with the specific team; however, we find these aggregate data useful in conceptualizing the framework presented in Figure 11-1. This framework of proportional representation has heuristic value in visualizing interaction patterns between majority and minority groups both within teams as well as within the sport as a whole. It should also be noted that the proportional representation may, in time, shift from one racial group to another. Thus, during the 1950s and 1960s professional basketball not only began integrating blacks but the proportion ratio has moved from a uniformly white sport to a "tilted group" in which the majority of the players are black. However, in the sports of professional baseball and football, this race relations cycle has apparently stopped short of tipping toward a black majority. We shall speculate about the reasons for these proportions later in this chapter.

Proportional Representation: Interactional Consequences

The value of studying black and white proportions in sport stems from the fact that numerical modifications are significant in group interaction (Simmel, 1950). For the present analysis we do not deal with the absolute numbers, but rather with the relative proportion of blacks and whites. The following discussion is admittedly speculative and has yet to be studied empirically; however, some of the issues are guided by previous research on the relative numbers of males and females in industrial contexts (Kanter, 1977). The proportional representation of blacks and whites are considered in terms of three aspects of interaction—visibility, informal interaction, and role performance.

Visibility. When the first members of a minority group are integrated into a sport, they are particularly visible and their behavior takes on added symbolic significance. For example, under these circumstances they are subject to extra scrutiny, conversation, questioning, and gossip. Breaking the "color barrier" may force the token minority person or persons to restrict their behavior to a prescribed role that meets a particular image, stereotype, or behavior that is prescribed for minorities by the majority group. This heightened visibility is illustrated by the example of Jackie Robinson when he was the first black baseball player introduced into the National League. Branch Rickey, president of the Brooklyn Dodgers, took special care to select a black who could accept the taunts and indignities that would go with being the first black in the League. Robinson's success in this highly visible position was based on his ability to endure the taunts plus his outstanding athletic ability. This heightened visibility is illustrated by other examples of precedent-setting athletes such as Janet Guthrie the female auto racer and Jack Johnson the black boxer who became a heavyweight champion in 1908.

Informal interaction. With the admission of a minority member to a team, the informal interaction and conversation will be changed. The token member is likely to be on the periphery of the team socializing, excluded from in-group humor, and generally treated as an outsider. Because of the presence of the minority member or members, the team members are likely to be more guarded in their conversation that would be offensive or be misinterpreted. Also, the actions of the minority members, especially if they are tokens, will initially tend to be subdued and conventional.

Role performance. In the skewed or tilted group, in which the minority is underrepresented, the role performance is likely to be rigidly defined and constricted (a "role entrapment"). Jackie Robinson, for example, was expected to be a "model black." This requirement that the minorities be better than the majority has given rise to a subtle form of discrimination—equal opportunity for superior ability. On the other hand, when the proportional representation on the team is more balanced, the members of the racial or ethnic groups can assume more varied roles, and they have the social support from their own group that allows them to be more expressive and assertive of their subcultural style.

While we have speculated that the proportional representation of players on a team have important implications for social interaction on a team, we also assume that fan support will vary with the racial composition of a team. Perhaps the student body and alumni of a primarily white college or university will not identify as closely with a team that is predominantly black. Similarly, some white spectators of professional basketball may become disenchanted with teams in which the white players are tokens.

We do not know all the social dynamics that result in some sport contexts having a higher percentage of minorities than others, or why the proportion of the minority group shifts up to a point and then stops. No doubt there are a number of variables that need to be taken into consideration. In part, the differences are a result of the opportunity to learn a sport. For blacks, the game of basketball is a part of their urban subculture. They have ample opportunity to learn the game and they excel in it. On the other hand, ice hockey is less available to racial minorities, as are sports that require an extensive period of private club training at considerable financial cost, for example, tennis, swimming, golf, and gymnastics. Furthermore, the type of fans that patronize a sport may be a factor in the type of players recruited. Perhaps the majority and minority ratio in team sports also depends on the complexity of the game. Thus, football and baseball have a greater division of labor and specified roles than basketball. Consequently, the effect of bias against minorities playing some positions (i.e., "white positions") would limit the proportion of blacks on these teams. In the following section we focus on the issue of the patterning in athletic positions according to race.

STACKING OF PLAYING POSITIONS

Loy and McElvogue (1970) first explicated the stacking phenomenon by synthesizing two theoretical perspectives—the concept of centrality developed by Grusky (1963) and Blalock's (1962) propositions on discrimination. Grusky contended that the formal structure of an organization is based on three interdependent dimensions: spatial location, nature of the task, and the frequency of interaction. These dimensions are incorporated in the following statement: "All else being equal, the more central one's spatial location: (1) the greater the likelihood dependent or coordinative tasks will be performed, and (2) the greater the rate of interaction with the occupants of other positions" (pp. 345–46). Blalock's contribution was the development of a number of theoretical propositions concerning occupational discrimination. Two of these propositions were the following: (1) "The lower the degree of purely social interaction on the job . . . , the lower the degree of discrimination," and (2) "To the extent that performance level is relatively independent of skill in interpersonal relations, the lower the degree of discrimination" (pp. 245–46). Combining the concept of centrality with these propositions on discrimination, Loy and McElvogue (1970) hypothesized that racial segregation in professional team sports is positively related to centrality (p. 7). Thus, we would expect to find few blacks playing in the central positions.

In their analysis of football, Loy and McElvogue defined the central positions as quarterback, center, offensive guards, and linebackers, and in baseball the catcher, and infielders. Pitchers were excluded from the analysis because comparable data on the pitchers were not available; moreover, because they do not play every day, they might be considered part-time players. The rationale for defining these positions as central is based on the spatial centrality of the position on the playing field or formation, and the high degree of interdependency of these positions with other team positions (i.e., in football, handling the ball, leading the play, and in baseball, handling the ball, put outs, etc.). According to the Loy and McElvogue hypothesis, blacks will be underrepresented in these positions; in other words, they will be "stacked" in the noncentral or peripheral positions. This pattern of exclusion from the central positions could represent a form of discrimination. Tables 11-1 and 11-2 report the distribution of blacks and whites by central and noncentral positions in professional football (both offensive and defensive) and baseball. Although this distribution does not manifest complete segregation of blacks from central positions, they are notably underrepresented.

TABLE 11-1 Central and Noncentral Playing Positions in Professional Football by Race, 1968

	RACE	
POSITION	WHITE (N = 220) (%)	BLACK (N = 66) (%)
	OFFENSIVE TEAMS	
Central	45	6
Noncentral	55	94
	DEFENSIVE TEAMS	
	WHITE (N = 192) (%)	BLACK (N = 94) (%)
Central	38	6
Noncentral	62	94

Source: Adapted from Loy and McElvogue, 1970, pp. 12-13.

TABLE 11-2 Central and Noncentral Playing Positions in Professional Baseball by Race, 1967

POSITION	RACE	
	WHITE (*N* = 132) (%)	BLACK (*N* = 55) (%)
Central	71	35
Noncentral	29	65

Source: Adapted from Loy and McElvogue, 1970, p. 10.

Because these data were collected in the late 1960s, it should be noted that more recent research findings have generally been consistent with the original hypothesis (Scully, 1974; Dougherty, 1976; Leonard, 1977; Polack, 1980). For example, Leonard modified the original research procedure for professional baseball players by including an analysis of the playing positions of the regular players, including Latins, for the 1977 season. These data, displayed in Table 11-3, show the continued pattern of underrepresentation of blacks in the central positions of baseball; interestingly, the representation of Latins in the central positions is more similar to whites than the blacks.

TABLE 11-3 Central and Noncentral Positions in Professional Baseball by Race, 1977*

POSITION	RACE		
	WHITE (*N* = 111) (%)	BLACK (*N* = 68) (%)	LATIN (*N* = 26) (%)
Central	79	35	69
Noncentral	21	65	31

*Excludes nonstarters, pitchers, and designated hitters.

Source: Adapted from Leonard, 1977.

The continuity of the stacking phenomenon in football in the last decade is also substantiated by the findings of Eitzen and Yetman (1977) on professional football players; data on race and playing position are presented in Table 11-4. The determination of central positions is somewhat different than in the original Loy and McElvogue study (e.g., guards were added in the category of offensive line), yet it remains clear that racial stacking has continued in professional football.

Similarly, Schneider and Eitzen (1979) studied a sample of sixteen major university football teams in the 1978 season. Although these teams did not represent a true representative sample of all major universities, they did represent five major conferences, nine teams that were in the top twenty at the end of the 1978 season, and a total of 730 players. The stacking phenomenon is also present in collegiate football as shown in Table 11-5. Blacks are underrepresented in the kicker/punter, quarterback, offensive line, and linebacker positions. The stacking of blacks in the noncentral positions approximates the pattern in professional football and provides continued support for the original Loy and McElvogue hypothesis.

TABLE 11-4 The Distribution of White and Black Professional Football Players by Position (1975)

	WHITES		BLACKS		TOTALS
POSITION	*N*	%	*N*	%	*N*
Kicker/Punter	78	99	1	1	79
Quarterback	84	95	3	4	87
Offensive line	209	76	66	24	275
Linebacker	151	74	53	26	204
Defensive front four	107	52	97	48	204
Receiver	101	45	125	55	226
Running back	70	35	131	65	201
Defensive back	70	33	144	67	214
Totals	870	58	620	42	1490

Source: Adapted from Eitzen and Yetman, 1977, p. 5. Because 42 percent of professional football players in 1975 were black, this provides the dividing line for establishing whether blacks are overrepresented or underrepresented at a given position.

TABLE 11-5 The Distribution of White and Black College Football Players by Position (1979)

	WHITES		BLACKS		TOTALS
POSITION	*N*	%	*N*	%	*N*
Kicker/Punter	24	100	0	0	24
Quarterback	37	95	2	5	39
Offensive line	149	91	14	9	163
Linebacker	75	84	14	16	89
Defensive front four	72	59	49	40	121
Receiver	44	44	55	56	99
Running back	27	33	54	67	81
Defensive back	41	36	73	64	114
Totals	469	64	261	36	730

Source: Adapted from Schneider and Eitzen, 1979, p. 139.

Does the stacking phenomenon also occur in basketball? Initially it might appear that the concept of centrality would not be applicable because the specific division of labor, zones, and positions of responsibility are less evident in basketball than in baseball and football. However, Eitzen and Tessendorf (1978) have taken a different position. They argue that the positions in basketball do have variations in responsibility, leadership, and physical and mental demands. For example, one of the guards is usually the playmaker of the team—he sets the plays, provides leadership, and is the "floor general." The center is expected to handle the ball well, rebound well, block out opponents under the basket, and be a pivotal person in the offensive pattern, whereas a forward is expected to be quick, have good hands, and shoot well. In short, a good case can be made for specific zones of responsibility and differential competencies in the game of basketball. In this context, Eitzen and Tessendorf hypothesized that "blacks will be disproportionately found at the forward position because the essential traits required are physical rather than mental and underrepresented at the guard and center positions, the most crucial positions for leadership and outcome control" (p. 119). Their study utilized data from team brochures and the NCAA Official Basketball Guide for the season 1970–1971; the sample included 274 college and university teams. The expected proportions of players in basketball would be 40 percent at the guard positions, 40 percent forwards, and 20 percent centers. The findings from this study support the original hypothesis; the blacks were overrepresented at the forward positions (with 53 percent) and underrepresented at the guard (33 percent) and center (14 percent) positions (see Table 11-6).

TABLE 11-6 The Racial Composition of Playing Positions in College Basketball

	POSITION		
RACE	FORWARD (N = 1120) (%)	GUARD (N = 1110) (%)	CENTER (N = 499) (%)
White	36	44	20
Black	53	33	14

Source: Adapted from Eitzen and Tessendorf, 1978, p. 120.

Explanations for Stacking

In the original Loy and McElvogue (1970) study, the explanation for the stacking or underrepresentation of blacks in some team positions rested upon the spatial location of the position that was also linked to the interdependence and the interpersonal skill required of that position vis à vis other positions. Such positions were defined as central. However, Edwards (1973b) posits that spatial centrality is incidental to more important factors, that is, the relative importance of the position to controlling the outcome of the game and leadership responsibilities. In his view, the "factor of 'centrality' itself is significant only insofar as greater outcome control and leadership responsibilities are typically vested in centrally located positions. . . ." (p. 209). Accordingly, this explanation would rest on the assumption that coaches feel blacks tend to lack the ability, skills, and attitudes to meet the demands of the central positions in terms of fulfilling the responsibilities and leadership requirements that are directly related to the success of the team. This interpretation is also consistent with the stereotype thesis of stacking in professional football presented by Brower (1972): "People in the world of professional football believe that various football positions require specific types of physically and intellectually endowed athletes. When these beliefs are combined with the stereotype of blacks and whites, blacks are excluded from certain positions" (p. 27). Both the leadership and the stereotype explanations seem to be applicable to the underrepresentation of blacks in the sports of football, baseball, and basketball. In general, the "black positions" are considered less crucial in terms of decision-making, assuming responsibility, and leadership. Underlying these explanations is the assumption that white coaches, athletic administrators, and owners have a negative perception of blacks' ability; in short, they are discriminatory toward blacks by tending to place them in playing positions with less demand for leadership and responsibility.

In addition to this discrimination explanation, there are other interpretations for the underrepresentation of blacks in certain playing positions. One such explanation is based on the notion that blacks are socialized toward specific playing positions because in their youth they emulate black "role models," and the latter are disproportionately located in the noncentral positions (McPherson, 1975). Thus, the ratio of blacks to whites in playing positions that may have originated through discrimination is perpetuated through the learning of sport roles. In short, the black youth may segregate themselves as they are socialized into sports. Additionally, as they enter higher levels of competition, they may choose to play at a noncentral position, hoping to improve their opportunity to play in accordance with the white coach's stereotype of the abilities of black athletes.

Another explanation for the unequal distribution of blacks and whites at playing positions is based on inherited physical and psychological differences by race. In other words, according to this interpretation, there are some positions for which whites and blacks are "naturally" suited. For example, perhaps blacks are more adept at automatic and reactive types of physical actions that would be required in the forward position in basketball, that is, rebounding, shooting, quickness, or the speed and agility of a running back, wide receiver, or a defensive back in football. A number of studies have attempted to research this issue, but the results have not documented the notion of either blacks or whites having natural or endowed aptitudes to play particular positions (Curtis and Loy, 1978; Eitzen and Tessendorf, 1978; Phillips, 1976). A combination of the discrimination and socialization interpretations seems to be more valid. We shall return to the consideration of race and physical ability later in the chapter.

SOME CORRELATES OF PLAYING POSITION

The effects of the stacking phenomenon go beyond a mere cross-tabulation of playing positions by race. For example, among football players, about three fourths of the endorsement spots on television, radio, and newspapers go to players in the central positions (Eitzen and Yetman, 1977). This fact may be the result of advertizing agencies employing white players because they assume the market will identify more with white players. On the other hand, the central positions are often the focus of media coverage, and the players in these positions gain more fame, which provides the opportunity for making commercials. In either case, there are more financial opportunities in endorsements for players in the central positions. The opportunity for financial returns are also more limited for football players in the noncentral positions because their playing careers are shorter. We do not know whether the shorter careers are a result of discrimination against blacks in the latter part of their careers who have lost some of their skills or because of increased injuries to players in these positions, which require speed and agility. Whatever the cause or causes, Eitzen and Yetman (1977, p. 4) report that in 1975 only 4 percent of the players in the NFL in the positions of defensive back, running back, and wide receiver (predominantly black positions) were in professional football for ten or more years, whereas 15 percent of the quarterbacks, centers, and offensive guards (predominantly white positions) continued at least ten years. The shorter active career not only reduces the opportunity for earnings as a player, it also limits the accumulation of retirement benefits.

In Chapter 9 ("Social Stratification and Sport") we pointed out that one career opportunity for former athletes is in the coaching ranks. Although most coaches have been athletes, the percentage of coaches who are black is far less than the proportion of blacks in collegiate or professional sports. Whereas the proportion of black football players in the NFL between 1973 and 1979 increased from 36 to almost 50 percent, only about 6 percent of the assistant coaches in the NFL are black and there were no black head coaches in 1980. Similar statistics are evident in professional baseball, where the blacks have excelled for three decades, but there have been few black managers—Frank Robinson (Cleveland Indians in 1974 and San Francisco Giants in 1981), Larry Doby (Chicago White Sox in 1978), and Maury Wills (Seattle Mariners, 1980). However, in professional basketball, which is dominated by black players, as many as seventeen head coaches have been black in recent years. Few major college basketball and football coaches are black; most collegiate coaching staffs include at least one black assistant coach.

Because we have determined that blacks are underrepresented in central positions in several team sports and, furthermore, that a low proportion of the head coaches are black, it should not be surprising to find that there is a relationship between playing position and coaching position. In 1975 Massengale and Farrington (1977) analyzed biographical data on 869 head and assistant football coaches from major colleges and universities. The collegiate playing position of each coach was classified as being central or noncentral; quarterbacks, guards, centers, and linebackers were considered to be central positions. Although a minority of the playing positions in football are central positions (four of the eleven offensive and usually no more than four of the defensive positions), a majority of the coaches had played at a central position. Furthermore, 65 percent of the head coaches had played a central position. An examination of Table 11-7 shows that the coach's former playing position is related to the coaching hierarchy, with a slight majority, 51 percent, of the assistant coaches having played at a noncentral (peripheral) position. Although some of the assistant coaches will move up the coaching hierarchy, we assume this mobility will be selective and probably will reflect the importance of centrality. An obvious explanation for this differential opportunity in coaching positions is that, because the central positions are the leadership and decision-making positions, presumably these players have the potential for more successful coaching careers.

TABLE 11-7 Former Player Position of Major College Football Coaches

	CENTRAL (N = 460) (%)	NONCENTRAL (N = 409) (%)
Head coaches	65	35
Assistant head and coordinators	63	37
Assistant coaches	49	51

Source: Adapted from Massengale and Farrington, 1977, p. 113.

Similar data are available that demonstrate a linkage between the central positions in baseball and opportunities for becoming a manager. Scully (1974) reports that 68 percent of the managers in baseball between 1871 and 1968 were former infielders. Because few blacks played these positions, they did not have the same opportunity to develop the qualities considered important for the position of manager.

UNEQUAL OPPORTUNITY FOR EQUAL ABILITY

In the previous section we discussed the proportion of blacks that occupy central and noncentral playing positions in football, baseball, and basketball. Most researchers have concluded that some form of discrimination is evident in the pattern of exclusion of blacks from the positions of leadership and responsibility. Another probable form of discrimination that has been disclosed by several studies is unequal opportunity for equal ability; that is, blacks must be better than whites to be admitted and remain on athletic teams. For example, Rosenblatt (1967) studied the batting averages of professional baseball players from 1953 to 1965 and found that the black averages were about twenty to twenty-one percentage points higher than the white averages during this period of time.

Rosenblatt concluded

> The superior Negro is not subject to discrimination because he is more likely to help win games than fair to poor players. Discrimination is aimed, whether by design or not, against the substar Negro ball player. The findings clearly indicate that the undistinguished Negro player is less likely to play regularly in the major leagues than the equally undistinguished white player (p. 53).[1]

Eitzen and Yetman (1977) tested the "unequal opportunity for equal ability" hypothesis among collegiate basketball players. Table 11-8 presents the percentages of blacks among the top five scorers of their teams. These data, gathered on collegiate players from 1958 to 1975, show that the higher the scoring rank on the team, the greater likelihood it would be occupied by a black player. Between 1958 and 1970, over 60 percent of the black players were among the top five scorers on collegiate basketball teams. In summary, the Eitzen and Yetman research corroborates the Rosenblatt hypothesis in collegiate basketball as well as in baseball.

Johnson and Marple (1973) extended the unequal opportunity for equal ability hypothesis to professional basketball. Black players generally have higher

TABLE 11-8 Percentage of Blacks among the Top Five Scorers on Collegiate Basketball Teams

YEAR	PERCENTAGE OF BLACKS AMONG TOP FIVE TEAM SCORERS
1958	69
1962	76
1966	72
1971	66
1975	61

Source: Eitzen and Yetman, 1977, p. 12.

[1]Published by permission of Transaction, Inc. from TRANSACTION, Vol. 4, No. 9, Copyright © 1967 by Transaction, Inc.

TABLE 11-9 Experience and Performance Records of Professional Basketball Players by Race for the 1970–71 Season

EXPERIENCE	0–9 POINTS PER GAME		10–19 POINTS PER GAME		20+ POINTS PER GAME	
	BLACK (%)	WHITE (%)	BLACK (%)	WHITE (%)	BLACK (%)	WHITE (%)
Rookie	53	47	63	36	33	67
Two to four years	56	44	65	35	78	22
Five or more years	43	57	59	42	63	37
Total *N*	92	84	74	44	27	14

Source: Adapted from Johnson and Marple, 1973, p. 12.

scoring averages than the white players, which seems to support the "blacks must be better" thesis. However, they also found that among the marginal players (less than ten points per game) who are at least in their fifth year in professional basketball, only 43 percent are black, compared with 57 percent of the whites in the same marginal category (Table 11-9). This finding suggests that marginal white ball players are retained on the team longer than marginal black players. Thus, these data indicate that black players must be better to play and remain in professional basketball. As we pointed out in our discussion of professional football, the length of time one plays a professional sport has financial consequences for both present earnings and retirement income, as well as for potential careers in coaching.

If a black player must be better, is this evident when they are recruited for college? Yes, according to one study of the recruitment of athletes at a major university in the Big Eight Athletic Conference. During the 1974 recruiting year, Evans (1979) studied the recruiting procedures for football players at Kansas State University. Table 11-10 provides a comparison of the high school football experi-

TABLE 11-10 High School Football Experience According to Race

EXPERIENCE	BLACK (*N* = 25) (%)	WHITE (*N* = 66) (%)
Played more than two years on varsity teams	92	71
Played more than two years on first team	72	53
Received letters more than two years	88	57
Received recognition as little All-American	28	12
Received recognition on All-State team	80	58
Received recognition on All-City or All-County teams	72	52
Made first team on All-City or All-County teams	94	64

Source: Adapted from Evans, 1979, p. 4.

ence of the recruits and indicates that the black players had earned more high school athletic letters and more recognitions than the white players. In general, the black recruits were more experienced players even before they enrolled in college. More importantly, these data indicate that if a black wants to play on a predominantly white team, he must be a better athlete than most of his white teammates.

One interpretation of these findings is that coaches discriminate against blacks in their recruiting practices. A coach may recruit outstanding black players because he must do so to be competitive with other coaches who are recruiting black players. However, when he has filled his "quota" of blacks, he stops; thus the less capable black player is not recruited. This "quota" system may reflect the expectations of fans or alumni who might be critical of a team consisting predominantly of blacks. An additional explanation suggested by Yetman and Eitzen (1972) is that many black athletes come from high schools with inadequate academic standards. Thus, a coach will strive to recruit an excellent athlete with at least an adequate academic background; see cell I in the following diagram. Coaches no doubt also attempt to recruit an outstanding athlete who is a marginal student (cell II), or even a marginal player who is an adequate student (cell III), but coaches are least likely to recruit a journeyman player with a marginal academic background (cell IV). The journeyman black athlete is more likely to fall in the latter category because of a less advantaged high school preparation and thus is less likely to be recruited than the white athlete.

		Athletic Skill	
		Excellent	Marginal
Academic Background	Adequate	I (Recruit)	III (Recruit)
	Marginal	II (Recruit)	IV (Nonrecruit)

EXPLANATIONS FOR BLACKS' PARTICIPATION IN SPORT

Much of the discussion in this chapter has focused on the overrepresentation of blacks in some sports, their exclusion from other sports, and underrepresentation in certain playing positions. We have devoted some attention to the explanations for these findings; now in this section we shall present a more extended discussion of the two primary explanations. The excellence of blacks in some sports, particularly basketball and some track events, has been so superior that a persistent common explanation is that racial differences account for the variances in athletic performance. One viewpoint is that blacks are naturally superior based on the notion of a "survival of the fittest;" that is, the black athletes are the offspring of the fittest blacks who survived the trip from Africa and the slavery period.

Edwards (1973b) refutes the natural superiority argument by pointing out that the studies of racial superiority are based on nonrandom samples of elite black athletes. Furthermore, he counters the "survival of the fittest" theory with the argument that

> Sociological and demographic knowledge indicates that inbreeding between whites and blacks in America has been extensive, not to speak of the influences of inbreeding with various other so-called racial groupings. Therefore, to assert that Afro-Americans are superior athletes due to the genetic makeup of the original slaves would be as naive as the assertion that the determining factor in the demonstrated excellence of white pole vaulters from California over pole vaulters from other states is the physical strength and stamina of whites who settled in California (p. 198).

If the racial superiority theory is valid, we should find variations in performance based on the degree of "blackness." Yet, so far as we know there are no studies indicating that some physical skills such as jumping ability varies along a gradient of color from very dark to very light.

Another problem associated with studying the physical endowment theory involves appropriate samples. If we are interested in nonelite athletes, the wide range of differences within each racial group and overlap between them will not make any difference in performances in the general population. On the other hand, to study elite competitors who constitute less than one percent of the population, we would need very large samples of both athletes and nonathletes. This type of research endeavor has not yet progressed very far. To elaborate this point further, the dearth of black swimmers has often been attributed to a lack of buoyancy among blacks. Although there is some question about the validity of this argument, if it is valid it would hardly explain the lack of swimmers at the elementary and junior high school levels. Surely the selective process for identifying elite swimmers has not trickled down to this low level of competition. Parenthetically, the lack of buoyancy among blacks would hardly explain their absence on the diving teams. However, we hasten to point out that the factors that help explain the absence of black swimmers or divers in childhood (such as lack of opportunity to participate in swim clubs) will be important determinants of identifying elite swimmers and divers in later adolescence. This assumption is based on the fact that elite athletes will have had the early training experience. As noted earlier in the chapter, the racially linked physical explanation has not been verified by empirical data. Furthermore, as Edwards (1973b, p. 198) has pointed out, one consequence of the notion that blacks are superior physically is that it reinforces the stereotype of black intellectual inferiority. The more likely explanations for black performance are grouped under the broad classification of social and cultural reasons.

The position of a minority group in the overall social structure of society is an important determinant of how the members of the minority group are oriented toward the institutions of society, including sport. Although members of the lower class, which includes a relatively large proportion of minority group members, share the general values of society, "they have stretched these values, or developed alternative values, which help them adjust to their deprived circumstances" (Rodman, 1963, p. 209). Thus, their overall view of the world, significant others, and opportunity structure contain the potential for a different pattern of socialization into sport roles.

To provide some empirical support for the hypothesis that members of minority groups are differently socialized into sport roles, McPherson (1975) studied the backgrounds of ninety-six elite white athletes and seventeen elite black athletes who participated in the 1968 Olympic Track and Field Trials. Differences in significant others and the social situation between the athletes are outlined as follows:

> Compared to white athletes, the black athletes: (a) before high school, received more encouragement (positive sanctions) from the mother than the father, thereby suggesting that matriarchal domination is present; (b) before high school, considered their peers to be most influential as role models; (c) in high school, received the most encouragement to participate in sport from track coaches and peers; (d) more frequently reported that they had an idol in high school; and that the idol was a successful track and field athlete (100 percent of the blacks indicated that their idol was an athlete, whereas only 81 percent of the whites indicated that their idol was an athlete); and (e) in college, received the most encouragements from peers, track coaches, and the father. Compared to white athletes, the black athletes: (a) came from larger families (4.5 children compared to 2.4 children for whites); (b) were from a lower socioeconomic background (none of the fathers had a college degree whereas 25 percent of the fathers of the white athletes did); (c) were raised in large cities to a greater extent (56 percent to 29 percent); (d) were more involved in other sports before specializing in track and field; (3) were involved in track events at an earlier age (75 percent of the blacks were competing by the end of elementary school whereas only 25 percent of the whites were competing at this time; and, (f) developed their first interest in track in the neighborhood and home, rather than in the school as the white athletes had (McPherson, 1975, pp. 965–66).

Phillips (1976) maintains that athletic ability is equally distributed in all racial groupings, that motivation to excel is basically equal across races, but that unequal access to facilities, coaching, and organized athletic programs is the main cause of racial variations in sport participation. Basically, Phillips argues that black overrepresentation in boxing, basketball, baseball, football, and track and field is explainable in terms of differential opportunities. More specifically, blacks tend to excel in sports where the facilities, coaching, and programs are available in the public schools. Similarly, blacks tend to be underrepresented in sports that have a club nexus such as tennis, golf, and swimming. He concedes, however, that his "thesis fails to explain why blacks in track and field overwhelmingly dominate the sprints, high hurdles, long jump, and triple jump events while they are almost totally absent in such events as the shot put, discus, pole vault, javelin and long distances" (p. 50).

The prominence of black distance runners from Kenya contravenes the argument that blacks are genetically disadvantaged for distance events. The cultural aspect is also highlighted by the fact that Japanese constitute less than 1 percent of the American population but yet represent over 20 percent of the top judo competitors in the United States (Phillips, 1976, p. 46). It seems clear that subcultural variations, processes of social learning and role modeling, geography (no alpine skiers from Somali), and historical accidents (cricket in India from the British colonial influence) are explanatory factors for many of the observed patterns of sport participation across racial and ethnic groupings.

We have noted that sport is often perceived to be a sphere of society where all ethnic and racial groups have an equal opportunity. It would seem foolhardy for a coach in a competitive situation not to play the best performers, regardless of their racial or ethnic background; yet, several studies and journalistic accounts have documented that practice. It appears that sport reflects some of the discrimination found in the rest of society, but that the orientation of members of minority groups toward sport is the consequence of a differential socialization process into the sport roles. In reality, both the discrimination and socialization models are partial explanations of the differential sport behavior of the racial groups.

SPORTS FOR BLACKS: OPPORTUNITY OR FRUSTRATION?

One explanation for the success of blacks in sports is offered by Edwards (1973b), who argues that blacks, like whites, are taught to strive for that which is defined as the most desirable among potentially achievable goals (p. 201). Because the avenues of achievement in many occupational areas are limited to blacks, and because sport is one area that has been available, they have devoted a disproportionate amount of their talent and energy to sports. Whites, on the other hand, have many avenues of opportunity and a variety of role-models available to them. Accordingly, "black athletes dominate sports in terms of excellence of performance where both groups participate in numbers" (Edwards, 1973b, p. 202).

Sport, then, is an activity in which many black youngsters commit their time and energy; it becomes a part of their ethnic subculture, and the dream of making it to "the bigs" is held by many black youngsters. Furthermore, the few blacks that do make it to the big leagues provide ample fuel for these dreams. Interviews with black major league baseball players yielded the following responses to the question of "Do you feel that as a young man you focused future aspirations and channeled much of your energies toward a career in competitive sport, particularly baseball?"

> It has been an avenue for me out of the ghetto. Hadn't I played baseball, I would have probably finished school, but I doubt seriously I would be doing exactly what I wanted to do. Blacks just don't get an opportunity to do what they always want to do.
>
> . . . I think baseball has been a helleva education to me—to meet people, to come in contact with them, to see things as they really are and on different levels both financially, economically, socially, whatever. I could have never gotten this education in no institution nowhere. I know the value of it.
>
> No doubt about it. I feel by being a professional athlete has opened up a lot of doors whereas if I wasn't one probably people would not even look at me or sit down and talk with me.
>
> Very definitely. I escaped through sports. For poor Blacks there aren't many alternative roads. Sports got me into college and with college I could have alternatives. But, without sports, I would not ever have gotten into school. I liked sports. I had ability at baseball, so I've tried to make the most of it. It has given me a good life. I've worked hard at baseball to get away from the way of life I led growing up.
>
> . . . We have a nice apartment. I have nice clothes and a nice car. I like having money and I like spending it. I like luxury. When you get out of the ghetto, the good life is very attractive to you.

> Yes, I think so. It's helped a lot of Blacks. There ain't too much other things you can do. There are other things, but you don't have the finances to do it. All the white kids' families are pretty wealthy. They get a chance to go to college and get the best job. But Blacks—they don't have the money to send their kids to school to get an education and a good job (Nabil, 1980, pp. 62–63).

For these players the dream came true; however, as we pointed out in Chapter 9, many black athletes feel that the emphasis on sports can be a "jock trap" for blacks. That is, they devote so much of their time, energy, and ego to sport that they fail to develop other skills, particularly their academic aptitudes, that are important for other career possibilities. This trap is evident when examined in light of the following statistics regarding opportunities for professional athletes.

> In professional football, there were 1144 active players during the 1975–1976 season. Of those, 432 or 38% were black. In professional basketball, there were approximately 286 players during the 1976–1977 season, and of those, about 171 or 60% were black. In baseball, there were nearly 600 players on the rosters for the 1977 season and about 285 of the players were black. What these figures show is that at the present time, there are fewer than 900 blacks making their living in the three major professional sports. If we add to that number, the black professional athletes from other sports along with black coaches, trainers, and minor league baseball players, it is doubtful that it would be increased much beyond 1500. Since there are over 24 million blacks in the United States, this means that professional sport provides opportunities for 1 of every 18,000 (Coakley, 1978, p. 295).

Although these numbers may change slightly, they do not present an optimistic picture of opportunities in sport for young blacks. Indeed, as we have previously noted in Chapter 9, Arthur Ashe, a former black tennis professional, and Walt Frazier, a black professional basketball player, have advised black youth against committing themselves entirely to athletics.

In one sense, the black professional superstars provide misleading role models. Consequently, black youth are often successful in school sports and receive considerable praise and recognition. Yet, all but a very small percent are sorted out of the athletic stream and are left with an inflated athletic role that is inadequate for gaining employment; consequently, they feel frustrated, cheated, and hostile. Even among blacks who have had a measure of athletic success, the inconsistency between the praise they receive for their athletic skills and the social injustices they experience as a result of being black can leave them embittered (Olsen, 1968). They are likely to have the feeling that there should be an equity between their athletic status and their racial status.

Numerous examples can be cited to illustrate this inconsistency in recognition that is given to black athletes; we noted earlier the cases of Jack Johnson and Jackie Robinson. We could add to the list Paul Robeson, Henry Aaron, Lee Elder, Tommie Smith, and John Carlos, who broke barriers and gained recognition for their athletic excellence but who were caught in the bind of having their behavior narrowly prescribed (a role entrapment) because they were black. Additionally, some black athletes perceive themselves as marginal persons because they are not fully accepted by either the white or black communities. Thus, they may feel forced to live by the white man's rules and to "make it" in the establishment world lest they be viewed as "radicals" or "ungrateful blacks," yet among blacks they might be called "Uncle Toms." Black athletes have handled this dilemma in a number of ways. Some have been able to fulfill their athletic role and take the criticisms of their ethnic subculture. Others have tried to accommodate both roles and absorb the criticisms that come from both the athletic establishment and the black community. Finally, some black athletes have tried to escape the pressures by dropping out of sports completely. Perhaps none of these responses is completely successful, and we wonder about the long range physical and mental health consequences of this conflict experienced by black athletes (cf. Edwards, 1973a; Edwards, 1973b, p. 180; Eitzen and Sage, 1978, p. 239).

CONCLUSION

In this chapter we have examined the interaction between two major social phenomena—the status of blacks in our society and the social institution of sport. It is evident that participation of blacks in the sport world has been unique and requires analysis apart from the usual experience of white athletes. Presumably, further analysis might be extended to other ethnic groups, though the research in this regard is less developed. In some respects the consideration of the black athlete is an extension for the two previous chapters (Chapters 9 and 10). In this portion of the book we are focusing on the way our society ranks people on such criteria as wealth, power, prestige, gender, and race and the consequences of these rankings in the sport milieu. Additionally, this analysis incorporates the study of social change that is evident in shifting roles of females and minorities. Thus, the conflict perspective is often useful in analyzing contradictory values, roles, and subcultures, and the redistribution of power associated with these social phenomena.

The escalation of females and blacks in our consciousness through sports has also revealed other internal contradictions and conflicts within society. Some skeptics might argue that these changes only create more disharmony and violence. We do not take this pessimistic and deterministic view; more specifically, in our analysis of blacks in sports we find some evidence of improvement in the status of blacks in the sport world. Previous segregation has a variety of causes, but it ultimately is antithetical to a more humanistic climate in sports. When individuals "must live by the code or get out" merely because of their skin color, they are likely to feel frustrated and hostile. Hopefully, in some measure our presentation in this chapter has clarified certain patterns in sport that are not evident in the mass media. Although we do not expect that sport will be flawless when it is located within a societal framework of inequality, we do believe that increased understanding of the causes of social disharmony has the potential to produce a more humane environment within the world of sport.

CHAPTER 12
Structural Strains within the Coaching Role and Collective Violence

In this chapter we consider two aspects of sport that involve conflicting and ambiguous social expectations. On a personal level, coaches frequently find themselves in a situation in which contradictory expectations in their occupational role produces an inducement for deviant behavior. On a group level in sport, ambiguities and strain also develop that result in a breakdown of the traditional norms that structure people's behavior; under these conditions of structural strain collective violence may erupt. In the second section of this chapter we focus on some preconditions for collective violence in sport.

THE COACHING ROLE: STRUCTURAL STRAINS TOWARD DEVIANCE

In sociological terms, the concept of role strain indicates conflicting social expectations for a person holding a particular social position. We have already pointed out the conflicting expectations and ambiguities associated with the role of the female athlete and the black athlete. Coaches also frequently find themselves in a position of conflicting social expectations and strain (see Chapter 2 for the defense mechanisms used by coaches to cope with defeat). Conflicting expectations are common in other occupational situations; however, the strains in the coach's role involve inducements toward deviant behavior which facilitate success—a good win-loss record. Before analyzing the strain in the coaching role in more detail, we provide some background to coaching as a career.

As part of his analysis of occupations and professions. Everett C. Hughes (1971) defines a career as a "running adjustment between a man and the various facts of life and of his professional world. It involves the running of risks, for his career is his ultimate enterprise, his laying of bets on his one and only life" (p. 401). A career is defined as being broader than one's occupation; it should be viewed as a progressive adjustment of one's occupation throughout the life cycle. Careers may develop upward, downward, and shift from one route to another. As a consequence, the notion of "process" implies that a career often twists, turns, and passes through different stages that parallel the life cycle. One's self image, education, age, occupational preparation, family background, and other factors influence the career pathway.

In examining the coach's role within the framework of a career, there are several contingencies to consider—level of the sport (junior high, high school, college, university, professional), type of sport, and institutional context of the sport (degree of pressure on winning, type of contract). In general, a career in coaching achieves it highest level of prestige and monetary reward by advancing through the coaching ranks to the major university in a revenue sport and to the professional levels. Correlatively, the social pressures on the coach to produce winning teams are likewise greater, and the structural strains toward deviance are likely to increase.

At the secondary school level, a coach will usually also be a teacher; career evaluation is likely to be confounded at this level by the assignment of diffuse responsibilities. Nevertheless, at the high school level coaches are hired for the following reasons:

1. To reorganize the athletic program toward a reemphasis of the "major" sports
2. To win
3. To gain state ranking with the team
4. To bring new recognition to the school and community through winning and state ranking
5. To work for all-star and all-state recognition for some of the boys on the team
6. To satisfy the Booster Club
7. To win championships
8. To appease unhappy "barbershop quarterbacks" (Sabock, 1973, p. 95).

These goals suggest that sport in the secondary schools is moving toward formal sport, in which the emphasis is on winning and the social pressures mount to "win at any costs" even if it means "bending the rules." Furthermore, the criteria for hiring secondary school coaches and the structural strains imposed on the coach can be dysfunctional to the educational objectives of school systems. Consequently many coaches feel alienated from the values and life style of the academic community (Massengale, 1974).

With the progression to the more formalized levels of coaching (such as large high school, college, university, and professional sports), the evaluation becomes more focused and specific. The foremost standard for evaluation becomes the coach's win-loss record, and coaches of revenue-producing sports at major universities may be hired and fired on that basis alone. University committees and athletic directors who select coaches will, of course, consider the coach's organizational abilities, rapport with players, public image, knowledge and experience in coaching, and recruiting ability, but these constitute measures of the coach's presumed ability to win games. In short, at major universities coaches of football and basketball are not primarily hired for their character-building abilities.

The importance of winning enhances the gate receipts, the chances of profitable television coverage, and encourages the alumni to give money. For example, after the firing of Alex Agase, Purdue University's football coach, in 1976, the university's president cited the growing financial problems associated with maintaining a strong competitive role in intercollegiate competition. President Hansen praised Agase for his integrity and honesty, but his fourth consecutive losing season (18–25–1 overall) and attendance at home games had taken their toll (*Toledo Blade*, November 27, 1976, p. 7). Big-time sports are big business, and the scoreboard and turnstiles determine the career progression of coaches in these situations. This emphasis reflects the commercialism and performance orientation of formal sport in American society. It also approximates the emphasis placed on success in general in contemporary American society.

If a coach has a mandate to win a high percentage of his or her contests, this results in a considerable amount of strain and tension surrounding the coaching role, because few coaches can win all the time. Thus there is *limited control* with *complete liability* over the contest outcome (Edwards, 1973b). The limited control over the outcome of athletic competition reflects the indeterminacy of sport ("In this league on any given day any team can defeat any other team"). This indeterminacy results in the tension and excitement that make sporting events interesting at the same time as it makes coaches' jobs and future careers insecure and problematic. This strain sometimes erupts into verbal and physical outbursts by coaches; perhaps the confrontations of the former Ohio State football coach, Woody Hayes, with reporters, photographers, and players would be examples.

In the effort to win games and reduce the role strain, coaching procedures are utilized that are rational and irrational, legitimate and illegitimate. We have previously referred to the use of superstition and magic as irrational attempts to manage the unpredictability of sport and to reduce the gap between the controlled and uncontrolled aspects of the game. On the other hand, rational attempts to control the outcome of games include such methods as extensive game preparation, well-trained assistant coaches, motivation of players, and the recruitment of highly skilled players. These are logical, good coaching methods that contribute toward the achievement of a greater control over game outcomes. However, because there is seldom complete control over the outcome and the coach is ultimately responsible for defeats, there is the strain to do everything possible in order to win. Thus the structural strain inherent in the coaching role motivates coaches to use not only these rational and irrational procedures, but also illegal or deviant practices. These social processes can be illustrated as follows:

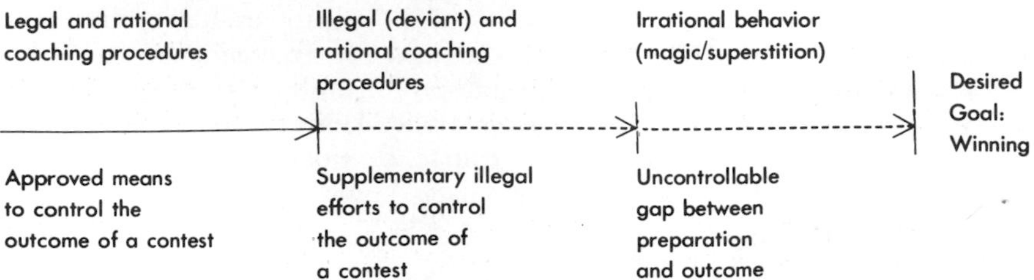

Deviant coaching practices are likely to emerge out of the strain and tensions of achieving the socially acceptable outcome—victory. The desired end sometimes serves to justify the use of *any* means, legal and illegal, rational and irrational. The coach who does not use illegal coaching procedures is placed at a disadvantage, a fact that provides a greater impetus to use these tactics ("everyone else is doing it"). Parenthetically, if a team's competitors are relatively weak, there is already a large measure of control over the game outcome (the "gap" is less) and consequently less likelihood of illegal methods being used. Moreover, sport is often a reflection of fundamental characteristics of the society. The administration of the Vietnam War, corporate business practices, and the revelations of Watergate suggest that deviant behavior to achieve desired ends is not peculiar to the world of sport.

The structural strain toward illegal but efficient means of improving one's chances of victory is only one of the modes of adaptation between ends and means discussed by Robert Merton (1938). In his essay, "Social Structure and Anomie," Merton suggests several distinctive patterns of relations between ends and means. The following paradigm utilizes a modification of Merton's scheme when applied to sport. In the conformity and retreatism forms of adaptation, the means and ends are consistent, while in ritualism the end is rejected and the means becomes the primary objective of the contest. In these forms of adaptation there is no strain or inconsistency. The primary focus of Merton's original essay was on the nonconformist mode of adaptation, which in our context is the desire for success or winning and the role strain that predisposes the coach to use illegitimate means to win. This does not mean that coaches are necessarily psychologically predisposed toward deviant behavior. The explanation for the behavior rests in the social structure of the coaching role.

MODE OF ADAPTATION	MEANS	GOAL	RESULTING BEHAVIOR
Conformity	+	+	Highly efficient and legal coaching; weak opponents; achievement of the goal by legitimate means
Nonconformity	−	+	Use of efficient and illegal or illegitimate coaching techniques to win; "win at all costs;" "winning is everything"
Ritualism	+	−	Emphasis on participation rather than winning in informal sport; "it's not whether you won or lost but how you played the game"
Retreatism	−	−	Rejection of the goal and means of sport; aversive socialization away from sport

The primary goal, a winning tradition, is the "product" being sold by a business organization, the athletic department. This is often not the desired objective of athletic directors and university presidents, but it represents the economic facts of life.

> In a special report for the November issue, the *Oklahoma Business* magazine took a look at the amounts the two state schools shell out for winning football.

> The amounts reported to the magazine by the respective schools for football were surprisingly moderate—$1.9 million in fiscal 1975–76 at Oklahoma and $1.6 million for OSU in the same period.
>
> However, both schools readily admitted that the amounts all depend upon which figures are listed under which columns.
>
> For example, all revenues from Big Eight TV and bowl games are lumped into the "general" category at OSU.
>
> So it is more accurate to look at the entire sports budget, which comes to $5.1 million at Oklahoma and $2.7 million at OSU.
>
> Football accounts for about 75 percent of the revenue at each school, with the remaining 25 percent coming from basketball, wrestling, and other sports.
>
> If you take the combined $7.8 million revenue at both schools, only 38 corporations in Oklahoma during fiscal 1975–76 had higher revenues (*Toledo Blade*, December 12, 1976, p. D7).

In the management of a major athletic department, an outstanding athlete is valuable "property." The NCAA allows a college player to receive a financial grant-in-aid in the form of books, tuition, board, and room. However, because the very best athletes are likely to eventually sign professional contracts, some are enticed to sign with an agent for additional financial support. This practice is strictly forbidden by NCAA rules prior to the completion of one's eligibility. The payments and services provided by the agents to the players must eventually be returned with additional legal fees at the time when the first professional contract is consummated, and thus some players become financially beholden to their agents. College coaches have also been offered money to encourage their players to sign with a particular agent. The extent to which college players sign prematurely with an agent is not certain, but professional scouts suggest that it is a common practice in college football, and "one college basketball coach said he thinks 50 percent of the blue-chip basketball players are paid by agents" (Lauck, 1977b, p. 11). Furthermore, it has been reported that "nearly 20 former and current college basketball coaches have said that they were offered money or other gratuities by agents to influence their players" (Lauck, 1977c. p. 17). Dean Smith, former Olympic basketball coach and the North Carolina basketball coach "said he was offered a bribe of $2^1/_2$ percent of a player's contract by a New York agent who wanted to sign one of his players" (Lauck, 1977a, p. 29). While payments by agents may not be controlled by coaches, the financial arrangements are clearly illegal by NCAA rules and represent a form of under-the-table payments for players who continue to be defined as amateur and who participate on a college or university team. The growth and development of professional sports and the possibilities of a lucrative contract provide the context and impetus for illegal deals with agents. This relatively recent development in collegiate athletics has led to penalties by the NCAA in several cases. Charles White of Southern California and Billy Sims of Oklahoma, both Heisman Trophy winners, have admitted to early signing with agents, but neither they nor their institutions were penalized because the violations were detected after they had ended their collegiate careers.

Major university players can also receive under-the-table financial support from alumni or others by selling their allotted player tickets. Harold Henson, a former All-American at Ohio State University is reported to have said it "goes on everywhere, including Ohio State" (*Bowling Green Daily Sentinel-Tribune*, November

13, 1976, p. 11).[1] Former Buckeye players Tim Fox and Rick Middleton supported Henson's allegation regarding the exchange of tickets for cash in violation of NCAA rules. Fox is reported to have said that players and assistant coaches traded season tickets for cars.

The area in which the coach or assistant coaches are most likely to resort to NCAA rule violations is in recruiting. In order to win consistently, coaches must have superior athletic talent. Other coaches are, of course, recruiting many of the same outstanding players. A "blue chip" high school player may be deluged by 200 college offers. Thus, "college coaches often become involved in bidding wars for the services of the most talented prospects. One inducement leads to another, then another—each subsequent one more attractive, and quite possibly, more unethical or illegal than the last" (Nixon, 1976a, p. 21) The illegal offers may come from alumni rather than from the coaching staff, and apparently coaches and alumni do not operate entirely independently of each other. The following case illustrates the range of violations uncovered at the University of Kentucky in 1976 by NCAA investigators.

> The NCAA said that two UK assistant football coaches made cash payments to players "for successfully performing certain plays" during games.
>
> The report also told of a booster who provided an athlete with an apartment for a year free of charge and loaned the athlete furniture for the apartment.
>
> In another case, the NCAA said, "A student-athlete, over a two-year period, received the benefit of alcoholic drinks at no cost to him at a local bar."
>
> Another athlete and his sister were given a free ride home in a private airplane, and the parents of some athletes were offered transportation to the school's football games.
>
> Other violations listed included:
>
> Entertaining a prospective athlete at a race track; arranging free motel rooms for parents of young men who were injured; providing recruits with as many as three free trips to the Lexington campus; transporting the father of a prospective basketball player to the school when his son paid an official visit; holding organized off-season football practices; selling complimentary tickets for away games and giving the money to athletes. . . .
>
> The NCAA report didn't distinguish between football and basketball violations, but the wording of the report indicates that at least 18 were in the football program and more than six were identified with basketball (Klein, 1976, p. 3).

Many of the violations in collegiate athletics are not clearly attributable to structural strain toward deviance among coaches. Some are an organizational type of deviance as discussed in Chapter 7. Nevertheless, the temptation to use deviant means (as defined by the NCAA) to achieve a desirable goal (recruiting outstanding athletes and victories) is evident in a series of recent NCAA rule violations. Numerous citations of improper inducements for prospective athletes and excessive recruiting expenses are apparent in the NCAA Enforcement Summary (Committee on Interstate and Foreign Commerce, House of Representatives, 1978). The cases cited involve excessive fringe benefits, clothing, cash, tryouts, use of credit cards, free loans, free transportation, and excessive entertainment.

Although the NCAA is likely to deal with these violations, the attempt by coaches to stretch their control over the uncertainty of games and to thus secure

[1]Reprinted by permission of United Press International.

victories has also led some of them to dominate their athletes' lives far beyond the athletic realm. The need to win sometimes leads the coach to assume (or presume) unquestioned authority over the players. Such domination by coaches over the lives of the athletes may make the athletes "feel like efficient robot-like machinery programmed to manufacture consistent victories" (Nixon, 1976a, p. 21). It is also in this context that coaches and athletic trainers may be enticed to play athletes who are injured and thus further aggravate their injuries "for the good of the team." Furthermore, in this unpredictable environment, there is the temptation for coaches and trainers to provide drugs such as amphetamines, pep pills, and steroids for hormonal manipulation. These drugs may stimulate performance and biologically engineer the athlete, but they are also physically and mentally destructive.

Although these strains on the coaching role are most evident in the revenue sports, they are likewise apparent in other sports as increased resources are put into them with the concomitant expectation that the coach will produce victories. Additionally, with the advent of Title IX (see Chapter 10) and the emphasis that is being placed on upgrading sports for females, we can anticipate similar consequences for those coaches. The amount of strain inherent in the coaching role tends to vary with the amount of resources diverted to the sport and the resultant expectations to produce results. Consequently, the structural inducements toward deviance will reflect these differential investments by the sponsors of the team.

COLLECTIVE VIOLENCE IN SPORT

Violence is regarded as a threat to society or subsystems in a society. It involves risk taking, a condition for fear, and a change in the usual pattern of social relationships (Neal, 1976). More specifically, violence is likely to involve the injury, damage, and destruction of lives and/or property. Collective violence, like other forms of social behavior, tends to assume a pattern that is subject to theoretical analysis and explanation.

Since the Boston Tea Party and the inception of the American Revolution, violence has been a recurring feature of American society. Slavery was maintained through overt and covert use of violence. The Ku Klux Klan conducted terrorism throughout many areas of our society well into the twentieth century. Immigrant and ethnic groups in the large cities found that the "melting pot" was not free of conflict. The labor movement has often been involved in violence to achieve the proclaimed rights of laboring men and women. In the frontier and rural regions of America, a "dead Indian was a good Indian," and the use of vigilantes, the "law of the gun," and lynchings were mechanisms of social control. More recently, in the 1960s we have witnessed the violence of the Vietnam War, assassinations, brutality directed at civil rights demonstrators, and urban riots. As H. Rap Brown said, "violence is as American as cherry pie."

These specific examples of social stress have been accompanied by fundamental social changes with reverberating consequences. Rapid population shifts to urban and industrial centers have had both social organizational and social psychological effects. The processes of urbanization, industrialization, and geographical mobility have ruptured traditional feelings of community and ties with family and religious institutions. In many ways, this underlying social transition contributed to the breakdown of the social "rules of the game." Values have changed and the traditional social supports are no longer available to many people. Thus the individual's sense of meaning, control, and purpose is no longer well defined.

With the decline of traditional forms of community, new sources of identification have arisen, including new forms of communal living, religious cults, meditation groups, and a nostalgia for the past. For many people, the rise of commercialized sport served as a means of generating new social meanings and identity. Thus athletic teams that represent high schools, colleges, universities, and cities are supported by dedicated and committed fans (from the term "fanatic"). This identification with a sport team may be psychologically functional as a compensation for the loss of community and social supports resulting from urbanization.

These social changes have had their social costs in the changing forms of work and the meaning of work. For many people, assembly-line work is not intrinsically satisfying. Work has become increasingly instrumental, and the "deprivations experienced in work are made up or compensated for in non-work activities" (Kando and Summers, 1971, p. 314). Sport and other forms of leisure may become means of "letting off steam" and reducing job tension in a leisure setting. For others, sport may also serve as a restoration of tension and excitement, a pleasurable contrast to the routinized aspects of their workaday life. Thus, sport may serve a compensatory function for people's uncertainties, disappointments, boredom, and monotony. This compensatory function of sport, coupled with the need for identification, is likely to result in spectators who demand excellence and vicarious success not available to them in other spheres of their life.

Although sport contests are, by definition, structured and rule-bound, they are played within a social context where the structure is tenuous and may be easily upset. As Lüschen has aptly pointed out, if "sport teams are points of identification with other systems, such as schools, communities, and nations, rivalries coming from other sources may be introduced into a sport contest and thus lead to . . . severe conflict" (1970a, p. 28). The source of rivalry between athletes and spectators may also be crystallized around racial, ethnic, religious, economic, political, or social strains inherent in a society.

The ethnic, economic, and political overlays of riots associated with sport contests are illustrated in the "soccer war" between Honduras and El Salvador in 1969. Prior to 1969, large numbers of people from overpopulated El Salvador had illegally migrated to rural, economically underdeveloped, and sparsely populated Honduras. This migration increased the friction between the two countries, and the Hondurans resented the economic superiority of El Salvador. Furthermore, there were frequent disputes over the ill-defined border between the two countries. In this context of international tension, riots accompanied all three World Cup soccer games between the two countries. The third World Cup game culminated in a severance of economic and political relations between the countries and the mobilization of military forces (Smith, 1975, p. 305). Other instances of economic, religious, political, and ethnic conflicts have been associated with sport-related riots among soccer fans in England, Scotland, and Italy.

Evidence indicates that crowd support for legal and illegal violence at athletic contests contributes to the escalation of tensions that may result in crossing the tipping point between an orderly continuation of the contest and the encouragement of violence. Smith (1976) reports that young hockey players generally perceive that their illegal behavior in hockey is supported by fathers, teammates, coaches, mothers, and nonplaying peers. Many fans demonstrate their greatest enthusiasm during fights between players. Furthermore, the build-up of tension and excitement is greatest when the teams are approximately equal in performance and the game outcome is important as, for example, in a league championship.

In short, athletic competition draws together participants and crowds under conditions in which the usual rules, norms, and division of labor are easily disturbed and thus lead to aggressive and violent confrontations. In sociology, the term *collective behavior* designates such relatively unstructured situations. Most examples of violence in sport would be classified as collective behavior, particularly unruly crowd behavior, riots, and aggressive behavior on the part of players and fans. These forms of behavior include the breakdown of socially structured behavior, emergent norms, and a relative absence of social control mechanisms. More specifically, violent crowd behavior is likely to include the following characteristics: (1) the situation involves many people in face-to-face contact with one another; (2) most of the behavior evolves in an unplanned fashion; (3) the crowd activity is transitory and short-lived; and (4) there is considerable cooperation among the crowd members (Berk, 1974, p. 7; see also Perry and Pugh, 1978).

Aspects of Sport That Encourage Violent Behavior

The fundamental ingredients for collective behavior are often present in sport contexts. Not only are sport situations conducive to hostile outbreaks, the mechanisms for social control are also tenuous. Objects of attack—opposing players, fans, and referees–umpires—are readily accessible. Basketball coaches are known to bait referees to provoke a technical foul in order to "fire up" the players and fans. George Allen, the ex-Washington Redskin football coach, admitted that "he had encouraged a free-for-all in 1966 while he was coaching the Los Angeles Rams—'just to get 'em going. Just to get 'em all together . . . Because unless you get 'em all together, unless you have that, you aren't going to be a winner. It's all part of winning' " (Tutko and Bruns, 1976, p. 16). Additional factors that may promote violence include creation of increased intergroup hostility by the news media, high expectations of team success, and conscious efforts to heighten crowd excitement ("spirit") through rallies, pageantry, cheerleaders, and school songs.

In hockey and football a great deal of violent behavior is considered a normal part of the game and is sometimes encouraged to promote gate receipts.

> The pros and cons of on-ice violence were even debated in the courtroom in 1975, when Boston's Dave Forbes was charged with aggravated assault with a dangerous weapon—his hockey stick. His victim was Henry Boucha of the Minnesota North Stars, who almost lost an eye when Forbes attacked him with his stick after they had scuffled on the ice. Forbes testified that Boucha was the real culprit, claiming that Boucha hit him with a "sucker punch" from behind, and that he felt he had to retaliate or Boucha would think "he could walk all over me." Fighting back, Forbes said, is an integral part of the game, taught to players as youngsters, and a player who doesn't fight back is an easy mark.

> Boston coach Don Cherry admitted that he may have contributed to the violent outbreak by his locker room talk before the game. "The pressure was really on," he testified. "We'd been losing games. We really had to win—it was an explosive game." He said he felt his job was in jeopardy. "The pressure was on me and if the pressure is on me, it's on the players." So he told them before the game: "If you don't get going, you're all going to be gone (to the minor leagues). It has always been my philosophy to win at all costs." He later added, of course, that he didn't motivate his players to injure competitors.
>
> Before the trial (which ended with no verdict), National Hockey League president Clarence Campbell defended fighting as "a well-established safety valve for players," and even as an essential ingredient for the economic well-being of the game. "If violence ceases to exist, it will not be the same game," he said. "Insofar as fighting is part of the show, certainly we sell it. We do not promote it. We tolerate it and we bring it under disciplinary control which we believe satisfies the public" (Tutko and Bruns, 1976, p. 17).

Even basketball, originally a "no contact" sport, has become physical.

> Vanderbilt coach Wayne Dobbs says flagrant violence is becoming all too common in Southeastern Conference basketball.
>
> "I sometimes feel that college basketball is becoming like ice hockey . . . the more blood, the better the show," Dobbs said.
>
> In a game here with Auburn last Monday, Vanderbilt freshman Mark Elliott suffered a gash in his scalp—that later took five stitches to close—after being elbowed by an Auburn player.
>
> A foul was called against the Auburn player, but Vanderbilt coaches contend a flagrant foul—which required ejection from the game—should have been called. The coaches have sent a game film to the SEC office.
>
> Also Monday night, a total of four players were ejected as the result of fights which broke out in games at Kentucky and Georgia.
>
> Dobbs said his criticism is not intended to single out any team, but focuses on the SEC as a whole. He added that Kentucky, which he considers the SEC's most physical team, has not been guilty of such violence with Vanderbilt.
>
> "They were physical when they beat us by 40 points at Lexington, but they didn't take a cheap shot all night," Dobbs said.
>
> "I'm for this kind of tough, aggressive play. I like to coach it. But when we take a kid like Mark Elliott and endanger his life by putting him on the basketball court in our conference, it's gone too far," the coach said . . . .
>
> Dobbs said SEC basketball is "10 times more physical than when I first came to Vandy seven years ago" (*Toledo Blade*, February 20, 1977: Sec. E, page 7).

Promoters are often willing to condone aggressive and violent behavior to provide the fans with the "entertainment" they want, and sports commentators encourage fans to focus their attention on the "physical" aspects of the game. Consequently, as fans are taught to expect violence, their tolerance for it increases. There is a danger that the desire for a "good fight" and "a lot of action" can easily lead to violence or mayhem. The tragedy of Darrel Stingley, former receiver for the New England Patriots football team, illustrates the need for regulation of physical violence. Jack Tatum, an Oakland Raiders' defense back, broke Stingley's neck in a 1978 exhibition game. Although Tatum was not trying to cause permanent injury, after the accident he wrote a book (*They Call Me Assassin*) in which he describes how to intimidate and hurt opposing players. Special promotional schemes such as free beer nights tend to draw fans to the stadium with extraneous motivation. For example, in the Summer of 1977, the Chicago White Sox promoted a "disco demolition night." Thousands of fans, many of them teenagers, were admitted to a doubleheader with a disco record and 98 cents; the promotional gimmick was to blow up the records on the field between the games. Unfortunately, the promotion backfired when fans began throwing records onto the field, and between the games a mob of 7000 spectators swarmed onto the Cominskey Park field and began tearing up the bases, setting fires, and destroying the batting cage; the second game was eventually called off. Other accounts could be cited of violent outbreaks between fans and players in hockey, football, and basketball. Collective violence spreads through the spectators as a form of contagion and is often initiated by player actions. Sport by its very nature is structured and regulated by rules that provide the framework within which tension and aggressive impulses are expressed. As defined by the rules, the game is concluded at a specified time; the hostility is resolved by the elation of the victory or by the agony of defeat. In any event, the tension is gradually dissipated; however, when the rules are disregarded the spectators may become confused as an aggressive mood becomes contagious. Basketball officials recognize the need to control aggression; when the game is getting "too physical," they call fouls more readily to re-establish control of the game. The rules maintain the structure of the game. When violence occurs in the playing area, it has the potential of spreading to the stands, where the fans become participants in the violence following the breakdown of the order of the game. Collective actions by fans pose a serious threat to order, safety, and property:

> ITEM: With less than a minute remaining in a game between the Vikings and the Cowboys in Bloomington, Minn., Dallas takes the lead on a disputed touchdown pass from Roger Staubach to Drew Pearson, virtually assuring a Vikings' defeat, and disappointed fans to go bonkers. One end of the field becomes a rain of whisky bottles, golf balls, beer cans, flasks; at the other, two police officers stop fights among drunks. A whisky bottle, lofted from the stands, strikes referee Armen Terzian in the head, knocking him semiconscious and opening his forehead. . . .
>
> ITEM: Chris Chambliss sends the Yankees into the World Series with a ninth-inning home run against the Royals. Fans pour onto the field, knock Chambliss down before he reaches second base, maul him at third base, practically prevent him from scoring. Then they proceed to tear up hundreds of feet of infield and outfield grass and the padding on the walls. . . .
>
> ITEM: Fans at Foxboro, Mass., descend onto the field after their Patriots beat the Jets, 41–7. Teenagers tackle friends and strangers. Beer bottles fly. An old woman is struck in the head by a bottle. Two men have fatal heart attacks; someone urinates on an ambulance attendant who is trying to save one of them by mouth-to-mouth resuscitation. Twenty-three people go to jail, 30 to the hospital (*Toledo Blade*, December 12, 1976, p. 3).

Collective violence often occurs at the end of athletic contests. Consequently, many urban high schools have been forced to play their games in the afternoons and in some cases in the absence of spectators. Games held at night are often the prelude to bottle throwing, assaults, looting, and vandalism under the cover of darkness.

One theory of aggressive behavior posits that the observation of, and participation in, aggressive activities has a cathartic effect by venting pent-up (some people would argue these are inborn) hostilities. To determine the merit of this theoretical assumption, Goldstein and Arms (1971) used behavioral measures of hostility among male spectators at a competitive aggressive sport (football) and at a competitive nonaggressive sport (gymnastics). The results indicated that hostility increased significantly after observing the football game, regardless of the desired outcome, while no such increase in hostility was found for those observing the gymnastics competition. One methodological difficulty of this study is the possibility that more hostile observers may be attracted to a football game than to a gymnastics meet. Nevertheless, the preponderance of evidence from other scientific studies indicates that aggression tends to produce more aggression rather than serve as a catharsis for its release (Fisher, 1976).

Leuck et al. (1979) replicated the Goldstein and Arms study with more research on spectator behavior at collegiate basketball games. They reported that males, college students, and irregular attenders tended to be more aggressive as spectators. A likely explanation for the higher level of aggression among males is that this form of behavior has traditionally been more socially acceptable with male than females; also basketball has been more associated with male than female participation. The reason why students had higher levels of aggression than nonstudents may be explained by the greater degree of psychological involvement and identification with the team by students. Because students are a part of the university, the team is a symbolic representation for them. Finally, the occasional attenders manifested higher levels of aggression than season ticket holders, which might be explained by the fact that season ticket holders attend each game and become accustomed to the stress of the game. An alternative explanation is that many of the students are not season ticket holders and, as we have noted, the students would be expected to identify strongly with the team. More importantly, Figure 12-1 indicates that the aggression level in each subgroup increases with the progress of the game. This finding corroborates the Goldstein and Arms study in contradicting the notion that sport events serve as a catharsis that reduces aggressive impulses.

Several field studies have identified the conditions that are conducive to collective violence at athletic events; the data suggest that the likelihood of collective violence increases with the addition of each of the following conditions:

1. High expectations of a team victory. This is frequently enhanced by the mass media.
2. Strong attachment to "their" team. The team attachment is increased if there are overlays of economic, political, religious, or ethnic characteristics. This is more important if the teams are traditional rivals.
3. High levels of tension and excitement. This collective excitement is often promoted by cheerleaders, bands, and the promotional staging of the contest.
4. Hostile acts between opposing teams and coaches are frequent, intense, and poorly regulated (for example, baiting of officials).
5. Game officials are perceived to be biased, lax, or incompetent.
6. Law enforcement officials seem hesitant, sparse, and ineffective (Nixon, 1976b, p. 27).
7. The occurrence of violence varies directly with the level of competition (junior high, high school, collegiate, and professional) and the importance of the game, as in a regu-

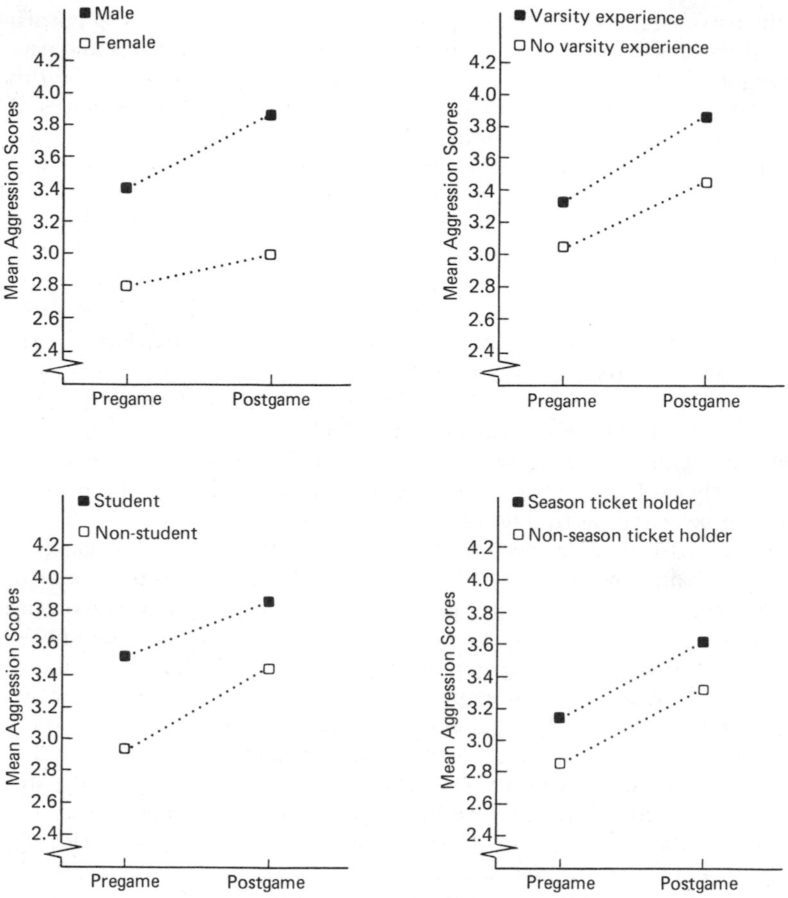

FIGURE 12–1 Pregame and postgame aggression levels of various subgroups (*Source:* Adapted from Leuck, Krahenbuhl, and Odenkirk, 1979, p. 47).

lar season game compared to an intense play-off or championship game (Lewis, 1977, p. 6).

Bryan and Horton (1976) conducted an extensive study of fan aggression associated with seventy-nine sport events in one university community in the academic year 1974–1975. Based on their data they offer the following hypotheses regarding the likelihood of collective violence:

1. Spectator violence and aggression will be more likely to occur during and after team sport spectacles than for individual sports. Spectators can more easily identify with teams than with individuals.
2. Spectator violence and aggression will be more likely to occur if and when the losing team becomes frustrated and aggressive. Anger causes anger.
3. Spectator violence and aggression will be more likely to occur when one or more of the competing teams is sponsored by a large school. Small schools provide more legitimate

opportunities for student self-display; urban spectators seek more strongly for individual identities in spectatorship.

4. Team members are likely to exhibit more violence and aggression if spectators are present. The presence of spectators changes the nature of the game from "play" to "display."
5. Spectator violence and aggression are more likely to occur at the end of a game rather than during its actual progress. The crowd, with no common focal concern, becomes a mob characterized by certain aleatory factors which contribute to aggressive outbursts.
6. Spectator violence and aggression are more likely to occur at homecoming games than during other, more typical contests. More time and effort are given toward the development of in-group solidarity and out-group hostility by the sponsoring schools.
7. Spectator violence and aggression are more likely to occur at games which are played between traditional rivals (for the same reason as number 6).
8. Patterns of spectator violence and aggression at college sports events will be similar to those which occur at high school games. "More education" is not a deterrant to fan aggression.
9. Spectator violence and aggression are more likely to occur when the competing teams are from neighboring communities or schools than when the schools are geographically separated. Propinquity contributes to rivalry, with certain exceptions (p. 23).

As part of a comprehensive study of fan behavior, Dewar (1979) analyzed factors associated with fights among spectators at professional baseball games. Thirty-nine fights were observed in nineteen of the forty games studied. The probability of a fight occurring was associated with the following factors:

1. Thirty-three of the thirty-nine fights took place on Friday, Saturday, or Sunday.
2. The majority of the fights occurred at night games.
3. Two out of three fights occurred when the attendance was 80 percent of the stadium's capacity or greater (larger crowds are also more likely on the weekends).
4. Most of the fan hostility took place in the bleachers and right field grandstand sections. These were the least expensive seats; this finding suggests that the socioeconomic status is associated with the fights.
5. The average number of fights was greater in June, July, and August and when the temperature was higher. Similar data from criminology indicate that physical assaults are more likely to occur in warm and humid weather. The implication of these findings is that irritability increases in hot weather.
6. Fighting is more likely in the late innings of the game. These are the "clutch" innings and thus the fans are more likely to be provoked to anger. No doubt the consumption of alcoholic beverages also contributes to the pattern of fan violence at the later stage of an athletic contest.
7. Twenty-four of the fights followed offensive rallies for the home team. Presumably the rallies contributed to rising expectations of a victory for the home team and increased the commitment of the fans in the late innings of the game. As noted previously, a deeper level of involvement in the game by the fans increases the probability of confrontations.

The associations cited in these studies do not warrant the conclusion that they are direct cause and effect relationships; however, they provide a starting point analyzing fan hostility and thus yield descriptive data from which theoretical frameworks can emerge. We outline several theoretical perspectives applicable to collective violence in sport in the following sections.

The Contagion Theory of Collective Violence

According to this theory, crowds initially show their agitation and volatility by "milling," the process wherein individuals become increasingly tense, uneasy, and excited. With increased excitement, emotion, and reciprocal stimulation, people are more likely to act impulsively under the influence of a common impulse or mood. If this process escalates in intensity, a *social contagion* stage emerges that involves a rapid and nonrational dissemination of a mood (Blumer, 1939). This social contagion stage often induces participants to become active participants in collective behavior. Furthermore, the collective excitement in a crowd may involve the process of circular reaction. Thus, when a person becomes restless, agitated, or excited these emotions and behavior become a model that influences others, and when one sees that other people have been influenced he or she in turn is further stimulated (Perry and Pugh, 1978). The mutual interstimulation results in a circular spiral of feelings and actions.

One precipitous and hostile incident that included fans and players occurred in 1972 at Minnesota University in a showdown game with Ohio State University for the Big Ten Championship. Reports of this contest emphasize how spectators can become an angry mob. Pregame warm-ups by the Minnesota team included demonstrations of ball handling, passing, and dribbling drills to the heavy cadence of rock music. This pregame showmanship was designed to "psych up" the team and the crowd. Observers report that these demonstrations served to build up tension and rapport in the crowd of over 17,700 fans. The game itself was played fiercely by both teams and remained under control until the final period. In the last twelve minutes, when Ohio State took the lead and the Gophers faced probable defeat, the crowd begin to throw objects on the floor in protest against the turn of events. The incident that touched off the riot resulted from a flagrant foul committed by a Minnesota player who then became involved in a fight with the player he had fouled. This scuffle set off a contagion of emotion that spread through the arena and ultimately included both teams and many members of the crowd.

The Convergence Theory of Collective Violence

Whereas the contagion theory is helpful in examining some crowd behavior and suggests that individuals are transformed into unruly crowd participants after being "infected" by social contagion, "convergence theory argues that the crowd consists of a highly unrepresentative grouping of people drawn together *because* they share common qualities" (Milgram and Toch, 1968, p. 551). For example, a high school athletic contest may bring together a large number of young spectators who are predisposed to engage in volatile and lawless behavior. Moreover, such an aggregation of spectators may include an unusually large number of males who are inclined to express their machismo through attacks on players, spectators, or officials. As noted previously, the disco demolition night in Cominskey Park brought together a unique crowd of spectators who were oriented toward destruction. Similarly, Marsh and Harré (1978) have analyzed the participants in British soccer riots. These fans consist primarily of young adolescents who are in the nonacademic track at school and who lack the opportunity for the development of a sense of worth and personal value in school or work. The peer network of the "football holligans" affords them an opportunity for a measure of success and prestige. Marsh and Harré argue that these riots are characterized by less violence and chaos than often portrayed in the British media; that is, much of their seemingly violent behavior represents ritualistic and highly stylized forms of machismo within a working-class environment of youth.

The Emergent Norm Theory

Both the contagion and convergence theories of crowd behavior contend that there is a "oneness" between individuals in the crowd. This unanimity is a result of a common impulse of excitement that "infects" the crowd (contagion theory) or the uniformity of background characteristics among the crowd members (convergence theory). On the other hand, Turner and Killian (1957) have proposed that the motive, attitudes, and behavior of individuals in a crowd are not uniform. Rather, common standards or norms *emerge* from interaction between the crowd members. The *emergent norm theory* emphasizes that collective behavior, like other forms of behavior, develops through social interaction and the emergence of social norms that apply to the situation at hand (Smith, 1975). Thus, different norms may emerge according to a particular time and place. This theory is not mechanistic and deterministic. In one situation, the emergent norm that guides fan behavior may be to harass the officials or opposing players; however, in another context a norm may develop that justifies the throwing of debris, bottles, and dangerous objects. This point has practical implications for crowd control; presumably sport events might be staged within a setting where seating facilities, traffic flow, public address announcements, and other situational arrangements can pre-establish norms or guide the emergence of norms that would deter aggressive behavior on the part of both fans and athletes.

Value-Added Theory

Although the three theoretical perspectives just discussed are different, they are not necessarily mutually exclusive. That is, the fans in an arena or stadium may have background characteristics that predispose them to volatile behavior (convergence theory); similarly, they may at a given time become emotionally aroused and communicate this excitement among themselves (contagion). Furthermore, there may emerge among the fans behavioral expectations (emergent norms) of how to respond in an ambiguous situation after they have become excited. Smelser's (1962) *value-added theory* is more comprehensive and incorporates several of the hypotheses from the theories discussed previously. Smelser's theory attempts to explain how broad societal conditions provide a foundation for violence. In his theory, the likelihood of violence increases when several factors come together; furthermore, as these factors are added, alternative possibilities are reduced. There are six determinants or stages in this process.

1. Structural conduciveness involves the general conditions that "set the stage" for collective violence to occur. Structural conduciveness may take a variety of forms; Michael

Smith (1976) lists four categories: (a) the presence of ethnic, religious, class, national, regional, or other cleavages; (b) the unavailability of alternative avenues of protest for grievances, or the unavailability of appropriate targets to blame; (c) conditions that are conducive to the rapid communication of hostile beliefs; and (d) the accessibility of objects of attack which determines whether or not an incident will occur and the form it will take (pp. 205–6). Sport contexts provide ample opportunities to observe these conditions. The fans and players of the opposing teams provide an immediate rivalry and a source of potential antagonism (for example, games between rival cities or countries). These rivalries may be more intense if there are social class, religious, or ethnic differences between the contestants. Other aspects of conduciveness for violence in sport include the physical characteristics of the setting–stadium or arena and the proximity of opposing fans, players, and officials.

2. Structural strain describes contradictions or ambiguities within various parts of society. The very nature of sporting events is that the outcome is unpredictable. Structural strain is evident when norms that define social interaction break down and new norms emerge. The strain is manifested in the ambiguity of which norm to follow (the old norm or the new norm). Structural strain is also promoted by a dissonance between what fans want to happen (a victory) and what actually occurs (a defeat).
3. Generalized belief is the emergence of an explanation for the structural strain—for example, "the lousy official," "that dirty player," "they threw the bottles." A generalized belief then emerges concerning appropriate action to cope with the difficulty posed by the structural strain. This stage will likely include contagion and an emergence of new norms.
4. Precipitating factor refers to a specific event or action that confirms the generalized belief, dramatizes its importance, and initiates the collective action. The precipitating factor must take place within the context of the preceding determinants of collective behavior. Precipitating events often include violent action by a player and unpopular decisions by an official (Boire, 1980).
5. Mobilization for action refers to the availability of people at the scene of the precipitating event for action. This mobilization would include the presence of crowd leaders and predisposed followers, the composition of the crowd, and physical surroundings that may influence the social organization of the crowd.
6. Social control mechanisms refer to the relative absence or presence of means of restraint. Such social control actions may include: a restriction of communication in the crowd so that continued action between leaders and followers is difficult; a decisive and an impressive display of force; and isolation of the area so that people can leave but not enter (Boire, 1980, p. 32).

The value-added perspective means that each of these determinants of collective violence adds its value to the preceding stage, thus increasing the probability (i.e., predictability) of collective disorder. With each additional determinant, the range of behavior is narrowed and funnelled toward a specific action that can only be halted by an effective social control. These stages are illustrated in the following diagram.

As we have suggested, the value-added perspective is comprehensive and incorporates aspects of other theoretical perspectives. Yet it is not a complete model of collective behavior because its focus is primarily on sociological determinants; clearly, psychological determinants are also relevant—each person may react dif-

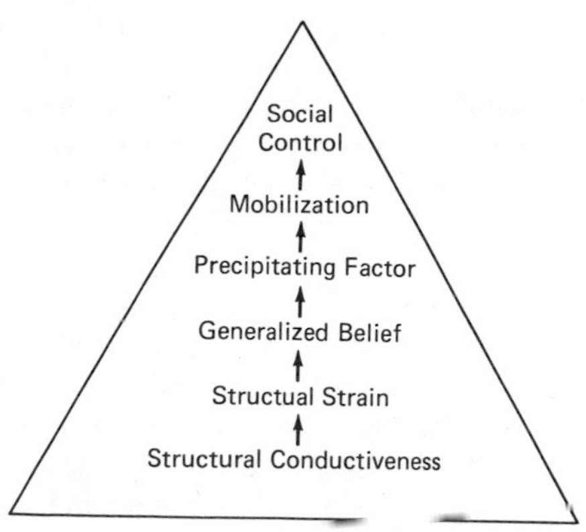

ferently to the specific situation, strains, emerging beliefs, precipitating factors, mobilization, and social control agents (Boire, 1980, p. 36). Nevertheless, the Smelser model does provide a framework for systematizing, classifying, and explaining many of the descriptive facts that have been accumulated from studies of collective violence in sports. Some of these facts were listed earlier in the chapter—for example structural conduciveness and strain will be evident when fans have a strong attachment to "their" team, when the teams are traditional rivals, when there is a high expectation of victory by both teams, when the contest is poorly officiated, when there is a baiting of officials, near the end of the game when the outcome is ambiguous, and when spectator involvement is high. Furthermore, a generalized belief about an appropriate action, a precipitating event, and mobilization can be seen in such examples as the Ohio State–Minnesota basketball game and in the disco demolition night at Comiskey Park.

In summary, we have considered collective violence in sport within a general societal context. In many respects, American society has a history of violence, particularly under conditions of rapid social change in which the norms and values are ambiguous or contradictory (structural conduciveness). In some respects the world of sport has probably become a compensatory area for social identification and meaning that is no longer available in the more traditional areas of family, religion, and work. The mass media have also assisted in the fans' identification with "their" team. These changes further enhance the probability of violence in athletic contexts. Some violence in sport seems to be a normal part of the game. Excessive violence between players seems to be a function of the liberalization of rules and rule interpretations, partly in response to the desires of the fans for action and to enhance the franchise owners' interest in increasing attendance. A more serious type of violence involves not only players but fans as well. When the "rules of the game" collapse on the playing floor, ambiguity may be expressed in the breakdown of norms within the arena and among the spectators. Under these conditions the basic nature of sport—that it is governed by the rules—becomes distorted. It is ludicrous to talk about sportsmanship when the total ambience of a particular sporting event bespeaks hostility and violence.

CONCLUSION

In this chapter we have considered two aspects of sport that are rooted in the ambiguities and structural strains of sport. On a personal level, we have looked at the stresses that impinge on the coaching role, which involves limited control but complete liability over the outcome of a contest. This dissonance creates a strain that may be alleviated by deviant behavior, that is, illegitimate and illegal attempts to gain an advantage over the opponent. In a broader context we have examined the controversial topic of violence in sport. By the examination of previous incidents of collective violence in sport, we can identify a number of factors that are conducive to violence. Moreover, these descriptive facts and examples can be embedded within the several theories of collective behavior. Smelser's value-added model is probably the most comprehensive theory of collective behavior and generally incorporates elements of the contagion, convergence, and emergent norm theories. Collective violence contains the potential to destroy the most fundamental and basic characteristics of sport. One might argue that deviant behavior and violence are the warp and woof of American society, and we should expect them in the athletic arena. We are reluctant to accept this argument; rather, we believe that continued analysis of these structural strains contain the potential for a better understanding and a modification of these conditions.

CHAPTER 13
Sports and the Mass Media

Prologue

Notre Dame's Cyclone Beats Army

Outlined against a blue-gray October sky, the Four Horsemen rode again. In dramatic lore they are known as Famine, Pestilence, Destruction and Death. These are only aliases. Their real names are Stuhldreher, Miller, Crowley and Layden. They formed the crest of the South Bend cyclone before which another fighting Army football team was swept over the precipice at the Polo Grounds yesterday afternoon as 55,000 spectators peered down on the bewildering panorama spread on the green plain below.

A cyclone can't be snared. It may be surrounded, but somewhere it breaks through to keep on going. When the cyclone starts from South Bend, where the candle lights still gleam through the Indiana sycamores, those in the way must take to storm cellars at top speed. Yesterday the cyclone struck again as Notre Dame beat the Army, 13–7, with a set of backfield stars that ripped and crashed through a strong Army defense with more speed and power than the cadets could meet.

This famous quote, originally published in the *New York Herald Tribune*, October 19, 1927, was authored by Grantland Rice, prototypical sportswriter and sportscaster of the 1920s and 1930s—the Golden Age of Sport. The emergence of the mass media, particularly the newspaper and radio, provided a rapid means of informing the public about the happenings in sport, and thus sport flourished. The commercial interests who controlled the mass media quickly realized that the reading and listening publics were interested in sport. Writers and broadcasters promoted both sport and the media by embellishing the games through the use of imagery, metaphors, and the creation of heroes—the Babe, the Gipper, the Manassa Mauler, the Four Horsemen, the Yankee Clipper, and the Galloping Ghost. Writers and broadcasters not only promoted sport into a major entertainment business in the 1920s through their creative use of metaphors and hyperbole, but they also served their own entrepreneurial interests by "selling" sport. In short, a reciprocal affinity developed between the mass media and sport.

SPORT AND THE MASS MEDIA: AN AFFINITY

This affinity between the image makers and sport entrepreneurs sold radio time and newspapers while selling sport to the public. In recent years this relationship has become more significant as large blocks of television time are being devoted to sport, with some of these events selling commercials at over $500,000 per minute. A symbiotic relationship exists between the mass media and sport that is beneficial to both social segments. Although this relationship may not be equal in nature (because it is more beneficial to sport than to the media), both the media and sport serve their own interests by protecting and promoting each other.

The symbiotic relationship between sports and the mass media is evident in the large chunks of broadcast time allocated to sports coverage and the generous coverage of sports news in daily newspapers. Visitors from abroad commonly remark that the newspapers in the United States, the bastion of capitalism, devote more space to sports affairs than to business news. In fact, "many metropolitan dailies now carry more news about sports than any single subject. If a man from Mars were to judge our interests from the space devoted to them in newspapers, he'd think that sport was our main preoccupation" (Klein, 1979, p. 18). It is estimated that about 30 percent of the persons buying daily newspapers do so primarily for the sports section (Edwards, 1973b, p. 4).

The link between television and sports is even stronger than with newspapers in the sense that television buys, supports, and controls sports events in subtle and not so subtle ways. Pete Rozelle, the Commissioner of the National Football League, suggests that "the spectacular rise in player salaries and in player employer benefits over the last decade or so is directly related to the entertainment value of the game—the money paid by TV rights" (Subcommittee on Monopolies, 1975, p. 49). Roone Arledge, President of ABC Sports, puts it more boldly: "So many sports organizations have built their entire budget around television that if we ever withdrew the money the whole structure would just collapse" (quoted in Runfola, 1974, p. 6).

Corporate sport has clearly become a branch of the entertainment industry and thus must put on a good show to remain financially solvent. Evidently, the television audience agrees that bigtime sport is good entertainment; the total number of network hours devoted to sports has increased dramatically from 650 hours in 1961 to over 1300 hours in 1980. Fortunately for sport, commercial money has been available to cover the escalating cost of television coverage. For example, the television networks had no difficulty in finding sponsors who were willing to pay $275,000 for a thirty-second commercial in the 1981 Super Bowl. The NBC network easily sold its twenty-three minutes of commercial time available in the telecast of the 1981 Super Bowl for a total of some $12 million. Small wonder, then, that NBC was willing to pay $6 million to the National Football League for the contract to broadcast the game. The size of the television royalties has increased so rapidly that the numbers soon become outdated and mind-boggling. For example, in 1978 the National Football League received $162 million from the networks for broadcasting rights.

Television is also critical for professional baseball. About 25 percent of the revenues in professional baseball comes from television contracts, including both network contracts and local affiliates. About 66 percent of major league baseball games are carried on television, approximately 1400 games out of a schedule of 2100 games. Professional baseball sells a national network package that includes the Saturday Game of the Week, Monday Night Baseball, the All-Star Game, the Championship Series, and the World Series. This contract is yielding $93 million over the period of a four-year contract for professional baseball.

Television contracts are even more critical for professional basketball. The National Basketball Association has a four-year network contract for $48 million in television rights. Each NBA team derives approximately $800,000 annually from its national contract; local television contracts yield an additional $100,000 annually for the average NBA team (Subcommittee on Communications, 1979, p. 2370). Television revenues represent the difference between operating at a profit or a loss for at least 75 percent of the teams in the National Basketball Association.

Sports and television have become so inextricably linked that it is difficult to separate the two in the mind of many passive consumers of corporate sport.

> Television needs sports, therefore, as much as sports need television, since both function as powerful socializers for the habit of passive consumption. Televised pro sports have become an advertising medium for *macho* related sports products like beer, cigars, cars and men's toiletries. Sports watching has developed to such a high degree that many fans are now passive participants and super consumers of sport and sport related products (Runfola, 1974, pp. 7–8).

Sports represent a particularly desirable form of programming for corporate sponsors because it is noncontroversial in the sense of politics or religion; sports coverage on television also delivers a desirable audience in terms of demographics—young, mobile, and upscale consumers. Moreover, conversation about sports represents a social lubricant, as a contemporary lingua franca, within the business world. Sports jargon permeates the corporate world and takes on significance as primordial metaphors—team spirit, the ball is in your court, get on the ball, the need to score, game plan, and so on. In brief, "televised sport has thus become little more than a vehicle for consumers. The exploitation of sports stars in the merchandising of products and the adaptation of commercial copy to the metaphor of sport are but two of the many devices advertisers use to establish fan identification with commercial products. The Olympic Games are particularly valued as a 'wholesome sales vehicle' for the peddling of goods and services because the fan views the games in a nationalistic frame of reference" (Runfola, 1974, p. 10).

DIFFERENCES AMONG THE MEDIA

The evolution of corporate sport is intertwined with the various stages of the communications revolution running from the print era through the electronic age. Each stage of the evolution represents a separate dimension of sports experience with its own sensory validity; each presents a different version of the sports contest and a unique information environment. David Voigt (1977) distinguishes four types of experience for the sports spectator: "The first is the game on the field and consumed by spectators in attendance; second, the game as displayed in newspapers and sport journals; third, the game as presented via radio; and fourth, the game as presented by television" (p. 3).

Using communications theory developed by Marshall McLuhan (1966), Voigt points out that the medium of print transmits sports information primarily through the eye with a linear imagery that offers the reader an illusion of individualization. The sports announcer on the radio, by comparison, is able to manipulate the feelings of the listener with a more direct and immediate communication. Thus, the radio announcer can be "a super *shaman*, a magical leader who evokes vivid sporting trances for eager fans" (Voigt, 1977, p. 13). With the onset of television, sports information is communicated in a multisensory modality with a nonlinear format; the TV viewer can become persuaded that he or she is a participant in the contest. "TV presents us with the problem of fusion, or con-fusion, between an imagined world and one we really believe exists" (Cummings, 1975, p. 74).

Interestingly, some sport purists eschew television coverage in favor of the softer medium of radio; they believe that radio stimulates more of the mind, imagination, and fantasy. The radio listener creates his own media event, albeit with the creative efforts of the announcer. Moreover, it is easier for the radio listener to conjure heroic images of athletes because one does not see favorite players on the screen spitting, pulling at their crotch, cheek bulging from tobacco, wiggling in designer uniforms, and other ignoble postures and behaviors. In addition, some fans take a hybrid position by combining radio announcing with silent television coverage in an attempt to get the best of two media.

It is interesting to note that the increasing popularity of television as a medium for sports coverage has *not* been at the expense of the sportspage in the daily newspaper; in fact, television seems to have fed the appetite of the sports fan for more personalized coverage of their favorite teams in the local newspaper.

> The expansion of the sports section was not curtailed by the growth of television. Instead, as with the advent of radio before it, television has *reinforced* rather than replaced the print media. We think it likely that the longer stories found in 1975 were providing details and expert commentary on events witnessed by fans the day before, and that TV coverage whetted fan appetites for reactions they could compare with their own. Similarly, the explosive growth of professional basketball's coverage on the sportspage was concurrent with the rise of basketball on television. Although some sportswriters feel that newspapers should respond to TV by moving into the open territory—the vast number of sporting events fans cannot see in their living room—those who want to sell papers continue to give attention to the big events that have largest fan appeal, even though those are the very same games covered by television. . . .
>
> The sportspage is a crucial part of this expanded role. The changed face of sport owes much to the revenues produced by television, but that medium is ill-suited to equip the sports fan with the detail he (and increasingly she) needs to follow favorite teams and to discuss their fate. There are too many teams, too many games, too much local variation for network television to fill the needs of the fan. It is the big city newspaper that provides the information for those endless arguments and debates on the

most frequently discussed subject at work or play. And it is only natural that in filling that need, the paper reflects the changing social reality of sport: an expanded role for sport in a leisure-oriented society, and for sport organized for nationwide competition between professional teams (Lever and Wheeler, 1978, pp. 25, 29).

THE SPORTSWRITER

Both corporate spectator sports and individual leisure sports took shape in the United States between 1870 and 1900. During this period, professional baseball and college football emerged as mass spectator sports while tennis, golf, and cycling were gaining popularity as recreational sports (Paxson, 1917). Sports reporting as a separate genre emerged during this same period; newspaper publishers, as always, were anxious to sell papers and thus covered the events that were deemed newsworthy:

> As sport grew, so did the sportspage. The big sporting events had always been covered by the press, but they were spasmodic: an occasional big fight, a championship crew race, or the leading harness race of the day. It was not until sport itself became more formally organized, with league competitions and routinized schedules of competition, that anything like a sporting *section*, as distinct from an occasional news story, was possible. But by the turn of the century, the leading newspapers were giving recognition to the growing interest in sport by organizing and routinely reporting sporting news. (Lever and Wheeler, 1978, p. 1).

Although sports reporting initially took the form of sensationalism, it soon took on respectability as an integral section of the newspaper. The size of the sportspage grew in size from 9 percent of the total paper in 1900 to about 17 percent by 1975 (Lever and Wheeler, 1978, p. 4). The role of the sportspage is seen more clearly when analyzed in terms of the ratio of sports news to other general news stories. In 1900, sports news comprised about 15 percent of all general news coverage; by 1975 sports coverage had increased to almost 50 percent of the coverage devoted to local, national, and international news stories (i.e., excluding comics, society page, entertainment, etc.). Research suggests that the sportspage has about five times as many readers as the average section of the newspaper (Lever and Wheeler, 1978, p. 5). The three dominant spectator sports of football, basketball, and baseball account for about half of the total coverage in the sports section of the current metropolitan daily. The salience of the sportspage reflects the general societal trends toward mass leisure and consumption.

The pre-World War II era is considered the Golden Age of sportswriters—Grantland Rice, Damon Runyon, Quentin Reynolds, Paul Gallico, Ring Lardner, and Bob Considine. Besides being superbly skilled as creative writers, they lived in a romantic, fantasy world. "They wrote as though athletes were gods descended from Olympus. Their athletes were always kind to small children and dogs, chivalrous to ladies. They won because their hearts were pure. . . . The gosh-wow school of writing remained in style for years and the hero-worshipping American public loved it" (Dolgan, 1977, p. 23).

This fantasy approach to sportswriting was eroded in the 1950s in the face of competition from television. A new realism became evident in sports writing. The big change occurred, however, during the societal unravelling of the 1960s. During this period, sportswriters tended to assume the posture that their subject matter was not really that significant in the bigger picture of life. "In their zeal over this discovery, this new school of humor writers, who came to be known as the chipmunks, mocked athletes and held everything they did in irreverence. They delighted in showing that successful athletes were often boobs in private life, and vice versa" (Dolgan, 1977, p. 26).

The radical school of sportswriting did not concern itself with the technical side of the game—statistics, analysis, and prediction; rather they turned to investigative journalism and life style reporting. It should also be noted that this critical approach to sportswriting in the newspaper was paralleled by a series of popular books about sports in a decidedly critical vein. In the late 1960s and 1970s, a number of books provided behind-the-scene accounts of the world of sport. When books by such writers as Jack Scott, Harry Edwards, Robert Lipsyte, Larry Merchant, and Leonard Schecter reached the public, they were criticized for being controversial and disloyal for exposing unsavory aspects of sport. This advocacy style of journalism generally exploited the disillusionment of some professional athletes while attacking the sports establishment. Furthermore, when conflicts developed between players and management over player rights, salary negotiations, and reserve clauses, the athletes found that writers can be a valuable means of taking their cause to the general public. It is commonly suggested that these writers exaggerated the controversies in sport in order to sell their books—perhaps the way magazines publish exposés of movie personalities to gain subscribers. Although it is likely that some of these writers engaged in exaggeration and hyperbole, traditional sportswriters have perpetuated the happy myths of sport to provide the public with what they want and thus sell newspapers.

During the last half of the 1970s, the chipmunks were eclipsed by a more conservative style of sportswriting. Even some of the leading lights among the critical newspaper writers, such as Wells Twombly of the *San Francisco Examiner*, swung to more conventional fare during the post-Vietnam era. The current posture is still realistic but is more optimistic; debunking is passé as an end in itself. It appears that the average reader of the sports page is more interested today in the nuts and bolts of athletic contests than in complex issues of political economy facing corporate sport:

> Contrary to the hopes of some and the fears of others, this increased coverage of professional teams has not been devoted to their social, business or political problems, nor even to the "human interest" side of sports reporting. The words and stories remain firmly anchored, as they have throughout the century, on players and their actions on the field. The complexities of collective bargaining, player contracts, tax incentives for management, and stadium construction and financing receive little if any more attention in 1975 than did the business side of sport earlier in the century. Of course there is a "new breed" of journalism and a critical literature on sport that is more visible now than in the days of Grantland Rice, but it remains of only limited significance in quantitative terms. In part this is a function of the severe demands for coverage of the vastly increased number of sporting events. . . . Sport remains an escape, an enjoyment, a source of relief from the minor aggravations and the boredom of everyday life. Although socially responsible journalism may require more detailed investigative reporting and the bringing of a more subtle and knowledgeable appreciation of the

> world of sport to its readers, there is no evidence of a growing public clamor for such reporting. And at least so far as the *Chicago Tribune* goes, the vast bulk of coverage remains focused, as it always has, on the playing field and the athletes who inhabit it.
>
> We noted that in some respects, 1925 and 1975 looked "more alike" than the intervening period. The so-called "Golden Era" of sport in the twenties has been reborn, though this time with more emphasis on professional team sports than ever before. Indeed, far from sporting interest cresting during the twenties, we are just now beginning to experience the full reach of sport, participant as well as spectator, into the life of the society (Lever and Wheeler, 1978, pp. 28–29).

Although the hatchet man is no longer prominent among sports writers, the perennial conflicts over what to report still remains. Is a story substantial enough to justify losing contacts for future stories and scoops? "The clubhouse syndrome, in which writers talk to padded lummoxes at length in hopes of picking up some nuggets of wisdom, may cost a lot of writers their independence. This could be the biggest stumbling block to objective, sophisticated sportswriting" (Dolgan, 1977, p. 36).

Sports journalists are dependent on the sports establishment for their "copy" in the sense that they need access to athletes, coaches, managers, team officials, and to back regions of the locker room and executive suite for scoops. This access rests in a delicate state of tension because the sports establishment views it as a privilege rather than a right. If a sports journalist is indiscrete in his or her reporting, this can be interpreted as disloyalty and thus result in a freezing out from the communication network. The negative response of the baseball establishment to Jim Bouton subsequent to his publication of *Ball Four* exemplified the response to writers who violate the sanctity of the clubhouse.

The sportswriter who takes the party line of the baseball establishment is called a "house man." A sportswriter spends many hours travelling with the team and fraternizing with club officials as part of the search for a good story. The tendency, then, is to be accommodating and agreeable, to write stories that will not displease the players or club officials, and in this way keep the channels of communication open. It should also be noted that there are other rewards for becoming a house man.

> When reporters become "house men"—the name for writers who almost always support a team's management—important stories are usually leaked to the "homers" first. Many teams still pay the reporter's expenses including meals and transportation in return for press coverage. Even if sports editors prevent the freebies, it is extremely difficult for sportswriters to remain objective when they socialize and travel with a team. Sportswriters tend to get emotionally involved because of this close association as members of the traveling sports family. This further serves the interest of management. According to Glenn Dickey, sports columnist of the San Francisco *Chronicle*, "Coaches and owners usually manipulate writers more by giving them the feeling of being on the inside than anything else."
>
> There are less subtle methods by which sportswriters are ingratiated by the sports establishment. Fringe economic benefits are often necessary because of the relatively low salaries of sportswriters. Accommodating sports teams keep regular writers in side money with program article and yearbook assignments. Some reporters even pick up pocket money by helping with play by play sheets. Friendly owners have also been known to show their appreciation to accommodating sportswriters (or sports editors) by a regular allotment of tickets and a generous Christmas gift (Runfola, 1974, p. 19).

The job of the sportswriter seems to be getting more difficult in the sense that sports celebrities are becoming more resistent to what they perceive as intrusions from the press. An increasing number of star athletes refuse to grant interviews, and a few teams have closed their locker rooms to journalists except for a brief period following a game. It might be conjectured that some sport celebrities have become enamored with the more glamorous medium of television and "believe that they have outgrown their need for their old 'contract' with the newspapers" (Klein, 1979, p. 18). The irony in this context is that sportswriters may have no alternative other than to feed the monster they helped to create.

THE SPORTS ANNOUNCER

The sports announcer has three constituencies to please in addition to the listener or viewer—the owner of the sports franchise, the corporate sponsors who buy the advertising time, and the owner of the television or radio station. In the best of all worlds, the sports fan will get interesting play-by-play coverage; the team owner will acquire new fans who are willing to buy tickets for home games; the corporate sponsors achieve more profit through increased sales, and the station owner is able to increase the demand from advertisers for air time. In the real world, however, sportscasters continually experience conflict in meeting the differing expectations of the four constituencies (Emrick, 1976).

Because sports announcers at the local level are commonly employed by the sports franchise whose games are being aired, there is inevitable pressure to be a promoter as well as a reporter. In addition to play-by-play commentary, the sports announcer is expected to plug upcoming home games, advertise regional ticket outlets, promote special events such as bat day or ladies' day, and push the sale of team souvenirs and yearbooks. This huckster role is commonly called "shilling." It might be noted in this context that Harry Caray had a contract when he was announcing the Chicago White Sox games that included a bonus for drawing fans into the stadium. In a national television interview, Caray noted that "the White Sox had a total attendance of 495,000 the year before I came. I had an agreement whereby I received $10,000 for every 100,000 fans above the 500,000 mark" (Emrick, 1976, p. 35). Given this commercial orientation, then, it is quite clear that the announcer's role is markedly different from the objective journalism of a reporter assigned, say, to the police beat.

In his book entitled *Kiss It Goodby*, Shelby Whitfield (1973) explains some of the pressures that he experienced from the owner of the Washington Senators when he was announcing their games during the 1969 and 1970 seasons. For example, the team owner was irritated if Whitfield made any negative comments on the air about the temperature or humidity on the day of the game. One club official even suggested that Whitfield fabricate favorable weather forecasts for upcoming games. Whitfield balked: "I've got to draw the line here. I've got a reputation to protect. You just can't expect me to go on and say the weather's going to be great when every forecaster in town, every newspaper, every radio station and every TV station is calling for a monsoon!" (p. 73).

Similarly, Whitfield was instructed not to announce scores of games involving rival teams and not to give attendance data when the crowd was unimpressive.

The team owner was particularly sensitive about the fact that the attendance for Senators' games was generally poor on Saturday afternoons. Whitfield recalls one Saturday game in May 1969 when the gate was 12,728 against a visiting team low in the league standings. It just so happened that this attendance figure represented a record Saturday crowd since the team had started nine years earlier in Washington:

> We duly reported this fact on the air, and Short raised hell. I had a message to call him after the game.
>
> "Look Whitfield. Don't ever say that a crowd of 12,728 is a good crowd."
>
> "Well, Bob," I said, "by comparative standards. . . ."
>
> "Look goddammit, I said it was a bad crowd! Don't say a thing about the crowd tomorrow if there aren't 25,000!" (pp. 74–75).

When the carrot was not sufficient, the team owner was not averse to use of the stick; Whitfield was instructed to back up the hearse in the sense of threatening that the franchise might be moved to a more appreciative city if attendance is poor:

> He wanted me to intimidate the Washington fans into coming out to the ballpark. "Tell those damn people in Washington that they had better get their asses out to the park or they won't have a club to watch." I'd balk. "Goddamn it," he'd continue. "I am telling you to say it, and if you don't, I'll get someone who will. I don't care what words you use or how you say it, but do it" (pp. 73–74).

The issue concerning house men or shills is more relevant to baseball announcers than football announcers because baseball is telecast through local affiliates (except for the Saturday Game of the Week), whereas in professional football the NFL signs a national contract with the networks. In this situation, an old adage sometimes applies—"Whose wine I drink, his song I sing." Runfola (1974) suggests that "house announcers have become as much a part of baseball as hot dogs and peanuts. There is a sprinkling of reliable announcers who inform rather than film-flam . . . but the vast majority of baseball announcers are little more than hucksters and apologists for the games they cover" (p. 25).

The case of Red Barber is an interesting exception in this connection. After some thirty-five years as a baseball announcer, Barber paid the price for candor in his reporting of the last game of the 1966 season when he asked the TV cameras to show the small number of fans (413) in attendance at Yankee Stadium. It was the smallest crowd in the history of the stadium, and a club official had instructed the camera crew not to follow foul balls into the stands. Barber commented over the air, "I don't know what the crowd is today—but whatever it is, it is the smallest crowd in the history of Yankee Stadium . . . and this smallest crowd is the story, not the ball game" (quoted in Runfola, 1974, p. 32). Four days later, Red Barber was fired.

The precarious role of the sportscaster is illustrated in a recent controversy involving the owner of the New York Yankees, George Steinbrenner, and Tony Kubek, an announcer for NBC's Baseball Game of the Week. Kubek had made some critical comments regarding Steinbrenner's treatment of Yankee personnel and his approach to ownership of a sports franchise. The Yankee owner was provoked when he read Kubek's comments in a Florida newspaper, perhaps especially because it came from a former Yankee player and a national telecaster. Steinbrenner responded with a threefold counterattack.

> First, Steinbrenner made copies of the article and mailed them to major league owners with this note: "How's this for the mouth that bites the hand that feeds it."
>
> Next, he whipped off memos to NBC executives and filed a complaint with commissioner Bowie Kuhn.
>
> Finally, he instructed his players through an intermediary—not to talk to Kubek (Taylor, 1978, p. 3).

Steinbrenner's reference to "the mouth that bites the hand that feeds it" reveals a yearning for the "house man" type of announcer, the shill who hears no evil and sees no evil. Kubek was insightful in noting the economic nexus in his response to Steinbrenner's actions: "If he can influence the other owners, my job is at stake. There's millions of dollars at stake . . . if he's starting a blackball procedure I certainly want to have something to say about it, not just for me but for the cause of journalistic integrity" (quoted in Taylor, 1978, p. 3).

EX-ATHLETES AS ANNOUNCERS

Some observers feel that former athletes have a special advantage as announcers in the sense of "having been there" and being able "to tell it like it is." They can give the impression of offering the fan an inside view of strategies, respective team strengths and weaknesses, and locker room scuttlebutt. The listener feels that inside dope is being transmitted and that the human dimension is being considered.

> In terms of entertainment value, ex-football players turned commentators provide insight into the game from their first hand experience, and they have almost incalcuable entertainment value. Listening to the ex-players explain the plays has more than informative value for an audience. Fans also hear what appears to be privileged inside information. It is almost as if the fan is listening to "shop" conversations among "the boys." The boys, often as super or super-super stars, have been viewed by many fans in games over the span of the past 20 years. Viewers are familiar with them due to this exposure on TV. Retired and out of uniform, they are mortals, but special ones. The fans have the privilege of eavesdropping on the conversation and joking, possibly only among peers. This they share along with millions of other fans. In this sense, television not only brings the "gods" into one's living room, but lifts the fan to the privileged sanctuary of the broadcast booth.
>
> The ex-players, in broadcasting The Game itself, frequently show insight into aspects of the game that they didn't themselves play, i.e., a quarterback commenting on linebacker play, a lineman commenting on pass defense, etc. This causes further interest and creates the illusion of having "inside" knowledge on the part of the viewers. The announcers sometimes show a spontaneous enthusiasm for the game they are watching that is expressed in colorful language. Citing a defense player "red dogging" (rushing the passer), one commentator very suddenly and very excitedly said, "There's the dog!" (Givant, 1976, p. 38).

On the other hand, journalists may view the ex-athlete announcer as an amateur debasing the standards of a professional:

> What lapse of sense prompted the rise of the ballplayer–broadcaster? Was it the thought that former jocks would lend some special perspective, perhaps even spill a little locker-room insight? There's a thought that belongs in the Wrongo Notion Hall of Fame. The average fan in the bleachers has a better built-in gauge of baseball than any former ballplayer. . . . Baseball requires ballplayers to play it, broadcasters to say it (Boyer, 1980, p. 4).

INTRUSION OF TV INTO SPORTS

In certain respects television and sports have become two sides of the same coin. The financial support from television for sports has become so substantial that rules, format, and scheduling have been molded and adopted to meet the commercial interests of television. "It has been suggested that once a sport, league, or team has had its 'product' bought by television for use as programming, that entity can seldom exist thereafter, at least in the same style or manner, without the financial support of television. Similarly, television has become dependent upon sports to fulfill many of its programming needs" (Parente, 1977, p. 128). Sport is the one type of programming that is able to generate large television audiences on the otherwise dead periods of Saturday and Sunday afternoons.

The intimate relationship between sports and television can be explained in terms of four basic propositions:

> 1. For many sports, television rights payments represent a substantial portion of gross revenue.
> 2. Broadcast revenue is normally a stable source of income that is less subject to the changing whims of fan allegiance than is typically the case with attendance.
> 3. Television is one of the few sources of income for many organizations that has potential for increase. Many teams and events have little room for growth in attendance and little opportunity to raise ticket prices which are about as high as the market might bear.
> 4. The decision-makers in sports have apparently found it easier to change the nature of their sport to appeal to the desires of television rather than to the wants of the live spectator.
>
> Of the reasons stated above, the fourth is, perhaps, the most interesting. Prior to the sixties, changes in sports generally were made to improve the sport itself either for "sporting" reasons or to make it more interesting to spectators in order to stimulate attendance. Gradually, entrepreneur types of sportsmen saw an opportunity for greater profits by making slight changes within their sports to appeal to the desires of television. These changes seldom affected attendance adversely, although there were some notable exceptions. Eventually, sports unabashedly began "marketing" themselves for television (Parente, 1977, p. 129).

The revenues derived from television have not been without cost to the world of sport; many observers have commented on the various ways in which the mass media have intruded upon the nature of sport. Rules, playing surfaces, scheduling of contests, and the flow of the game itself have been altered to accommodate television. One example of these encroachments involves the intrusion of unnatural pauses in the flow of the game to accommodate commercial messages. One highly publicized instance of this symbiosis was brought to light in 1967 when a soccer referee admitted that he called an injury timeout whenever a network producer signaled him by means of a concealed beeper underneath his uniform.

Other examples of intrusion include the conversion of PGA golf from match to medal play to increase the likelihood that prominent golfers would be available to the television cameras throughout the match, the introduction of tie-breakers into tennis to prevent prolonged deuce games, the shortening of halftime breaks in professional football to fit the time slot of television programming, winner-take-all boxing matches, the substitution of a broken center line in hockey to provide better visibility on television, Monday night football, and World Series play during the evening hours (Runfola, 1974; Parente, 1977).

The influence of television on sport is well illustrated by the case of the 1976 World Series (Loomis, 1976). The New York Yankees were irritated by the fact that they had to wait five days after the last game of the regular season before starting the play-off series in order to accommodate a starting date on Saturday for the benefit of television. Then, once the play-off series was finished, the Yankees had to begin World Series play within 30 hours. Fortunately, the series ended on a Thursday night; if a Friday game had been necessary, the Yankees and Reds would have started the game at 6:00 P.M. in order to avoid a conflict with a presidential campaign debate on television between Ford and Carter that was scheduled for 9:30 P.M. It might also be noted that the movement of World Series games to an evening hour to bolster the television audience changes "the summer game" even more into the "fall classic" as temperatures dip to 30 degrees on October nights in the northeast.

In addition to dictating the day of the week and the hour at which athletic events are scheduled, television also affects the very process of the contest through such scheduling decisions. Since entering into financial agreements with television, team owners, leagues, and athletes have lost autonomy and control over the dynamics of the sport. For example, in 1967 television demanded that the major league baseball all-star game in Anaheim, California, be played at 4:00 p.m. in order to have the game shown in the East during prime viewing time. Because of the glare of the sun (and perhaps because of all-star pitching), the batters were only able to produce three runs in fifteen innings (Nixon, 1974, p. 126).

Another case in point involves the hockey contest for the gold medal between the U.S.S.R. and the U.S.A. in the 1980 Winter Olympics. The Olympic officials scheduled the event for 5:00 p.m. on a Friday. The TV network made the decision not to broadcast the game live because of the loss of audience due to the time slot; consequently, the game was taped and transmitted beginning at 8:00 P.M. prime time after most viewers had already learned of its outcome through earlier news reports. Much of the game's excitement was thus lost in the translation.

The extent to which the video component of television mediates the flow of a contest has been studied by communications researchers. A study by Brien Williams (1977) is interesting in this connection; his research involved a content analysis of videotapes of six National Football League games from the 1975 season. His research documented that sports telecasting tends to focus on individual action as contrasted with team effort; for example, the camera coverage focuses attention on the ball and ball-carriers with relative neglect of the supporting cast and subtleties of the game. The video coverage of individual player action was typically accompanied by biographical and personalized commentary from the announcing team.

Williams' research showed that 82 percent of the camera shots involved game action; 11 percent of the coverage was devoted to game-related content such as coaches and players on the sidelines; and 7 percent of the camera shots involved material unrelated to the game (e.g., cheerleaders or signs displayed by spectators in the stands). Williams (1977, p. 138) also reported that "Sound mixtures and levels were highly manipulated, particularly when crowd noise and sounds from the field were used literally to 'orchestrate' live action, thus inducing notions of excitement as well as aurally communicating the force of physical contact."

Communications researchers have also analyzed the content of the sports announcers' narration on television. For example, Bryant et al. (1977) did a content analysis of the videotapes from six professional games during the 1976 season. They found that 72 percent of the broadcasters' statements were descriptive in nature; 27 percent were coded as *dramatic interpretations* of the action with the remaining 1 percent coded as humor. This finding clearly documents the fact that announcers spend considerable time attempting to embellish the action within a contest.

> It would seem that the sportscaster serves not only to fill in the knowledge gaps left by the limitations of the visual dimensions of television, but to add histrionics to the "human drama of athletic competition." It would also appear that the sports announcer's dramaturgy is already rather stylized, with a great deal of reliance on a relatively small number of dramatic motifs. There is, however, some variation within networks which appears to be rather consistent (p. 149).

The role of the announcer in dramatizing sports on television has been studied in an experimental context by communications researchers. For example, Comisky et al. (1977) conducted some laboratory research in which 139 university students rated a series of hockey videotapes on several dimensions, including the perceived degree of action involved and the entertainment value. The findings showed that the students' degree of enjoyment was directly related to their perception of aggressiveness and even violence in the game. The researchers' initial discovery concerning the influence of the TV announcers in generating excitement is particularly interesting.

> After examining videotapes of several ice hockey games for various types of violent interactions, we selected two segments that we had tentatively identified as containing different degrees of aggressiveness: one with normal play and the other with aggressive exchanges. We had selected these segments while watching the monitor in much the same manner that the typical sports fan observes televised sports, with at least a moderate amount of attention given to both the audio and visual portions of the presentation. Upon more systematic examination of the audio and video tracks of our segments, however, we discovered that the segment that we had initially identified as showing aggressive action contained only a little explicitly violent behavior. The announcers, however, had managed to convince us that we were witnessing rough and tough ice hockey at its best, with the action threatening to turn into fisticuffs at any minute, when in fact there was little action. The segment that we had identified showing normal action, on the other hand, actually presented several very rough incidents (hard checks, etc.). The announcers, however, when play was intense, had let the action carry the game with little commentary of a dramatic sort (Comiskey et al., 1977, p. 151).

SPORTS TELECASTING

On the surface it might appear that the spectator at a live sporting event has a more intense experience of the contest than the television viewer due to the focused immediacy of the action and the social facilitation or contagion from the crowd. Moreover, one might suggest that the spectator in the stadium or arena views the contest with relatively immaculate perception unalloyed by the embellishment of the announcing team. Nevertheless, it is also true that the relatively distant stadium seat combined with extraneous activity by neighboring fans (e.g., drinking, ordering refreshments from vendors, etc.) can result in a less accurate perception of the contest than that of the television spectator.

The television viewer, on the other hand, is exposed to a media event orchestrated by a producer, director, technical staff, and a team of announcers. "In choosing from among the several close-ups, long shots, replays, cutaways and various segments of action at his disposal, the director is certainly an editor of the game. Moreover, yet another crew, the sportscasters, is in charge of embellishing the drama of the affairs, thereby making it more palatable to the action-hungry audience" (Comisky et al., 1977, p. 150). The sophisticated technology that is used in TV sportscasting has come to represent a type of sensory validation. Increasingly, the viewer waits upon a replay, slow-motion shot, or analysis from the announcer before responding to a particular segment of the game action.

The power of television to mediate the sports experience is evident in the curious fact that several stadia have installed giant closed-circuit television screens in strategic locations inside the stadium in order to replay selected action for special isolation shots or slow motion runs. At least three cities currently have these super screens in their stadia—Los Angeles, Kansas City, and New Orleans. The size of the screen in New Orleans' Superdome is thirty-four feet measured diagonally. This mediating power of electronic media is also evident in the large number of fans who bring portable radios and even television sets to the stadium to verify their visual impressions. It appears that the live spectator cannot compete with the sensory stimuli experienced by the TV viewer with the multiplicity of camera angles, special effects, and announcers.

Since the 1950s, television has had a significant impact on American society. It has influenced family life, study habits of students, books read, leisure-time pursuits, and general life style. Our electronic society is filled with visual and auditory stimuli from the media. Television has progressed from black and white to color, including exciting graphic presentation, and to sophisticated electronic recording devices. Consequently, the television camera has contributed to the visual imagery of sport. "Television has done to sport, in a sense, what film has to drama: transformed it into a new electronic medium" (Cummings, 1975, p. 73). Through the electronic eye, we have become accustomed to specific segments of athletic performance being isolated, blown up, slowed down, repeated, and otherwise detached from the overall sport configuration. Through devices such as the instant replay, "Sport provides heroic images and television provides those images with exposure" (Cummings, 1975, p. 76). This new reality provided by television is dramatically described by ex-Green Bay Packers football player Jerry Kramer.

> Over and over and over, perhaps twenty times, the television cameras reran Bart's touchdown and my block on Jethro Pugh. Again and again, millions of people across the country saw the hole open up and saw Bart squeeze through. Millions of people who couldn't name a single offensive lineman if their lives depended on it heard my name repeated and repeated and repeated. All I could think was, "Thank God for instant replay" (Kramer, 1968, p. 262).

Jerry Kramer's big play became the climax of his football career, and he became the first hero of the instant replay era. The national networks use as many as fifteen television cameras plus videotape and slow-motion units in their game plan to capture such big moments as that of Jerry Kramer's key block. "The phenomenon of the replay is related to both our penchant for stopping time, reliving great moments, holding them in immortal tape present . . . and to our need for expert analysis, to see it again to make sure" (Cummings, 1975, p. 76).

The TV coverage of the 1980 Winter Olympics exemplifies the technological virtuosity *and* inherent limits of sports telecasting (Klein, 1980). Obviously, not all the events could be covered live in the allotted fifty-two hours of coverage; moreover, some of the events are not exciting spectator fare for the uninitiated. In any event, except for some telecasts of hockey games shown in their entirety, the TV coverage of the 1980 Winter Olympics basically amounted to fifty-two hours of highlights with the prosaic interludes expunged.

> For the most part, it was entertainment of a high order. Even if skiing, skating and sledding leave you cold, you're not enamored with the way the Olympics are organized and executed, it was impossible not to be seduced. ABC was technically brilliant, as always, the Lake Placid vistas were beautiful and the tug of nationalism is strong. The 12-day duration of the games permitted the kind of sustained spectator involvement that rarely occurs in sports and made us care about the outcome of events with which we previously had only a nodding acquaintance.
>
> Make no mistake, though; what we saw wasn't winter sports as they are but as only a rich, efficient and experienced American television network can present them. With but few exceptions—most notably the U.S. hockey team's incredible victory over the Soviet Union's—the drama of the games stemmed from the application of the broadcaster's art (Klein, 1980, p. 9).[1]

THE 24-HOUR SPORTS NETWORK

In 1979 the Entertainment and Sports Programming Network (ESPN) began offering sports on television on a 24-hour basis. ESPN is generally provided to cable subscribers for no additional cost as a "foundation service." The Getty Oil Company is the chief funding source for this innovation in sports broadcasting. The potential market for ESPN is presently limited to the 15 million homes which are wired for cable service out of the 74 million homes with television in the nation. It is estimated that the number of cable hookups will triple by 1985 (Middleton, 1979, p. 7).

---

[1]Reprinted by permission of *52 Years of Olympic Highlights* by F. Klein, © Dow Jones & Company, Inc. 1980. All Rights Reserved.

The new sports network carries exotic fare in addition to the bread and butter sports—water polo, table tennis, frisbee, karate, kayaking, women's field hockey, lacrosse, golf lessons, fishing, horse jumping, motorcycle racing, and even the player draft for the National Football League. It is now possible for a sports addict to watch, for example, football games from Saturday morning to Monday night. This 24-hour sports network supplements the 1300 hours of sports carried by CBS, NBC, and ABC on a national basis per year. In addition, local television affiliates and independent networks carry other sports events of regional interest.

ESPN has a contract with the National Collegiate Athletic Association to broadcast about 350 collegiate sports events over the course of a year. The sports network pays a university or college about $3,000 for a major athletic event; by comparison the ABC network pays about $533,000 for a nationally televised game and $401,000 for a regional appearance (Middleton, 1979, p. 6). Although ESPN broadcasts games for some twenty universities who do not appear on network telecasts, most of the collegiate football games carried by ESPN involve well-known institutions.

The NCAA contract with ESPN specifies that no institution may have more than four of its athletic events aired on ESPN over the course of a year—a maximum of one in football, two in basketball, and the remaining one from the so-called minor sports. The NCAA contract with the ABC network stipulates that no university football team may be covered more than five times over two consecutive years; moreover, the contract requires ABC to broadcast less glamorous games each season—four games in Division II and three games in Division III (Middleton, 1979, p. 7).

CONCLUSION

A mutual interdependence emerged between sport and the mass media during the 1920s and 1930s. This period was marked by rapid expansion in the coverage of sports in newspapers and on the radio, the emergence of big-time collegiate sport, and the birth of professional sports. In this era the media promoted sport, and sport sold the media. A symbiosis developed wherein newspapers became a device for promoting sports, and sport spectacles became a means for selling newspapers. The marriage between sports and the mass media paralleled broader societal trends toward consumerism and the development of the advertising industry. The promotion of sports heroes by newspaper writers and radio announcers played a large part in increasing the attendance at sports events.

The role of the sportswriter and the importance of the sports page has not been attenuated by the powerful presence of television. In fact, the sports writer feeds off major sports telecasting by providing followup analysis of a more individualized nature tailored to a particular geographic region. The style of sports writing has alternated over the years between objectivity and subjectivity; the happy myth maker and "house man" style of reporting was eclipsed by the critical muckrakers of the late 1960s, while a more objective analytic posture is characteristic of current sports reporters in newspapers. Nevertheless, there is still a lack of clear consensus concerning the role of the sportswriter.

The role of the journalist in the sport world is similar in some respects to that of a journalist in the political or economic sphere. He or she has a responsibility to provide the public with the realities of the situation, because the public needs to be informed in order to engage in the political process. The exposure of the behind-the-scene realities of Watergate by Bob Woodward and Carl Bernstein of the *Washington Post* is a case in point. From a journalistic perspective, the exposure of the sexual exploits of political leaders is not relevant unless these activities involve the use of public money or influence the political decision-making. In the realm of sport reporting, we do not see very much significance in published accounts of the private activities of athletes, although the behavioral scientists might be interested in these activities from the standpoint of how the social structure of sport may promote these forms of behavior.

The relationship between sport and the mass media took a quantum leap with the diffusion of television in the 1950s. Television proved to be a very powerful medium for promoting sports at all levels. For example, during a Sunday afternoon in the fall, about 750,000 fans are in attendance at professional football games in the United States, while at the same time about *22 million* households around the country are watching one of these games on television. "Television, therefore, provides access to the sport for a large number of people, and televised football has become a popular source of television entertainment. That popularity, in turn, is a significant source of revenue for the football league itself" (Committee on Commerce, 1978, p. 9).

We have discussed the ways in which television has the potential to disrupt the very *process* of sports contests due to a marketing emphasis on sports as a product. The symbiotic relationship between sports and the mass media has become skewed with the increasing dependence of sports for television revenues. Perhaps the most unfortunate part of the sport–TV relationship is the willingness of a major university football coach and athletic director to acquiesce to the TV networks requests. Are the television dollars more important than the educational goals of the university, the physical and mental well-being of players, and the desires of students, fans, and alumni?

> Why have sport events started, paused, and ended on cue from TV directors? Why did soccer referee Peter Rhodes once wear an electronic beeper on his shoulder, and signal an injury on cue to allow time for a one-minute commercial? Why do teams call time-outs at relatively inopportune stages in the game? Why has red-dogging—or close pursuit of the passer—been prohibited in football All-Star games? Why have athletes and coaches submitted to TV interviews during an intensive preparation for important games and after agonizing defeats? Why has tennis sought to limit the length of matches through changes in its scoring system? Why have numerous other sports made changes in the rule of play, their physical facilities, and the kinds of uniforms worn by players?
>
> The justification for such concessions and modifications has been MONEY, and most prominently, money from television contracts. The commercial success of professional and big-time amateur sport depends crucially today upon the television dollar (Nixon, 1974, p. 237).

We find ourselves in a dilemma at this point. Many sport fans enjoy the opportunity to watch televised athletic events that they would not otherwise be able to observe. Furthermore, most fans are probably willing to pay a little more for after-shave lotion to help pay for the network advertising of such events. Nevertheless, the television dollars are "soft money" that can be withdrawn very quickly when the market is saturated. Perhaps sport has become too dependent on easy money from television—like wild animals in our national parks that become dependent on handouts from tourists for their sustenance. The television medium is a double-edged sword; it can inspire and it can corrupt. If the sports establishment does not regain some sense of autonomy vis à vis television, sports could evolve into a form of studio entertainment.

It is not unreasonable to ask in this context whether we are reaching the saturation point in televised sport, especially with the seasons bumping into one another and overlapping with a consequent fracturing of the audience. It is now common to see as many as thirty sports offerings over the course of a week in a television schedule. Given this smorgasbord, will the sports fan become resistant to shelling out cash for live attendance at sports events? Only the most competitive teams in the established leagues are able to draw a break-even level of attendance; the marginal teams survive only by virtue of league television contracts on a pooled basis. The death of the World Football League, the World Hockey League, the American Basketball Association, and World Team Tennis indicates that only the best product will draw a live audience and attract a national television contract. As Yogi Berra once observed, "If the fans don't want to come to the game, who's going to stop them?"

It is commonly assumed that the linkage between the mass media and sports is antithetical to *active* physical participation; a common stereotype in this context is a Joe Fan drinking his six-pack laying back in an easy chair. In reality, however, empirical research shows a clear *positive* relationship between active sports involvement and consumption of sports through the mass media. One might suggest that television affords the amateur an opportunity to watch experts in action, particularly in individual sports such as tennis and golf. Television provides role models for citizen athletes trying to improve their skills (Coakley, 1978, p. 192). In this respect, then, one cannot generalize that sports telecasts appeal only to passive "super spectators."

CHAPTER 14
The Political Economy of Sports

About 730,000 people attend professional football games in the United States on a given Sunday afternoon, while another 22 million households are watching one of the games on television.

In 1978 the National Football League received approximately $162 million from the three television networks for broadcasting rights. A one-minute commercial during the 1981 Super Bowl cost the sponsor $500,000.

In 1977 a contract was signed between ABC television and the National Collegiate Athletic Association which guarantees the payment of $118 million over a four-year period for coverage of collegiate football games.

AMPEX Corporation was prepared to supply $15 million of television equipment for the 1980 Summer Olympics in Moscow. The Levi Strauss Corporation made a commitment of $12 million in the form of television commercials, donation of team uniforms, and other promotional activities associated with the 1980 Summer Olympics.

ABC television was awarded television rights for the 1984 Olympic Games at the price of $225 million. More than 200 hours of air time is planned which amounts to about $1 million per hour of television coverage.

A boutique catalogue advertised a designer jogging suit—pullover top at $58; matching shorts, $46; and matching pants at $66.

NIKE, the number two producer of running shoes, reported corporate earnings of about $360 million in 1980.

Corporate sponsors contributed over $400,000 in 1979 to have their names associated with the New York City Marathon.

The world famous Davis Cup tennis tournament will be renamed the NEC Davis Cup next year. The NEC represents the Nippon Electric Company which has agreed to sponsor the event over the next three years with $950,000 a year in prize money alone.

The news items listed here suggest that sports are now big business. In addition to being an industry unto itself, sport also stimulates economic activity in a variety of other enterprises such that the sports complex now represents a business of about $100 billion annually in the United States. Loy et al. (1978) have outlined eight components of the sports complex:

> This industry includes (1) large corporations that manufacture sporting goods in an estimated 10.5-billion-dollar industry; (2) clothing manufacturers who produce practical, attractive athletic attire to be worn while playing or consuming sport (e.g., swimsuits, tennis clothes, footwear); (3) architects, building contractors, and consulting engineers who design, construct, or remodel stadiums, games sites, ski resorts, etc., at a large profit (see Auf der Maur, 1976); (4) concession owners and operators who engage in a million-dollar industry selling food and beverages at sporting events; (5) part-time entrepreneurs such as those who recover golf balls from ponds and lakes for resale in a million-dollar business, much of which is illegal; (6) bookies and betting syndicates who handle over one billion dollars a year in wagers on professional and college sport events; (7) agents and lawyers who represent the contractual and commercial interests of athletes; and (8) various forms of the mass media, especially television, which sell commercial time to business corporations which can then advertise their products to a relatively homogeneous set of potential consumers. Within the sport world itself, a large number of personnel directly receive incomes in exchange for services in the production of sport; these include athletes, coaches, field and business managers, scouts, trainers, officials, maintenance personnel, publicity officers, sportwriters and sportcasters, etc. (pp. 256–57).

SPORTS AS A PUBLIC POLICY ISSUE

Serious issues of political economy within the world of sports are emerging with increasing frequency. One can hardly pick up a newspaper without reading about public policy issues in the sports industry that affect the general public as well as the fan. The sports industry involves a broad array of legal issues that intersect the political and economic institutions. Consequently, one sees increasing legislative and judicial activity in big time sports, as well as government intervention through its regulatory agencies. A congressional committee noted the increasing litigiousness within the world of sports in the opening paragraph of its *Inquiry into Professional Sports* (House Select Committee, 1976a).

> The past decade has seen a radical change in the public face of professional sports. Once the traditional sports page preoccupation was with the hopes engendered by the opening of training camps, or box scores and statistics, or the rise of new heroes and the fall of old reliables, or harmless gossip and mythmaking. Now the American sports fan is presented with an almost daily barrage of socio-legal crises which threaten to, and at times succeed in, over-shadowing the efforts and accomplishments of the athletes on their respective fields of play (p. 1).

We can expect to see more governmental reports of this type as the society in general becomes more bureaucratized and litigious, as the fans become more vocal as consumers, and as we experience the steady-state era compounded by the energy crisis. Nevertheless, the public still tends to view sports as a pure phenomenon devoid of political and economic ramifications.

> It will be difficult for the public to understand the dynamics of change within Sportsworld unless it is aware that a relationship exists between government and sports, and understands that issues of Sportsworld are issues of public policy, the outcome of which is decided by the political process. The public is not likely to voice its policy preferences in an attempt to influence policy decisions if it lacks this perspective and continues to believe in the purity of sports myth. In essence, the public, despite its great interest in sports matters, will not be represented when issues of public sports policy are decided. It is important, therefore, that the public understands clearly the process and the arguments which are utilized in achieving agenda status for sports issues (Johnson, 1978, p. 321).

PROFESSIONAL SPORTS AND THE GOVERNMENT

The regulatory agencies of the United States government have been active in professional sports since 1922 when the Supreme Court ruled that baseball was immune to antitrust laws on the grounds that it was not engaged an interstate commerce. Eventually, the position has emerged that professional sports are a type of public trust that deserves some of the protections afforded a public utility while simultaneously enjoying some of the perquisites of private industry as a species of commercial entertainment. Michael Roberts (1977, p. 16) suggests that the separation between sport and state in the United States has been a history of cozy sweetheart contacts. He argues that some politicians will do anything for "Jockdom" and that the governmental agencies have been "mindlessly obsequious" in dealing with the sports establishment.

The political clout of sport entrepreneurs flows from substantial economic resources; however, it also stems from occasional myopia on the part of some legislators. Johnson (1979) notes in his connection that the influence of the sports establishment involves "the campaign contributions which they are capable of making, and their ability to award much-sought-after franchises to 'deserving' cities. It has been charged that this last source of power is used to reward members of Congress for cooperation on crucial legislative issues" (p. 111). Moreover, in 1971 Congressman Lionel Van Deerling of California suggested the success of the sports establishment in Congress may be due to "reluctance of many Congressmen to risk antagonizing club owners in their cities" lest a franchise be moved out of their home district (*Congressional Record*, September 25, 1971, p. 33407).

It is relevant to note in this connection that the National Football League awarded a new franchise to New Orleans shortly after Senator Long from Louisiana (and Senator Everett Dirksen) had shepherded a bill through Congress authorizing the merger of the American and National Football Leagues. As noted elsewhere in this chapter, this piece of legislation was approved with *blitzkreig* speed and involved use of political clout.

> The *Congressional Quarterly* magazine reported that the tactic of adding the merger bill to the investment tax credit bill was actually devised by Senator Long along with Congressman Hale Boggs. Long and Boggs were both members of the critical Conference Committee that accepted the amendment. And both men were from Louisiana. New Orleans did not have a professional football team at the time the merger was being considered, but was thought to be high on the list of likely cities for future expansion. The bill, as proposed and enacted, conditioned antitrust immunity for the merger

on their being *more* teams in the combined league than had participated in the two separate leagues (Sobell, 1977, pp. 392–93).

During 1951–1978, the United States Congress deliberated on almost 300 legislative items concerning sport (Johnson, 1979). Congress tended to view sports in a somewhat idyllic and romantic image until the mid-1960s; it was pretty much assumed that the business of sport is the business of America. For example, a Congressional report in 1952 dealing with the monopoly power of baseball noted that "in many respects, professional baseball typifies the basic ideals of the American people. Fairness and clean competition are the passwords of the sport. It is the melting pot of men of all races, religions and creeds" (*Subcommittee on Monopoly Power*, 1952, p. 9). Similarly, in 1953, Senator Edwin Johnson of Colorado suggested that "If the free world and Iron Curtain countries could compete on the baseball diamond, plans for war would disappear from the face of the earth like an early-morning dew" (*Congressional Record*, March 20, 1953, p. 2151).

The profit motif of professional sports gradually became evident to congressmen and senators with the move of the Dodgers and Giants to the West Coast in 1958, with the movement of the Milwaukee Braves to Atlanta, with the purchase of the New York Yankees by CBS in 1964, and especially with the loss of two baseball franchies from Washington, D. C. This growing disenchantment was exemplified in Senator Marlow Cook's bill to establish a Federal Sports Commission as a regulatory mechanism in response to the "mass commercialization of sports" (Senate Committee on Commerce, 1972, p. 102). The concern of the Congress reached its peak in 1976 with the House Select Committee's (1976a, 1976b) comprehensive Inquiry into Professional Sports; the two summary volumes on these hearings cover a total of 1187 pages.

Johnson's (1979) excellent analysis of the relationship between Congress and professional sports clearly documents that the history of professional sports in the United States is largely a series of public policy issues that have been decided through the political process—antitrust rulings, league mergers, collective bargaining agreements, reserve clauses, sports broadcasting, and public subsidy of sports facilities. The power of the sports establishment with governmental agencies has weakened over the past fifteen years; Congress has become particularly solicitious about protecting the public's right of access to sporting events. The cash nexus of professional sports has been exposed by a series of franchise transfers which disregarded the public interest, a skein of management–labor disputes, and the explosion of salary levels for professional athletes. The increasing visibility of profit-making motivations on the part of owners, who seemingly disregard the interest of the fans and the quality of the game, has resulted in a more realistic image on the part of legislators.

PROFESSIONAL SPORTS AS A BUSINESS

Professional sports are unique as a business in the United States; no other enterprise has the same operating privileges. Federal antitrust legislation prohibits the formation of business combinations (cartels) to the end of restraint of trade. Professional sports leagues are cartels in the sense that they carve out geographical markets and establish the entry and working conditions of the players. A new club can enter the market only with the permission of the existing franchise owners; similarly, a sports team can relocate only with approval from the league. This control over the market flow is unparalleled in Americal business.

Professional sports are also distinctive in the sense that workers cannot ply their trade in an open market because team owners have exclusive bargaining rights with players from the time of selection in a player draft. From a purely business perspective, these league rules are collusive and anticompetitive in nature. Gerald Scully (1978), a professor of Economics at Southern Methodist University, points out the peculiar characteristics of professional sports as a business enterprise.

> No other occupation in America, except perhaps conscription into the military, is as restrictive. To enforce player contracts, leagues have resorted to a number of anticompetitive labor practices, such as black-listing. Such activities would be per se illegal for any other business in America.
>
> Leagues establish collusive agreements which govern the selection, contractual arrangements, and distribution of players. Collectively, these powers create a condition of monopsony in the player market. Monopsony is a technical economic term applying to the monopolization of labor markets, and is a condition which exists when there are restrictions on with whom individuals may contract employment. The effect of monopsony is that an individual receives a salary less than that which would be competitively established. The magnitude of the salary is unimportant; the term applies as long as the employment restrictions result in a salary below the market value of the individual's services (pp. 433–34).

At this point it is relevant to note that monopolistic practices also occur in sports at the amateur level. These activities are evident in the activities of individuals, associations, institutions such as universities, conferences, and leagues with respect to scheduling, postseason games, enforcement procedures, Olympic tryouts, broadcasting, eligibility, and territorial jurisdiction.

> Amateur and professional sports entrepreneurs engage in monopolistic practices when they acquire exclusive negotiation rights for prospective athletes' skills, require the signing of a common contract containing reserve or option clauses which bind athletes to a franchise for an unreasonable amount of time, jointly sell broadcasting and telecasting rights to their sporting contests, ban or blacklist players who played for competing leagues, ban the telecasting of games within the "territory" of another league member, merge with rival leagues, and extract excessive concessions from municipalities seeking professional franchises. The enjoyment of such powers may be a result of either formal antitrust exemptions provided by the courts (exemplified by professional baseball) or Congress (professional sports television policy), congressionally issued charters (the USOC), or unchallenged tradition (as in the case of the NCAA) (Johnson, 1978, p. 329).

The three basic sources of revenues for the team owners are admissions, broadcasting rights, and concessions. "In all these areas, teams are essentially monopolistic: for each sport, only one team in any city has the right to sell tickets to major-league professional contests, to offer broadcasts of contests, and to sell food, beverages, and souvenirs to those in attendance at its games" (Noll, 1974,

p. 6). Moreover, each league has regulations ostensibly designed to equalize the relative strength of the teams in the league with respect to player ability—hence the policies governing player drafts, trades, reserve clauses, player options, and free agency.

The assets of a professional sports franchise involve three types of tangibles in addition to the intangible factor of public goodwill: (1) contract rights over players and other personnel; (2) franchise rights granted under the agreement of the league; and (3) ownership of the equipment and materials associated with each team. Each owner has the power to make many decisions concerning the staffing and operation of the club; however, major decisions are shared with other owners in the league. It is understood, for example, that a strong majority of the league owners is required for approval of a new franchise or the transfer of a team from one city to another.

No uniform pattern of sharing admission revenues exists across leagues; the distribution of admission revenues equally across teams within a league is commonly proposed as a means of creating parity among teams with large and small attendance pools. The data on admissions suggest that "in all sports, most of the teams in the half-dozen or so largest metropolitan areas are among the most successful, and few teams in these areas draw badly even when their record is poor" (Noll, 1974, p. 154). In professional hockey and basketball, the income from ticket sales are not shared with the visiting team; in the National Football League the home and visiting teams share on a 60–40 basis; in professional baseball the gate is split on approximately an 80–20 basis.

THE PLAYER RESERVE CLAUSE

Player equalization is a prime concern in professional sports in order to prevent dynasties that can kill fan interest. It is commonly asserted, for example, that the domination by the Cleveland Browns of the All-American Conference during 1946–1949 led to the demise of that league in 1950. On the other hand, during recent decades we have seen other super-teams which seemingly had no deleterious effects on the health of their respective leagues—the New York Yankees, Green Bay Packers, Boston Celtics, and Montreal Canadiens. In any event, all professional sport leagues in the United States have had some type of reserve clause which basically grants the team owner an exclusive option for renewal of a player's contract.

The reserve clause was first instituted in the late nineteenth century as part of professional baseball "to prevent a practice known as 'revolving,' whereby a player would jump from club to club in response to higher salary offers. Club owners claimed then, as they do today, that such actions would ultimately destroy professional sports" (Demmert, 1973, p. 21). From the players' perspective, on the other hand, "the reserve system is designed to hold salaries down, stifle dissent, and allow the owner to dictate lifestyle if he so desires" (Garvey, 1979, p. 92). The players view the reserve clause as a restrictive measure that determines where and for whom an athlete shall play over the course of a career.

The perpetual reserve clause meant that a professional athlete could ply his trade with only one employer who, as the sole buyer of his services, held the balance of power in contract negotiations. In this context, Senator Sam Ervin compared professional athletes to serfs and peons during the 1971 Senate hearings on the proposed merger of the National and American Basketball Associations.

> Many years ago, the term 'chattel' was used to denote the legal status of slaves. That is, they were considered a type of chattel which was owned as a piece of furniture or livestock was owned. This use of the term 'chattel' applied to human beings and the condition it stands for are so abhorrent that we don't even like to acknowledge that they ever existed. Yet, in a real sense that is what these hearings are about today—modern peonage and the giant sports trusts (Sobell, 1977, p. 83).

During the last decade professional athletes launched a series of attacks on existing employment practices in professional sports; their legal actions have resulted in greater personal control over their contractual conditions. Basically, they were challenging the player draft and the reserve-option system through which the owners could dictate the working conditions of professional athletes. Once a particular team had selected a player in the draft, it could claim exclusive bargaining rights with the athlete. The reserve clause prevented many other teams from bidding on the services of a player, and it prohibited a player from negotiating with another team regardless of professional, financial, or personal reasons.

Until recently, baseball and hockey had a permanent reserve clause in the sense that a player could join another team only if the parent club released, traded, or sold him to another franchise. In football and basketball, on the other hand, the reserve clause was not perpetual because a player could announce his intention to play out his option after a prescribed length of service. The club that signed such a free agent was then required to compensate the team losing the services of the player according to compensation rules prescribed by the league.

It should be noted that if a player had a single-year contract with a team owner, the club had the power to terminate a player's contract if the player was viewed as being of little value to the franchise. Thus, the team owner had the right, but not the obligation, to employ an athlete for the length of the contract. Now that multiyear contracts have become common, the pendulum has swung toward the players. For example, the Yankees signed Don Gullett to a six-year contract for $2.1 million in 1976. Since that time he was able to pitch only one full year and was officially released at the end of the 1980 session; he remains on the Yankee payroll with his salary intact. Basically the same scenario applies to Wayne Garland, who was signed by Cleveland in 1976 for a ten-year contract at $2.3 million; arm troubles prevented him from regaining the pitching form that he had in Baltimore, but his salary continues to be paid at the original rate.

In the next section, we trace the recent history of the reserve clause in professional sports in the United States. The history is basically one of legal conflict in which the courts have increasingly tilted toward the interests of professional athletes.

Professional Baseball

As originally instituted in baseball in 1879, the reserve clause dictated that baseball team owners could reserve a certain number of players, originally fourteen, for their own teams who were not eligible for hiring by other clubs. The clause was struck down in several court cases early in the twentieth century; however, the tide turned toward the owners in the landmark case of the *Federal Baseball Club v. the National League* in 1922. The Supreme Court under Oliver Wendell Holmes ruled that the antitrust laws did not apply to baseball because "the business is giving exhibitions of baseball, which are purely state affairs," and thus are not governed by Federal laws for interstate commerce (*House Select Committee*, 1976c, p. 10). Consequently, the reserve clause was viewed as compatible with antitrust legislation. The Supreme Court has not seen fit to extend this antitrust exemption to any professional sport other than baseball.

In the 1953 case of *Toolson v. New York Yankees*, the Supreme Court acknowledged that there was no sound rationale for exempting baseball from antitrust legislation. In this case the Supreme Court reasoned, however, that because baseball had been allowed to develop for thirty years under this understanding, it would be unwise to reverse the Holmes decision as a complex structure had been built upon it. The Court then noted that it was up to the Congress to determine the future legal status of professional baseball. The issue surfaced again in 1969 with the Curt Flood case.

Curt Flood had played for twelve years as a superstar for the St. Louis Cardinals when he was traded in 1969 to the Philadelphia Phillies without having been consulted concerning his interests. Curt Flood sardonically noted that he had been given less personal consideration than "a foot-shuffling porter"; he was officially informed of the trade by the following letter:

> Dear Curt:
> Enclosed herewith is Player Report Notice #614 covering the OUTRIGHT assignment of your contract to the Philadelphia Club of the National League, October 8, 1969. Best of luck. Sincerely yours, Bing Devine, General Manager (Sobell, 1977, p. 58).

Curt Flood's case came before the Supreme Court in 1972, when the issue of the reserve clause was again side-stepped. The court did not rule on Flood's argument that the reserve clause was illegal; basically, it reiterated its 1953 position that the remedy for problems such as Curt Flood's would have to be found in Congressional action. By the time of the 1972 nondecision, Flood had retired from baseball in 1971 as property of the Washington Senators. He subsequently lived for some years in Europe as a disillusioned expatriate.

One year later, in 1973, a significant change took place in professional baseball with the insertion of a compulsory arbitration provision in a collective bargaining agreement between team owners and the players' union. Catfish Hunter exploited this grievance mechanism a year later when he requested arbitration on the grounds that the Oakland Athletics had failed to provide all of his compensation in the form in which he requested it—half of the salary in a taxfree annuity—as specified in his contract. The arbitration panel ruled in favor of Hunter, and thus Catfish became legally free to sign a multimillion dollar contract with the New York Yankees.

The landmark case of Andy Messersmith stemmed from his inability to secure agreement with the management of the Los Angeles Dodgers concerning his 1975 contract. Among other items, Andy Messersmith was requesting a no-trade condition or at least the right to approve any trade in which he would be involved. Consequently, he played the 1975 season without a contract. The players' association then contended that Messersmith would become a free agent at the end of the 1975 season.

The owner disagreed and asked a Federal district judge to review the case who, in turn, sent it to an arbitration hearing. Ultimately, it was decided "that the renewal clause was for only one year (not perpetual) and that after that year there was no contractual bond between player and club" (*House Select Committee*, 1976c, p. 13). A Court of Appeals reaffirmed the ruling; the Messersmith case effectively killed the reserve clause in professional baseball; the legal decision in this case basically allows players currently under contract to play out their option year and thus become free agents. An extended strike by baseball players in the summer of 1981 revolved around the issue of compensation to the former team of a baseball player when he plays out his option and signs a contract with a new team.

Now that the reserve clause is dead in professional baseball, the wealth of the individual franchise owners is becoming a disequilibrating factor. In this context, George Steinbrenner and the New York Yankees offer an interesting case study of an independently wealthy owner and a lucrative sports franchise. Steinbrenner signed ten free agents between 1975 and 1980 at a total cost of about $33 million. This jumbo payroll is possible because some franchises are "more equal" than others due to larger attendance pools and more lucrative media markets. Although some of Steinbrenner's free agents turned out to be failures on the playing field, the free-spending policy has paid off at the gate; the home attendance of the Yankees increased from 1.2 million in 1972 to 2.6 million in 1980. George Steinbrenner's initiative with free agents over a six-year period is outlined in the following list:

1975	Catfish Hunter	$3.35 million over five years
1976	Reggie Jackson	$2.90 million over five years
1976	Don Gullett	$2.10 million over six years
1977	Rich Gossage	$2.75 million over six years
1977	Rawley Eastwick	$1.00 million over five years
1978	Luis Tiant	$740,000 over two years
1978	Tommy John	$2.5 million over three years
1979	Rudy May	$1.00 million over three years
1979	Bob Watson	$1.70 million over three years
1980	Dave Winfield	$15 million over ten years

Professional Football

The reserve clause in professional football was first challenged in 1960 when the American Football League emerged as a competitor of the National Football League. Interleague competition evolved in the sense that a player had the right to sign with either the NFL or AFL team which had drafted him. After this initial contract, an athlete could then theoretically play out his option and become a free agent in both leagues; however, the team owners had a gentlemen's agreement not to sign another team's free agents either within or between leagues. For the first three years during which the dual leagues were in operation, no raiding of players occurred between leagues or within a league.

The dam broke, however, in 1963 when the Baltimore Colts signed a free agent (R. C. Owens) from the San Francisco 49ers, both NFL teams. In response to this breach, the NFL owners instituted the so-called Rozelle Rule to prevent such raiding in the future.

> The Rozelle Rule states:
> "Any player, whose contract with a League club has expired, shall thereupon become a free agent and shall no longer be considered a member of the team of that club following the expiration date of such contract. Whenever a player, becoming a free agent in such manner, thereafter signed a contract with a different club in the League, then, unless mutually satisfactory arrangements have been concluded between the two League clubs, the Commissioner may name and then award to the former club one or more players, from the Active, Reserve, or Selection List (including future selection choices) of the acquiring club as the Commissioner in his sole discretion deems fair and equitable; and such decision by the Commissioner shall be final and conclusive" (Committee on the Judiciary, 1975, p. 20).

The situation became more complicated in 1966 when the New York Giants (NFL) signed Pete Gogolak as a free agent from the Buffalo Bills (AFL). Shortly thereafter, Roman Gabriel of the Los Angeles Rams (NFL) announced that he would be signing with the Oakland Raiders (AFL); similarly, it was announced that John Brodie and Jim Ninowski would soon be signing as quarterbacks in the NFL (Sobel, 1977, p. 385).

Within three months, the AFL and NFL began their public merger talks (June, 1966). Because the Sherman Antitrust Act was a barrier to such a merger, Senators Long and Dirksen introduced a bill in Congress to authorize the merger on September 9, 1966. The Senate Judiciary Committee recommended that the bill be passed two weeks later without holding any public hearings. The Senate enacted the bill on September 26, 1966, with no debate. The Senate report noted that the merger would not diminish the rights of football players; in fact, the committee report suggested that the merger would increase players' salaries as well as increase the overall employment opportunities for athletes. Not surprisingly, the Committee also noted that without the merger, "there was danger that some of the less favorably situated franchises in both existing leagues faced dissolution or transfers to other cities" (Sobel, 1977, p. 386).

Michael Roberts (1977, pp. 16–17) suggests that the prompt exemption of the AFL–NFL merger from antitrust legislation is another example of collusion between governmental agencies and the sports establishment. In this context, Roberts refers to a speech Senator Everett Dirksen gave to the Washington Touchdown Club in 1977 upon receiving the "Mr. Sam Award" for outstanding service by a public official in the interests of sports.

> At the Touchdown Club rostrum, Dirksen delivered a play-by-play account of the legislative Super Bowl resulting in his enshrinement. He characterized the defensive signals called by the opposition captain, Representative Emanuel Celler, as delaying tactics. "The clock was ticking toward the end of the game, and the Senate grabbed the ball," said Dirksen. Then: "In the huddle I motioned to Senator Russell Long that now was the time for the long bomb and for him to run like hell for the goalpost. Some people accused us of a sneakplay or an endaround play, but it wasn't. I just faded back to pass to Russell Long heading for the goal line with Celler watching the clock."

> Dirksen tempered his braggadocio by confessing that he hadn't really been at the top of his form: The Senate team, he admitted, had not been able to surpass its feat of 1962, when the NFL wanted a quickly crafted antitrust loophole to permit collective negotiations with the television networks. That year it took just 12 days between introduction and enactment of the bill. The quarterback of the "world's greatest deliberative body" apologized to his fans for taking a bit longer to push the merger bill across the goal line. . . .
>
> In his fulsome paean to camaraderie between pols and captains of athletic industry, Dirksen left the impression that the lawmakers had nothing on their minds but the obvious worthiness of whatever pro football wants (Roberts, 1977, pp. 16–17).

The Rozelle Rule was undermined in 1974 by a federal district judge in the Joe Kapp case with the ruling that the Rozelle provision was illegal and that the standard player contract violated the antitrust laws. The reserve clause in professional football was definitively voided in 1975 by the ruling of another federal judge who declared it illegal and enjoined the owners of NFL teams to cease the enforcement of the Rozelle Rule. In 1977 the NFL players' union reached a five-year collective bargaining agreement with the owners' association in an attempt to reduce conflict and expensive legal action. As part of this agreement, the Rozelle Rule was watered down with provisions specifying that the team losing a free-agent veteran would be compensated by a number of draft choices in proportion to the salary of the departing player. Moreover, a player is to be guaranteed 110 percent of his salary during the year in which he plays out his option.

Professional Basketball

The reserve clause was first challenged in professional basketball in 1961 when the Syracuse Nationals of the National Basketball Association took legal action against Dick Barnett to prevent him from jumping to a Cleveland team in the rival American Basketball League. Barnett claimed that the reserve clause in the NBA, which was identical to baseball, was unreasonable because it was permanent. The owner of his contract argued that the reserve clause involved only a one-year renewal. The court ruled against Barnett, noting that the constraint was "reasonable, practical, just and in accord with principles" (House Select Committee, 1976c, p. 14).

The next significant court action in professional basketball concerning the reserve clause occurred in 1975 when the players' union of the NBA went to courts in an attempt to prevent the merger of the National and American Basketball Leagues on the grounds that it would produce a monopoly. The Players Association also asked the court to ban the player draft and to outlaw the reserve clause on the grounds of restraint of trade. The court ruled against the players' union. Nevertheless, only a year later and no doubt in response to the dismantling of the reserve clause in baseball and football, the owners and players of the NBA reached a voluntary agreement on the liberalization of the reserve clause as part of a new collective bargaining agreement (House Select Committee, 1976c, p. 19).

> A team which drafts a player has one year to sign him. If the player is not signed he may be drafted a second time and that team has 1 year to sign him. If he does not sign after a year he becomes a free agent and may be signed by any team without compensation or penalty.

> Except in certain instances for rookies or where specifically agreed to by a veteran, option clauses are eliminated. Hereafter until the end of the 1980–1981 playing season a player who completes the term of his contract may negotiate with any other club in the league. The club that signs the free agent must compensate the old team. If an agreement on compensation is not reached, the Commissioner may award the prior team players and/or draft picks and/or cash.
>
> After the 1980–1981 season and until the end of the 1986–1987 playing season the compensation rule is abolished. Instead, during that period a veteran free agent may negotiate with any club. However, his prior club has the opportunity to substantially match the new offer (right of first refusal) and if it does, the player remains with the old club. Disputes over equivalency of offers will be taken to arbitration.
>
> The NBA agrees to pay an indemnity of $4.3 million to the players that brought the suit plus attorneys' fees and costs totalling in excess of $900,000 (House Select Committee, 1976c, p. 19).

Professional Hockey

Up until 1974 the National Hockey League had a permanent reserve clause similar to that of baseball. The emergence of the World Hockey Association in 1972 led to litigation because, at that time, all minor league teams had affiliations with the NHL. When the teams of the WHA began play it had 345 players on its twelve teams; over 200 of them were subject to reserve clauses stemming from their contracts of the previous year. As would be expected, the NHL entered the courts in an attempt to prevent league-jumping. "Of four actions that came to decision in 1972, the WHA won three and arguably gained greater benefit from the fourth which the NHL technically won" (House Select Committee, 1976c, p. 13).

In a case involving Gerry Cheevers, the court reviewed the reserve clause and the affiliation agreements between the NHL and minor leagues and ruled that this set of arrangements restrained trade in professional hockey. In the same year the court ruled in favor of the New York Islanders (WHA) with a decision that NHL contracts violated the Sherman Antitrust Act. Similarly, in a suit brought forth by a WHA franchise in Philadelphia, the court ruled that the NHL violated antitrust legislation because its affiliation with minor league teams gave it overwhelming control over the supply of players available for play in the new league. The last case in 1972 involved a suit by the NHL attempting to block Gary Peters from jumping to the new league. The court enjoined Gary Peters from entering the new league until he had played out his option in a final year of service in the NHL. In this case the NHL effectively abandoned its defense of a perpetual reserve clause when it argued that Peters should have been blocked from league jumping for three years to coincide with the terms of a collective bargaining agreement between the league and the players union.

The issue was settled in 1973 when the NHL abandoned its perpetual reserve clause in favor of a one-year option clause coupled with a player equalization condition involving compensation to the parent team as determined by compulsory arbitration. A neutral arbitrator then rules on the appropriate compensation for the team losing the player's services by committing future draft choices, assignments of other players' contracts, and/or cash payment.

SPORT REFORM MOVEMENTS

The conflict between sport entrepreneurs and the fans is becoming increasingly overt over the transfer of sport franchises, the trading of star players and the loss of local favorites through free agency, the cost of tickets and parking, and high-priced junk food at stadium concessions. Increasingly, fans view themselves as powerless in the face of franchise owners. Fan loyalty is fractured by franchise transfers such as the movement of the Nets and Giants from New York to New Jersey. More and more we see calls for a Federal Sports Commission to regulate the sports industry and to protect the interests of the consumer. Moreover, fans now realize that the escalation of multimillion dollar contracts for players are inevitably passed through to the customers.

The plan to move the Oakland Raiders to Los Angeles in 1980 spawned a "Save Our Raiders" movement among the local fans. Activists distributed thousands of "Fan Survival Kits" requesting participation in a protest wherein fans withdrew their attendance from the first five minutes of a nationally televised game in Oakland. The organizers requested that the spectators congregate outside the stadium during this interim for a protest meeting that would include local celebrities and musicians donating their time. The hope was that this action would produce a media event to gain publicity for their cause.

In the last decade or so, the public has made sporadic efforts to organize as an interest group within the world of sport. The most systematic attempt occurred in 1977 when Ralph Nader, inspired by success in other spheres of consumer advocacy, attempted to mount a sports consumer association on a nationwide basis under the acronym of FANS—Fight to Advance the Nation's Sports. The association would be designed to protect the general interests of sports fans and taxpayers vis à vis the interests of the owners and players. An association of this type would ostensibly negotiate with the sports establishment on matters such as ticket prices, the location of new sports facilities and franchises, exert pressure for the disclosure of accounting data from team owners, organize spectator boycotts as a form of protest, and lobby with legislators for the general interests of the fan.

As a consumer movement, FANS was short-lived; it disbanded in the fall of 1978 after only a year of operation, during which it failed to reach its membership goals. Moreover, it experienced financial difficulty stemming from too few fee-paying members; its demise was also due to a poor reception on the part of the media, owners, and players (Diamond, 1977; Saxe, 1977).

The interests of the public are somewhat more diffuse than those of the owners and the athletes. The enthusiasm of the general public for sports sometimes leads to manipulation, and the lack of organization on the public's part makes them vulnerable to exploitation. For example, "Intercity and interstate rivalry (a virtual sports war is raging between New Jersey and New York) for attractive sports events and professional franchises keeps the general public and its representatives divided in their attempts to negotiate with sports entrepreneurs" (Johnson, 1978, p. 335).

The fans tend to view sports through a romantic and particularistic lens which blinds them to the fact that they do not have a lobby comparable to the league's or players' associations. Although representatives of the players' unions commonly assert a mutuality of interests between the fans and the public vis à vis the monopolistic power of the franchise owners, the fact is that the economic interests of the players commonly coincide with the owners at the expense of the public.

> When this is the case, players' representatives will either testify with the owners, as was the case in hearings held in Miami in 1978 on the effects of antiblackout legislation, or will be silent, as was the case in 1978 when the Ways and Means Committee considered and rejected the administration's tax proposal to disallow the purchase price of (season) tickets as a business tax deduction for entertainment activities. In such cases, it appears that the public is without a voice in the policymaking process of professional sports (Johnson, 1979, p. 112).

The conflict of interests inherent in various components of the sports world is laid bare in activist organizations that have emerged among sport reformers. For example, Sports For The People attempts to expand the opportunities for sports participation among the less privileged members of our society.[1] This association attempts to diffuse the philosophy that sport is a basic right for all individuals. Similarly, the Women's Sport Network functions as a coalition for research and advocacy of women's sports. The Women's Sport Network is a branch of Sports For The People and works in conjunction with the YWCA in New York City. It has a membership of female athletes, coaches, physical educators, and community organizers. This coalition is presently compiling an inventory of sports facilities and programs and will basically function as a resource center for women in the New York City area.

SPORT FROM A CONFLICT PERSPECTIVE

A conflict framework is commonly used to analyze issues of political economy in the sports industry. Jean-Marie Brohm (1978), for example, is explicit in viewing corporate sport through the lens of Marxism.

> While the national and international sports system is rapidly being colonised by state monopoly capitalism, the capitalist groups have in their turn developed a veritable sports industry, based not only on the production of articles and commodities linked to the practice of sport, but also the provision of sports services. The sports system has thus given rise to its own industry on a capitalist basis. The capitalist system, as we know, obeys the laws of the expansion of capital. In order to maintain the average rate of profit in the face of inter-capitalist competition, owners of capital seek virgin areas for investment and the extraction of surplus value. The constant equalization of the rate of profit explains the dizzy slide of capital from one sector of economic activity to another and the opening up of new areas for the accumulation of capital. This bears out the basic law of capital as Marx stated it: "accumulate, for ever accumulate!' To meet the difficulties caused by over-capitalization and over-production in traditional industrial sectors, capital is invested in 'marginal' sectors such as services, tourism and

---

[1]The address of Sports For The People is 834 East 156th Street, Bronx, New York 10455.

> sport. This explains the sudden expansion of the sports industry during the 1960s. Eventually, through a promotional sales strategy, the sports industry finds its way into every part of the food, clothing and leisure industries (p. 134).

One does not have to be a Marxist to perceive elements of class conflict within the world of sports. The separate class interests of owners, players, and fans underlie current controversies over the relocation of sport franchises, public subsidy of sports facilities, free agency, tax shelters, television blackouts of home games, the legality of sport on cable television, and players' objections to artificial turf. These issues clearly indicate that sport is heavily involved with the "cash nexus" as a component of the entertainment industry. Sport entrepreneurs must struggle for their share of the entertainment dollar by marketing their product in a very competitive industry.

From the Marxist perspective, the power of the sport entrepreneurs (the ruling class) is derived from the superior economic resources available to franchise owners for legal support, lobbying, and access to the media. The robber barons of sport are viewed as controlling the means of sport production. They are able to develop political support through propaganda in the mass media, which commonly results in favorable treatment from governmental agencies. The different interests of the owners and players result in a form of class consciousness that reflects their respective economic position; each becomes a "class of itself" through their respective organizations—trade associations and player unions. The superior resources of the owners enables them to induce false consciousness among the general public by emphasizing the apolitical and integrative aspects of sports, sport as a meritocracy and agency for social mobility, and by basically presenting sport as a mirror of society.

Much of the theoretical writing on sport in North America is informed by a conflict perspective (cf. Gruneau, 1975; Kidd, 1980; Petrie, 1975; and Scott, 1971). Marxist critiques of sport are prevalent in France, Germany, and Italy. On the other hand, much of the empirical literature on sport in North America reflects an implicit functionalist perspective that focuses on the more salutary consequences of sport for the larger society. The last decade or so has produced a plethora of sport polemics in a more popular vein (cf. Durso, 1971; Hoch, 1972; Meggysey, 1971; Parrish, 1972; and Shaw, 1972).

The newspapers are replete with complaints about greedy owners, tax evaders, super-brat athletes, and lightweight hitters who play out their option only to be signed by other teams at salaries equal to top executives of leading corporations, while the tab is picked up by the fans through an increase in ticket prices. The idols have fallen. We no longer see sports reporters writing in mythic terms *a la* Grantland Rice—"Outlined against a blue-gray October sky, the Four Horsemen rode again." The average fan knows as much about the salary packages and investment schemes of contemporary athletes as they do about batting averages and votes for the Heisman Award. Nevertheless, the perennial attraction of sport is strong enough to outweigh the occasional profanations.

It should be pointed out in this context that not all intellectuals see a need for serious reform within professional sports. Perhaps the feeling is that the cure can sometimes be more painful than the disease. Dowling (1977) suggests that the overall history of governmental efforts at reform does not inspire confidence; consider, for example, the boomerang effects that resulted from governmental interventions in the oil industry and agribusiness or the bonanzas created for the medical industry through Medicare. Dowling offers the following assessment:

> But, of course, one knows where the real sin of sports lies; sports is partly a business and partly the purveyed dreams of boyhood innocence and glory. The two are hard to reconcile. I wish one could ignore the business part, but the sports pages won't allow it. What was once merely escapist entertainment has now become an adjunct of the "dismal science," a job for Ralph Nader. The curious thing is this: Sports is probably more equitable, more consumer oriented and more honestly run than enterprises far more essential to our welfare. Yet there seems to be no alternative (given what sportscasters call momentum) but to continue to denigrate and meddle with the dream until it ceases to give us any pleasure. Sports is a business that manufactures and sells dreams, and I have to wonder whether dream factories don't merit more lenient treatment than they are getting. Escapism, too, is in the public interest (p. 52).

Bethell (1980) also suggests that the consumer movement has been a mixed blessing for Everyman. He points out paradoxically that Common Cause may have done more harm than good as a public-interest lobby tinkering with the political process. In a similar vein, William Gaylin et al. (1978) published a book entitled *Doing Good: The Limits of Benevolence.* These authors show how governmental attempts to improve human services tend to result in undesirable forms of coercion; the beneficiaries can become "prisoners of benevolence." Therefore, they propose the principle that governmental programs "ought to be evaluated, not on the basis of the good it might do, but rather on the basis of the harm it might do. Those programs ought to be adopted that seem to be the least likely to making things worse" (p. 145).

SPORT FROM A FUNCTIONALIST PERSPECTIVE

As we discussed in Chapter 3, the functionalist perspective on social life focuses on the mechanism of order and equilibrium rather than coercion and conflict. Functionalist theory emphasizes the collectivity rather than the individual; consequently, it tends to focus on social solidarity and cohesion. According to functionalist theory, the basis of social order is moral consensus—shared values, sentiments and traditions. Society is viewed as a type of organism wherein the whole is greater than, and different from, the sum of its parts. Society is a social system that results in common advantages that could not be achieved by individuals acting alone.

The functionalist perspective on sport is evident in the thinking of both scholars and laypersons. For example, the physical educator's ideal of a sound mind in a sound body is obviously functional for the larger society. Similarly, the internalization of the work ethic, self-discipline, and team work transfers from the playing field to the economic and political spheres. In some respects, youth sports do prepare one for the larger game of life. Although it cannot be proven that the Battle of Waterloo was won on the playing fields of Eton, many would agree that the personality characteristics emphasized in competitive sports help to prepare one for life.

Moreover, it can be argued that sport is the one element of popular culture that appeals to all social strata. Sports are less class-linked than other aspects of the mass media (Loy et al., 1978, p. 298). Sport provides a wholesome form of spectator entertainment for a broad segment of society, and a healthy form of exercise for a smaller proportion of society. By virtue of this common denominator function, sports facilitate social integration. Moreover, in a largely impersonal society, sports as a topic of conversation facilitate social access among strangers.

Harry Edwards (1973) has delineated the "Sports Creed' as it exists in America—fitness, character development, discipline, competition, religiosity, and nationalism. This value cluster correlates nicely with the traditional American achievement ethic; the sports creed reinforces the American Dream and is thus functional for societal integration. Although some elements of the sports creed sometimes get skewed in the sphere of institutionalized athletics (as revealed in periodic scandals), it is clear that sports reinforce the American way of life and thus serve to legitimate the larger social system.

As noted in Chapters 3 and 9, the values inherent in the sport subculture are isomorphic with the larger society—particularly vis à vis the economic, political and religious institutions. In other words, there is a certain amount of overlap and mutual reinforcement among these institutions. For example, in both institutionalized sport and the world of work, a strong emphasis is placed on investments and returns, competition, and the importance of individual motivation. Both sport and the free enterprise system are based on the concept of meritocracy and a latter day form of social Darwinism.

In the functionalist perspective, the rules of the game are public and fair in athletics, economics, and politics; success is based on individual motivation and ability. If one adheres to the rules and works hard, it is possible to succeed. On the other hand, in both sports and the larger game of life, not everybody can be a winner; therefore, it is important to be a good loser (sportsmanship). The loser will have another opportunity; be prepared, the system is not at fault. "A quitter never wins, and a winner never quits."

According to this perspective, both sports and society benefit from the competitive process in which one pits his or her skills against others, with the best rising to the top. In this context it is commonly thought that sport is the one area of social life in which only ability and effort count—a meritocracy writ small. Any mother's son can rise to become a pitching star for the New York Yankees; race and humble birth are not barriers within the world of sport.

In sum, one can argue that sport, like any other cultural element, emerges and continues out of collective interests and needs (Coakley, 1978, p. 17). Sport contributes to pattern maintenance of the larger society by instilling values, norms, and motivation appropriate to membership in the society. Similarly, sport contributes to tension management in society by providing an intense form of entertainment for a broad segment of the population that helps individuals to become recreated for their instrumental duties as worker, parent, student, and community member. Moreover, sport contributes to the maintenance of society by helping the individual adapt, adjust, and conform to societal expectations. Sport discipline helps to restrain egotism while developing a spirit of team work—"There is no 'I' in team," and "Who passed you the ball when you scored?"

CONCLUSION

In this chapter we have analyzed professional sports in the United States as a business enterprise and its characteristics as a component of the recreational industry. In particular, we have discussed professional sports within the context of political economy—specifically with respect to corporate sports vis à vis the courts and the regulatory agencies of the federal government. We have also discussed various attempts to reform the world of sports as a part of the consumer movement and as part of grass roots political activism.

This chapter discusses in detail the ways in which professional sports franchises benefit from public subsidies and carry out several monopolistic practices. These practices have been defined as legal by the courts and Congress. The general assumption seems to be that the peak-and-valley nature of the sports business flowing from the unpredictability of win-loss records and concomitant fan support necessitates some inducements for investment in team ownership. "The owners have simply taken advantage of the fact that sport in American society has traditionally been defined as an activity *apart* from everyday affairs" (Coakley, 1978, p. 215).

In concluding this chapter, we wish to emphasize that the world of sport reflects an ethos or world view inherent in the larger society; consequently, an analysis of sports provides insights into the society at large. For example, the philosophical foundation of institutionalized sport is a meritocratic perspective on social inequality that correlates with the ethos of modern industrial society. Within a meritocratic philosophy, the emphasis is more on equal opportunity in the process of *recruitment* than on inequalities of *rewards*. From this perspective, then, social stratification, inequality, and hierarchy are not problematic as long as the system remains open and provides opportunity for all to compete for positions and rewards. "An open system is necessary so that the most qualified—the most useful—persons in a society will come to occupy the most important positions" (Gruneau, 1975, p. 130). Thus, one can see that the Sports Creed is eminently compatible with the meritocratic value system of a free enterprise economy.

The affirmation of meritocracy within both sport and the larger society is a key example of the way that radical sports critics view sport as reinforcing the ideological hegemony (domination) of the conventional wisdom in the larger society.

> Recent egalitarian criticisms of sport are far more radical than their meritocratic counterparts, in that they challenge the whole concept of rationalized competition and suggest that the popularity of sport aids in the "ideological hegemony" of ruling groups. This hegemonic process operates at two levels: (a) a social psychological level wherein sport involvement is seen to inculcate a belief in inequality through meritocracy; and (b) an institutional level, wherein the apolitical mythology of sport's "ludic" foundations ostensibly eliminates the exposure of athletes to any radical political framework (Gruneau, 1975, p. 132).

The concept of hegemony derives from the Marxist theory of Antonio Gramsci (1971) wherein *cultural forces* are analyzed as sources of coercion that supplement the economic forces of oppression as conceived by Karl Marx. As outlined by Gramsci, ideological hegemony, or the rule by ideas, is more effective than overt political power; the consent of the masses that the ruling class achieves through intellectual and moral direction is the ultimate form of coercion. "No regime could sustain itself by exercising control and domination over the masses; it will need the 'ideological consent' of the masses" (Salamini, 1979, p. 368). *Hegemony* is the process by which control is exercised through a subtle transformation of human consciousness whereby the consent of the masses is achieved through an internalization of the existing social order as the natural state of things. Consequently, the individual comes to want to do what he or she has to do as common sense knowledge.

Thus, "hegemony refers to ideological dominance exercised by a ruling class through its intellectual and moral leadership. This leadership is objectified in and exercised through the religious, educational, and cultural institutions of society" (McQuarie, 1980, p. 248). The cultural hegemony of the establishment is diffused through the mass media, schools, and ancillary institutions such as sport. Although the concept of hegemony is identified with a Marxist perspective, conventional sociological analysis also highlights the resonance among sports, religion, economics, and politics.

As analyzed earlier, institutionalized sport diffuses and reinforces the values of the larger society and socializes the participants with a distinctive world view. Similarly, the multiplicity of aphorisms used by coaches in the training process are expressive of the conventional world view—"Nobody ever drowned in sweat," "Live by the code or get out," "An ounce of loyalty is worth a pound of cleverness." From the perspective of conflict theory, then, the world of institutionalized sport is a species of hegemony in the sense that it is built on the internalization of values and norms that represent the quintessence of the ideology dominating the larger society.

The basic purpose of this chapter, then, was to delineate the ways in which professional sports are related to the economic and political institutions; we have attempted to provide theoretical underpinnings for these interrelationships. In the following chapter, we extend our analysis of the political economy of sports by means of three case studies showing the ways in which sports are embedded in the political and economic spheres. Although sport is commonly viewed as an island unto itself, the courts and Congress have initiated periodic interventions in the world of sport over the past sixty years in the United States. Moreover, professional athletes and team owners are increasingly turning to the courts and regulatory agencies of the government for redress of perceived grievances. Consequently, professional sports are now taking on the form of a public utility. It is unlikely, however, that the regulatory agencies will be any more successful in mediating the disparate interests of team owners, athletes, and the general public than they have been in regulating other public utilities.

CHAPTER 15

The Political Economy of Sports: Three Case Studies

In the previous chapter we outlined some economic and political aspects of sport in modern society. In the present chapter we offer three case studies that demonstrate the variety of relationships between sport, economics, and politics. These interinstitutional relationships illustrate why various writers refer to "the political economy of sports."

CASE 1: THE OLYMPIC GAMES

The modern Olympic movement began in 1896 under the leadership of Baron Pierre de Coubertin, who established the forerunner of today's International Olympic Committee. The Baron was interested in overall educational reform in France and, particularly, in building a stronger nation through physical fitness and sport programs in French schools. As a result of his travel throughout Europe and North America, de Coubertin gradually came to the belief that sports could serve as a means of establishing international goodwill and mutual understanding to the ultimate end of world peace. He viewed the revival of the Olympic Games as laying a foundation for friendship and cooperation through sports contests (Strenk, 1979, p. 139). On a more pragmatic level, de Coubertin was also distressed by the dismal performance of France in recent military efforts, especially vis à vis Germany. "France needed strong physical specimens to deal with her more numerous neighbors across the Rhine, and de Coubertin offered his country a means of obtaining them" (Lowe et al., 1978, p. 114).

De Coubertin (1978) was utopian in his stance toward the peace-making role of the Olympics: "Wars break out because nations misunderstand each other. We shall not have peace until the prejudices which now separate the different races shall have been outlived. To attain this end, what better means than to bring the youth of all countries periodically together for amicable trials of muscular strength and agility. The Olympic Games, with the ancients, controlled athletes and promoted peace. It is not visionary to look to them for similar benefactions in the future" (p. 127). De Coubertin was also idealistic concerning the nature of competition at the Olympics: "The most important thing is not to win but to take part, just as the most important thing in life is not the triumph but the struggle. The essential thing is not to have conquered but to have fought well" (quoted in *President's Commission*, 1977, p. 1).

The Olympic Games have fallen short of de Coubertin's vision in the twentieth century; the Games have been contaminated by national self-interest, pecuniary overlays, ideological demonstrations, and jurisdictional conflicts. The Olympic Games have proven to be a microcosm of the larger social structure—"Given all these factors, sports will continue to remain political. The idea of unpolitical sports is, and always has been, a myth. Modern sports are, indeed, a 'war without weapons' " (Strenk, 1979, p. 140).

Unfortunately, it is not true that athletics, like music and other fine arts, transcend the world of politics. We have outlined a sampling of the political conflicts that have emerged in the nine Olympic Games since World War II (Espy, 1979).

1948 Germany, Japan, and Italy banned from participation in the Summer Games at London by the victorious allies.

1952 Controversy concerning the validity of both of East and West Germany participating in the Summer Games at Helsinki. Soviet Union introduces the Cold War into the Olympics by housing its athletes apart from the Olympic Village.

1956 Controversy concerning the validity of both mainland and Nationalist China participating in the Summer Games at Melbourne. Lebanon, Iraq, and Egypt withdraw from the games in protest over the Suez Canal.

1960 Protest against participation of South Africa and Taiwan in Summer Games at Rome. Controversy over commercialism in the Olympics stemming from the expenditure of $30 million by the Rome Organizing Committee.

1964 Indonesia and North Korea withdraw from Summer Games in Tokyo due to political differences with International Olympic Committee. A challenge emerges concerning the participation by Taiwan and South Africa.

1968 Black athletes in the United States organize a boycott of the Olympic trials. Tommie Smith and John Carlos raise clenched fists in black power salute and lower their heads during the national anthem on the victors' stand; Olympic Committee strips them of their medals and bans them from future Olympic competition. South Africa is "disinvited" from Olympic participation in Mexico City Games in response to protest from black African nations.

1972 Arab terrorists kidnap and murder eight Israeli athletes at the Summer Games in Munich. Two black American medal winners in track (Vince Matthews and Wayne Collett) stage a low profile demonstration on the victor's stand to protest the casual attitudes of white Americans toward black Americans; Olympic Committee bans them from future Olympic competition.

1976 Thirty-two nations boycott Summer Games in Montreal in protest over New Zealand's sports relations with South Africa. Taiwan and South Africa barred from participation based on political considerations.

1980 The United States leads a boycott of the Summer Games in Moscow as a protest against the Soviet Union's intervention in Afghanistan, thus effecting the first large-scale boycott of the Olympics in the modern era.

It is interesting to note in this connection that political demonstrations of an affirmative nature have not been criticized by the International Olympic Committee even though nationalistic expression violates the spirit of the Olympics (Thirer, 1978). In fact, three recent Olympians from the United States were lionized for what could be considered jingoistic behavior. In the 1972 Olympic Games George Foreman walked around the ring waiving an American flag after having won a gold medal in boxing. Bruce Jenner, similarly, ran around a track at the 1976 Olympic Games waving an American flag after having won a gold medal in the decathalon. Even more dramatically, Jim Craig wrapped himself in a large American flag on the ice after the USA won the gold medal in hockey at the 1980 Winter Games. The mass media, especially television, are a stimulus for such "positive" demonstrations.

The Economics of the Olympics

The issue of economic excess within the Olympic Games first emerged in connection with the 1960 Summer Games at Rome. For some years prior to 1960, Avery Brundage, the long-term President of the International Olympic Committee, had been suggesting a de-escalation of the Olympics on the grounds that they were becoming unmanageable. As more events were added to the schedule every four years, the cost of mounting the Olympic Games increased. At the 1960 Summer Games, Brundage lamented that the "Games have become 'Big Business' with obvious danger to Olympic ideals" (Espy, 1979, p. 73).

The cost of mounting the Olympic Games is startling; Los Angeles was able to hold the 1932 Summer Games for about $6 million, but by 1976 this figure had escalated to almost $1.5 billion in Montreal. It is estimated that the 1976 Games cost each taxpayer in Montreal about $726; alternatively, it has been suggested that Montreal's investment in the Olympics could have been spent on low-rent housing for 120,000 citizens or free public transportation for ten years (Loy et al., 1978, pp. 280–81). Canadian officials had hoped that the private sector could have financed the bulk of the cost of the 1976 Olympics in Montreal through the selling of rights as official supplier. "For example, such firms as Coca-Cola paid $1.3 million plus all the free coke the athletes could drink to be an 'official supplier'; Pitney-Bowes paid $350,000, and Adidas shoes paid $500,000. The list was endless. Beyond the commercial contributions, the organizing committee had planned to sell commemorative coins and stamps, to hold lotteries, and to gain revenue through the sale of television rights" (Espy, 1978, p. 160). The best estimate is that the Soviet Union spent about $2 billion to stage the 1980 Summer Games and was not averse to seeking donations of equipment from Western corporations and royalty income from "official suppliers."

NBC purchased the rights to televise the 1980 Summer Games for $85 million. ABC was awarded the contract to broadcast the 1984 Olympics for a whopping $225 million—$125 million for production and support facilities and $100 million for television rights. ABC plans more than 200 hours of Olympic television coverage in 1984, which results in a cost of about one million dollars per hour of coverage. The $225 million paid by ABC for the contract to televise the 1984 Olympics represents a dramatic increase over the $13.5 million paid by the same network for the broadcasting rights to the 1974 Olympics.

The Winter Games have been a continuing source of controversy both in terms of cost and potential environmental injury to rural areas in which they are held. It is estimated that the 1948 Winter Olympics at St. Moritz did not exceed $5 million in cost; the 1964 event at Innsbruck saw an increase in cost to over $100 million. The 1968 Winter Olympics at Grenoble cost over $400 million, while the event in 1972 at Sapporo soared to about $700 million, which represents an investment of some $700,000 per competitor. "The sheer logistics of endeavoring to stage a Winter Olympics in or near a city environment escalates all costs, traffic control, parking, housing, sanitation, transporting, and multiple other administrative problems, in almost a direct ratio to the size of the city, and far out of proportion in relation to the events themselves" (Subcommittee on Transportation and Commerce, 1976, pp. 32–33).

The Winter Olympics have also been tainted by commercialism in the form of product endorsement. It is commonly believed that winter competitors receive remuneration from sporting goods manufacturers for openly advertising their products, especially at victory ceremonies. This form of commercialism leads to controversy about the amateur status of Olympic athletes. Olympic Rule 34 specifies that "no commercial advertising is permitted on equipment used in the Games nor on the uniforms or numbers"; moreover, Rule 54 specifies that "the display of clothing or equipment marked conspicuously for advertising purposes will normally result in immediate disqualifications or withdrawal of credentials" (Nafziger, 1978, p. 169).

Sporting goods manufacturers in Japan, Austria, Germany, France, Switzerland, Finland, Canada, the United States, and other nations compete vigorously for their share of the winter sports market. Sports equipment is a big business that is zealously pursued through the advertising medium of the Olympic Games, especially via the worldwide television coverage. It has been estimated, for example, that the 1972 Winter Games in Sapporo led to the sale of 16 million pairs of skis (Brohm, 1976, p. 163).

Similar issues surround endorsements at the Summer Games. For example, at the 1968 Olympic Games in Mexico City, it became known that two of the leading manufacturers of track shoes (Adidas and Puma) had paid Olympic athletes to wear their products. "In the process of investigation it was revealed that manufacturers were in the habit of paying athletes to use their equipment, and that such payments had become a major source of income for athletes" (Espy, 1979, p. 120). The controversies concerning endorsement and advertising have led to cynical comments concerning "shamateurism." Moreover, such abuses lead to suspicions that sport at all levels has now become a business enterprise; the reality of profit has displaced the philosophy of sport as a disinterested end in itself.

Boycott of 1980 Summer Games

It is interesting to compare American justifications for the boycott of the 1980 Summer Games in Moscow with the rhetoric that had been offered four years earlier in support of having the 1980 Winter Games in Lake Placid, New

York. In March 1976, the Congressional Subcommittee on Transportation and Commerce conducted hearings on the proposal for the 1980 Winter Olympics because the Lake Placid Olympic Organizing Committee was requesting a $50 million subsidy from the Federal government as cost-sharing in the support of the Winter Games. As part of these Congressional hearings, a representative of the Lake Placid Committee testified that

> the Olympic Games is an impressive and rather wonderful title representing the world's greatest sports spectacle. . . . But, also, just as the Olympic Games are the greatest sports spectacle in the world, they are, at one and the same time, one of the world's greatest movements for peace. It is fitting that in these troubled times, the United States, world leader in the search for peace has been designated the host country for the 1980 Olympic Winter Games. It is here on this field of friendly rivalry, forgetting for the moment politics and many other problems that beset us, that the world's greatest nations meet on a common ground—athletic endeavor (Subcommittee on Transportation, 1976, p. 14).

Similarly, in September, 1977, the Congressional Subcommittee on International Organizations conducted hearings on the desirability of hosting the 1984 Summer Olympic Games in the United States, specifically in Los Angeles. As part of these hearings, the House and the Senate affirmed that "the Olympic Games further the cause of world peace and understanding," and that "the nation hosting the Games performs an act of international goodwill" (Subcommittee on International Organizations, 1977, p. 1). During these hearings, Michael Harrigan, former Executive Director of the President's Commission on Olympic sports, testified concerning the international value of the Olympic Games:

> The important thing here is that this is an argument for the Olympic Games to be held in the United States. Only the United States can turn the clock back to games that are free from politics. . . there is no doubt in my mind that hosting the Games in 1984 will be an act of leadership on the part of the United States which will be felt around the world. I am convinced that the peoples of the world will know that they will be able to come and enjoy the Games for the purposes that they were originally conceived. The Olympic movement needs leadership to survive; I believe the United States can provide it in a big way by hosting the 1984 games (Subcommittee on International Organizations, 1977, p. 5).

During these same hearings, John C. Argue, President of the Southern California Committee for the Olympic Games, offered the following tribute to the Olympic Games:

> The Olympics are clearly the greatest sports event in the world, and more than that, represent a great festival of youth and a powerful force for good and peace. The Olympics are not perfect, as nothing run by mere men (and women) is; however, the Olympics do represent a great concept and stand for what is best in the world. The Olympics are worth preserving (p. 25).

It might be noted that the American boycott of the 1980 Summer Games was mobilized in a "conservative" context, whereas the attempted boycott of the 1968

Summer Games by black American athletes was initiated by a "radical" philosophy. Harry Edwards, a black sociologist, was a prime mover of the 1968 protest. He argued what does it profit black athletes to win hundreds of medals for the United States while their brothers and sisters were being bombed in churches, being bitten by police dogs, fired upon with high pressure water hoses, confined to ghettos, and generally being treated as second-class citizens. Edwards and others involved in the 1968 Olympic Project for Human Rights were strongly criticized for injecting politics into the Olympics. Edwards (1980) reflects on his experience with the 1968 Olympic protest in his autobiography entitled *The Struggle That Must Be*. Edwards finds it ironic that twelve years after he was criticized as a black radical for leading a protest against the Olympics, the President of the United States led a multinational boycott of the Summer Games in Moscow. President Carter corroborated Edwards' proposition that sports are indeed political.

President Carter wrote a letter to the United States Olympic Committee to explain the administration's rationale for the boycott of the 1980 Summer Games in Moscow. His letter took note of the "meaning of sacrifice" of world-class athletes who had to forego participation. The President also reaffirmed "the desirability of keeping governmental policy out of the Olympics, but deeper issues are at stake"; among these issues was "access to a major part of the world's oil supplies." Mr. Carter also expressed support for the movement to establish a permanent site for the Summer Games in Greece to minimize political contamination in the future. An excerpt from President Carter's letter to the U.S. Olympic Committee is reproduced here.

> I want to reaffirm my own personal commitment to the principles and purposes of the Olympic movement. I believe in the desirability of keeping Government policy out of the Olympics, but deeper issues are at stake.
>
> In the Soviet Union international sports competition is itself an aspect of Soviet government policy, as is the decision to invade Afghanistan. The head of the Moscow Olympic Organizing Committee is a high Soviet Government official.
>
> The Soviet Government attaches enormous political importance to the holding of the 1980 Olympic Games in Moscow and if the Olympics are not held in Moscow because of Soviet military aggression in Afghanistan, this powerful signal of world outrage cannot be hidden from the Soviet people, and will reverbrate around the globe. Perhaps it will deter future aggression.
>
> I therefore urge the USOC, in cooperation with other National Olympic Committees, to advise the International Olympic Committee (IOC) that if Soviet troops do not fully withdraw from Afghanistan within the next month, Moscow will become an unsuitable site for a festival meant to celebrate peace and good will. Should the Soviet Union fail to withdraw its troops within the time prescribed above, I urge the USOC to propose that the Games either be transferred to another site such as Montreal or to multiple sites, or be cancelled for this year. If the International Olympic Committee rejects such a USOC proposal, I urge the USOC and the Olympic Committees of other like-minded nations not to participate in the Moscow Games. In this event, if suitable arrangements can be made, I urge that such nations conduct alternative games of their own this summer at some other appropriate site or sites. The United States Government is prepared to lend its full support to any and all such efforts." (Carter, 1980, p. 51).

The Future

It is easy to become cynical about the negative aspects that have become a part of Olympic competition and to be patronizing about the noble ideals behind the Olympic Games. It is clear that the Olympic Games have always been political; however, there are different forms and degrees of politicization. Sugden and Yiannakis (1980) have identified four types of politicization in the Olympic context; the four types are listed here in ascending order of progressively more severe consequences for the Olympic movement.

1. The quest for national prestige in which nations seek to make their mark in the world community by achieving success at the Games.
2. The use of the Games by the host nation as a means of showcasing its political ideology and culture.
3. The use of athletic competition as a means for granting diplomatic recognition/nonrecognition to favored or delinquent nations.
4. The use of the Games in a manipulative fashion to coerce a nation to alter its internal or external political/military activities.

In recent decades we see a marked increase in the latter two, more severe types of political activity at the Olympic Games. Nations at all stages of economic development are attempting to use the games for political objectives; the worldwide television coverage provides an attractive propaganda vehicle. Reforms are needed to denationalize the Games and to establish superordinate patterns of identification on a transnational basis. "The question that we must confront therefore (in view of twentieth century political realities) is not whether the Games and politics are intertwined, but *what level of politicization* can we live with, without perverting or destroying the Games, and the noble ideals upon which they rest" (Sugden and Yiannakis, 1980, p. 1; see also Seppanen, 1981).

CASE 2: SPORTS TELECASTING

Television Contracts

As discussed in Chapter 13, sports telecasting is a lucrative enterprise for both the television networks and professional sports. The revenues that sports franchises receive from television contracts represent a lifeline for corporate sport in its present form. Consequently, professional sports leagues have instituted a number of policies governing television coverage that are designed to protect their economic interests. These protective mechanisms involve a number of issues in political economy that have been reviewed in the courts and in Congress, particularly with respect to monopoly and restraint of trade.

Within professional sports, competition over television coverage has been restricted in two basic ways (House Select Committee, 1976c, p. 9). First of all, the courts have granted sports leagues the exclusive right to control *national* broadcasts of sports events. This power was granted to professional sports leagues by Congress in September 1961 through Public Law 83-331. This piece of legislation empowers professional sports leagues to pool their broadcasting rights in order to sell the contract as a package to the highest bidder among the networks. Each team in the league then derives equal shares of the revenues derived from the pooled contract.

Secondly, each team has exclusive rights to broadcast all *home* games that are not in the national package, as well as the power to prevent the broadcasting in its home territory of any game not in the national package. Because professional teams have local monopolies or compete with only one other professional team in its market area, these provisions produce a local monopoly in broadcasting that can be more important to a club than league television contracts on a national basis.

The passage of Public Law 83-331 by Congress represents a legislative achievement for professional sports that is second in importance only to the 1922 exemption of baseball from federal antitrust laws. As noted previously, the 1961 Sports Broadcasting Act enables professional sports leagues to sell their national TV rights on a package basis without violating antitrust laws. In effect, a sports league can then function as a cartel, with the three major networks competing against themselves for the national contract. Although the networks clearly must pay a higher price under this pooling system, the networks can pass on the cost to the commercial sponsors, who in turn pass it through to the consumer. This arrangement results in greater revenues for sports franchises, a lock on national broadcasting rights for the major networks, and the elimination of competition from independent and regional networks.

Prior to the passage of Public Law 83-331, the broadcasting system in professional sports involved a decentralized system with considerable competition among the television networks. Each club negotiated a separate TV contract; in addition to ABC, CBS, and NBC, an independent network was also participating in the broadcasting of professional sports. "Thus, in 1960 and 1961, for example, the ABC network telecast AFL games, NBC telecast Baltimore and Pittsburgh of the NFL, and CBS telecast the remaining NFL teams other than the Cleveland Browns, who were telecast by Sports Network. With all the competing telecasts, in 1961 the fourteen NFL clubs averaged $250,000 in broadcast revenues. Without such competition, they averaged $1.1 million in 1964" (Horowitz, 1977, p. 163). Under the pre-1962 pluralistic system of broadcasting, highly successful teams and franchises located in the larger metropolitan areas were able to negotiate more lucrative television contracts than the less fortunate clubs.

Professional football, baseball, and basketball currently have national TV contracts on a pooled basis; their annual share of the national television contract on a per team basis in 1978–1979 was $5.8 million for football, $970,000 for baseball, and $880,000 for basketball. Each team also negotiates local television contracts on a regional basis. Within professional football and basketball, each team generated an additional $200,000 in 1978, on the average, from local broadcasting contracts. In professional baseball, the annual revenues from local broadcasting contracts in 1978 ranged from about $350,000 to $2.5 million, depending on the market area.

In addition to the pooling privilege which represents a type of monopoly, the courts have upheld the principle that franchise ownership includes exclusive television rights within the club's market area (generally defined in terms of a 75-mile radius). This unusual degree of market control is legally protected for two basic purposes: "first, in order to permit a member to protect its home gate receipts against the broadcast competition of *either* its own home games or those of other league members; and second, to assure each club a home territory broadcast monopoly" (Horowitz, 1977, p. 162). This restriction on television competition has not been extended to radio broadcasting because it is not generally considered a threat to attendance at home games.

The courts have defined this protection of local gate receipts through broadcasting restrictions as a reasonable restraint of trade. This legal exemption enables a sports franchise to exclude local television coverage of a competing game when the club is playing at home as well as to withhold television coverage of its own games that are not sold out. However, as will be discussed later, cable television is eroding the control that sport franchises have over television coverage of the same sport in its market area.

It can be argued that the legal exemptions provided by Congress and the courts in the sphere of sports broadcasting work to the advantage of the television networks and sports franchises at the expense of the general public:

> Professional team sports and television have enjoyed a pleasant and profitable relationship. Insofar as consumers ultimately pay some or all of a television sponsor's advertising costs through higher prices than would otherwise obtain, conventional telecasts of sports events are by no means 'free' to the public, nor does the public have an inherent 'right' to be offered a steady diet of sports events via conventional television. Indeed, the concern of Congress and the FCC with protecting the latter right translates into a protection of the 'rights' of a comparatively small set of sponsors and the television networks to be able to monopolize the sports-broadcast industry, and thus offer to nonfractionated television audiences whatever sports programming they want to offer them. It is equally true that, although professional team sports have a special place in our society, the leagues and clubs have no inherent 'right' to supracompetitive profits, and to the special exemptions from antitrust laws which would protect and/or create broadcast monopolies that could be exploited to yield those supracompetitive profits (Horowitz, 1977, p. 167).

Television Blackouts

In September 1973, Congress enacted Public Law 93-107 specifying that any professional game being broadcast by a television network under a league contract could not be blacked out if the contest was sold out 72 hours before the game. This law was passed in the public interest. The legislation contained a sunset provision specifying that the provision would expire at the end of 1975; since that time the National Football League has observed the law on a voluntary basis. The other professional sports leagues have not volunteered to abide by the provisions of Public Law 93-107, which is largely due to the fact that relatively few of their games are telecast via a national contract.

Since the original blackout legislation in 1973, the Federal government has published an annual report concerning the consequences of the antiblackout law (Committee on Commerce, 1979). The data show that the antiblackout law has had a negative impact on *season* ticket sales—a decrease of about 14 percent. It is also evident that the law has resulted in an increase in the number of "no-shows"—ticket holders who do not attend the game. About 8 percent of ticket holders for a sellout game do not attend when the game is telecast due to the 1973 law. In general, however, the antiblackout law does not appear to be an economic threat to the well-being of professional football, the only sport that has actually been affected by the law (Siegried and Hinshaw, 1977a, p. 646). The law has obviously been beneficial for sports fans; a substantially larger number of fans can now view their hometown heroes in sellout contests which would have otherwise been blacked out. The antiblackout law resulted in 109 home games being televised locally in 1973, 86 sold-out home games televised in 1974, and 75 sold-out home games televised in the 1975 season (Siegfried and Hinshaw, 1977b, p. 170). When given a choice of watching a home team game or another game on television at the same time, viewers prefer the home team game by a 5-to-1 margin.

The right afforded to owners of professional teams to deny telecasting of home games that are not sellouts implies a position on the part of the courts that the public does not have an inherent right to television coverage of sports events; however, the intervention of Congress via the antiblackout law was designed to maximize public access to television coverage. Interestingly, in this context Horowitz (1977) suggests that "the seemingly well-intentioned sporadic attempts to legislate the telecasting of various sports events represent rather presumptuous efforts on the part of legislators to interfere with the free-market system through state interventions that would be unthinkable in any other industry in our capitalistic society" (p. 162). As noted in the preceding chapter, the regulatory agencies of government tend to conceive of professional sports as a hybrid industry somewhere between a public utility and a free enterprise corporation.

Moreover, although the antiblackout law was passed in the public interest, the law can have an unanticipated consequence that affects the economic interests of the public. As Horowitz (1977, p. 165) points out, the increased number of games televised in a club's home territory resulting from the antiblackout law presumably increases the size of the television audience, and thus would logically raise the value of the league's TV contract that is sold to the networks. Because the networks will then have to pay more to the league for the television rights, the added costs have to be passed through to the corporate sponsors of the television commercials, who in turn pass on the incremental cost to the general public in the form of higher prices for the products.

Cable Television

Cable television was originally designed to improve the television reception for subscribers living in remote areas where television transmission was problematic. In recent decades, however, cable systems have spread to all regions of the country, including large metropolitan areas, and now offer a wide variety of programming, particularly in sports. The secondary transmission of sports via cable television (CATV) represents another issue of political economy within the world of sports. Presently, about 18 million homes are wired for CATV, approximately 25 percent of the homes with television sets. It is projected that by 1990 over half of the homes with television sets in America will be subscribers to CATV. More than thirty cable networks are presently operating in the United States—including networks that offer sports, news, and religion on a twenty-four-hour basis. "Most cable systems are capable of offering 12 or more channels of broadcast services; a few offer as many as 36 channels. Cable television's capacity to provide an abundance of channels through recent technological innovations has transformed it from a mere tool to improve television reception into a broadband communications vehicle" (Subcommittee on Communications, 1979, p. 2).

Cable owners are not required to be licensed by the FCC; the law requires only that the cable owners register with the Federal Communications Commission. As a nonwritten product, sporting events are not covered by copyright laws; consequently, cable networks can simply pick up sports broadcasts from the public air waves and export them to other regions. Professional sports leagues have been vigorously opposed to CATV because, among other reasons, it infringes on their much cherished right of exclusive market control in the home region.

Conclusion

The economic power of television plays an increasingly dominant role in professional sports. The substantial revenues derived from television contracts have encouraged sports leagues to adopt rules that restrict competition in the sale of broadcasting rights; these rules are also designed to protect the live attendance at home games of professional teams (Siegfried and Hinshaw, 1977a, p. 645):

1. An outside game could not be telecast in a third team's home territory when the home team was also televising an away game in its home territory.
2. An outside game could not be telecast in a third team's home territory when that team had a home game.
3. The clubs' television broadcast rights were pooled so that the league negotiated with the television networks for the sale of the collective rights.
4. "Blackout" agreements were made under the pooled arrangement which prevented the telecasting of a game at the same time and in the same area in which the game was being played.

When these rules have been challenged or threatened in recent years, the professional sports leagues have appealed to Congress and the courts for support. The leagues have been generally successful in securing legal reinforcement for the first three restrictions noted in the previous list; however, Congress has been reluctant to adopt legislation restricting the secondary transmission of sports telecasting via cable television, much to the disappointment of the sports establishment. It might also be noted that Congress ruled against the fourth restriction noted in the list when it passed Public Law 93-107, which permits local televising of professional sports contests that are sold out 72 hours in advance of game time.

This relationship works to the benefit of sports fans in the sense that the number of hours of sports coverage on a nationally televised basis has doubled between 1961 and 1980 (from 650 hours per year to over 1300 hours), in addition to any increases in the coverage offered by local stations and independent networks. This plethora of sports fare is available to the viewer free of charge (Horowitz, 1977, p. 168).

CASE 3: PUBLIC SUBSIDY OF SPORTS FACILITIES

The public subsidy of sports facilities for professional franchises is probably the most controversial issue within the political economy of sports. The taxpayers subsidize professional sports through construction bonds, stadia rents below the market value, taxes foregone on the land, and appropriation of public services to sports facilities in the form of water and sewage facilities, mass transit, law enforcement, and improvement of access roads. This use of public funds in support of private enterprise raises the critical question of *cui bono*, who benefits?

On the negative side, it is commonly argued that sport impressarios are the prime beneficiaries and that the public is getting ripped-off. These critics suggest that many franchise owners are not paying a fair share for their facilities. Although a new sports facility might benefit a few people in the form of new jobs, all taxpayers are, in effect, subsidizing the facility. Critics also suggest that many of the dollars that allegedly flow from a sports facility enter the pockets of the team owners in the form of parking, concessions, promotional ventures in the form of yearbooks and memorabilia, advertising revenues from team publications, radio and television royalties, membership fees in elite stadium clubs, and even blocks of free tickets that can be used for wooing other members of the power elite.

As for tax revenues, some argue that the main benefits are for the owners and not the general public. In this context it is interesting to note that the owners of the new Madison Square Garden—the Gulf and Western conglomerate—recently offered to sell the arena to the City of New York for one dollar in an attempt to get the arena off the tax rolls of the city; the city of New York presently receives about $3.7 million each year in real estate taxes from the Madison Square Garden. The great majority of the fifty-three new or remodeled sports facilities in the United States are not self-supporting and cost the taxpayer in terms of subsidy. Increasingly, such facilities are considered successful if they can generate enough income to pay *half* the operating costs of the facility. Critics also point out that sport entrepreneurs could be more spartan in their design of stadia and arenas. The basic cost of construction can reach $3900 per seat in a stadium when unnecessary luxuries are added. For example, the bill is run up by items such as a $1 million waterfall, $5 million for a scoreboard, and luxurious VIP suites (Surface, 1977: p. 10).

The economic picture is particularly grim for recently constructed sports facilities. For example, the domed stadium in New Orleans was originally scheduled to cost $35 million; however, this figure had expanded to $163 million by the time of its completion in 1975. The total will increase to about $325 million when the interest on the bonds has been paid. The state of Louisiana guarantees the annual bond payment of $11 million. It costs about $13 million per year to operate the Superdome—about $37,000 per day! It is expected that the facility will run an annual deficit between $5–7 million at least until 1984 (House Select Committee, 1976a, Part 1: p. 490). In other words, the taxpayers will be subsidizing the domed stadium to the tune of about $500,000 per month. The domed stadium was approved in 1966 through the Louisiana Superdome Authority as a capital investment by the taxpayers to construct a facility for major league sports, conventions, road shows, musical performances, and miscellaneous events. It was financed by a 4-percent tax on hotel rooms in the parishes of Orleans and Jefferson. The planners projected additional income from parking fees, rental fees, advertising revenues, and profits on concessions. The Superdome was basically conceived as a complement to tourism, which is the second largest industry in both the city and state.

The Economic Gains

On the positive side, it is commonly argued that major league sport franchises help to unite a community, lift the morale of the local citizens, and generally enhance the public image of a particular city. It is also argued that big time sports help to attract new business firms as well as conventions to the metropolitan area. Sport promoters also point out that a major league team functions as an economic multiplier by generating incremental business for hotels, restaurants, night clubs, department stores, airlines, taxis, and other retail outlets. For example, a 1954 study estimated that out-of-town visitors to Baltimore Orioles games spent as much as $8.3 million over the course of a baseball season (Okner, 1974; p. 328). Similarly, it is estimated that the 1976 Super Bowl pumped an additional $40 million into the economy of Miami, and that the 1980 Super Bowl yielded an extra $35 million for New Orleans. The Secretary-Treasurer of the Louisiana Superdome Authority, William J. Connick, presented the following case for the social benefits of the new domed stadium in New Orleans:

> The justification of the Superdome is reflected in the stabilization of the city of New Orleans, for as a result of the Superdome the Greater New Orleans area now has a hotel–motel inventory of over 20,000 hotel rooms.
>
> Thirteen thousand of these rooms have been built since the Superdome's commission was established in 1966. As an example of the industrial growth this year, the opening of the new Hyatt Regency, the Hilton Hotel, and the addition to the 4-year-old Marriott reflects a combined capital outlay of $170 million, more than the cost of the Superdome itself.
>
> Tourism is the State's and the city's second largest industry. The three hotels that I have mentioned will have an annual payroll of some $12.3 million, and represent over 2,000 new jobs. New Orleans as an example reflecting the impact of tourism has as many bartenders and waiters as we have longshoremen.
>
> The reality of the Superdome has made Louisiana a better tourist State. The Louisiana Superdome was the host of the Lions International Convention and through 1981 the Superdome will house some 61 major conventions. It is not to say that that is the only conventions that will be held in the community. These are conventions that are committed to the Superdome itself, and reflect a substantial amount of revenue not only to the community as a whole, but also to the district itself.
>
> Since 1975 future convention bookings in the Greater New Orleans area exceed $100 million per year through the early 1980's.
>
> I don't want to confuse the issue by giving the understanding that the overall benefit to the community as a whole is a plus. I do think it is fair to recognize that the growth of the hotel-motel industry and the activity in the community has substantially increased since the announcement of the Superdome, because we have increased the hotel-motel inventory from some 6,500 hotel rooms to what we have today, which is right at 20,000.

These hotel rooms are capital outlays by investors and not the superdome and it is to their benefit to have activities in these hotels as frequently as possible. This activity not only gives a benefit to the community as a whole but also is a direct dedicated source of revenue to the building itself.

What I am trying to relate to you is that the overall economic spin of activity in the Greater Metropolitan New Orleans area has been not only stabilized by the reality of the Superdome, but it has been complemented as far as the overall good of the community is concerned. . . .

I don't want to play a shell game and I don't want to misrepresent two very real understandings. No. 1, we are in deficit. We shall be in deficit as far as direct revenues and debt service is concerned from revenues associated with activities solely related to the Superdome itself.

However, the economics of the Superdome reflects that the benefit to the community as a whole is substantial, and I will liken it or give you an analogy as contrasted to the Houston Astrodome.

The first year that the Houston Astrodome was opened some $95 million new sales were generated that were reflected in the genreal sales tax revenue of Harris County in Houston that was not available prior to the Astrodome, and the activity in the Greater New Orleans area, since the first year of operation, and we were 1 year old yesterday, again reflects over $90 million of new sales in our community have taken place since the Superdome (House Select Committee, 1976a, Part I, pp. 490–91, 498–99).

CONCLUSION

In the introductory portion of this book we noted the interrelationship between sport and the other institutional segments of society. In the last two chapters we focused on the linkage between sport and the political and economic institutions. For example, sport has assumed increasing *political* significance within international relations. This is illustrated by the politicalization of the Olympic Games. Additionally, the staging of the Olympics has *economic* ramifications that are worthy of analysis. Moreover, the examination of sports telecasting and the public subsidy of sports facilities are examples of the economic nature of formal sport in modern societies. Yet, it is evident in these cases that professional sports are political as well as economic spheres of interest. Increasingly, the Congress, courts, and regulatory agencies are involved in the negotiations that take place between owners, managers, athletes, and the various segments of the public.

CHAPTER 16
The Religious Dimensions of Sport

At first glance it might seem that religion and sport have little in common. Religion ostensibly deals with the supernatural, the transcendent, and the sacred, whereas sport is seemingly embedded in the physical, mundane, and earthy dimensions of the human condition. Such an impression is simplistic, however, both in terms of religion and sport. The purpose of this chapter, then, is to analyze the interconnections and parallelisms between religion and sport as two forms of human experience. We shall see that both forms of human expression are in some important respects cut from the same cloth. Many writers have noted religious dimensions in the world of sport; Harry Edwards (1973b), for example, has delineated a series of parallelisms between sport and religion:

> Sport has a body of formally stated beliefs, accepted on faith by great masses of people across America's socioeconomic strata.
>
> Sport also has its "saints"—those departed souls who in their lives exemplified and made manifest the prescriptions of the dogma of sport.
>
> Sports also has its ruling patriarchs, a prestigious group of coaches, managers, and sportsmen who exercise controlling influence over national sports organizations.
>
> Sports has its "gods"—star and superstar athletes who, though powerless to alter their own situations, wield great influence and charisma over the masses of fans.
>
> Sport has its high councils, controlled or greatly influenced by patriarchs who make and interpret the rules of sports involvement.
>
> Sport has its scribes—the hundreds of sports reporters, sports telecasters and sports broadcasters whose primary duties are to record the ongoing history of sports and to disseminate its dogma.
>
> Sport has its shrines—the national halls of fame and thousands of trophy rooms and cases gracing practically every sports organization's headquarters.
>
> Sport also has its own "houses of worship" spread across the land where millions congregate to bear witness to the manifestation of their faith.

> Sport has its "symbols of faith"—the trophies; game balls; the bats, gloves, baseballs, and so forth, that "won" this or that game; the clothing, shoes, headgear or socks of immortal personages of sports.
>
> Sport has its "seekers of the kingdom," its true believers, devotees and converts (pp. 261–62).[1]

A SOCIOLOGICAL PERSPECTIVE OF RELIGION

In order to perceive the religious dimension of sport, it is first helpful to explicate the sociological nature of religion. Sociology has long been interested in the role of religion within everyday life, particularly with respect to its relationship with the family, economy, state, and education. Classical sociology viewed religion as an important cultural fact that permeates all social institutions. Although cloaked primarily in spiritual terms, religion has worldly consequences which represent the central focus of the sociologist.

One cannot fully understand the writings of sociologists on religion without an awareness of Karl Marx's pervasive influence. In many respects Western social thought reached a watershed in the writing of Karl Marx; his thought has profoundly influenced the writing of social scientists in addition to its implications for revolution. Zeitlin (1968, p. viii) has suggested that social theorists of the twentieth century have been writing with the ghost of Marx looking over their shoulder. Marx's influence continues to be very evident in general sociology as well as in sport sociology; the Marxist critique of contemporary sport will be discussed later. At this point let us consider his perception of the role of religion within society.

Marx basically viewed religion as a historical stage of human unfulfillment. Human beings create a fictional utopia in an afterlife to compensate for current deprivations. Heaven provides fulfillment absent on earth. Religion will continue to exist as long as the productive process results in alienation. The exploitation inherent in industrial capitalism is the cause of religion as it existed in the mid-nineteenth century. The radical social reformer should, therefore, work to accomplish the socialist revolution rather than attempt to debunk the illusion of religion through debate. Once the productive system is reformed, religion will wither away. The following passage summarizes Marx's position on religion:

> Religious distress is at the same time the expression of real distress and the protest against real distress. Religion is the sigh of the oppressed creature, the heart of a heartless world, just as it is the spirit of an unspiritual situation. It is the opium of the people.
>
> The abolition of religion as the illusory happiness of the people is required for their real happiness. The demand to give up the illusion about its condition is the demand to give up a condition which needs illusions. The criticism of religion is therefore in embryo the criticism of the vale of woe, the halo of which is religion (Marx and Engels, 1959, p. 263).

Max Weber is the sociologist most closely identified with an analysis of the role of religion in everyday life. Weber's famous monograph entitled *The Protestant Ethic and the Spirit of Capitalism* (1946) focused on the interconnection between the Calvinist tradition within Protestantism and the flowering of capitalism in the West. He documented the affinities between the two value systems and concluded

---

[1]Harry Edwards, *Sociology of Sport* (Homewood, Ill.: Dorsey Press, 1973). Reprinted by permission.

that the worldly discipline inherent in this strain of Protestantism contributed to the remarkable material success of this economic system in the nineteenth century. Weber clearly showed that the flow of influence between religion and economics is reciprocal and contrasted with Marx's more unilateral perspective that has come to be termed *economic determinism.*

Another sociologist of this period, Durkheim, believed that religion was based on an important distinction between the realms of the sacred and the profane. As a sociologist, Durkheim (1954) was attempting to develop a general theory of religion that could be used to analyze and compare all religions. Basically he argued that what is common to all religions is not a conception of supernatural beings and powers but rather some conception of sacredness. All religions focus on objects and activities that are set apart as nonordinary and special, as commanding respect, reverence, and transcending the workaday world. The sphere of the profane, on the other hand, involves commonplace elements, the mundane side of life. The realm of the sacred, then, constitutes *The Elementary Forms of Religious Life* (Durkheim, 1954).

Contemporary sociologists continue to analyze the role of religion in social life. Sociologists generally conceptualize religion as a symbol system dealing with ultimate questions of human existence. Because the manifest purpose of religion is not amenable to scientific observation, sociologists focus on the consequences of religion, many of which are unintended. For cross-cultural analysis, religion is commonly defined substantively in terms of beliefs, ethical codes, and rituals. Many sociologists prefer, however, a functional definition of religion which permits them to analyze nonsupernatural belief systems as a species of religion (e.g., communism, humanism, and scientism). In this context, Milton Yinger (1970) defines religion as "a system of beliefs and practices by means of which a group of people struggles with the ultimate problems of human life" (p. 7).

Sociologists tend to focus on meaning, ultimate concerns, transcendence, and sacredness as the core experiences of religion; in this framework, supernatural elements are not an essential element of the definition of religion. The contemporary anthropologist Clifford Geertz (1966) defines religion in a phenomenological sense that emphasizes the experiential process which can include both supernatural and humanistic systems:

> Religion is (1) a system of symbols which acts to (2) establish powerful, pervasive and long-lasting moods and motivations by (3) formulating conceptions of a general order of existence and (4) clothing these conceptions with such an aura of factuality that (5) the moods and motivations seem uniquely realistic (p. 4).

Andrew Greeley (1972) suggests that the human person experiences a strain toward the sacred in the sense that any person, process, or belief that provides meaning and purpose in life tends to take on sacredness in the form of respect and reverence:

> One might argue that man has a tendency to socialize his ultimate systems of value. Even if one excludes the possibility of a transcendent or a supernatural, one nevertheless is very likely to treat one's system of ultimate explanation with a great deal of jealous reverence and respect and to be highly incensed when someone else calls the system of explanation to question or behaves contrary to it. It is precisely this tendency

> to sacralize one's ultimate concern that might well explain the many quasi-religious phenomena to be observed in organizations which officially proclaim their non- or even anti-religiousness (Greeley, 1972, p. 9).

Viewed in this light, then, one can say that all persons are religious in the sense that all persons have ultimate concerns. If one does not adhere to a conventional religious tradition, the tendency is to evolve a functional equivalent by sacralizing one ultimate value system. In this context, Milton Yinger (1970) observes, "To me, the evidence is decisive: human nature abhors a vacuum in systems of faith" (p. vii). The prominent American theologian H. Richard Niebuhr (1960) points up the perennial meaning-giving function of religion on both sacred and secular contexts:

> It is a curious and inescapable fact about our lives, of which I think we all become aware at some time or another, that we cannot live without a cause, without some object of devotion, some center of worth, something on which we rely for our meaning. . . . (p. 118).

The sociologist Thomas Luckmann (1967) points out in his book entitled *The Invisible Religion* that the modern person is a "consumer of interpretive schemes" (p. 113). In a pluralistic secular society, one can be "into" many things. A recent cartoon presents two men talking at a cocktail party; a conventional looking man is depicted as saying to a bohemian-like fellow, "I used to be into experience, but now I'm into money." The array of meaning systems currently available in the West boggles the mind; Greeley (1972, p. 70) suggests that modern man assembles a meaning system in a manner analogous to the selection of components for a stereo system. The spate of pop psychology books on self-improvement and the proliferation of human potential therapies can be viewed as a quest for meaning in secular society—transcendental meditation, yoga, nude therapy, Esalen, encounter groups, EST, I'm OK, you're OK, bioenergetics, biorhythms, body wisdom, postural dynamics, T-groups, *ad multiplicandum.*

A THEOLOGICAL PERSPECTIVE ON PLAY

At least since the medieval era, theologians have analyzed elements of transcendence within the domain of play and sport. A basic assumption of contemporary theologians is that "God talk" must begin with an analysis of the human condition. The transcendent is mediated through historical experience within a cultural context. The transcendental dimension "can be uncovered by looking more closely at our self-experience, which includes gradations of conscious awareness moving from a vague mood to a carefully articulated self-awareness. . . . This analysis lays the foundation for the claim that religious experience is not confined to one area of our lives, but is the essential, if often eclipsed, depth dimension of all our experience" (Bacik, 1980, p. xiii).

It is interesting to note that the nature of play has been analyzed within a religious context as early as the Golden Age of Greece. In his *Nicomachean Ethics*, Aristotle discusses play with respect to human happiness. He views expressive behavior in instrumental terms, that is, in a recreationist perspective as the reciprocal of work:

> It follows that happiness does not consist in amusement. Indeed it would be paradoxical if the end were amusement; if we toiled and suffered all our lives long to amuse ourselves. For we choose practically everything for the sake of something else, except happiness, because it is the end. To spend effort and toil for the sake of amusement seems silly and unduly childish; but on the other hand the maxim of Anacharsis, 'Play to work harder,' seems to be on the right lines, because amusement is a form of relaxation, and people need relaxation because they cannot exert themselves continuously. Therefore relaxation is not an end, because it is taken for the sake of the activity. But the happy life seems to be lived in accordance with goodness, and such a life implies seriousness and does not consist in amusing oneself (Aristotle, 1976, p. 327).

An interesting theological perspective on play is found in the writings of the medieval theologian Thomas Aquinas. Aquinas is well known for the recovery of Aristotle's philosophy from the Golden Age of Greece and the incorporation of classical Greek thought into medieval scholastic philosophy. Aquinas follows the Nicomachean Ethics of Aristotle in defining human virtue as a golden mean between two extremes; for example, courage falls between cowardice and rashness. In the context of play, Aquinas defined the rule of life for a happy person as a disposition falling between the empty buffoon and humorless boor. Aquinas argued that "unmitigated seriousness betokens a lack of virtue because it wholly despises play, which is as necessary for a good human life as rest is" (quoted in Rahner, 1972, p. 2).

Aquinas also follows Aristotle in defining *eutrapelia* as an essential attribute of the human ideal—that is, a nimbleness of mind and spirit that predisposes one toward play as part of a nobly formed character. The contemporary German theologian Hugo Rahner calls *eutrapelia* "the forgotten virtue." Interestingly, the Greek etymology of this term involves a root meaning of "well-turning." In his *Man at Play*, Rahner (1972) views eutrapelia as a spiritual nobility which enables one to pursue lovely and relaxing activities in the form of play with detached seriousness:

> He who plays after this fashion is the 'gravemerry man'. . . . I am trying to make plain that such a man is really always two men in one; he is a man with any easy gaiety of spirit, one might almost say a man of spiritual elegance, a man who feels himself to be living in invicible security; but he is also a man of tragedy, a man of laughter and tears, a man, indeed, of gentle irony, for he sees through the tragically ridiculous masks of the game of life and has taken the measure of the cramping boundaries of our earthly existence (p. 27).

In this connection, it is interesting to note that the European theologian Romano Guardini (1937) has analyzed the spirit of play inherent in religious liturgy. Liturgical worship is a type of sacred play in which the human spirit wastes time for the sake of God with utter abandonment. Guardini points out that the elements of the liturgy transcend purely utilitarian considerations (i.e., gestures, colors, vestments, materials, symbols, vestments, vessels, prayer, and dance). The formality and rhythm of the rituals are foreign to everyday life: "It is in the highest sense the life of a shield in which everything is picture, melody and song. It is a pouring forth of the sacred, God-given life of the soul; it is a kind of holy play. . ." (Guardini, 1937, p. 106).

Another European theologian, Gerardus Van Der Leeuw, has analyzed play as a species of religious phenomena; his analysis of play is set within the context of the religious dimensions of art. In his *Social and Profane Beauty: The Holy in Art*, Van Der Leeuw (1963) outlines the aesthetic of play from a theological perspective. He conceptualizes the theatre, dance, music, and the plastic arts as the play of the human person, as a game. The encounter of man with God through these media is seen as sacred play. Play points beyond itself—downward to the everyday rhythms of life and upward to the highest levels of existence. Van Der Leeuw views play as a metaphor of religious life which involves a meeting between the human person and a greater personal power.

Contemporary American theologians have also been active in analyzing the spiritual significance of play. Robert E. Neal's *In Praise of Play* (1969) represents a significant theological analysis wherein the human person is viewed as basically a playful being and where religion is seen as a playful human response to God in the form of dance, ritual, and myth-telling. The playful person leads a divinized life:

> . . . the play self is the creation of one who experiences that coalescence of discharge and design which leads to the significant identity and meaningful and graceful movement of adventure. Play is distinguished from work by those elements of peace, freedom, delight, and illusion that occur in the modes of story and game. And much of what appears to be play may be a perversion of play, while some of what is not commonly associated with play may be exemplary. It is possible for adventure to capture totally the life of the mature adult, and this full play is the realm of new harmony of discharge and design, and religion is the play response to it" (p. 97).

Neale views the experience of the sacred as an expression of psychic harmony; however, the contemporary secular person has instituted barriers to experience the sacred. As a result of this desacralization, the secular person seeks a tenuous security in the world of work. This rejection of the sacred precludes the opportunity for profound play. Much of contemporary play is partial because it does not involve the total person. Neale then argues in ironic fashion that the retreat from the sacred is accompanied by increased interest in unplayful forms of spectator sport.

Neale views commercial sport as analogous to the bread and circuses of the Roman era—as a quasi-religion. This vicarious form of play does not involve the total person and is therefore inauthentic; nevertheless, it does represent a yearning for deeper spiritual meaning. "The conclusion is that fascination for the sacred is intrinsic to man and cannot be abolished. If an attempt is made to live secularly, the religious response will occur. . ." (p. 114). Failing to recognize the fundamental need for transcendence, modern man falls into minor forms of worship, among which are corporate spectator sports.

In a similar vein, the American theologian David Miller (1970) has published a monograph entitled *Gods and Games: Toward a Theology of Play*. Miller viewes nonseriousness as the highest form of seriousness. Within the world of play, the emphasis should be on celebration, not cerebration. Play involves "body-seeing, body-knowing; seeing with the whole body, with the wholeness of the body. It is learning the joy of the expansion of consciousness" (p. 140). Human play is a form of creation, a personalized physical expression of a particular individual. Play is living in the world of "as if," as a physical metaphor pointing to more profound human meaning.

A lyrical discussion of the religious dimensions of sport can be found in *The Joy of Sports* by the American theologian Michael Novak (1976). This popular author argues that sport is a type of natural religion in both a phenomenological and institutional sense (p. 19). As a form of human consciousness, sport involves religious-like elements of asceticism, commitment, mystery, destiny, profound fellowship, awe, aspiration for perfection, and a respect for powers beyond oneself. Similarly, as a social institution sport encapsulates transcendence through liturgy-like rituals impregnated with symbolic meaning, celebration, myths, heroes, music, temples, vestments, and temporal cycles akin to seasonal rites which resonate in the human spirit with profound meaning. The liturgical aspect of sport spectacles with vestments, rituals, and pageantry bespeak a sacred type of celebration involving a sense of anticipation and reverence. Novak develops the image of "sport as religion" from the perspective of a theologian and philosopher. He sees sport as emanating from a natural impulse for freedom, symbolic meaning, and the pursuit of perfection. Sport is a natural religion in the sense of involving asceticism, a sense of awe and fate, a quest for community and for participation in the rhythms of nature, and a respect for the mystery and power of one's own being.

A PHENOMENOLOGY OF PLAY

The elements of transcendence within the context of play have been imaginatively delineated by Johann Huizinga (1950) in his monograph entitled *Homo Ludens: A Study of the Play Element in Culture*. The basic thesis of this classic work is that human play antedates civilization; that is, civilization evolved out of the context of play. Man the player (*homo ludens*), not man the maker (*homo faber*), represents the distinctive characteristic of the human person as well as the wellspring of higher forms of culture.

Huizinga's work is relevant to the present discussion of sport and religion because of his insightful phenomenology of play. Play is viewed as a primordial form of human behavior that transcends the everyday world and is not reducible to biological or utilitarian needs. Play is supralogical and autonomous, a reality unto itself. Ordinary life is set aside and suspended during pure play; the player is immersed in an interlude. Human awareness is narrowed; self is submerged; and one is caught up with the creative tension, rhythm, and rapture of play. Huizinga emphasizes both the individual and social functions of play:

> [Play] adorns life, amplifies it and is to that extent a necessity for both the individual—as a life function—and for society by reason of the meaning it contains, its significance, its expressive value, its spiritual and social associations, in short as a culture function. The expression of it satisfies all kinds of communal ideals (p. 9).

Play takes on elements of the sacred in the sense that it is set apart in time and place. This demarcation or set-apartness of play and sport invariably evolves into a structure designed to reproduce the experience. This repetitive quality frequently takes on a ceremonial or ritual form (Harris, 1981). Sport sites invariably take place within special spatial arrangements (sacred space)—stadia, arenas, courts, diamonds, gridirons, and field houses. This type of consecrated space signifies "forbidden sports, isolated, hedged round, hallowed, within which special rules obtain. All are temporal worlds within the ordinary world, dedicated to the performance of an act apart" (Huizinga, 1950, p. 10).

Play and sport can be compared to the stage and the altar in the sense that a mythic or mystic activity is repeated or re-presented in a ritual form. It is no accident that the first forms of the theatre in England emerged out of the mystery plays that formed part of the liturgy. In the liturgy, theatre, and sport, a performance or contest is acted out on a narrow slice of space. This type of rite is not merely imitative, however, because the acting out of the physical activity enables the worshipers, audience, or spectators to participate vicariously in the sacred event itself (Huizinga, 1950, p. 15).

Any deviations from the ordained order of play marks a break in the interlude, thus breaking the spell and robbing the player of the illusion. This conjunction between play and order is significant in an aesthetic sense.

> Play has a tendency to be beautiful. It may be that this aesthetic factor is identical with the impulse to create orderly form, which animates play in all its forms. The words we use to denote the elements of play belong for the most part to aesthetics, terms with which we try to describe the effects of beauty, tension, praise, balms, contrast, variation, solution, resolution, etc. (Huizinga, 1938, p. 10; see also Lowe, 1977).

Play and sport are transcendent in the sense that they are beyond the experience of everyday life. Amidst the seemingly random sounds and movement of the profane world, sport can represent a limited perfection in the sense of order:

> The athlete is a man apart. The beauty and grace of his body, his coordination, responsiveness, alertness, efficiency, his devotion and accomplishments, his spendid unity with his equipment, all geared to produce a result at the limits of bodily possibility, set him over against the rest of men. Mankind looks on him somewhat the way it looks on glamorous women, the worldly successful, and the hero. These enhanced themselves by reordering their minds and bodies, and thereby realized bodily attainable great goals. We sense in them a power which we also sense in their perverted forms—in the prostitute, the criminal, and the villain. They are at the end points of the spectrum of human promise; they define our boundaries, good and ill. The athlete has a particular fascination for most men because, in addition to his athletic prowess, he provides a conspicuous illustration of the fact that even the young can sometimes be superb (Weiss, 1969, p. 85).

This experience of perfection within the finitude of a game is experienced at one time or another as a peak experience by many athletes. This moment of glory can result from a feeling of awesome power and delicate control with courage conquering fear such that one loses consciousness of self but ends up with a sense of self-affirmation. The prominent American philosopher Paul Weiss (1969) has described this experience very vividly:

> It is a great accomplishment to turn a body from a creature of vagrant stimuli, insistent appetites, and poorly focused objectives, into one which is taut and controlled, and directed toward a realizable excellent end. It is a great accomplishment to have made oneself willing to see how to deal well with the obstacles and challenges that one's body, other men, and nature provide. It is a great achievement to make oneself ready and willing to discover the limits beyond which men cannot go in a rule-governed, bodily

> adventure. It is a great achievement to have found one way in which men, as possessed of finite bodies involved in finite situations, can become self-complete (p. 84).

Sport as a vehicle for peak experiences has been much discussed. The concept of peak experience was elaborated by the psychologist Abraham Maslow (1971). As applicable to sport, peak experiences are characterized by submersion of the self, self-validating moments, lack of consciousness regarding time and space, wonder and awe, unity of awareness, clarity of perception, loss of anxiety, and a feeling of having been graced. Beisser (1977, p. 205) has referred to this type of rapture within sport as a type of "madness" in the sense of ecstasy—one is caught up into something greater than oneself, with the self becoming fused with the environment, when supposed limits are exceeded and the full potential of existence seems within reach, and where the action is all-encompassing.

Most accounts of peak experiences in sport refer to dramatic breakthroughs in terms of breaking records or great plays in a championship series. Such "highs" can be experienced, however, in more modest settings. For example, a physical educator recalls an intercollegiate baseball game in which he participated as a freshman at a liberal arts college:

> One rather chilly April afternoon in Oberlin, Ohio, during my freshman year in college, I walked up to the plate to face an Ohio Wesleyan pitcher for the third time. The game itself was insignificant, since we were well down in the standings. The particular time at bat mattered little, since this was the second-to-last game of the season and I was neither in danger of losing my starting position nor in contention for any batting titles. In a word, it was somewhere around my millionth trip to the plate since my father introduced me to the cult some eighteen years earlier in my playpen. Who would ever have expected what was to happen?
>
> The first pitch was a slider down and away, and I let it pass. The second was a fastball, shoulder high, to the outside part of the plate. The ball literally floated toward me. It moved ever so slowly and silently into my hitting area. It was as if someone had turned a picture into slow motion and shut off the sound. Waiting for the ball was a delicious experience—not anxious, not boring, not overly eager—just peacefully ready. I don't remember trying to swing the bat. It just happened. Effortlessly, smoothly, powerfully it arced toward the ball, which was now suspended, motionless over the outside corner of the plate. I can still see the ball and bat at the moment of impact, both of them so large. They surely must have expanded on the spot. The ball was propelled on the fly toward left-center field and, as I now mechanically ran toward first, the ball was caught on the run by the left fielder.
>
> Was the experience important or worthwhile? Surely not in terms of what is good and useful in life. I did not even get a hit! It is merely part of the story of one person. You know, I had never seen a ball and bat look like that before. I had never taken a swing that required no effort. I had never waited at the plate so peacefully. I did not know that baseball could be like that! And with these gifts came the promise that there was still more to come. How could I ever give enough to baseball? How could I ever exhaust its riches? (Kretchmar, 1976, p. 169).

It should be noted that peak experiences can also be experienced by the spectator:

> The stadium offers a nostalgic opportunity, in a fragmented age of science and secularism, to recreate the oneness of a religion past. This clarity. . . combined with total

> absorption in the play, is like restoring God to heaven and putting all in its proper place (Beisser, 1977, p. 207).

It is also relevant to note that a community of players (true believers) commonly emerges out of a satisfying sporting experience; this bond is affirmed by the ritual or ceremonial dimension of sport. It seems that the feeling of having been apart together, or having gone to the mountain to share peak experiences, and of having drunk deeply from the cup of physical expression produces a desire to perpetuate the sacred spell or enchantment beyond the delimited time and place of the discrete event. Such a community of players frequently develops a distinctive lore and even elements of secrecy. Within this new social circle, the norms and expectations of everyday life are submerged under a new form of ultimacy.

Slusher (1967, p. 64) has observed that pure sport can produce "a type of mysticism that is quiet, peak and flowing with care" for the members of the team. This experience of a spiritual community can emerge from the mutual involvement of teammates through joint effort and cooperation resulting in an awareness that being is being with others. This openness of individual to individual is described in the ideal terms vis à vis a crew team:

> It is intimately felt in the common rhythm of the rowers; each one of them feels within himself the same movement of transcendence toward a common goal, on the horizon of a common world, and feels it with the other rowers. In this conception, however, being for others has been replaced by being with others. It reveals the coexistence of consciousnesses without explaining it (Salvan, 1962, p. 66).

In the conclusion of his monograph that was first published in 1938, Huizinga expresses regret about the "play-element in culture" that had formed the original foundation of other cultural forms such as art, poetry, philosophy, law, and the theatre. Today civilization is no longer played; in fact, it is very difficult to determine where play ends and nonplay begins. The bureaucratization and regimentation of technological culture has removed sport further and further from the play sphere such that it has now become a category unto itself, neither play nor work. The organic ritual roots of sport have been several; thus it has become profane and unholy.

> The ability of modern social techniques to stage mass demonstrations with the maximum of outward show in the field of athletics does not alter the fact that neither the Olympiads nor the organized sports of American universities . . . have, in the smallest degree, raised sport to the level of a culture-creating activity. However it may be for the players or spectators, it remains sterile. The old play-factor has undergone almost complete atrophy. (Huizinga, 1938, p. 198)

A contemporary theologian, Harvey Cox (1969), has echoed Huizinga's focus on the importance of play for the human person. According to Cox, we have paid a dear price for material affluence:

> While gaining the whole world, he has been losing his own soul. He has purchased prosperity at the cost of a staggering impoverishment of the vital elements of his life. These elements are festivity—the capacity for genuine revelry and joyous celebration; and fantasy—the faculty for envisioning radically alternative life situations.

> Festivity and fantasy are not only worthwhile in themselves; they are absolutely vital to human life. They enable man to relate himself to the past and the future in ways that seem impossible for animals (p. 25).

MAGIC, SUPERSTITION, AND SPORT

The mass media and popular sport literature (e.g., Bouton, 1970, and Kramer, 1969) suggest that magical practices are quite prevalent in high intensity sports. It is clear that many team rituals and ceremonies unite the team members in a manner analogous to religious rites that promote cohesion among the believers—for example, team prayers, communal meals, a common hotel on the road, team parties, attendance at a movie the night before a contest, and common street clothes worn to and from a contest. In addition to these practices designed to promote espirit de corps and morale, many individual practices of a magical-type are invoked by a given athlete to improve performance. In this latter context, superstitions are commonly used to reduce anxiety. Superstition can be defined as a "belief that one's fate is in the hands of unknown external powers governed by forces over which one has no control" (Johoda, 1969, p. 139).

It has often been observed that sport is an area of human activity fraught with magic and superstition due to the inherent indeterminacy of sport. This unpredictability of sport is captured in clichés such as "the ball takes funny bounces," "too close to call," "a toss-up," "a game of inches," and the notoriety of sport "goats" who are thought of as the cause of a loss in an important game due to a single misplay.

It should be emphasized that the relationship between religion and magic is complex, and it is difficult at times to determine where one begins and the other ends. A wag once defined magic as the other guy's religion. In this context it might be helpful to define religion and magic in an ideal manner in terms of the basic characteristics underlying these forms of human behavior as outlined in Table 16-1.

TABLE 16-1 Comparative Dimensions of Magic and Religion

DEFINING CHARACTERISTICS	MAGIC	RELIGION
Nature of evidence	Not empirical, not open to scientific test	Not empirical, not open to scientific test
Basic goals	Pragmatic, mundane, worldly, instrumental: health, success, victory	Other-worldly, transcendent, immanent; salvation, grace, wisdom
Mentality	Control, manipulation, practical, get the job done	Nonmaterial means, awe, reverence, mystery, submission
Theoretical scope	Narrow frame of reference cook book, how to do it manual, specific techniques	Grand theory, all-encompassing framework, diffuse approaches, open-ended

Source: Adapted from Malinowski, 1948; Nottingham, 1971; and Greeley, 1972.

The "gap theory" of magic can be seen in Malinowski's (1948) classic description of the fishing practices among the natives of the Trobriand Islands. He observed that magical practices were used only when the men fished on the dangerous high seas; no magic was invoked prior to fishing in the more tranquil waters of the lagoon. Malinowski thus theorized that magic emerges in situations when chance and insecurity reign and when rational means of control are not available. Magic functions, then, to "bridge the gap" and allay the anxiety associated with the unknown and uncontrollable:

> Thus magic supplies primitive man with a number of ready-made ritual acts and beliefs, with a definite mental and practical technique which serves to bridge over the dangerous gaps in every important pursuit or critical situation. It enables man to carry out with confidence his important tasks, to maintain his poise and his mental integrity in fits of anger, in the throes of hate, of unrequited love, of despair and anxiety. The function of magic is to ritualize man's optimism, to enhance his faith in the victory of hope over fear. Magic expresses the greater value for man of confidence over doubt, of steadfastness over vacillation, of optimism over pessimism (p. 90).

The question of whether athletes are more superstitious than the general population has been addressed in sociological research. For example, Spaulding's (1975) survey of college students reported that athletes were less likely to admit to a general belief in magic and superstition (31 percent versus 48 percent); however, the varsity athletes in his sample did report a high incidence of superstitious practices among their teammates. For instance, 96 percent of the athletes agreed with the statement that "I have noticed some of my teammates are superstitious," and 60 percent affirmed that "my coach is superstitious." Spaulding suggests that the common perception of superstition among these athletes, despite their skepticism about these practices, may be due to the influence of the coach. This perception of the coach as superstitious might be interpreted in the context of the coach's role, which involves heavy accountability for the outcome of a contest over which the coach has little control (see Chapter 12 for a detailed analysis of the role of the coach).

A more ambitious research project by Gregory and Petrie (1972, 1975) compared the incidence of superstition among college athletes of both sexes across six sports vis à vis a control group of nonathletes. Their research replicated Spaulding's (1975) finding that the athletes were not more inclined than nonathletes in the realm of general superstition, but the athletes did enumerate more superstitions pertaining to sport than the nonathletes. In general, Gregory and Petrie found that superstition was more prevalent in team sports than in individual sports (due perhaps to social influence and the greater degree of uncertainty), that some superstitions are linked to a particular sport (e.g., not stepping on chalklines), and that females in general tend to be more superstitious than males.

George Gmelch (1972) has traced the use of magical practices in professional baseball in the form of taboos, fetishes, and rituals designed to reduce anxiety and to increase a sense of personal control. Interestingly, he observed relatively few superstitious practices related to the defensive aspect of baseball, in which the average success rate in fielding percentage is .975, as compared to an abundance of superstitions associated with batting, in which the success rate is only .245. This pattern clearly supports Malinowski's theory that magic emerges in human behavior as a response to unpredictability and uncertainty. We would speculate that the higher the level of competition and involvement by the players, the greater the likelihood of superstitious behavior.

It is interesting to note that superstitions may be used in sport *prior* to a contest to reduce anxiety as well as *after* a game in an attempt to explain a defeat. Moreover, one can distinguish between sorcery as magical practices in sport used to bring about a desired result (a base hit), as contrasted with taboos that are observed as a means of warding off undesirable results (fumbling the ball). Sorcery might include fetishes such as old bats or balls, religious medals, or horseshoes in the locker; taboos, on the other hand, might include never shaving or having one's picture taken before a contest, not changing equipment in midseason, never mentioning that a no-hitter is in progress, and not stepping on chalk lines on the field.

The recent increase in expressions of conventional piety among professional athletes might also be interpreted within Malinowski's framework as an attempt to reduce anxiety about performance. A syndicated column in the sports page of a Sunday newspaper carried the headline, "Religion is Sweeping Sports" (Lyon, 1978). The article dealt in particular with how athletes within boxing and baseball had found religion. Postgame interviews with star athletes frequently include testimony of personal faith suggesting that God is alive and well in the locker room. Reporters tend to be uneasy with this new form of piety:

> It is, after all, the most personal of relationships. What a man believes is his business and no one else's. So we think nothing of standing in front of a naked athlete and asking him what pitch he hit, how much money he makes, even whether he knows if the guy in the stall next to him is still running around with that stewardess in Atlanta. But how do you ask him if he believes in God without both of you feeling uncomfortable? (Lyon, 1978, p. 5).

It might be noted in this context that references to God are received more graciously subsequent to victory than defeat. A few years ago, a syndicated article carried the headline, "Reggie Gives Credit to the Man." In a game at the end of a close pennant race, Reggie Jackson reported, "I prayed to God that I'd hit a homerun. If you let me hit one, I'll tell everyone you did it" (Richman, 1977, p. 16). No cynical response was reported on the part of the manager or owner after he hit the homerun.

Various explanations have been offered for the recent spread of religiosity in the form of Fellowship of Christian Athletes, Pro Athletes Outreach, and Baseball Chapel. Some observers view religiosity in athletes as a means of sloughing off personal problems or, more crudely, as rabbit foot's path to the World Series. The fame and fortune of star athletes are viewed as leaving a void—the "bitch goddess of success" (William James' term) does not bring fulfillment. Loneliness and fear of failure (easily measured competency) may create a need for social support in the form of religious fellowship.

We read that prayer service is conducted every Sunday morning in the locker room of the New York Yankees under the sponsorship of the association Baseball Chapel. The comments of some of the athletes concerning the functions of these prayer meetings are interesting:

Bucky Dent: "It's the best way to share with my teammates because we're together, hearing speakers give insights on their lives. Some of them have really good things to say which you can apply to your own life."

Dick Howser: "They can get wrapped up too much in baseball. There are other things in life. The pressures of pro ball are so great that I think most players would enjoy attending services like this."

Ron Guidry: So I go to the Chapel when I can to spend a few minutes with the Lord. I talk to him in my own special way. The Chapel gives me the freedom of mind to talk to him and get things off my shoulder."

Johnny Oates: The physical is the easy part of the game. It's the mental part that's tough. So any time you can put your mind at ease, this game is easier. That's one of my goals in the Chapel—to clear the cobwebs out" (Breig, 1980, p. 16).

THE RADICAL HUMANIST CRITIQUE OF SPORT

A reader might suggest that an analysis of the religious dimensions within sport is fine as far as it goes; however, it is also necessary to consider the objective, historical, and institutional ramifications of sport. Sport is embedded in a broader sociocultural context, which invariably alters the nature of sport as a form of human experience. Paraphrasing Marx, a contemporary critic might argue that the need is to *change* the world of sport, not simply to understand it in an abstract sense.

Critics of contemporary sport tend to follow one of two traditions in their analysis: (1) writings in the spirit of Max Weber with a focus on bureaucratization, instrumentalism, the cult of efficiency, and disenchantment in the sense of an eclipse of pure play within competitive athletics, and (2) writings in the spirit of Karl Marx with a focus on commercialism, economic exploitation, ideological masking, and consequent alienation of the individual athlete. One perspective emphasizes the iron cage of bureaucracy, and the other focuses on the economic infrastructure of sport. Both of these critical traditions are humanistic, however, because they highlight the debasement of the human spirit.

Many sport critics argue that sport has been contaminated by commercialism, technological fixation, organizational overkill, and an overlay of evils from the larger society—racism, sexism, elitism, and nationalism (cf. Brohm, 1978; Edwards, 1973a; Hoch, 1972; Scott, 1971; Tutko and Bruns, 1976). The basic argument is that formal sport has become suffused with extrinsic values; the religious dimensions are being squeezed out as the technocratic mentality of corporate sport has trickled down even to the Little League. The athlete is increasingly being treated like a biological machine; physiological and psychomotor concerns reign supreme. Increasingly one sees a fetishism about swimming faster, jumping higher, kicking farther, throwing longer, and hitting harder. The cult of performance is evident in a lust for productivity in the form of records, medals, won–loss records, attendance figures, television ratings, and profit—all at the expense of the personal satisfaction of the individual athletes.

The specialty of sports medicine now includes human factors specialists, humanic engineers, physicians, and other technocratic encrustations. One can see the analogue of time and motion studies within the world of sport—cardiopulmonary measures, treadmill tests, body fat indicators, stopwatches, and various measures of human energy. Spontaneous joy and playfulness in physical expression recede in the face of training regimens and robotlike self-mastery; even eating is redefined as a "training table."

The erosion of pure sport is evident in both capitalist and socialist countries. In his monograph entitled *Sport in Soviet Society*, James Riordan (1977) reports that children as young as age seven are enrolled fulltime in sport schools which combine athletic training with the regular academic curriculum. In 1975 there were 4938 young people's sport schools in the Soviet Union with a total enrollment over 1,633,000 children.

> The aim of the schools is to use the best of the limited facilities available to give special and intensive coaching to children and young people in a particular sport so that they may become proficient, gain a ranking and graduate to an All-Union or Republican team. As the 1966 government resolution on the schools stressed these are 'special sports institutions and are intended to train highly qualified athletes.' The specialised gymnastics schools, for example, admit girls and boys from seven onwards; they are expected 'to pass from novice to master in six to seven years.'
>
> An examination of the sports pursued in the schools leaves no doubt that the chief targets for the schools' members are the Olympic sports (p. 337).

The mass media have made much ado about the success of female swimmers from East Germany in terms of questionable training methods. We hear reports about scientific weight programs, the alleged use of steroids to develop muscle tissue, and injections of male hormones. The training regimen for teenage swimmers in East Germany is said to include five hours of daily workouts and the use of a "current canal" (glass-bottomed pool) with a mechanically controlled flow of water that keeps a swimmer in a stationary position due to the counter-directional flow of the water.

The debasement of the distinctively human element of physical expression is poignantly evident in a recent comparison of human performance vis à vis animals:

> In an article in the September 1973 issue of *Paris-Match*, human beings were set alongside 'the most sporting species.' The ranking for the highjump works out as follows: the porpoise comes first with 6 metres, followed by the puma (4.50m), the salmon (3m), and man (2.3m). The speed champion is the cheetah, at 100 kilometres an hour, in front of the hare (74k.p.h.), and man is far behind at 37 k.p.h. Sporting vocabulary often borrows from the animal kingdom. Spitz is the 'hungry Olympic shark', whereas S. Gould becomes the 'dark mermaid.' W. Rudolph is the 'black gazelle,' and a wrestler is dubbed 'the Polish bull' etc. The mass media are particularly fond of this menagerie. The mythology of sport is thus peopled with hybrids, supermen, giants and gods who fight it out in a kind of pre-historic jungle (Brohm, 1976, p. 63).

Although careful delineation of time and space can be viewed as adumbrations of the sacred in a phenomenological analysis of sport, these same elements can be seen as levers for the repression of human spirit within the world of formal sport. In this context, Jean Marie Brohm's (1978) critique of contemporary sport is singularly well-titled—*Sport as a Prisoner of Measured Time*. The measurement of time and space in micro-precise units within the world of sports is analogous to an industrial mentality wherein persons are measured in commodity-like fashion in terms of productivity:

> Competition presupposes that labour has been equalised by the subordination of man to the machine or by the extreme division of labour; that men are effaced by their labour, that the pendulum of the clock has become as accurate a measure of the relative activity of two workers as it is of the speed of two locomotives. Therefore, we should not say that one man's hour is worth another man's hour but rather that one man during an hour is worth just as much as another man during an hour. Time is everything, man is nothing; he is, at most, time's carcase (Marx and Engels, 1975, p. 127).

Similarly, although a stadium can be viewed as a sacred space for the enactment of profound religious-like rituals, the same setting can become a repository of alienated persons—as bread and circuses or the opiate of the people. Corporate sport impressarios design superevents to the end of maximizing profit for the cartel. Here sport as a natural religion becomes transformed into mass entertainment, show biz, hoopla and hype, sexist skin parades, and a medium for gamblers. It is symbolic in this respect that even the organic link with mother earth has been severed in contemporary stadia with the installation of artificial turf.

CONCLUSION

In this chapter we have outlined a series of parallelisms and affinities between sports and religion. Both institutions have similar phenomenological manifestations—imitations of the sacred, ultimacy, and a quest for perfection. Sports are not merely a diversion; their power to exhilarate and depress shade into the sphere of the ultimacy characteristic of religion. In addition to religious-like institutional trappings such as heroes, shrines, symbols, rituals, and festival days, sport also instills quasi-religious qualities of heart and soul. With these considerations in mind, it has commonly been observed that sports represent a transcendent civil religion in secular society.

It is also evident that a symbiotic relationship exists between sport and religion in American society through which one serves the interests of the other (Eitzen and Sage, 1978, p. 111). For example, religious and magical practices are closely linked with athletics as a means of coping with the inherent unpredictability of sports contests and to reduce the anxiety stemming from the continued expectation of high performance. Both coaches and athletes invoke religion to cope with this type of stress. Similarly, institutional religion uses sports to further its mission. Religious congregations commonly sponsor athletic programs for youth and adults as a service to the members as well as to increase the social integration of the faith community. Moreover, religious leaders are perennially attracted to the moral development dimensions of the sports creed—clean living, self-discipline, and respect for authority. Furthermore, religious institutions have spawned a number of associations specifically for athletes: Fellowship of Christian Athletes, Athletes in Action, Pro Athletes Outreach, Baseball Chapel, and even a monthly periodical entitled *The Christian Athlete*.

The relationship between sport and religion can be generalized to include linkages with the political and economic institutions. All four institutions are functional for the maintenance of the existing social order by virtue of their regulative, social control, and integrative consequences. Their overlapping ideologies have a "conserv-ative" function within society; the process of reciprocal reinforcement among these four institutions is illustrated in the following diagram.

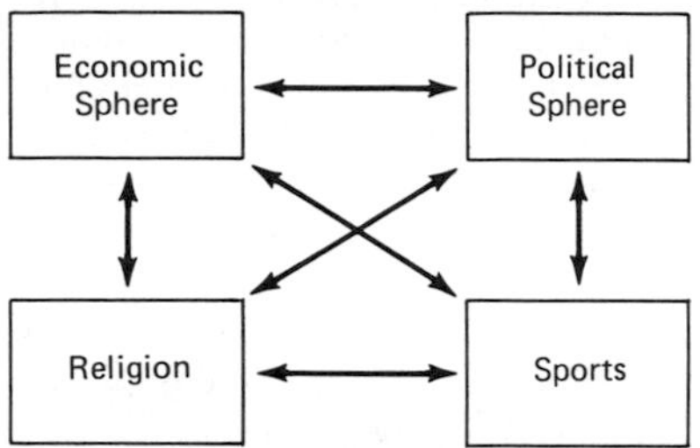

Each of the four institutions holds certain values in common which represent a type of transcendent *weltanschauung* in American society: moral development, self-discipline, fitness, work ethic, achievement orientation, meritocracy, loyalty, patriotism, sociability, efficiency, and social order. This value cluster also tends to reinforce the family and school systems; consequently, most parents desire that their children participate in sports even if they have no interest in sports personally. This same mentality is evident in the common practice of parents dropping their children off for Sunday School for "training" purposes without being church-attenders themselves.

CHAPTER 17
Lifelong Participation in Sport as Leisure

Prologue

In my fortieth year, I am riding on the 5:29 from my job in Manhattan to my home on Long Island, one of 90 million workers weary with the Monday blues. It is early in September, my birthday is half a week away. The scotch is swaying restlessly in my paper cup. Suddenly, I remember. Monday night: television. The Dodgers are at Montreal. My spirits lift. Tonight there is a treat. . . .

How could I be forty years old and still care what happens to the Dodgers? How could I have thrown away three hours of an evaporating life, watching a ritual, an inferior dance, a competition without a socially redeeming point? About the age of forty, almost everything about one's life comes into question. There is so little time to grasp and hold, it slides through fingers like the sand. It seems important, now, to concentrate. And so I asked myself: Is it time for sports to be discarded? Is it time to put away the things of childhood? (Novak, 1976, pp. *x-xi*).

Much of the research on involvement in sport and physical activity in this book has focused on youth and adolescence. This is the stage in the life cycle when the attitudes and skills associated with physical activity are usually developed (see Chapter 5). Research generally shows a correlation between participation in sport as a youth and encouragement from parents, peers, teachers, and coaches. Additionally, the research indicates that although many youths develop positive attitudes toward sport, others develop negative attitudes and are thus socialized away from sport. The increasing emphasis on high-level performance in high school sports soon closes off opportunities for sport participation by the less gifted. This emphasis on performance also seems to carry over into community-based sports such as Little League baseball, Pop Warner Football, and church league teams. It is also clear that when children experience failure and frustration within sport, their identity as an athlete is eroded, and thus they are likely to withdraw from subsequent opportunities for sport participation. In short, they define sport as an activity for the "good athlete"; they then avoid further embarrassment stemming from athletic failures (Ball, 1976; Harris and Eitzen, 1978). These attitudes, both positive and negative, are likely to carry over into adulthood (Snyder and Spreitzer, 1973, 1976). Additionally, research shows that persons who participated in organized sports as children and adolescents are more likely to have a self-perception of athletic ability and to identify with sport as adults. In short, at least some of the variation in adult participation in leisure sports is explained by the opportunity structure, role models, groups, and social influences that encourage learning the athletic role during childhood and adolescence. Having acquired this role as a youth, there is a likelihood of continued satisfaction with physical activity in adulthood.

The preponderance of research by exercise physiologists shows that involvement in sport and physical activity is correlated with physical and mental health among all age groups (see Chapter 6). Jack Wilmore (1980), an advocate of vigorous physical exercise, has noted

> Regular exercise is necessary to develop and maintain an optimal level of good health, performance, and appearance. It can increase an individual's physical working capacity by increasing muscle strength and endurance; by enhancing the function of the lungs, heart and blood vessels; by increasing the flexibility of joints; and by improving the efficiency or skill movement.
>
> For many adults with sedentary occupations, physical activity provides an outlet for job-related tensions or mental fatigue. It also aids in weight control or reduction, improves posture, contributes to a youthful appearance, and increases general vitality. Active individuals appear to have fewer heart attacks than their less active counterparts. Furthermore, if an active individual does suffer an attack, it probably will be less severe and his chances of survival are greater.
>
> Additionally, more than 50 percent of lower back pain or discomfort is due to poor muscle tone and flexibility of the lower back and to inadequate abdominal muscle tone. In many instances, this disability could be prevented or corrected by proper exercise. And finally, much of the degeneration of bodily functions and structure associated with premature aging seems to be reduced by frequent participation in a program of proper exercise (p. 5).

In Chapters 6 and 10 we presented data that suggest a positive relationship between sport participation and mental health. We have also tested the hypothesis that a similar relationship is evident between sport participation and psychological well-being among adults (Snyder and Spreitzer, 1974a). Earlier research has shown that social participation in general is positively related with psychological well-being and that people who are active in a variety of social activities tend to report a higher degree of emotional well-being (Robinson and Shaver, 1969). Following this lead, we tested the hypothesis that involvement in sport, as one form of leisure activity, is associated with reported life satisfaction and perceived happiness.

Data for this study were collected by means of a mailed questionnaire in a sample survey. A systematic probability sample (every *N*th name) was drawn from the City Directory for Toledo, Ohio. The sampling frame included the suburbs as well as Toledo proper. The research focused not only on the behavioral, affective, and cognitive dimensions of sport involvement, but also age, education, occupation, and social participation as predictors of psychological well-being. The *behavioral* dimension of sport involvement was quantified through questionnaire items designed to elicit the extent to which individuals actively participate in sports, spectatorship, talk about sports, read the sports page, and subscribe to or regularly read sport magazines. *Affective* involvement was quantified through four attitudinal items concerning the psychological meaning of sports to the individual respondent. The *cognitive* dimension was measured by having the respondents match a twelve-item list of sports personalities with their appropriate athletic sphere. This measure attempted to quantify the respondent's degree of knowledge about sports.

The data from this study, reported in Table 17-1, support the proposition that sport involvement is correlated with psychological well-being. Although the strength of the correlations is not striking, the pattern of the relationships is interesting. More specifically, sport involvement is a stronger predictor of well-being than are age, education, occupation, or general social participation. Furthermore, behavioral involvement in sport is more strongly correlated with psychological well-being than affective or cognitive involvement in sport. In addition, it should be noted that the same pattern of relationships was observed for the two separate indicators of psychological well-being reported—life satisfaction and perceived happiness.

TABLE 17-1 Summary of Relationships between Psychological Well-Being and Selected Predictor Variables*

PREDICTOR VARIABLES	LIFE SATISFACTION	PERCEIVED HAPPINESS
Age	.02	.04
Education	−.04	−.08
Occupation	.05	.01
Social participation	.12	.11
Cognitive sport involvement	.07	.07
Affective sport involvement	.15	.15
Behavioral sport involvement	.23	.24

*Gamma was used as the measure of association.

Source: Adapted from Snyder and Spreitzer (1974a), p. 32.

As we pointed out in the initial chapter of this book, there has been a marked increase in the salience of sport in our society. Furthermore, the prominence of sport is reflected in exercise participation levels that have reached unprecedented levels in the 1980s. Runners and joggers are a pervasive symbol of this fitness and slimness movement. The President's Council on Physical Fitness and Sports reports that approximately 55 percent of the American adults (eighteen years old and over) participate with some regularity in exercise and sport (Newsletter, 1979, p. 5). Yet, in spite of this fitness movement and its apparent advantages in physical and mental health, only one out of every five women, and 30 percent of the men report they are "very active" participants in some form of physical exercise (The Roper Organization, 1980, p. 83). Furthermore, studies generally show a pattern of disengagement from sport participation with an increase in age. For example, Gorden et al. (1976) studied almost 1500 adults ranging in age from twenty to ninety-four and found that as age increased there were marked decreases in leisure participation. Additional research shows that this age-related disengagement from sport pattern is also prevalent in cross-national data. Robinson (1967) studied sport participation in ten countries and found similar results; the degree of participation declined with age, although less for men than for women. An examination of his data on the United States reveals that 90 percent of the active adult participation in sports is performed by 20 percent of the population (p. 83). Similar results were reported by McPherson and Kozlik (1979); their analysis of 50,000 Canadian adults showed marked decreases in sport participation rates after age nineteen and age sixty-four—ages that roughly correspond to entering and leaving the labor force. In summary, this body of research shows a consistent pattern. Although the participation rates vary by sex, education and income, there is a consistent negative correlation between age and participation in sport and physical activity within all demographic groupings. In the following section we review some of the theoretical attempts to explain behavior of the aged.

THEORETICAL ORIENTATIONS OF AGING AND SPORT INVOLVEMENT

In social gerontology, several theoretical perspectives have been proposed as explanations for satisfactory adjustment to aging. One perspective, the activity theory, assumes that adjustment to aging is most successful if persons maintain as high a level of activity they had in middle age (Havighurst and Albrecht, 1953). When spheres of activity are lost, as through retirement or the death of a spouse, the individual should compensate by developing new interests, participating in additional activities, and initiating new roles (Bengston, 1973, p. 42). In short, according to this orientation, a satisfactory adjustment for the elderly requires them "to keep busy." This theoretical perspective assumes that self-esteem and life satisfaction are linked with the social support one receives from a variety of roles and activities.

A second perspective assumes that it is desirable to disengage gradually from involvement in the role of middle-age (Cumming and Henry, 1961). This process would presumably be functional for the society because these roles would then be filled by younger, more vigorous persons. Furthermore, this disengagement would be satisfying to the individual due to the release from the demands and pressures of performance in instrumental roles (Bengston, 1973, p. 43). However, the disengagement theory does not maintain that all or most roles are reduced. Indeed, some roles might be strengthened to compensate for disengagement from other roles; for example, upon retirement from work one might invest more time and energy in leisure pursuits.

A third perspective, the continuity theory, states that a satisfactory adjustment to the aging process is associated with an integration between stages of the life cycle (Atchley, 1977). This theory stresses the value of continuing activities in old age that were satisfying in middle-age. Thus, the focus is not on the number of role spheres one is participating in or disengaged from; rather, attention is focused on the desirability of maintaining continuity through the life cycle (Loy et al., 1978, p. 363). In general, research shows that youth who are successful in sport are more likely to maintain a continued involvement in sport in adulthood. The continuity theory does not, however, explain why many youthful sport enthusiasts soon disengage from sport in adulthood, or why some who did not participate earlier in athletics become physically active as adults.

Furthermore, neither the activity theory nor the disengagement theory provides an adequate explanation for the relationship between social activities, such as sport participation, and satisfaction in the later years of life. Additionally, these theoretical models do not explain why a disengagement from sport generally accompanies the aging process. Nevertheless, research showing positive correlations between mental health and involvement in sport across all ages supports the activity theory of aging. The primary deficiency in these theoretical approaches is that they focus primarily on the level of activity rather than on the meaning and degree of commitment to the activity. We will return to this point later in the chapter.

AGE DISCRIMINATION

One reason why involvement in sport tends to decrease in middle and old age is that our society has defined sport as a youthful activity. Admittedly, there are health factors that prevent some of the elderly from physical activity, yet in general they have been expected to express an interest in sport only as a spectator. These social expectations are reflected in the marked drop in activity of middle and older adults. Recent studies, however, show that with continued physical activity older persons can maintain a high level of physical strength and stamina. For example, one study shows that when training at the same intensity, frequency, and duration, older male runners (average age of fifty-eight) performed within 14 percent of men twenty-five years younger. The performance level was measured by cardiovascular endurance and physical work capacity. These older men performed about 100 percent better than their sedentary peer group. Furthermore, studies show that older swimmers who increase their practice time show almost no loss in endurance capacity. In general, for most people the loss of physical capacity with age is more a function of inactivity rather than aging (*Toledo Blade*, December 1, 1979, p. 10).

When social norms and sanctions are imposed on the older ages we find a form of stratification, in this case, age stratification, whereby older people are accorded less prestige, recognition, and status. When this age-grading limits the opportunities and range of behavior of older people, it becomes discriminatory. Thus, the admonition to "act your age" may be a subtle form of ageism by defining many forms of physical activity as inappropriate for the later stages of life. This age-grading has a negative effect and reinforces the stereotypes of mature adulthood as a sedentary stage of life. Thus, ageism in sport contexts may limit the opportunities for participation by inadequate programming and facilities on the assumption that such behavior is inappropriate or perhaps undesirable. Consequently, only in recent years have slow-break basketball leagues, masters sports events, and Senior Olympics been established; yet even these are primarily for older more gifted athletes. For those with average athletic ability, the social control mechanisms may constrain their involvement lest they appear foolish, and thus these programs commonly lack the "critical mass" of participants necessary for athletic programs for older people.

It is evident that the theoretical perspectives discussed thus far are limited in predicting physical activity at different stages of the life cycle. In the following sections we review additional social factors that help to explain the degree of commitment people have to physical activity; furthermore, these explanatory factors are generalizable to people of all ages.

SOCIAL BACKGROUND VARIABLES

Several studies of participants in sport and exercise programs indicate that involvement varies according to social background characteristics. Thus, we have cited research that demonstrates a reduction of participation with age, and a lower rate of participation is also evident for females when compared to males; moreover, participation rates are generally less for persons with lower levels of education and income (Purdy, 1980; see also Chapters 9 and 10). Although the analysis of such background correlates offers an incomplete explanation for the degree of adult participation in sport, such correlates provide important information that is helpful in understanding adult participation in sport and physical activities.

SOCIAL VALUES

One of the ironies of sport is that the emphasis on competition may lower the rate of participation. Some empirical research suggests that when the emphasis is on high-level competition and winning, there is generally a lower rate of continued large-scale participation in physical activity (Snyder and Spreitzer, 1979). The proposition that mass participation in sport is diminished when the social values emphasize competition might be further illuminated through cross-cultural research. For example, Galliher and Hessler (1979) argue that the emphasis on the collectivity in modern China results in a mass participation in sport ("friendship first, competition second"). They suggest that "unlike the massive levels of sports involvement in China, individualistic capitalism forces the masses away from sports participation through intense competition and highly restricted access to the means to pursue sports" (p. 18). Whether the degree of participation is the reflection of a competitive free enterprise ethos remains uncertain (cf. Riordan, 1978). Nevertheless, the perspective that focuses on cultural values is one possible explanation of adult participation in sport. The basic argument from this perspective is that the "product" orientation of corporate sport has suffused the sphere of recreational sport and results in a lower rate of participation in physical activity among the general population (i.e., increased spectatorism). Additional research is needed to assess the impact of the cultural values that were discussed in Chapters 3 and 4 on adult participation in leisure sports. Moreover, particular attention might be directed toward defining the optimal mix between the product and process aspects of sport participation. It is clear that competition is not necessarily dysfunctional for adult participation. Rather, the goal of recreation programs for adults would be to design the organizational arrangements so the competition can take place within age, sex, and skill levels at which all participants can experience some of the satisfactions and challenges of competition. When the social values define sports as primarily for those who are the "winners," the individual who has only a modicum of athletic ability is likely to feel embarrassed and unmotivated toward sport participation.

SPORT IDENTITY

Another relevant perspective focuses on an apparent need to find meaning in life by identification with, and involvement in, a major area of activity. Identity may be developed in one or several spheres—for example, family, work, voluntary associations, hobbies, and other leisure activities including sport. In fact, participation in sport for some people may have been, or may be, so salient that their identity is primarily sustained by their sport role. Several scholars have analyzed the need for identity and a sense of self-worth. For example, Ernest Becker (1971, p. 68) proposes the metaphor of an "inner newsreel" that passes in review before us the symbols that give us a feeling of self-esteem; consequently, we are continually testing and rehearsing the ways we are significant and important. Likewise, Glasser (1976) argues that our society has become an "identity society" in which people seek out roles that provide them an identity and a feeling of self-worth. To achieve identity requires an involvement with some segment of social life. In order to understand one's attachment to sport, it is important to determine the salience and meaning of the sport role as a source of identity and self-worth. When a person asks, "Who am I?" he or she is attempting to ascertain the roles that are a part of one's self identity (Kuhn and McPartland, 1954). We suspect that people's identity as an athlete is also related to the perception they have of themselves in terms of athletic ability. In all probability, participation in athletic activities is a source of continued support for an athletic identity. Conversely, for persons who do not perceive themselves as an athlete, the likelihood of participation in traditional athletic roles is negligible. The salience of one's sport identity will vary with the level of athletic performance and participation. The following excerpts from an interview with Jim Jacobs, six-time national singles and doubles handball champion, poignantly illustrate the personal stress he faced and the subsequent disengagement from active participation when a dissonance developed between his identity and performance.

> Jim: You know what happens . . . when you get older. I found it happen to me . . . in the nationals in 1965 when I won barely and from then on it would bother me terribly when I was by myself. From 1965 on I could perceptibly see that I was losing my talent. I couldn't hook the ball, I couldn't control the ball as well, my forearm got really tired. It started to happen in 1964 when though I won and I won only by the skin of my teeth. But what happens is, and it's very discouraging, you reach an age where you try to struggle to maintain a degree of excellence and you're going against nature. I found that happening when I was 36 or 37-years-old. It bothered me no little bit. Now I'm 48 and it doesn't bother me a bit because the precipice has been reached and passed, and I play so poorly that now I'm entertained by it.
>
> Interviewer: Why haven't you played in many Masters Tournaments?
>
> Jim: The reason I don't play in the Masters singles is I was once a very good player

> and I was proud of it; I was very proud of it, as I am today. Now young guys come to watch me, and at 48 I don't have any semblence of the skill that I had. It bothers me to play poorly in front of guys like Naty Alvarado who has heard I was a very good player, but when he sees me play I am embarrassingly bad. No one would know by the way I play now that I could ever play (*Handball Magazine*, August, 1978b, p. 76).

SPORT AS FESTIVAL

Although it is clear that active physical participation is a powerful source of identity, it should be noted that passive involvement in the form of spectatorship is also a potent source of at least transitory collective identification through vicarious experience as a fan. As has been frequently noted, large-scale sporting events can provide a sense of exhilaration, pagentry, drama, festivity, ritual, and ceremony that satisfy a "quest for excitement in an unexciting society" (Elias and Dunning, 1970). The theologian Michael Novak (1976) captures this vicarious nature of sport in his analysis of sport as a "natural religion."

The theological writings of Harvey Cox (1969) have some interesting implications for the sport sociologist. Cox argues that the play element in our Western culture (festivity and fantasy) has been slowly deteriorating during the past centuries of industrialization. Technological development has produced a more sober people, less playful and imaginative. The structured rhythms of factory and office have almost squeezed festivity and fantasy out of everyday life. According to Cox (1969), the human being is by nature *homo festivus* and *homo fantasia*—one who not only works and thinks, but who also plays, pretends, dreams, celebrates, prays, dances, sings, and tells stories. Cox suggests that the social and economic practices associated with industrialism and capitalism in the West have substituted thrift, ambition, diligence, and soberness for play, mirth, festivity, fantasy, and spontaneity. Imagination and uncalculated *joie de vivre* have been reduced in the face of deferred gratification, achievement, and a future orientation.

Cox defines festivity as the capacity for genuine revelry and joyous celebration, and he conceives of fantasy as a faculty for envisioning radically different life situations. According to Cox, festivity and fantasy are essential ingredients of human experience because they enable us to celebrate special occasions, to simply affirm the goodness of existence, to observe the memory of a hero or something sacred, and to experience vicariously the joy of others and the experiences of earlier generations. In summary, the need for ritual and festivity may be met via the vicarious involvement in sport spectaculars. Although this passive form of sport participation lacks the values of the physical dimension, it may serve modern man's psychological needs by providing a sense of exhilaration, excitement, and new experience that are otherwise lacking in his life.

ROLE CONFIGURATIONS

One's involvement with sport as a spectator in sport festivities or as an active participant are also influenced by the individual's overall role commitments to the family, work, community, and various leisure activities. These configurations vary not only from individual to individual but also by stages of the life cycle. The degree of commitment to each role is a function of investment (time, energy, money, and other resources) within each role, the skill level, and the overall negotiation that takes place within the individual regarding the constraints and resources, including satisfactions, that flow from each of the role segments. In short, the commitment to a role, such as leisure sport participation, is affected by one's investment in other interests besides sport; traditionally, for many people the work role has been a powerful influence on their identity. For example, introductions are usually made by giving a person's name and "what they do" (i.e., their occupation). Thus, work is a "master role" in the sense that it demands a heavy investment in time, energy and training, and most other roles are subordinate. Yet, Roberts (1970, p. 25) notes that "for many people leisure has now become such a central and dominant part of their lives that it is their behavior and attitudes toward work that are determined by their leisure rather than the other way around." Perhaps some workers tend to compensate for deprivations in the work context by investing heavily in leisure activities in order to achieve a sense of personal fulfillment that is not manifest in their work. Figure 17-1 outlines several spheres of activity and their corresponding roles; the diagram suggests that one's identity is constructed from the overall configuration of role commitments. These commitments will vary not only from individual to individual but also by the period of one's life cycle.

Identity	Family Role	Work Role	Leisure: Sport Role	Community Activities Role(s)
Childhood				
Adolescence				
Adulthood: young, middle years, retirement				

FIGURE 17–1 Spheres of activity, roles, and identity.

The following interview with another former nationally ranked handball player, Steve August, illustrates how the shifts in commitment may take place:

> Steve: Basically, what I'm not doing . . . is playing a lot of handball. I am playing. I play mostly tennis, some racquetball, occasionally handball. But I have found, for one reason or another, I am not able to play the way I was once capable of playing and somehow my ego will not allow me to play any other way, so at this point it is much easier for me to go to games in which no one expects anything of me and I really don't expect anything from myself.
>
> Interviewer: You say your ego won't allow you to play less than your best. What does your ego allow you to do now? How are you getting your satisfaction from life; from tennis?
>
> Steve: No, not really. My tennis, at this level, could hardly be expected to provide much ego gratification. As you know, we're all motivated one way or another to do the things that we do and a lot of what we do is motivated by a desire for a certain amount of self esteem or good self image. In all probability that is what motivated me to put the work I put in handball. When you put that kind of work in, you get something in return. The respect and the self-knowledge that I was the best at whatever I was doing in the world at the time was ego gratification enough to justify the work. At this point in my life I am receiving that self image or ego gratification in another way and because I am receiving it in another way the incentive is no longer there to put the tremendous effort I always felt that I had to put into handball. The other source I am

referring to is my work. As you know I am an eye surgeon and probably have spent the happiest three years of my life the last three years and that is primarily because I enjoy the work I do so much (*Handball Magazine*, June, 1978a, p. 6).

Steve August, like Jim Jacobs, has difficulty reconciling his level of performance with his identity as a handball player. Consequently, he has switched to tennis, an activity in which he has less identity invested (ego involvement) and in which other people do not expect a high level of performance from him. A personal negotiation has apparently taken place; he has shifted his primary identity from handball to his work (his new "master role"). He is investing commitment in his job from which he is now receiving his primary satisfactions.

COMPANIONSHIP

Social influence is an important factor in developing a commitment to leisure sports. Social influence is important because most people value the companionship, friendship, recognition, and respect they receive from others; there is a quest for community—a feeling of belonging. Often people are motivated to become involved, or remain involved, in sport because of encouragement from family and friends. In the sport context, mutual feelings are often expressed in the form of friendship, loyalty, and social approval; these sentiments are rewarding and thus reinforce participation in sports and physical activities. Golf and tennis partners may play at a regular time for many years; the social solidarity may become so strong that a deep sense of loss is evident when one of the participants is not able to play. The recent growth of leisure sports in the form of racquet clubs and road races are expressions of this sociability dimension. Many racquet clubs are designed to facilitate social interaction among the members; for example, they provide a snack bar, lounges, babysitters, and social events. Our observations of runners at road races indicate that the sociability factor is manifest in the warm-up period and during the informal social gatherings at the finish line. Road runners commonly participate in a circuit of races; consequently, a spirit of comarderie and friendship develops among the participants.

Crandall et al. (1980, p. 294) have examined a variety of motivations for leisure activities; their list of reasons is varied and includes both social and psychological dimensions. The following are cited as potential social motivations or satisfactions for leisure:

Enjoy companions
I feel I belong
Expected to by spouse
Expected to by children
Expected to by family
Expected to by friends
Meet new people
Be with a person of the opposite sex
Just to be with my friends
Escape family

Be with a group
To have power over others
Like being of help to others
Benefit to society
Prestige
Authority
Do something that will make others like and admire me

The social dimension of leisure activities has also been documented by Kelly (1978), who studied two communities and found that to "enjoy companions" and to "strengthen relationships" were among the most important reasons for leisure participation.

Moreover, our research on leisure sport activities among adults has shown the importance of sociability for sports activities. For example, in our sample of 202 racquetball players, 92 percent agreed with the following statement: "For me, sports are a way of getting together with friends and having a good time." A sample of 321 road runners expressed less sociability in their leisure participation, yet 76 percent agreed with this statement. These samples of adult participants also pointed to the influence of other people in initiating them into their leisure activity. For example, 45 percent of the runners said that "I started running because of someone's encouragement or influence," while 64 percent of the racquetball players were encouraged or influenced by someone to begin playing racquetball.

INTRINSIC AND EXTRINSIC REWARDS

In Chapters 2 and 5 we discussed the relationship between intrinsic and extrinsic rewards. Perhaps the single most important factor in developing a commitment to sport and physical activity is the sheer intrinsic enjoyment and pleasure. In Chapter 2 we discussed the intrinsic dimension as being autotelic, that is, an activity that is self-fulfilling and fun. On the other hand, the extrinsic dimension provides motivation to participate because of the anticipation of some external reward—a trophy, social prestige, money, or other "incomes." The optimal mix between these two forms of motivation has yet to be determined. Presumably unskilled performers will receive very little extrinsic reward for their athletic efforts; however, they may find the activity itself physically exhilarating. Perhaps as one's skill level increases the intrinsic enjoyment also increases, yet research shows that increased participation in physical activity results in a change in attitudes toward the activity. Consequently, the spirit of participation among skilled athletes tends to be serious and "professional"; thus the intrinsic motivation begins to diminish as one's skill level improves and the importance of winning athletic contests becomes increasingly important. In a study of adult softball league players, Purdy (1980) found that the experienced and competitive players were more "professionalized" toward the sport. In short, they took individual and team failures seriously, they prepared for the games in a serious worklike manner, and they manifested a greater need for extrinsic rewards. In some cases the involvement in physical activity may be reversed. That is, one may begin a physical regimen such as jogging for health reasons (an extrinsic motivation); however, with continued participation one may become hooked on the intrinsic returns and develop a commitment to involvement in the activity (positive addiction). We suspect, however, that serious road runners receive a strong dose of extrinsic rewards and satisfactions in the form of recognition, social support for the one's identity as an athlete, and the sociability dimension that surrounds participation in road races.

When we consider lifelong participation for the general population, the intrinsic rewards seem most important. Few middle-age and older adults can develop and maintain the high level of skill necessary to compete primarily for external rewards. Even elite athletes eventually retrench on their physical and temporal commitment to sport. Furthermore, the average adult does not develop the skill level necessary to attain satisfaction primarily from extrinsic rewards. Unfortunately, the socialization process associated with sport in our society emphasizes the extrinsic rewards, which are not conducive to lifelong participation in physical activity on a recreational basis.

SKILL LEVEL

As noted in the preceding paragraph, the world of sport places a high value on people who can demonstrate athletic skill and performance. Within the world of sport, one's level of competence becomes integrated with the athlete's self-concept with the result that athletes tend to evaluate their identity in terms of skill levels. Most people do not enjoy activities in which they are incompetent. Competence in sport is usually developed in childhood and adolescence and continues into adulthood. Logically, one can participate in sport and be unskilled; however, satisfaction is usually based on how well one performs. In short, most adults who are active sport participants have been, and are, good athletes. To encourage unskilled adults to engage in athletic endeavor requires programs to teach skills and institutional arrangements that place the emphasis on intrinsic rewards of physical activity, that is, the pure fun and enjoyment of the activity itself. Perhaps the recent popularity of jogging and racquetball reflects the ease of participation in these activities in terms of skill level. Most people who can walk can condition themselves to begin jogging; likewise, most people can have some positive feedback from racquetball without a long training period.

AVOIDANCE OF STIGMA, EMBARRASSMENT, DISAPPROVAL

Because the norms of sport are oriented toward skill and victory, many adults hesitate to engage in competitive sports because of the likelihood of being defeated and embarrassed. Many adults remember the negative sanctions they experienced in their youth. When people carry the wounds of aversive socialization from physical education teachers and coaches who labelled them as "gutless," "yellow," "loser," "failure" and "spastic," or at least as uncoordinated, they are not likely to have a positive attitude toward sport as a lifelong leisure activity. Gross and Stone (1964) define *embarrassment* as "whenever some *central* assumption in a transaction has been *unexpectedly* and unqualifiedly discredited for one of the participants" (p.

2). We suspect that many adults hesitate to enter athletic situations because they think they would look foolish, lose face, and feel embarrassed. Their incompetence defines them as unworthy performers. It is necessary to reduce the anxiety sourrounding one's level of performance in order to encourage adult participation in recreational sports.

A MODEL OF PLEASURE AND ENJOYMENT

In Chapter 2 we discussed the notion of "flow" as the feeling of intrinsic pleasure and enjoyment that one feels when there is an optimal challenge in relation to one's skill level (Csikzentmihalyi, 1975, pp. 38-49). The flow experience is dependent upon a balance between one's skill level and the social expectations of performance and is depicted in Figure 17-2 as the "flow channel." If an individual's skill level is low, but he or she is expected to achieve a high level of performance, the result will be a feeling of anxiety and perhaps embarrassment (see point A in Figure 17-2). Conversely, if a highly skilled person is participating at level 1 in terms of social expectations concerning performance, there will be an insufficient challenge with a likely result of boredom (point B in Figure 17-2). A high level of either boredom or anxiety is not conducive to continued participation. In the first case, to move into the flow channel the individual must substantially improve his or her skill or lower the level of competition (e.g., drop out of the "A" league and participate in the "B" league). In the second case, the bored individual must redefine the situation as "just for fun" or adopt a handicap (such as giving a number of points) to generate sufficient challenge to enter the flow state. This model focuses attention on several factors associated with lifelong participation in pleasurable activities. We suggest that recreation programs designed to encourage greater adult participation should focus on the section of the flow channel where the coordinates intersect at skill levels 1 and 2 and less than a level 3 performance expectation.

FIGURE 17–2
Flow model incorporating skill and performance expectations (*Source:* Adapted from Csikszentmihalyi, 1975, p. 49).

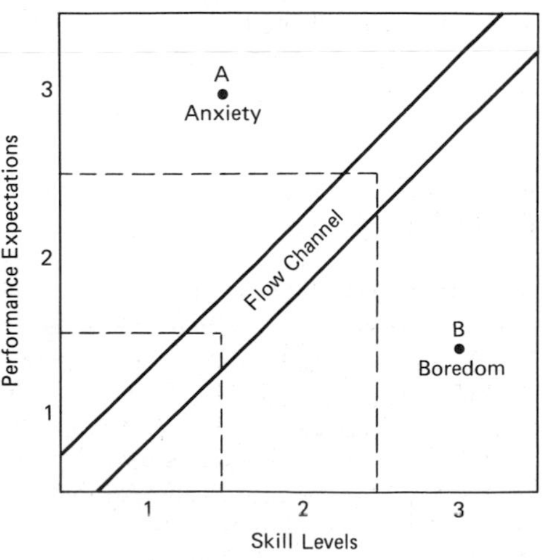

In summary, we have discussed the following factors as correlates of lifelong involvement in sport on a leisure basis:

1. Social values conducive to mass participation
2. The importance of sport within one's identity
3. The personal and social value of sport as a festive activity
4. The individual's overall configuration of roles
5. The relative importance of social factors in the form of companionship and friendship within the particular physical activity
6. The relative mixture of intrinsic and extrinsic rewards flowing from participation in the activity
7. One's skill level and physical condition
8. The desire to avoid stigma, embarrassment, and social disapproval

In the flow model we provide a graphic representation of the importance of skill level vis à vis expected level of performance. It is evident that a comprehensive model of adult participation in sport must consider both the overall "pay-offs" and "costs" that the individual experiences from this type of involvement.

COMMITMENT TO SPORT

In Chapter 5 we discussed the socialization process whereby one becomes involved in sport. We have incorporated this socialization process into the concept of commitment; that is, to be socialized into sport can also be a process of becoming committed to sport. In Chapter 5 (Figure 5-5) we provide a diagram of the elements of commitment that affect the degree of involvement in sport. Our discussion in the present chapter is an extension of these elements of commitment (see also Snyder, 1981). In the analysis of an individual's level of commitment to a particular activity, we need to determine the relative satisfaction and dissatisfaction that he or she receives from this sphere of activity. For individuals who are not involved in sport participation, one can assume that, based on the variety of factors we have outlined in this chapter, they do not receive sufficient satisfaction either to begin or continue active involvement in physical activity. In short, adult recreational sport programs must provide sufficient "pay offs" to encourage participation.

It will obviously be easier to recruit participants who have had a background of involvement in sports during their youth. Individuals who were successful in athletics during their youth have already developed some degree of physical skill and have presumably experienced some satisfaction from this involvement. On the other hand, the majority of adults have only modest athletic abilities and have not been particularly successful in the athletic sphere. In their overall role set, their involvement with sport is likely to have been primarily as a spectator. In order to develop a commitment to physical activity among these individuals, the rewards need to be increased by a greater emphasis on the social dimension and the intrinsic satisfactions of participation. Furthermore, programming should be varied to provide an opportunity to compete within one's skill and age level without undue feeling of embarrassment or anxiety. In short, we propose that creative programming can utilize the elements of commitment outlined in this chapter to increase the feeling of personal satisfaction and thus reinforce the willingness to invest time, energy, and money in leisure sport participation.

CONCLUSION

Research provides evidence of the physical and mental advantages of participation in sport and physical activity for people of all ages. Nevertheless, studies of adult participation show a rapid disengagement from sport, particularly among the middle- and older-aged. The theoretical perspectives from social gerontology—activity, disengagement, and continuity theories—focus on the activities in which individuals participate as they pass from middle into old age. However, these theories are limited in terms of explaining why some people remain active or disengage from certain roles. In part, the behavior of the aged is also determined by societal expectations. None of these theories of aging considers the relative importance of particular roles within the overall role set of the individual.

We suggest that the concept of commitment might be incorporated within existing theories to provide insight regarding the relative priorities which the individual places on various activities. The depth of commitments will be more critical in determining quality of life among adults than the mere membership in groups and organizations. We have suggested several elements of commitment that may be helpful in understanding commitment to a particular activity. We believe these elements of commitment determine adherence to and withdrawal from physical activity and participatory sports. More specifically, lifelong adult participation in leisure sports is influenced by elements of commitment such as fun and pleasure, pride, social approval, health and other extrinsic rewards, fellowship, and attempts to maintain a favorable self-concept.

Although this chapter dealt primarily with *active* participation in sport as a form of leisure, it is appropriate to point out that spectator sports serve some of the same functions as active involvement in sport. In this context, Spinrad (1981) has outlined several functions of spectator sports—hero identification, participation in folklore, and the comprehensive lore of statistics. Spinrad basically suggests that spectator sports represent a playful but engaging form of experience that offer a respite from the complexity of personal and social life. "Unlike most popular culture involvements it is a viable escape, partly because the experiences suggest a caricature of so many unstated features of regular societal processes. The result is a respite, a small-scale catharsis" (p. 363). The motivations for spectator sport as outlined by Spinrad are interesting heuristic insights; however, they are not anchored in a scientific theoretical tradition and are thus not amenable to testing. As is discussed later with respect to the classical theories of play, the motivations that are offered for spectator sport represent a type of pretheory at this point in time.

This chapter has basically addressed the question of why people play (we define leisure sports as being heavily permeated with the characteristics of play). As noted in several other places in this book, this quesion has been asked at least since the time of Aristotle (350 B.C.). Ellis (1981) has analyzed fifteen more or less separate theories concerning human motivation for play. These quasi-theories are traditionally discussed in textbooks on the philosophy of physical education and recreation; for example, VanderZwaag (1972) enumerates twelve theories purporting to explain why people are attracted to sport:

Cultural demand—one's culture places certain demands on the individual to play.

Sociability—the individual plays due to a natural desire to be a part of a group.

Outlet for aggression—play offers a socially acceptable way of displaying or releasing aggression.

Surplus energy—play is a means of letting off steam, a means of physical–emotional release that is satisfying to the individual.

Physical development—play is a means of facilitating physical fitness and conditioning, a sound mind in a sound body.

Surrogate competence—play is attractive for those who do not have the ability to recreate through other "higher" means, such as the fine arts or "cultural" pursuits.

Pursuit of excellence—play is another manifestation of the basic human desire to pursue excellence and self-identity.

Recreational stimulation—play is attractive as a stimulating form of leisure behavior.

Activity—play is a manifestation of the basic human desire to move with a purpose in mind, particularly with speed and agility.

Concreteness—sport is a delimited and visible form of recreation which is set apart from the everyday world.

Challenge—people need challenges, obstacles, and difficulty in order to make life interesting.

Competition—competition is an attractive challenge in the form of rivalry; sport offers a highly visible means of testing one's abilities.

According to VanderZwaag (1972) none of the theories listed here is a satisfactory explanation of human expressive behavior:

> Overall, if we examine the possible reasons why the individual is attracted to sport, we emerge with a gestalt effect. There is no simple answer. The individual himself is the important variable. He is probably attracted due to a complex of factors. Furthermore, at any given time in his life, a particular factor may be more significant than others. Later the 'weighting' of these factors may change. But we do feel that, in general, sport is attractive among the forms of recreation because sport offers activity, concreteness, a challenge, and competition (p. 121).

The theories of play that were reviewed by Ellis (1981) are basically the same as those presented by VanderZwaag. Ellis also finds them unsatisfactory as scientific theories. "They have lingered on, presumably because they were seen as innocent cognitive artifacts cluttering only the introductory chapters of our textbooks. . . . It is time to eliminate as many of them as we can so that we can get on with the task of determining why people play" (p. 480). According to Ellis, two modern theories of play are deserving of further scientific attention—play as competence motivation and play as information-seeking. These theories have emerged out of empirical research as contrasted with armchair speculation.

The theory of play as information-seeking basically suggests that play is a form of arousal-seeking stemming from a human need to interact with the environment in order to achieve an optimal level of stimulation and interest. Play is thus seen as a form of behavior concerned with maintaining a stimulating flow of information; once the human person has satisfied the more pressing needs of survival, he or she then tends to seek out interaction with the environment of a more challenging and complex variety. The theory of play as competence motivation can be viewed as a subtype of arousal-seeking. Here the focus is on the human propensity for curiosity, challenge, exploration, investigation, and wonder. The human person is viewed as having a need to produce effects in the environment, to demonstrate competency, and with a resulting satisfaction from the feeling of effectance. Stimulation and arousal flow from the uncertainty of outcome in the sense that the individual needs to test continually whether one can still produce the effect in the environment (i.e., mastery or success).

The motivation for play in general is likely to apply to lifelong participation in sport as a form of leisure because of the salience of intrinsic motivation in both forms of expressive behavior. Moreover, the theories of play as competence motivation and information-seeking seem to apply well to adult recreational sports such as competitive road runs, tennis and racquetball tournaments, and to quasi-sports such as backpacking, orienteering, white water canoeing, hang gliding, and mountain climbing. We suggest that the theories of play as competence motivation and information-seeking represent abstract theories that incorporate the elements of motivation and commitment outlined in this chapter for lifelong participation in leisure sports—sport identity, sport as festivity, sociability, avoidance of stigma, and sport as an autotelic experience. In particular, the flow framework of Csikszentmihalyi (1975) correlates nicely with Ellis' (1981) conceptualization of play as information-seeking and competence-motivation behaviors; that is, the satisfactions from play result from an optimal fit between the skill level of the individual vis à vis the challenge and uncertainty of the task being confronted.

This perspective on why people play represents a type of middle-range theory that falls between simple empirical generalizations and over-arching grand theories. A middle-range theory of play contains a few basic assumptions from which specific hypotheses can be logically derived and tested through empirical research (Merton, 1968, p. 68). A middle-range theory of this type differs from the "simple and sovereign" grand theories that were outlined previously; they explain everything and are thus not open to testing—for example, surplus energy, catharsis, and displacement of aggression. We suggest that teachers, coaches, and directors of recreation programs might profit from a study of these new theories of play in order to promote lifelong physical activity as a form of leisure for persons across the entire age range.

CHAPTER 18
Epilogue: The Sociological Image of Sport

In the initial portion of this book we emphasized the pervasiveness of sport in modern society. We also noted that sport as an institution is deeply embedded in the history of Western society; the importance of sport in our culture is reflected in many links with other social institutions and segments of society—the family, school, economy, polity, religion, mass media, leisure, and recreation. Portions of this book have been devoted to these social institutions in their relation to sport.

As sociologists, we find the analysis of sport to be worthwhile because it has the potential to expand our knowledge of a form of human behavior that spans the gap between the playful, spontaneous, and expressive and the formal, institutionalized, bureaucratic, and work-like dimensions of life. The sociological lens reveals new images of sport phenomena in the sense that it exposes for observation some previously unseen elements of sport. Indeed, we are elated when readers say, "Gee, I never thought about sport in this way before"; such is the nature of the educational process. This illumination of the several layers of sport reality is likely to reveal some of the unintended consequences of sport behavior; that is, sport behavior may have functions that are unobserved and unintended (i.e., they are latent). An important objective of the sociological perspective is that it allows us to observe these functions of social behavior in greater depth. Thus, the more superficial observations of sport are often exposed as inaccurate, and sociological analysis may have a "debunking" effect. These unintended consequences are often evident in the paradoxes and ironies of sport we have discussed throughout the book. To know something about the social world that was previously unknown is a primary goal for the educator. For such knowledge is necessary to broaden provincial perspectives that limit rational behavior and understanding. For the practitioner, this sociological perspective is important to promote a greater depth and understanding of the nature of sport that is necessary to design and implement strategies for effective sport programs.

THE SOCIAL CONTOURS OF SPORT

One of the books we have found particularly useful in describing the sociological perspective is Nisbet's (1976) *Sociology as an Art Form.* In this monograph the author explains the degree to which sociology, like the arts, constructs thematic representations of society. Nisbet (1976, p. 37) argues that there are several underlying and persistent themes in the social sciences of Western society. These themes include (1) the individual—his nature, mind, soul, and desires; (2) order and conversely perceptions of disorder, disintegration, and breakdown; (3) freedom; and (4) the phenomenon of change. These master themes in Western social thought are expressed in each of the social sciences, and within sociology they combine to form the more specific concepts of community, authority, status, the sacred, and alienation. According to Nisbet, these fundamental sociological concepts form the basic modes of describing and illuminating the sociological landscape.

In the present book we have not organized our discussion around these generalized themes or specific sociological concepts, yet the reader will note that much of the material in the book has incorporated these thematic and conceptual schemes. For example, if we focus on the sociological concepts suggested by Nisbet the following topics come to mind.

Community. As we noted in Chapter 4, industrial society is characterized by the emergence of secularity, rationality, specialization, and bureaucratization. Social critics often view these changes as dehumanizing and alienative; however involvement in sport may serve a compensatory function for modern man by providing a source of identification with a team. This social identification is apparent in educational institutions as well as with professional teams that represent urban communities. Furthermore, one important means of satisfying the quest for belonging and community is in the common sharing of values that are isomorphic with the sport subculture and the social relationships associated with informal and formal sport groupings. The evidence suggests that the growth of leisure sports serves this important sociability function for many people.

Authority. Within sport, particularly formal sport, the use of authority is readily apparent. The functioning of teams is based on the authority of the coach over players. Furthermore, the socialization process whereby people learn the sport role is based upon parents, coaches, and athletic officials exerting their authority over children and youth. In this process social values provide support and legitimation for the use of authority. The reader will also recognize the use of authority, and the related concepts of power and social control, in the study of sport and its relationship to the political, economic, and religious institutions.

Status. One of the early childhood motivations for participation in sport is that it results in recognition and social approval. This encouragement is often initiated within the family and is continued in the school and community athletic programs. Numerous studies cited in this book lend support for the function of sport as a means of enhancing one's ego and social status. Participation in sport is an important status symbol in our society, and the life styles associated with social class are reflected in the manner of sport involvement. One of the common assumptions about sport is that it has been an important means of social mobility. The contribution of the sociological perspective is demonstrated by a series of studies showing that this assumption should be qualified. Furthermore, participation in sport may be limited by discrimination based on race, sex, and age. Coaches, counselors, and parents might profit from research findings on this important topic.

The sacred. Both sport and religious experiences elicit a sense of awe, exhilaration, and peak experiences that transcend the workaday world. Indeed, critics have observed the parallels between sport and religion as a means of escaping the trials and tribulations of one's everyday living. Similarly, sport has its saints, rituals, sacred objects displayed in athletic halls of fame, scribes, and shrines. The human condition is problematic and uncertain, but so also is sport, and indeterminacies seem to elicit religious, magical, and superstitious practices. We can also observe the correspondence between sport and the sacred in the playfulness and joy of physical exertion that is akin to the shouts of praise and joy of the worshipper.

Alienation. In the nineteenth century, Weber, Durkheim, and Marx all viewed the social changes of that period with alarm, though they differed on what should be done about them. Weber saw the increasing rationalization and bureaucratization as an "iron cage" from which there was no escape, while Durkheim perceived these changes as causing *anomie* (i.e., a normlessness) and a breakdown of social integration. In a similar vein, Marx argued that these social changes associated with industrialization were economically exploitive and alienating to the workers. Likewise, critics of bureaucratic sport have argued that athletes are often cogs in the athletic machine to be "used," exploited, then discarded. The contemporary critic suggests that the competitiveness of sport promotes a dominant ideology that is product-oriented and meritocratic, which results in character traits such as acceptance of authority, obedience to rules, self-discipline, and subjugation of self for the good of the team. In short, according to this argument, sport is functional for the maintenance of the status quo view that benefits from the powerlessness and alienation of the workers (players).

In summary, the social landscape is illuminated by these themes and conceptualizations which are useful in the analysis of the sport context. To carry the art metaphor one step further, we might add that the social portrait is another form of sociological expression (Nisbet, 1976, p. 68); that is, sociological writings often provide descriptions of various social types such as the blue collar worker, student, bureaucrat, intellectual, delinquent, call girl, and the aged. These portraits emphasize traits which persons in a social category or occupation are commonly thought to possess or exhibit. In the present book, sociological portraits have not been explicitly drawn, yet attention has been given to such social types as the athlete, and more specifically, the female athlete, black athlete, former athlete, coach, and spectator.

SOCIOLOGICAL IMAGES OF SPORT

In the previous section we outlined some basic sociological themes that are useful in highlighting the contours of sport. The subject matter of sociology can also be examined from different angles or perspectives. In fact, relying on the work of Ritzer (1975), we suggest that there are three sociological images or paradigms that are helpful in the sociological analysis of sport, and each of these perspectives is useful for seeing some portion of the social dimension of sport.

Social facts. The focus of this image is on social phenomena such as groups, societies, institutions, positions, roles, norms, values that are external and coercive for the individual. This perspective views the individual as basically determined by these social structures and institutions. Using this image of sport, we would focus on content such as the values that are associated with the sport subculture, the social influences that are external and coercive to the individual and that promote sport participation and its influence on the participants. The study of sport and the mass media, economic, political, legal, and religious structures fall within the context of this perspective. Questions concerning the way sport may be functional or dysfunctional to the society would also be subsumed by the social facts paradigm.

Social definition. This paradigm assumes an image of the subject matter that emphasizes the way in which people's actions are influenced by their subjective interpretations (rather than being determined by external social facts). This approach also emphasizes that behavior is based on one's understanding of the situation and interaction with others. The overarching theme of this perspective is that man is "an active creator of his own social reality" (Ritzer, 1975, p. 89). Using this view of sport, we have examined such topics as the affective meanings and symbols people attach to sport, the importance of one's self-perceptions of athletic ability, and the self-negotiation and reflection that take place within individuals when faced with conflicting social expectations, for example, the feminine role versus the athletic role, the desire to play fairly versus the pressure to win at all costs, and the attempts to save face when one confronts failure or loss of athletic skills. In more unstructured sport contexts, the social definitionist perspective is particularly appropriate. Thus, informal sport and play situations tend to be fluid, uncertain, and emergent wherein meanings and behavior are processual and constructed at the moment. This perspective would apply to a pick-up game of baseball or touch football, in which the rules and manner of play are adjusted during the game to meet the affective desires and abilities of the players.

Social behavior. The social behaviorist's view of man operates on the assumption that an individual's actions are determined by external stimuli that provide positive or negative reinforcement. Thus, behavior is determined by the give and take process of personal investments (costs) and rewards; in short, behavior is based on the degree of reciprocity in interpersonal exchange. If rewards are minimal relative to the investments, one is not likely to find the behavior satisfying or enjoyable, that is, a negative reinforcement. The continuation of social relationships will be determined by the balance of perceived rewards and costs. Within sport this paradigm has utility in highlighting behavior such as using rewards to induce sport behavior as a part of socialization into sport. Conversely, the use of negative reinforcements in the form of criticism, sanctions, and embarrassment will tend to dissuade one from sport participation. In general, we find it likely that the degree of one's commitment to sport is largely determined by the rewards and satisfactions that accrue from one's involvement in sport.

In summary, each of the three perspectives is suitable for viewing some facet of sport. The social fact perspective is most appropriate for a broad societal view of institutions and how they are interrelated with the institutional aspects of sport. The social definition framework is better able to deal with the social construction of reality and meanings from a social psychological perspective. On the other hand, the social behavior viewpoint is helpful in viewing the contingencies of reinforcement via reward and punishment among individuals in sports contexts. Consequently, to achieve an adequate explanation of the variety of behavior associated with sport, the use of all three paradigms is helpful at some time or another. The following diagram provides a summary of some concepts and topics we have discussed and the paradigm most appropriate for the analysis of these topics. In some cases more than one paradigm may be helpful in examining a topic.

Social Fact	Social Definition	Social Behavior
The nature of formal sport	Informal sport as recreation	Positive and negative reinforcements
Sport and values	Socialization into sport	Socialization into sport
Cultural variations in sport	Socialization via sport	Sport and identity
Sport within educational institutions	Sport and identity	Role conflicts in sport
Sport and economic, political, and religious institutions	The meaning of sport	Lifelong participation
Sport and mass media	Role conflicts in sport	Intrinsic and extrinsic motivation

These sociological images help explain different facets of sport behavior. Thus, they represent general theoretical orientations that can help explain cause and effect relationships; such is the nature of science. It has often been observed that nothing is as practical as a good theory. A philosopher of science once observed that more lives have been saved by the knowledge derived from the basic science of astronomy as applied to navigation than all the books ever written on the applied art of ship building. A good theory enables one to control and manipulate the environment. In comparison to the powerful theories of physical science, many of the theoretical frameworks of sport sociology are still basically at a descriptive level of understanding. Nevertheless, the social scientific study of sport is a valuable complement to popular approaches to the topic if for no other reason than to expose half-truths and simplistic assumptions. In this context, Peter Park (1969) has suggested:

> To be sure, science does not have a monopoly on explanation. Explanations of one kind or another are constantly preferred by the man in the street without the benefit of science, and a common sense explanation, too, imparts understanding of sorts. Science, after all, has its beginning in common sense, and there are rudimentary similarities in the logical structure between common sense explanation and the scientific variety. The latter, however, stands apart from the former in its persistent adherence to explicit and systematic rules of reasoning and operation (p. 17).

CONCLUSION

In the introduction to this book we pointed out that sociology attempts to understand and explain social life in a systematic and scientific manner. Sociological concepts and frameworks help to order the fragments of social life that are being observed. In this chapter we have discussed several master concepts and three fundamental images of the sociological landscape that we feel are useful avenues for focusing on the social dimensions of sport. The scholarly analysis of sport discloses several layers of reality and thus has the potential to further our understanding of this segment of society. The salience of sport for sociological study is manifest in the many forms of participation and spectatorship as well as the complex interlocking relationships between the political, economic, legal, and religious spheres of society. The increasing politicalization and commercialization of sport likewise contribute to an increase in the growth of the mass media and litigation associated with the sport milieu. We suggest that the relationship between sport and other societal institutions will be increasingly evident in the future.

Although the bureaucratization of sport is likely to continue, we are heartened by the marked increase in recreational and leisure sports. Admittedly, these are often promoted and perhaps distorted by the commercialization of sport (e.g., marketing of running shoes, racquets, warm ups, etc.); nevertheless, the fitness and health movement is an encouraging sign for the achievement of one cardinal aim of education—a worthy use of leisure time. Consequently, in recent years we, the authors of this book, have devoted much of our research toward a greater understanding and expansion of lifelong leisure pursuits. Indeed, our personal views are that the primary value of sport and physical activity lies in the extent to which they can provide intrinsic fulfillment as a form of recreation on a lifelong basis. Hopefully, this book will contribute to this objective.

References

ALBINSON, JOHN G.

1973 "Professionalized attitudes of volunteer coaches toward playing a game." *International Review of Sport Sociology* 8(20.2): 77–87.

1976 "The 'professional orientation' of the amateur hockey coach," in Richard S. Gruneau and John G. Albinson (eds.), *Canadian Sociological Perspectives*. Reading, Ma.: Addison-Wesley.

ALLEN, NEAL

1964 *You Can't Beat the Hours*. New York: Harper and Row.

ALLISON, MARIA, AND GUNTHER LÜSCHEN

1979 "A comparative analysis of Navaho Indian and Anglo basketball sport systems." *International Review of Sport Sociology* 14(3-4): 75–86.

AMATEUR HOCKEY ASSOCIATION OF THE UNITED STATES

1973 *Official Guide*. Bloomington.

AMDUR, NEIL

1971 *The Fifth Down*. New York: Coward, McCann and Geoghegan.

1976 "East German women's success stirs U.S. anger." *The New York Times* (August 1): Section 5, p. 3.

AMERICAN ALLIANCE FOR HEALTH, PHYSICAL EDUCATION, AND RECREATION

1968 *Desirable Athletic Competition for Children of Elementary School Age*. Washington, D.C.

ANDERSON, DEAN, AND GREGORY P. STONE

1979 "A fifteen year analysis of socio-economic strata differences in the meaning given to sport by metropolitans," in M. Krotee (ed.), *The Dimensions of Sport Sociology*. West Point, N. Y.: Leisure Press.

ARISTOTLE
1952 "Poetics," in W. J. Bate, *Criticism: The Major Texts*. New York: Harcourt, Brace and Co.
1976 *The Ethics of Aristotle: The Nicomachean Ethics*. London: George Allen and Unwin Ltd.

ASHE, ARTHUR
1977 "An open letter to black parents: Send your children to the libraries." *The New York Times*, February 6, 1977, Section 5, p. 2.

ASHWORTH, KENNETH
1980 "Gresham's law in the marketplace of ideas: Are bad degrees driving out the good?" *The Chronicle of Higher Education*, October 6, 1980, p. 64.

ATCHLEY, ROBERT
1977 *The Social Forces in Later Life*. Belmont, Ca.: Wadsworth.

AUF DE MAUR, M.
1976 *The Billion-Dollar Game: Jean Drapeau and the 1976 Olympics*. Toronto: James Lorimer.

AUXTER, DAVID
1973 "A philosophy of developmental physical education," in Robert A. Cobb and Paul M. Lepley (eds.), *Contemporary Philosophies of Physical Education and Athletics*. Columbus, Ohio: Charles E. Merrill Co.

AVEDON, ELLIOTT M. AND BRIAN SUTTON-SMITH
1971 *The Study of Games*. New York: Wiley.

AVENTI, ADRIAN F.
1976 "Alternative stratification systems: The case of interpersonal respect among leisure participants." *The Sociological Quarterly* 17 (Winter): 53–64.

AXTHELM, PETE
1970 *The City Game*. New York: Harper and Row.

BACIK, JAMES
1980 *Apologetics and the Eclipse of Mystery*. South Bend: University of Notre Dame Press.

BAIN, LINDA L.
1976 "Play and intrinsic values in education." *Quest* 26 (Summer): 75–80.

BAKER, ANDREA
1976 "Continuities in sociological thought: From real estate agent to marijuana smoker." *Case Western Reserve Journal of Sociology* 8 (September): 32–50.

BALBUS, IKE
1975 "Politics as sports: The political ascendency of the sports metaphor in America." *Monthly Review* 26 (March): 26–39.

BALCHAK, THOMAS
1975 "A study of the use of sport and the image of athletes as depicted in the writings of Gilbert Patten 1900-1925." Masters thesis, Bowling Green State University.

BALL, DONALD W.
1976 "Failure in sport." *American Sociological Review* 41 (August): 726–39.

BARBER, RED
1970 *The Broadcasters*. New York: Dial Press.

BATE, WALTER JACKSON
1952 *Criticism: The Major Texts*. New York: Harcourt, Brace.

BECKER, ERNEST
1971 *The Birth and Death of Meaning*. New York: The Free Press.

BECKER, HOWARD
1960 "Notes on the concept of commitment." *American Journal of Sociology* 66 (July): 32–40.
1963 *Outsiders: Studies in the Sociology of Deviance*. New York: The Free Press.

BEISSER, ARNOLD
1967 *The Madness in Sports: Psychosocial Observations on Sports*. New York: Appleton-Century-Crofts.
1977 *The Madness in Sports*. Bowie, Md.: Charles Press.

BENAGH, JIM
1976 *Making It to Number One*. New York: Dodd, Mead and Co.

BEND, EMIL
1968 *The Impact of Athletic Participation on Academic and Career Aspiration and Achievement*. Pittsburgh: American Institutes for Research.

BENEDICT, RUTH
1934 *Patterns of Culture*. New York: Mentor Books.
1946 *The Chrysanthemum and the Sword: Patterns of Japanese Culture*. Boston: Houghton-Mifflin.

BENGTSON, V. L.
1973 *The Social Psychology of Aging*. Indianapolis: Bobbs-Merrill.

BERGER, PETER L.
1963 *Invitation to Sociology: A Humanistic Perspective*. Garden City: Doubleday and Co.

BERGER, PETER L. AND B. BERGER
1972 *Sociology: A Biographical Approach*. New York: Basic Books.

BERK, RICHARD A.
1974 *Collective Behavior*. Dubuque, Iowa: William C. Brown.

BERLIN, PEARL
1974 "The woman athlete," in E. Gerber, J. Felshin, P. Berlin, and W. Wyrick (eds.), *The American Woman in Sport*. Reading, Ma.: Addison-Wesley.

BERSCHEID, E., E. WALSTER, AND G. BOHRNSTEDT
1973 "Body image, physical appearance, and self-esteem." Paper presented at the meetings of the Americal Sociological Association, New York, 1973.

BERST, S. DAVID
1979 Personal communication.

BETHELL, TOM
1980 "Taking a hard look at Common Cause." *The New York Times Magazine* (August 24): 34–38, 42–46.

BETTS, JOHN
1974 *America's Sporting Heritage 1850-1950*. Reading, Ma.: Addison-Wesley.

BLALOCK, H. M.
1962 "Occupational discrimination: Some theoretical propositions." *Social Problems* 9 (Winter): 240–47.

BLUMER, HERBERT
1939 "Collective behavior," in Robert Park (ed.), *An Outline of the Principles of Sociology*. New York: Barnes and Noble.

BOERSEMA, JAMES
1979 "Baseball: Oriental style." *Soldiers* 34 (June): 28–31.

BOIRE, JUDY A.
1980 "Collective behavior in sport." *Review of Sport and Leisure* 5 (Summer): 2–45.

BOOKWALTER, KARL W. AND HAROLD J. VANDERZWAAG
1969 *Foundations and Principles of Physical Education.* Philadelphia: W. B. Saunders.

BOUTON, JIM
1970 *Ball Four: My Life and Hard Times Throwing the Knuckleball in the Big Leagues.* New York: Dell.

Bowling Green Daily Sentinel Tribune
1976 "Henson charges ticket frauds." November 13, p. 11.

BOYER, PETER
1980 "Keep the jocks off the air: Thank you, Vin Scully." Associated Press column in the *Toledo Blade*, October 24, 1980, page 4.

BOYLE, ROBERT H.
1963 *Sport: Mirror of American Life*. Boston: Little, Brown.

BRAILSFORD, DENNIS
1969 *Sport and Society*. Toronto: University of Toronto Press.

BREIG, J.
1980 "Baseball chapel provides scripture in the locker room." *Catholic Chronicle*, September 19, 1980, p. 16.

BRIM, ORVILLE G.
1966 "Socialization through the life cycle," in O. G. Brim and S. Wheeler (ed.) *Socialization after Childhood.* New York: Wiley.

BROHM, JEAN-MARIE
1978 *Sport: A Prison of Measured-Time*, trans. Ian Fraser. London: Ink Links Ltd.

BROOKOVER, W. S. THOMAS, AND A. PATERSON
1964 "Self concept of ability and school education." *Sociology of Education* 37 (Spring): 271–78.

BROSNAN, JIM
1963 "Little leaguers have big problems—their parents." *The Atlantic Monthly* 211 (March): 117–20.

BROVERMAN, I., D. BROVERMAN, F. CLARKSON, P. ROSENKRANTZ, AND S. VOGEL
1970 "Sex role stereotypes and clinical judgments of mental health." *Journal of Consulting and Clinical Psychology* 34 (February): 1–7.

BROWER, JONATHAN
1972 "The social bias of the division of labor among players in National Football League as a function of stereotypes." Paper presented at Annual Meetings of Pacific Sociological Association.

1979 "The professionalization of organized youth sport: Social psychological impacts and outcomes." *Annals of the American Academy of Political and Social Science* 445 (September): 39–46.

BROWN, ROSCOE C., AND BRYANT J. CRATTY
1969 *New Perspectives of Man in Action*. Englewood Cliffs, N. J.: Prentice-Hall.

BRYAN, CLIFFORD, AND ROBERT HORTON
1976 "Athletic events and spectacular spectators: A longitudinal study of fan aggression." Paper presented at the American Educational Research Association.

BRYANT, JENNINGS, PAUL COMISKY, AND DOLF ZILLMANN
1977 "Drama in sports commentary." *Journal of Communication* 27 (Summer): 140–49.

BUHRMANN, H.
1972 "Scholarship and athletics in junior high school." *International Review of Sport Sociology* 7: 119–31.
1977 "Athletics and deviance: An examination of the relationship between athletic participation and deviant behavior of high school girls." *Review of Sport and Leisure* 2 (June): 17–35.

BUREAU OF THE CENSUS
1976 *The United States Fact Book: The American Almanac*. New York: Grosset and Dunlap.

BURT, DAVID J.
1975 "The helmeted hero: The football player in recent American fiction." Paper presented at 1975 meeting of the National Popular Culture Association.

CARMACK, MARY AND RAINER MARTENS
1979 "Measuring commitment to running: A survey of runners' attitudes and mental states." *Journal of Sport Psychology* 1 (1): 25–42.

CARTER, JIMMY
1980 Letter of January 20, 1980 to Robert Kane, President of the U.S. Olympic Committee. Reprinted in the *Department of State Bulletin* 80 (March): 50–51.

CASADY, MARGIE
1974 "The tricky business of giving rewards." *Psychology Today* 8 (September): 56.

CHAMPOUX, JOSEPH
1973 "Self-concept, work, and non-work: An empirical examination of the compensatory and spill-over models." Paper presented at annual meeting of the American Sociological Association.

Chronicle of Higher Education
1980 "College sports expand, NCAA reports." November 3, p. 2.

CIALDINI, ROBERT, RICHARD BORDEN, AVRIL THORNE, MARCUS WALKER, STEPHEN FREEMAN, AND LLOYD SLOAN
1976 "Basking in reflected glory: Three (football) studies." *Journal of Personality and Social Psychology* 34 (September): 366–75.

CLAUSEN, JOHN A.
1968 "A historical and comparative view of socialization theory and research," in John A. Clausen (ed.), *Socialization and Society*. Boston: Little, Brown.

CLEAVER, CHARLES G.
1976 *Japanese and Americans: Cultural Parallels and Paradoxes*. Minneapolis: University of Minnesota Press.

COAKLEY, JAY
1978 *Sport in Society*. Saint Louis: C. V. Mosby Co.

COBB, ROBERT A., AND PAUL M. LEPLEY
1973 *Contemporary Philosophies of Physical Education and Athletics*. Columbus, Ohio: Charles E. Merrill.

COFER, C. N., AND W. R. JOHNSON
1960 "Personality dynamics in relation to exercise and sports," in W. R. Johnson (ed.), *Science and Medicine of Exercise and Sport*. New York: Harper.

COHEN, ALBERT
1955 *Delinquent Boys: The Culture of the Gang*. Glencoe, Il.: The Free Press.

COLEMAN, JAMES S.
1961 *The Adolescent Society*: New York: The Free Press.

COLEMAN, KEN
1973 *So You Want To Be a Sportscaster*. New York: Hawthorn Press.

COLLINS, GEORGE J.
1954 "League baseball and our children." *The Physical Educator* 11 (May): 37–39.

COMISKY, PAUL, JENNINGS BRYANT, AND DOLF ZILLMAN
1977 "Commentary as a substitute for action." *Journal of Communication* 27 (Summer): 150–59.

COMMISSION ON THE REVIEW OF GAMBLING
1976 *Gambling in America*. Washington, D.C.: U.S. Government Printing Office.

COMMITTEE ON COMMERCE, SCIENCE, AND TRANSPORTATION
1978 Fifth Annual Report of the Federal Communications Commission on the Effect of Public Law 93-107, The Sports Antiblackout Law. Ninety-Fifth Congress, United States Senate. Washington, D.C.: U.S. Government Printing Office.

COMMITTEE ON THE DISTRICT OF COLUMBIA
1974 Amend the Financing of the District of Columbia Stadium Act. House of Representatives, Ninety-Third Congress. Serial No. 93-94. Washington, D.C.: U.S. Government Printing Office.

COMMITTEE ON FINANCE
1976 Tax Reform Act of 1975. U.S. Senate, Ninety-Fourth Congress. Washington, D.C.: U.S. Government Printing Office.

COMMITTEE ON FOREIGN RELATIONS
1980 Participation in the 1980 Summer Olympic Games. House of Representatives, Ninety-Sixth Congress. Washington, D.C.: U.S. Government Printing Office.

COMMITTEE ON INTERSTATE AND FOREIGN COMMERCE, HOUSE OF REPRESENTATIVES
1978 *NCAA Enforcement Program, Part 2*, Attachment "I," Washington, D.C.: U.S. Government Printing Office.

COMMITTEE ON THE JUDICIARY

1975 Rights of Professional Athletes. Hearings Before the Subcommittee on Monopolies and Commercial Law, Ninety-Fourth Congress. Serial No. 59. Washington, D.C.: U.S. Government Printing Office.

CONGRESSIONAL RECORD

1953 March 20. 2151. Washington, D.C.: U.S. Government Printing Office.

1971 September 25. 3340. Washington, D.C.: U.S. Government Printing Office.

COOPER, LOWELL

1969 "Athletics, activity, and personality: A review of the literature." *Research Quarterly* 40 (March): 17–22.

CORBIN, CHARLES B.

1973 "College physical education and the vertical curriculum," in Robert A. Cobb and Paul M. Lepley (eds.), *Contemporary Philosophies of Physical Education and Athletics*. Columbus: Charles E. Merrill Publishing Co.

COSER, LOUIS

1974 *Greedy Institutions*. New York: The Free Press.

COX, HARVEY

1969 *The Feast of Fools: A Theological Essay on Festivity and Fantasy*. New York: Harper and Row.

CRANDALL, RICK, MONICA NOLAN, AND LESLIE MORGAN

1980 "Leisure and social interaction," in Seppo E. Iso-Ahola (ed.), *Social Psychological Perspectives on Leisure and Recreation*. Springfield, Il.: Charles C Thomas.

CRANDALL, RICK, AND KARLA SLIVKEN

1980 "Leisure attitudes and their measurement," in Seppo E. Iso-Ahola (ed.), *Social Psychological Perspectives on Leisure and Recreation*. Springfield, Il.: Charles C Thomas.

CRATTY, BRYANT J.

1973 *Psychology in Contemporary Sports*. Englewood Cliffs, N.J.: Prentice-Hall.

1974 *Psycho-Motor Behavior in Education and Sports*. Springfield, Il.: Charles C Thomas.

CROSS, GEORGE

1977 *Presidents Can't Punt: The OU Football Tradition*. Norman: Oklahoma University Press.

CSIKSZENTMIHALYI, MIHALY

1975 *Beyond Boredom and Anxiety: The Experience of Play in Work and Games*. San Francisco: Jossey-Bass Publishers.

CUMMING, ELAINE, AND WILLIAM HENRY

1961 *Growing Old: The Process of Disengagement*. New York: Basic Books.

CUMMINGS, RONALD

1974 "The Super Bowl society: Three archetypal heroes." Unpublished manuscript, Purdue University.

1975 "Double play and replay: Living out there in television land," in E. Snyder (ed.), *Sports: A Social Scoreboard*. Bowling Green State University: Popular Press.

CURTIS, J., AND JOHN W. LOY

1978 "Positional segregation in professional baseball." *International Review of Sports Sociology* 13 (1): 67–80.

DANFORD, HOWARD G., AND MAX SHIRLEY

1970 *Creative Leadership in Recreation*. Boston: Allyn and Bacon.

DAVIS, KINGSLEY, AND WILBERT MOORE

1945 "Some principles of stratification." *American Sociological Review* 10 (April): 242–49.

DECI, EDWARD L.

1972 "The effects of contingent and noncontingent rewards and controls on intrinsic motivation." *Organizational Behavior and Human Performance* 8: 217–29.

1975 "Notes on the theory and metatheory of intrinsic motivation." *Organizational Behavior and Human Performance* 15: 130–45.

DE COUBERTIN, PIERRE

1896 "The first Olympics." *Century* 53 (November): 53.

1978 "The Olympic games of 1896," in Benjamin Lowe et al. (eds.), *Sport and International Relations*. Champaign, Il. Stipes. Originally published in *The Century Magazine* 53 (November): 1896.

DE GRAZIA, SEBASTIAN

1962 *Of Time, Work, and Leisure*. Garden City: Doubleday.

DEMMERT, HENRY

1973 *The Economics of Professional Team Sports*. Lexington: D.C. Heath.

DENZIN, NORMAN

1976 "Child's play and the construction of social order." *Quest* 26 (Summer): 48–55.

DEPARTMENT OF COMMERCE

1975 *The Growth of Selected Leisure Industries*. Washington, D.C.: U.S. Government Printing Office.

DEPARTMENT OF LABOR

1973 "Careers in professional sports." *Occupational Outlook Quarterly* 17 (Summer): 2–5.

DEVEREUX, EDWARD C.

1976 "Backyard versus little league baseball: The impoverishment of children's games," in D. M. Landers (ed.) *Social Problems in Athletics*. Urbana: University of Illinois Press.

DEWAR, CAMERON

1979 "Spectator fights at professional baseball games." *Review of Sport and Leisure* 4 (Summer): 14–25.

DIAMOND, ARTHUR, M.

1976 "Hockey violence: Courts don't have the answer." *The New York Times*, December 19, 1976, Section S, p. 2.

1977 "Help for sports fans? Nader's idea is dissected." *The New York Times*, October 30, 1977, p. 2.

DODDS, PATT

1976 "Love and joy in the gymnasium." *Quest* 26 (Summer): 109–16.

DOLGAN, ROBERT

1977 "Sportswriting comes of age." *Sunday Plain Dealer Magazine*, August 14, 1977, pp. 22–36.

DOUGHERTY, JOSEPH

1976 "Race and sport: A follow-up study." *Sport Sociology Bulletin* 5 (Spring): 1–12.

DOWELL, LINUS J.

1971 "Environmental factors of childhood competitive athletics." *The Physical Educator* 28 (March): 17–21.

DOWLING, TOM

1977 "Don't touch that dream." *Skeptic* 21 (September/October): 20–23, 50–52.

DUBOIS, PAUL

1978 "Participation in sports and occupational attainment: A comparative study." *Research Quarterly* 49 (March): 28–37.

1979 "Participation in sport and occupational attainment: An investigation of selected athlete categories." Paper presented at the American Sociological Association, Boston.

DUNCAN, O., A. HALLER, AND A. PORTES

1968 "Peer influences on aspirations: A reinterpretation." *American Journal of Sociology* 74 (September): 119–37.

DUNNING, ERIC

1967 "Notes on some conceptual and theoretical problems in the sociology of sport." *International Review of Sport Sociology* 2: 143–53.

1971 "Some conceptual dilemmas in the sociology of sport." Magglinger Symposium on the Sociology of Sport. Basel, Switzerland; Birkhauser Verlag, pp. 34–37.

DURKHEIM, EMILE

1954 *The Elementary Forms of Religious Life*. Glencoe: Free Press.

DURSO, JOSEPH

1971 *The All-American Dollar: The Big Business of Sports*. Boston: Houghton-Mifflin Co.

1975 *The Sports Factory: An Investigation into College Sports*. New York: Quadrangle Books.

EDWARDS, HARRY

1970 *Revolt of the Black Athlete*. New York: Free Press.

1973a "The black athlete on the college campus," in J. Talamini and C. Page (eds.), *Sport and Society*. Boston: Little, Brown.

1973b *Sociology of Sport*. Homewood, Il.: Dorsey Press.

1980 *The Struggle That Must Be: An Autobiography*. New York: Macmillan.

EITZEN, D. STANLEY

1973 "Athletics in the status system of male adolescents: A replication of Coleman's *The Adolescent Society*." Paper presented at the Midwest Sociological Society.

1976 "Sport and social status in American public secondary education. *Review of Sport and Leisure* 1 (Fall): 139–55.

1979 *Sport in Contemporary Society*. New York: St. Martin's Press.

EITZEN, D. STANLEY, AND I. TESSENDORF
1978 "Racial segregation by position in sports: The special case of basketball." *Review of Sport and Leisure* 3 (Fall): 109–28.

EITZEN, D. STANLEY, AND GEORGE SAGE
1978 *Sociology of American Sport*. Dubuque, Iowa: Wm. C. Brown.

EITZEN, D. STANLEY, AND NORMAN YETMAN
1977 "Immune from racism?" *Civil Rights Digest* 9 (Winter): 3–13.

ELDER, GLEN H.
1968 *Adolescent Socialization and Personality Development*. Chicago: Rand McNally.

ELIAS, NORBERT, AND ERIC DUNNING
1970 "The quest for excitement in unexciting societies," in Gunther Lüschen (ed.), *The Cross-Cultural Analysis of Sports and Games*. Champaign, Il.: Stipes Publishing Co.
1972 "Dynamics of sport groups with special reference to football," in E. Dunning, (ed.), *Sport: Readings from a Sociological Perspective*. Toronto: Toronto Press.

ELLIS, MICHAEL
1981 "Motivational theories of play: Definitions and explanations," in Gunther Lüschen and George Sage (eds.), *Handbook of Social Science of Sport*. Champaign, Il.: Stipes.

EMRICK, MICHAEL R.
1976 "Major league baseball principal play-by-play announcers: Their occupation, background, and personal life." Ph.D. dissertation, Bowling Green State University.

ENDICOTT, WILLIAM
1979 "Born again ball players on the increase." *Los Angeles Times*, August 31, 1979, p. 1.

ERMANN, DAVID, AND RICHARD LUNDMAN
1978 "Deviant acts by complex organizations: Deviance and social control at the organizational level of analysis." *The Sociological Quarterly* (Winter): 55–67.

ESKENAZI, GERALD
1972 *A Thinking Man's Guide to Pro Hockey*. New York: E. P. Dutton.

ESPY, RICHARD
1979 *The Politics of the Olympic Games*. Berkeley: University of California Press.

EVANS, ARTHUR
1979 "Differences in the recruitment of black and white football players at a big eight university." *Journal of Sport and Social Issues* 3 (Fall/Winter): 1–10.

FAUNCE, WILLIAM A.
1963 "Automation and leisure," in Ervin O. Smigel (ed.), *Work and Leisure: A Contemporary Social Problem*. New Haven: College and University Press.

FEDERAL COMMUNICATIONS COMMISSION
1976 Third Annual Report of the Effect of Public Law 93-107, the Sports Anti-Blackout Law, on the Broadcasting of Sold-Out Home Games of Professional Football, Baseball, Basketball, and Hockey. Washington, D.C.: U.S. Government Printing Office.

FELTZ, DEBORAH
1979 "Athletics in the status system of female athletes." *Review of Sport and Leisure* 4 (Summer): 110–18.

FIELDS, CHERYL
1979 "What colleges must do to avoid sex bias in sports." *The Chronicle of Higher Education* 19 (December 10): 1, 13–16.

FINE, GARY ALAN
1978 "Preadolescent socialization through organized athletics: The construction of moral meanings in Little League baseball," in March Krotee (ed.), *The Dimensions of Sport Sociology*. West Point: Leisure Press.
1979 "Small groups and culture creation: The idioculture of Little League baseball teams." *American Sociological Review* 44 (October): 733–45.

FISHER, A. CRAIG
1976 *Psychology of Sport*. Palo Alto, Ca.: Mayfield.

FLOOD, CURT
1970 *The Way It Is*. New York: Trident Press.

FOLKINS, CARLYLE, AND WESLEY SIME
1981 "Physical fitness training and mental health." *American Psychologist* 36(4): 373–89.

FRAZIER, WALT
1977 "Talk about doctors instead of athletes." *The New York Times*, May 1, 1977, Section 5, page 2.

FREY, JAMES
1978 "The organization of American amateur sport." *American Behavioral Scientist* 21 (January/February): 361–78.

FRICK, FORD C.
1973 *Games, Asterisks, and People*. New York: Crown Publishers.

FRIEDENBERG, E.
1966 "The adolescent in high school athletics," in H. Becker (ed.), *Social Problems*. New York: Wiley.

FURST, TERRY R.
1971 "Social change and the commercialization of professional sports." *International Review of Sport Sociology* 6: 153–70.

GALLIHER, JOHN, AND RICHARD HESSLER
1979 "Sports competition and international capitalism." *Journal of Sport and Social Issues* 3 (Spring/Summer): 10–21.

GALLNER, SHELDON
1974 *Pro Sports: The Contract Game*. New York: Charles Scribner's Sons.

GARDNER, PAUL
1974 *Nice Guys Finish Last: Sport and American Life*. New York: Universe Books.

GARFINKEL, HAROLD
1956 "Conditions of successful degradation ceremonies." *American Journal of Sociology* 61 (March): 420–24.

GARVEY, EDWARD

1979 "From chattel to employee: The athlete's quest for freedom and dignity." *Annals of the American Academy of Political and Social Science* 445 (September): 91–101.

GAYLIN, WILLARD, IRA GLASSER, STEVEN MARCUS, AND DAVID ROTHMAN

1978 *Doing Good: The Limits of Benevolence*. New York: Pantheon Books.

GEERTZ, CLIFFORD

1966 "Religion as a cultural system," in Michael Banton (ed.), *Anthropological Approaches to Study of Religion*. London: Tavistock Publications.

GEORGE, JACK F.

1973 "The interscholastic athletic program can survive," in Robert A. Cobb and Paul M. Lepley (eds.), *Contemporary Philosophies of Physical Education and Athletics*. Columbus, Ohio: Charles E. Merrill.

GERBER, ELLEN W.

1974 "Chronicle of participation," in E. Gerber, J. Felshin, P. Berlin, and W. Wyrick (eds.), *The American Woman in Sport*. Reading, Ma.: Addison-Wesley.

GERBER, ELLEN W., JAN FELSHIN, PEARL BERLIN, AND WANEEN WYRICK

1974 *The American Woman in Sport*. Reading, Ma.: Addison-Wesley.

GERTH, H. H., AND C. W. MILLS

1958 *From Max Weber: Essays in Sociology*. New York: Oxford University Press.

GIVANT, MICHAEL

1976 "Pro football and the mass media: Some themes in the televising of a product." Paper presented at Annual Meeting of Popular Culture Association.

1978 "Pro football and the mass media: Some themes in the televising of a product." *Review of Sport and Leisure* 3 (Winter): 69–92.

GLADER, EUGENE

1978 *Amateurism and Athletics*. West Point: Leisure Press.

GLASSER, WILLIAM

1976 *Positive Addiction*. New York: Harper and Row.

GMELCH, GEORGE

1972 "Magic in professional baseball," in Gregory Stone (ed.), *Games, Sport, and Power*. New Brunswick: E. P. Dutton.

GOFFMAN, ERVING

1952 "On cooling the mark out: Some aspects of adaptation to failure." *Psychiatry* 15 (Nov.): 451–63.

1967 *Interaction Ritual*. Garden City, N.Y.: Doubleday.

GOLDSTEIN, JEFFREY, AND ROBERT ARMS

1971 "Effects of observing athletic contests on hostility." *Sociometry* 34 (March): 83–90.

GOODE, WILLIAM

1960 "A theory of role strain." *American Sociological Review* 25 (August): 483–96.

GORDON, C. WAYNE

1957 *The Social System of the High School*. Glencoe, Il.: Free Press.

GORDON, C., C. GAITZ, AND J. SCOTT
1976 "Leisure and lives: Personal expressivity across the life span," in R. Binstock and E. Shanas (eds.), *Handbook of Aging and the Social Sciences*. New York: Van Nostrand Reinhold Co.

GRAMSCI, ANTONIO
1971 *Selections from the Prison Notebooks*. New York: International Publishers.

GREELEY, ANDREW
1972 *The Denominational Society*. Glenview, N. Y.: Scott, Foresman and Co.

GREENDORFER, SUSAN L.
1976 "A social learning approach to female sport involvement." Paper presented at the 1976 Meeting of the American Psychological Association Convention.
1977 "Intercollegiate football: An approach toward rationalization." *International Review of Sport Sociology* 12 (3): 23–34.

GREENE, DAVID, AND MARK R. LEPPER
1974 "How to turn play into work." *Psychology Today* 8 (September): 49–54.

GREGORY, C. JANE, AND BRIAN M. PETRIE
1972 "Superstition in sport." Paper presented at Fourth Canadian Psychomotor Learning and Sports Psychology Symposium, University of Waterloo.
1975 "Superstitions of Canadian intercollegiate athletes: An intersport comparison." *International Review of Sport Sociology* 10 (No. 2): 59–66.

GROAT, H. THEODORE
1976 "Community and conflict in mass society," in A. Neal (ed.), *Violence in Animal and Human Societies*. Chicago: Nelson-Hall.

GROSS, EDWARD, AND GREGORY P. STONE
1964 "Embarrassment and the analysis of role requirements." *American Journal of Sociology* 70 (July): 1–15.

GROVE, STEVEN, J. AND RICHARD A. DODDER
1979 "A study of functions of sport: A subsequent test of Spreitzer and Snyder's research." *Journal of Sport Behavior* 2 (May): 83–91.

GRUNEAU, RICHARD S.
1975 "Sport, social differentiation and social inequality," in Donald Ball and John Loy (eds.), *Sport and the Social Order*. Reading, Ma.: Addison-Wesley.
1976 "Sport as an area of sociological study: An introduction to major themes and perspectives," in Richard S. Gruneau and John G. Albinson (eds.), *Canadian Sport Sociological Perspectives*. Reading, Ma.: Addison-Wesley.

GRUSKY, OSCAR
1963 "The effects of formal structure on managerial recruitment: A study of baseball organization." *Sociometry* 26 (September): 345–53.

GUARDINI, ROMANO
1937 *The Spirit of the Liturgy*. New York: Sheed and Ward.

GUTTMANN, ALLEN
1978 *From Ritual to Record*. New York: Columbia University Press.

HAERLE, RUDOLPH K.

1974 "The athlete as 'moral' leader: Heroes, success themes and basic cultural values in selected baseball autobiographies, 1900-1970." *Journal of Popular Culture* 8 (Fall): 392–401.

1975a "Career patterns and career contingencies of professional baseball players," in Donald Ball and John Loy (eds.), *Sport and Social Order*. Reading, Ma.: Addison-Wesley.

1975b "Education, athletic scholarships, and the occupational career of the professional athlete." *Sociology of Work and Occupation* 2 (November): 373–403.

HALE, CREIGHTON

1959 "Athletics for pre-high school age children." *Journal of Health, Physical Education and Recreation* 30 (December): 19–21, 43.

1971 "Athletic competition for young children." Paper presented at Conference on Sport and Deviancy, Brockport, New York.

Handball Magazine

1978a "Two who quit." 28 (June): 75–80.

1978b "Jim Jacobs." 28 (August): 71–80.

HANFORD, G. H.

1974 *The Need for and Feasibility of a National Study of Intercollegiate Athletics*. Washington, D.C.: American Council on Education.

HANKS, MICHAEL P.

1979 "Race, sexual status and athletics in the process of educational achievement." *Social Science Quarterly* 60 (December): 482–96.

HANKS, MICHAEL P., AND BRUCE K. ECKLAND

1976 "Athletics and social participation in the educational attainment process." *Sociology of Education* 49 (October): 271–94.

HANNEN, JOHN

1976 "Editors notebook." *The Toledo Blade*, November 26, 1976, Section D, p. 3.

HARDY, STEPHEN H.

1974 "The medieval tournament: A functional sport of the upper class." *Journal of Sport History* 1 (Fall): 91–105.

HARING, DOUGLAS G.

1962 "Japanese national character," in Bernard Silberman (ed.), *Japanese Character and Culture*. Tucson: University of Arizona Press.

HARRIS, DONALD, AND D. STANLEY EITZEN

1978 "The consequences of failure in sport." *Urban Life* 7 (July): 177–88.

HARRIS, DOROTHY V.

1971 "The sportswoman in our society," in D. V. Harris (ed.), *Women in Sport*. Washington, D.C.: American Association for Health, Physical Education and Recreation.

1973 *Involvement in Sport*. Philadelphia: Lea and Febiger.

HARRIS, JANET C.

1981 "Sport and ritual: A macroscopic comparison of form." In John Loy (ed.), *Paradoxes of Play: Proceedings of the Association for the Anthropological Study of Play*. West Point: Leisure Press.

HART, M. MARIE

1971 "Women sit in the back of the bus." *Psychology Today* 5: 64–66.

HAVIGHURST, R., AND R. ALBRECHT

1953 *Older People*. New York: Longsman, Green.

HEIN, FRED V.

1973 "Competitive athletics for children," in Robert A. Cobb and Paul M. Lepley (eds.), *Contemporary Philosophies of Physical Education and Athletics*. Columbus, Ohio: Charles E. Merrill.

HEINILA, KALEVI

1966 "Notes on the inter-groups conflicts in international sport." *International Review of Sport Sociology* 1: 31–40.

1974 "Ethics of sport." *Research Reports* 4: 1–71.

HENNINGER, DANIEL

1980 "NBC's silent Saturday: Some kind of ballgame." *The Wall Street Journal*, December 23, 1980, p. 14.

HERMAN, ROBIN

1976 "The Soviet Union views sports strength as a power tool." *The New York Times*, July 11, 1976, Section 5, p. 15.

HEWITT, JOHN, AND RANDALL STOKES

1975 "Disclaimers." *American Sociological Review* 40 (February): 1–11.

HILL, PETER, AND BENJAMIN LOWE

1974 "The inevitable metathesis of the retiring athlete." *International Review of Sport Sociology* 9 (No. 3): 5–29.

HOCH, PAUL

1972 *Rip Off the Big Game: The Exploitation of Sports by the Power Elite*. New York: Anchor Books.

HOLLINGSHEAD, A. B.

1949 *Elmstown's Youth*. New York: Wiley.

HOROWITZ, IRA

1977 "Sports telecasts: Rights and regulations." *Journal of Communications* 27 (Summer): 160–68.

1978 "Market entrenchment and the sports broadcasting act." *American Behavioral Scientist* 21 (January/February): 415–29.

HORTON, JOHN

1966 "Order and conflict theories of social problems as competing ideologies." *American Journal of Sociology* 71 (January): 701–13.

HOUSE SELECT COMMITTEE ON PROFESSIONAL SPORTS

1976a *Inquiry Into Professional Sports: Part I*. House of Representatives, Ninety-Fourth Congress. Washington, D.C.: U.S. Government Printing Office.

1976b *Inquiry Into Professional Sports: Part II*. House of Representatives, Ninety-Fourth Congress. Washington, D.C.: U.S. Government Printing Office.

1976c *Professional Sports and the Law.* House of Representatives, Ninety-Fourth Congress. Washington, D.C.: U.S. Government Printing Office.

1977 *Inquiry Into Professional Sports: Final Meetings.* House of Representatives, Ninety-Fourth Congress. Washington, D.C.: U.S. Government Printing Office.

HOUSER, WILLIAM, AND L. B. LUEPTOW

1978 "Participation in athletics and academic achievement: A replication and extension." *The Sociological Quarterly* 19 (Spring): 304–9

HUGHES, EVERETT C.

1971 *The Sociological Eye: Selected Papers.* Chicago: Aldine-Atherton.

HUIZINGA, JOHAN

1938 *Home Ludens: A Study of the Play Element in Culture.* Boston: Beacon Press.

Human Behavior

1977 "Gay jocks." January, pp. 37–38.

INGHAM, ALAN, AND JOHN LOY, JR.

1974 "The structure of ludic action." *International Review of Sport Sociology* 9 (1): 23–62.

JACK, HAROLD K.

1973 "Philosophical considerations for junior high school physical education," in Robert A. Cobb and Paul M. Lepley (eds.), *Contemporary Philosophies of Physical Education and Athletics.* Columbus, Ohio: Charles E. Merrill.

JACKSON, C. O.

1961 "Just boys, not little adults." *The Physical Educator* 18 (May): 42.

JENKINS, DAN

1972 *Semi-Tough.* New York: Atheneum.

JOHNSON, ARTHUR

1978 "Public sports policy." *American Behavioral Scientist* 21 (February): 319–44.

1979 "Congress and professional sports: 1951-1978". Annuals of the *American Academy of Political and Social Science*, Vol. 445 (September): 102–15.

JOHNSON, NORRIS, AND DAVID MARPLE

1973 "Racial discrimination in professional baseball: An empirical test." *Sociological Focus* 6 (Fall): 6–18.

JOHNSON, WILLIAM

1971 *Super Spectator and the Electric Lilliputians.* Boston: Little, Brown.

JOHODA, GUSTAV

1969 *The Psychology of Superstition.* London: Penguin Press.

JOINT COMMITTEE ON INTERNAL REVENUE TAXATION

1975 *Tax Shelters: Professional Sports Franchises.* Prepared for the use of the Committee on Ways and Means, Ninety-Fourth Congress. Washington, D.C.: U.S. Government Printing Office.

JONES, JAMES, AND STEPHEN WILLIAMSON

1979 "Athletic profile inventory (API): Assessment of athletes' attitudes and values," in J. Goldstein (ed.), *Sports, Games, and Play.* New York: Wiley.

KAHN, ROGER

1971 *The Boys of Summer.* New York: Harper and Row.

KANDO, THOMAS, AND W. C. SUMMERS

1971 "The impact of work on leisure: Toward a paradigm and research strategy." *Pacific Sociological Review* 14 (Summer): 310–71.

KANDO, THOMAS M.

1975 *Leisure and Popular Culture in Transition*. St. Louis: Mosby.

KANTER, ROSABETH

1977 "Some effects of proportion on group life: Skewed sex ratios and responses to token women." *American Journal of Sociology* 82 (March): 965–90.

KAY, R., D. FELKER, AND R. VAROZ

1972 "Sports interests and abilities as contributors to self-concept in junior high school boys." *Research Quarterly* 43: 208–15.

KELLY, JOHN R.

1972 "Work and leisure: A simplified paradigm." *Journal of Leisure Research* 4: 50–62.

1978 "Leisure styles and choices in three environments." *Journal of Leisure Research* 21: 129–138.

KENYON, GERALD S.

1966 "The significance of physical activity as a function of age, sex, education, and socio-economic status of northern United States adults." *International Review of Sport Sociology* 1: 41–54.

1968 *Values Held for Physical Activity by Selected Urban Secondary School Students in Canada, Australia, England and the United States*. Madison: University of Wisconsin, Department of Physical Education-Men.

1969 "Sport involvement: A conceptual go and some consequences thereof," in Gerald S. Kenyon (ed.), *Aspects of Contemporary Sport Sociology*. Chicago: The Athletic Institute.

1970 "The use of path analysis in sport sociology with special reference to involvement socialization." *International Review of Sport Sociology* 5: 191–203.

1972 "Sport and society: At odds or in concert," in Arnold Flath (ed.), *Athletes in America*. Corvallis: Oregon State University Press.

KENYON, GERALD S., AND TOM M. GROGG

1969 Unpublished study, reported in G. S. Kenyon and B. D. McPherson, "Becoming involved in physical activity and sport: A process of socialization," in G. L. Rarick (ed.), *Physical Activity: Human Growth and Development*. New York: Academic Press, 1973.

1970 *Contemporary Psychology of Sport: Proceedings of the Second International Congress of Sport Psychology*. Chicago: The Athletic Institute.

KENYON, GERALD S., AND BARRY D. MCPHERSON

1973 "Becoming involved in physical activity and sport: A process of socialization," in G. Laurence Rarick (ed.), *Physical Activity: Human Growth and Development*. New York: Academic Press.

KERRANE, KEVIN

1974 "Reality 35, illusion 3: Notes on the football imagination in contemporary fiction." *Journal of Popular Culture* 8 (Fall): 437–52.

KIDD, BRUCE

1980 *The Political Economy of Sport*. Ottawa: Canadian Association of Health, Physical Education and Recreation.

KIDD, THOMAS, AND WILLIAM WOODMAN
1975 "Sex and orientations toward winning in sport." *Research Quarterly* 46 (December): 476–83.

KING, JOHN, AND PETER CHI
1974 "Personality and the athletic social structure: A case study." *Human Relations* 27 (February 1): 179–93.

KLAPP, ORRIN E.
1962 *Heroes, Villains, and Fools*. Englewood Cliffs, N.J.: Prentice-Hall.

KLEIN, FRANK
1976 "Race horse recruiting." *Tampa Times*, December 28, 1976, Section C, pp. 1, 3.

KLEIN, FREDERICK C.
1979 "The press' cozy relationship with sports." *The Wall Street Journal*, June 26, 1979, p. 18.
1980 "52 hours of Olympic highlights." *The Wall Street Journal*, February 29, 1980, p. 19.

KNEER, MARIAN E.
1976 "The role of student satisfaction in developing play skills and attitudes." *Quest* 26 (Summer): 102–8.

KNELLER, GEORGE, F.
1965 *Educational Anthropology*. New York: Wiley.

KOPPETT, LEONARD
1973 *The Essence of the Game is Deception*. Boston: Little, Brown.
1974 *All About Baseball*. New York: Quadrangle Books.

KOWET, DON
1977 *The Rich Who Own Sports*. New York: Random House.

KRAMER, JERRY
1968 *Instant Play*. New York: World Publishing Co.
1969 *Farewell to Football*. New York: World Publishing Co.

KRAUS, RICHARD
1968 *Public Recreation and the Negro*. New York: Center for Urban Education.

KRETCHMAR, SCOTT
1976 "Leisure: In defense of indefensible sports and sportpersons," in 1976 Proceedings of National College Physical Education Association for Men, University of Illinois at Chicago Circle.

KROLL, WALTER
1970 "Current strategies and problems in personality assessment of athletes," in L. E. Smith (ed.), *Psychology of Motor Learning*. Chicago: The Athletic Institute.

KUHN, M., AND T. MCPARTLAND
1954 "An empirical investigation of self attitude." *American Sociological Review* 19 (February): 68–76.

LA BARRE, WESTON
1962 "Some observations on character structure in the orient," in Bernard Silberman (ed.), *Japanese Character and Culture*. Tucson: University of Arizona Press.

LAHR, JOHN
1972 "The theatre of sports," in M. Marie Hart (ed.), *Sport in the Socio-Cultural Press*. Dubuque, Iowa: Wm. C. Brown.

LANDERS, DANIEL
1975 "Social facilitation and human performance: A review of contemporary and past research," in D. Landers (ed.), *Psychology of Sport and Motor Behavior II*. University Park: The Pennsylvania State University.
1976 *Social Problems in Athletics: Essays in the Sociology of Sport*. Urbana: University of Illinois Press.
1979 "Birth order in the family and sport participation," in March Krotee (ed.), *The Dimensions of Sport Sociology*. West Point: Leisure Press.

LANDERS, DANIEL, AND DONNA LANDERS
1978 "Socialization via interscholastic athletics: Its effects on delinquency." *Sociology of Education* 51 (October): 299–303.

LARSON, DAVID, ELMER SPREITZER, AND ELDON E. SNYDER
1975 "Youth hockey programs: A sociological perspective." *Sports Sociology Bulletin* 4 (Fall): 55–63.

LAUCK, DAN
1977a "Sports agents' slice may make pie sordid." *Toledo Blade*, February 3, 1977, p. 29.
1977b "Agents constantly signing college athletes still competing." *Toledo Blade*, February 5, 1977, p. 11.
1977c "Agents sent checks to lure cage star." *Toledo Blade*, February 7, 1977, p. 17.

LAYMAN, EMMA
1968 "The role of play and sport in healthy emotional development: A reappraisal," in G. S. Kenyon and T. M. Grogg (eds.), *Contemporary Psychology of Sport*. Chicago: The Athletic Institute.
1972 "The contribution of play and sports to emotional health," in J. E. Kane (ed.), *Psychological Aspects of Physical Education and Sport*. London: Routledge and Kegan Paul.
1974 "Contributions of exercise and sports to mental health and social adjustment," in Warren R. Johnson and E. E. Buskirk (eds.), *Science and Medicine of Exercise and Sport*. New York: Harper and Row.

LEE, ROBERT
1964 *Religion and Leisure in America*. New York: Abingdon Press.

LEONARD, GEORGE
1974 *The Ultimate Athlete: Re-visioning Sports, Physical Education, and the Body*. New York: Viking Press.

LEONARD, WILBERT M., II
1977 "Stacking and performance differentials of whites, blacks, and latins in professional baseball." Paper presented at the American Sociological Association.

LEONARD, WILBERT M., II, AND SUSAN SCHMIDT
1975 "Observations on the changing social organization of collegiate and professional basketball." *Sport Sociology Bulletin* 4 (Fall): 13–35.

LERCH, STEPHEN
1980 "The adjustment to retirement of professional baseball players." Paper presented at Annual Meeting of the North American Society for the Sociology of Sport.

LEUCK, M. R., G. S. KRAHENBUHL, AND J. E. ODENKIRK
1979 "Assessment of spectator aggression at intercollegiate basketball contests." *Review of Sport and Leisure* 4 (Summer): 40–52.

LEVER, JANET
1978 "Sex differences in the complexity of children's play and games." *American Sociological Review* 43 (August): 471–83.

LEVER, JANET, AND STANTON WHEELER
1978 "The *Chicago Tribune* sportspage: 1900-1975." Paper presented at 1978 meetings of the American Sociological Association.

LEWIS, GEORGE
1972 "Prole sport: The case of roller derby," in G. Lewis (ed.), *Side-Saddle on the Golden Calf*. Pacific Palisades, Ca.: Goodyear.

LEWIS, JERRY
1977 "Collective violence in sport: A sociological perspective." Paper presented to the Arts and Sciences, Kent State University.

LINDSAY, PETER
1973 "Attitudes towards physical exercise reflected in the literature of ancient Rome," in Earle Zeigler (ed.), *History of Sport and Physical Education to 1900*. Champaign, Ill.: Stipes.

LIPSET, S. M., AND E. C. LADD, JR.
1972 "The politics of American sociologists." *The American Journal of Sociology* 78 (July): 67–104.

LIPSYTE, ROBERT
1975 *Sports World: An American Dreamland*. New York: Quadrangle New York Times Book Co.
1979 "Varsity syndrome: The unkindest cut." *The Annals of the American Academy of Political and Social Science* 445 (September): 15–23.

LOCKE, L. F.
1973 "Are sports education?" *Quest* 19: 87–89.

LOOMIS, TOM
1976 "Mirrors of sport." *The Toledo Blade*, October 24, 1976, Section D, p. 3.

LOWE, BENJAMIN
1977 *The Beauty of Sport: A Cross-Disciplinary Inquiry*. Englewood Cliffs, N.J.: Prentice-Hall.

LOWE, BENJAMIN, DAVID KANIN, AND ANDREW STRENK
1978 "Olympian," in Benjamin Lowe et al. (eds.), *Sport and International Relations*. Champaign, Il.: Stipes.

LOWE, BENJAMIN, AND MARK H. PAYNE
1974 "To be a red-blooded American boy." *Journal of Popular Culture* 8 (Fall): 383–91.

LOY, JOHN W.
1969 "The study of sport and social mobility," in Gerald S. Kenyon (ed.), *Aspects of Contemporary Sport Sociology*. Chicago: The Athletic Institute.

LOY, JOHN W., SUSAN BIRRELL, AND DAVID ROSE
1976 "Attitudes held toward agonetic activities as a function of selected social identities." *Quest* 26 (Summer): 81–93.

LOY, JOHN W., AND ALAN INGHAM

1973 "Play, games, and sport in the psychosociological development of children and youth," in G. L. Rarick (ed.), *Physical Activity: Human Growth and Development*. New York: Academic Press.

LOY, JOHN W., AND GERALD S. KENYON

1969 *Sport, Culture and Society: A Reader on the Sociology of Sport*. New York: Macmillan.

LOY, JOHN W., AND JOSEPH F. MCELVOGUE

1970 "Racial segregation in American sport." *International Review of Sport Sociology* 5: 5–24.

LOY, JOHN W., BARRY D. MCPHERSON, AND GERALD KENYON

1978 *Sport and Social Systems*. Reading, Ma.: Addison-Wesley.

LOY, JOHN W., AND GEORGE H. SAGE

1968 "The effects of formal structure on organizational leadership: An investigation of interscholastic baseball teams." Paper presented at Second International Congress of Sport Psychology. Washington, D.C.

1972 "Social origins, academic achievement, athletic achievement, and career mobility patterns of college coaches." Paper presented at the Annual Meetings of the American Sociological Association.

LUCKMANN, THOMAS

1967 *The Invisible Religion*. New York: Macmillan.

LUEPTOW, L. B., AND B. D. KAYSER

1973–1974 "Athletic involvement: Academic achievement and aspiration." *Sociological Focus* 7: 24–36.

LÜSCHEN, GUNTHER

1967 "The sociology of sport: A trend report and bibliography." *Current Sociology* 15 (No. 3): 5–140.

1969 "Social stratification and social mobility among young sportsmen," in J. Loy and G. Kenyon (eds.), *Sport, Culture, and Society*. London: Macmillan.

1970a "Cooperation, association, and contest." *Conflict Resolution* 14 (March): 21–34.

1970b *The Cross-Cultural Analysis of Sports and Games*. Champaign, Il.: Stipes.

1972 "On sociology of sport: General orientation and its trend in the literature," in O. Grupe, D. Kurtz, and J. Teipel (eds.), *The Scientific View of Sport*. Heidelberg: Springer-Verlag.

LYND, ROBERT, AND HELEN LYND

1929 *Middletown*. New York: Harcourt, Brace.

LYON, BILL

1978 "Religion is sweeping sports." *The Toledo Blade*, January 22, 1978, Section D, p. 5.

MALINOWSKI, BRONISLAW

1948 *Magic, Science and Religion*. New York: Doubleday.

MALMISUR, MICHAEL C., AND NAOMI SCHMITT

1975 "Social adjustment differences between student athletes and student nonathletes as measured by ego development," in Daniel M. Landers (ed.), *Psychology of Sport and Motor Behavior*, University Park: The Pennsylvania State University.

MALONEY, T. L.
1970 "Attitudes toward Playing a Game and the Sport: Involvement of School Aged Adolescents." Unpublished Master's thesis, University of Western Ontario.

MALONEY, T. L., AND BRIAN M. PETRIE
1972 "Professionalization of attitude toward play among Canadian school pupils as a function of sex, grade, and athletic participation." *Journal of Leisure Research* 4 (Summer): 184–95.

MANGAN, J. A.
1973 *Physical Education and Sport: Sociological and Cultural Perspectives.* Oxford: Basil Blackwell.

MANTEL, R. C., AND L. VANDER VELDEN
1971 "The relationship between the professionalization of attitude toward play of pre-adolescent boys and participation in organized sport." Paper presented at the International Symposium on the Sociology of Sport, Waterloo, Ontario.

MARCIA, J. AND M. FRIEDMAN
1970 "Ego identity status in college women." *Journal of Personality* 38 (June): 249–63.

MARKS, STEPHEN
1977 "Multiple roles and role strain: Some notes on human energy, time, and commitment." *American Sociological Review* 42 (December): 921–36.

MARSH, PETER, AND ROM HARRE
1978 "The world of football hooligans." *Human Behavior* 1 (October): 62–69.

MARSHALL, STAN
1973 "A comprehensive philosophy of intercollegiate athletics for man," in Robert A. Cobb and Paul M. Lepley (eds.), *Contemporary Philosophies of Physical Education and Athletics*. Columbus, Ohio: Charles E. Merrill.

MARTENS, RAINER
1969 "Effect of an audience on learning and performance of a complex motor skill." *Journal of Personality and Social Psychology* 12 (July): 252–60.
1976 "Kid sports: A den of inquity or land of promise?" Proceedings of the National College Physical Education Association for Men, University of Illinois at Chicago Circle.

MARTIN, THOMAS W., AND KENNETH J. BERRY
1973 "Latent functions of competitive sport in post-industrial society." Paper presented at Annual Meeting of the Midwest Sociological Society.

MARX, KARL
1964 *Early Writings*. New York: McGraw-Hill.

MARX, KARL, AND FRIEDRICH ENGELS
1959 *Basic Writings on Politics and Philosophy*, ed. Lewis S. Fever. New York: Doubleday.
1975 *Collected Works: Volume 6*. London: Lawrence and Wishart.

MASLOW, ABRAHAM
1970 *Religions, Values, and Peak-Experiences*. New York: Viking Press.
1971 *The Farther Reaches of Human Nature*. New York: Viking Press.

MASSENGALE, JOHN
1974 "Coaching as an occupational subculture." *Phi Delta Kappan* 56 (October): 140–42.

MASSENGALE, JOHN D., AND STEVEN FARRINGTON
1977 "The influence of playing position centrality on the careers of college football coaches." *Review of Sport and Leisure* 2 (June): 107–15.

MCCAGHY, CHARLES
1976 *Deviant Behavior*, New York: Macmillan.

MCDILL, D., AND J. S. COLEMAN
1965 "Family and peer influences in college plans of high school students." *Sociology of Education* 38 (Winter): 112–26.

MCINTOSH, PETER
1979 *Fair Play: Ethics in Sport and Education*. London: Heinemann Press.

MCLUHAN, MARSHALL
1966 *Understanding Media: The Extensions of Man*. New York: McGraw-Hill.

MCPHERSON, BARRY D.
1972 "Socialization into the role of sport consumer: A theory and causal model." Ph.D. Dissertation, University of Wisconsin.
1975 "The segregation by playing position hypothesis in sport: An alternative hypothesis." *Social Science Quarterly* 55 (March): 960–66.
1978 "The child in competitive sport: Influence of the social milieu," in R. A. Magill, M. Ash, and F. Smoll (eds.), *Children in Sport: A Contemporary Anthology*. Champaign, Il.: Human Kinetics.

MCPHERSON, BARRY D. AND C. KOZLIK
1979 "Canadian leisure patterns by age: Disengagement, continuity or agism?" in V. Marshall (ed.), *Aging in Canada: Social Perspectives*. Pickering, Ontario: Fitzhenry and Whiteside.

MCQUARIE, DONALD
1980 "Utopia and transcendence: An analysis of their decline in contemporary science fiction." *Journal of Popular Culture* (Fall 1980): 242–50.

MEAD, GEORGE H.
1934 *Mind, Self and Society*. Chicago: University of Chicago Press.

MEGGYSEY, DAVE
1971 *Out of Their League*. New York: Paperback Library.

MEISSNER, MARTIN
1971 "The long arm of the job: A study of work and leisure." *Industrial Relations* 10: 239–60.

MERRIMAN, J. BURTON
1960 "Relationship of personality traits to motor ability." *The Research Quarterly* 31 (May): 163–73.

MERTON, ROBERT
1938 "Social structure and anomie." *American Sociological Review* 3 (October): 672–82.
1968 *Social Theory and Social Structure*, 3rd ed. New York: The Free Press.

MESSENGER, CHRISTIAN

1974 "Tom Buchanan and the demise of the ivy league athletic hero." *Journal of Popular Culture* 8 (Fall): 402–10.

METHENY, ELEANOR

1965 "Symbolic forms of movement: The feminine image in sports," in Eleanor Metheny (ed.), *Connotations of Movement in Sport and Dance.* Dubuque, Iowa: William C. Brown.

1972 "The symbolic power of sport," in Ellen Gerber (ed.), *Sport and the Baby.* Philadelphia: Lea and Febiger.

MICHENER, JAMES A.

1976 *Sports in America.* New York: Random House.

MIDDLETON, LORENZO

1979 "The cable connection." *Chronicle of Higher Education* 19 (December 3): 6–7.

MIHOVILOVIC, MIRO A.

1968 "The status of former sportsmen." *International Review of Sport Sociology* 3: 73–93.

MILGRAN, STANLEY, AND HANS TOCH

1968 "Collective behavior: Crowds and social movements," in Gardner Lindzey and E. Aronson (eds.), *Handbook of Social Psychology.* Reading, Ma.: Addison-Wesley.

MILLER, DAVID

1970 *Gods and Games: Toward a Theology of Play.* New York: World Publishing Co.

MINAMI, HIROSHI

1971 *Psychology of the Japanese People.* Toronto: University of Toronto Press.

MONDALE, WALTER

1980 Address before the U.S. Olympic Committee House of Delegates in Colorado Springs, Colorado on April 12, 1980. Reprinted in the Department of State Bulletin, 8 (May): 14–15.

MOORE, ROBERT A.

1966 *Sports and Mental Health.* Springfield, Il.: Charles C Thomas.

MORGAN, WILLIAM P.

1970 *Contemporary Readings in Sport Psychology.* Springfield, Il.: Charles C Thomas.

1973 "An existential phenomenological analysis of sport as a religious experience," in Robert Osterhoudt (ed.), *The Philosophy of Sport.* Springfield, Il.: Charles C Thomas.

1974 "Selected psychological considerations in sport." *Research Quarterly* 45 (December): 374–90.

1979 "Negative addiction in runners." *The Physician and Sportsmedicine* 7 (February): 57–69.

NABIL, PHILIP

1980 "The present-day Afro-American major-league baseball player and socioeconomic mobility in American society." *Review of Sport and Leisure* 5 (Winter): 49–68.

NACK, BILL

1976 "Spectator violence becoming part of sports scene." *The Toledo Blade,* December 12, 1976, Section D, p. 3.

NAFZIGER, JAMES
1978 "The regulation of transnational sports competition: Down from Mount Olympus," in Benjamin Lowe et al. (eds.), *Sport and International Relations*. Champaign, Il.: Stipes.

NAISMITH, JAMES
1941 *Basketball, Its Origins and Development*. New York: American Sports.

NATIONAL INSTITUTE OF LAW ENFORCEMENT AND CRIMINAL JUSTICE
1978 *Gambling Law Enforcement in Major American Cities: Executive Summary*. Washington, D.C.: U.S. Department of Justice.

NEAL, ARTHUR G.
1976 "Perspectives violence," in A. G. Neal (ed.), *Violence in Animal and Human Societies*. Chicago: Nelson Hall.

NEAL, PATSY
1972 *Sport and Identity*. Philadelphia: Dorrance.

NEALE, ROBERT E.
1969 *In Praise of Play: Toward a Psychology of Religion*. New York: Harper and Row.

NEULINGER, JOHN
1974 *The Psychology of Leisure*. Springfield, Il.: Charles C Thomas.

Newsweek
1977 "Keeping fit: American tries to shape up." November 23, pp. 78–86.

NICHOLSON, CONNIE SNYDER
1978 "A Study of Socialization and Sport Participation for Early Adolescent Females." Master's thesis, The University of Illinois.
1979 "Some attitudes associated with sport participation among junior high females." *Research Quarterly* 50 (December): 661–67.

NIEBUHR, H. RICHARD
1960 *Radical Monotheism and Western Culture*. New York: Harper and Row.

NISBET, ROBERT
1976 *Sociology As an Art Form*. London: Oxford University Press.

NISBETT, RICHARD
1968 "Birth order and participation in dangerous sports." *Journal of Personality and Social Psychology* 8 (4): 351–53.

NIXON, HOWARD L.
1974 "The commercial and organizational development of modern sport." *International Review of Sport Sociology* 9 (No. 2): 107–35.
1976a "Sport, socialization, and youth: Some proposed research directions." *Review of Sport and Leisure* 1 (Fall): 45–61.
1976b *Sport and Social Organization*. Indianapolis: Bobbs-Merrill.
1979 "Acceptance of the 'dominant American sports creed' among college students." *Review of Sport and Leisure* 4 (Winter): 141–59.

NOE, FRANCIS P., AND KIRK W. ELIFSON
1973 "The leisured poor: An absence of autonomy." Unpublished paper, Department of Sociology, Georgia State University.

NOLL, ROGER G.
1974 *Government and the Sports Business: Studies in the Regulation of Economic Activity*. Washington, D.C.: The Brookings Institution.

NOTTINGHAM, ELIZABETH
1971 *Religion: A Sociological View*. New York: Random House.

NOVAK, MICHAEL
1976 *The Joy of Sports: End Zones, Bases, Baskets, Balls, and the Consecration of the American Spirit*. New York: Basic Books.

NOVERR, DOUGLAS, AND LARRY ZIEWACZ
1974 "The athletic revolution reconsidered: An examination of the literature of athletic protest." Unpublished paper, Michigan State University.

NYQUIST, E. B.
1979 "Win, women, and money: Collegiate athletics today and tomorrow." *Educational Record* 60 (Fall): 374–93.

OBOJSKI, ROBERT
1975 *The Rise of Japanese Baseball Power*. Radnor, Pa.: Chilton.

OGILVIE, B., AND T. TUTKO
1971 "Sport: If you want to build character, try something else." *Psychology Today* 5: 60–63.

OKNER, B.
1974 "Taxation and sports enterprises," in R. Noll (ed.), *Government and the Sports Business*. Washington, D.C.: The Brookings Institute.

OLSEN, JACK
1968 *The Black Athlete: A Shameful Story of Integration in American Sport*. New York: Time-Life.

OPIE, IONA, AND PETER OPIE
1964 *Children's Games in Street and Playground*. London: Oxford University Press.

ORLICK, TERRY
1974 "The sports environment, a capacity to enhance, a capacity to destroy." Paper presented at the Sixth Canadian Symposium of Psycho-Motor Learning and Sports Psychology.
1975 "Games of acceptance and psycho-social adjustment." Paper presented at the Conference on Mental Health and Aspects of Sports, Exercise and Recreation.
1978 *Winning through Cooperation*. Washington, D.C.: Acropolis Books.

ORLICK, TERRY, AND CAL BOTTERILL
1975 *Every Kid Can Win*. Chicago: Nelson-Hall.

OTTO, LUTHER B.
1975 "Extracurricular activities in the educational attainment process." *Rural Sociology* 40 (Summer): 162–76.
1976 "Social integration and the status-attainment process." *American Journal of Sociology* 81 (May): 1360–83.

OTTO, LUTHER, AND DUANE ALWIN
1977 "Athletics, aspirations, and attainments." *Sociology of Education* 42 (April): 102–13.

PAGE, CHARLES H.
1969 "Symposium summary, with reflections upon the sociology of sport as a research field," in Gerald S. Kenyon (ed.), *Aspects of Contemporary Sport Sociology*. Chicago: The Athletic Institute.
1973 "The mounting interest in sport," in Charles H. Page and J. T. Talamini (eds.), *Sport and Society*. Boston: Little, Brown.

PARENTE, DONALD E.
1977 "The interdependence of sports and television." *Journal of Communication* 27 (Summer): 128–39.

PARK, PETER
1969 *Sociology Tomorrow*. New York: Pegasus.

PARRISH, BERNIE
1972 *They Call It a Game*. New York: Signet Books.

PATE, ROBERT M.
1973 "Physical education at the secondary school level," in Robert A. Cobb and Paul M. Lepley (eds.), *Contemporary Philosophies of Physical Education and Athletics*. Columbus, Ohio: Charles E. Merrill.

PAUL, ANGUS
1980 "Growing deficits force colleges to eliminate some varsity sports." *The Chronicle of Higher Education* 21 (September 15): 1,10.

PAXSON, FREDERIC
1917 "The rise of sport." *The Mississippi Valley Historical Review* 4 (September): 144–68.

PEARMAN, WILLIAM
1978 "Race on the sports page." *Review of Sport and Leisure* 3 (Winter): 54–68.

PEEK, CHARLES, J. STEVEN PICOU, AND EVANS CURRY
1979 "Interscholastic athletics and delinquent behavior: Appraisal or applause?" *Sociology of Education* 52 (October): 238–43.

PELTON, BARRY C.
1970 *New Curriculum Perspectives: Collegiate Physical Education*. Dubuque, Iowa: William C. Brown.

PERRY, JOSEPH B., AND M. D. PUGH
1978 *Collective Behavior*. St. Paul: West.

PETRIE, BRIAN M.
1971 "Achievement orientations in adolescent attitudes toward play." *International Review of Sport Sociology* 6: 89–101.
1975 "Sport and politics," in Donald Ball and John Loy (eds.), *Sport and the Social Order*. Reading, Ma.: Addison-Wesley.

PHILLIPS, JOHN C.
1976 "Toward an explanation of racial variations in top-level sports participation." *International Review of Sport Sociology*: 11 (No. 3): 39–53.

PHILLIPS, JOHN C., AND WALTER E. SCHAFER
1970 "The athletic subculture: A preliminary study." Paper presented at the American Sociological Association.
1971 "Consequences of participation in interscholastic sports: A review and prospectus." *Pacific Sociological Review* 14 (July): 328–38.

PIAGET, JEAN

1962 *Play, Dreams and Imitation in Childhood.* New York: W. W. Norton.

PICOU, J. STEVEN

1978 "Race, athletic achievement, and educational aspirations." *The Sociological Quarterly* 19 (Summer): 429–38.

PICOU, J. STEVEN, AND E. W. CURRY

1974 "Residence and the athletic participation–aspiration hypothesis." *Social Science Quarterly* 55 (December): 768–76.

PIETSCHMANN, RICHARD JOHN

1973 "Salaries in professional sports." *Mainliner: United Air Lines Magazine* 11 (December): 18–22.

PILAPIL, B., J. STECKLEIN, AND H. LIU

1970 *Intercollegiate Athletics and Academic Progress: A Comparison of Academic Characteristics of Athletes and Nonathletes at the University of Minnesota.* Minneapolis: University of Minnesota.

PILZ, GUNTER

1979 "Attitudes toward different forms of aggressive and violent behavior in competitive sports: Two empirical studies." *Journal of Sport Behavior* 2 (February): 3–26.

POLACK, LEE

1980 "Hegemony and the Stacking Process." Paper read at the North American Society for the Sociology of Sport.

PRESIDENT'S COMMISSION

1977 *The Final Report of the President's Commission on Olympic Sports: Executive Summary.* Washington, D.C.: U.S. Government Printing Office.

PRESIDENT'S COUNCIL ON PHYSICAL FITNESS AND SPORTS

1978 *Newsletter: Special Edition on National Physical Fitness Survey* (May).

1979 "Situation on exercise in the United States." *Newsletter* (July): 7.

PURDY, DEAN

1980 "Effects of socialization on attitudes toward failure and work in sport: An analysis of adult softball participants." *Sociological Symposium 30* (Summer): 1–19.

RAHNER, HUGO

1972 *Man at Play.* New York: Herder and Herder.

RAINVILLE, RAYMOND, AND EDWARD MCCORMICK

1977 "Extent of covert racial prejudice in pro football announcers' speech." *Journalism Quarterly* 54 (1): 20–26.

RARICK, G. LAWRENCE

1973 *Physical Activity: Human Growth and Development.* New York: Academic Press.

REAL, MICHAEL R.

1976 "Super bowl: Mythic spectacle," in Andrew Yiannakis (ed.), *Sport Sociology: Contemporary Themes.* Dubuque, Iowa: Kendall/Hunt.

REED, WILLIAM

1972 "An ugly affair in Minneapolis." *Sports Illustrated* 36 (February 7): 18–21.

REHBERG, RICHARD A.
1969 "Behavioral and attitudinal consequences of high school interscholastic sports: A speculative consideration." *Adolescence* 4 (Spring): 69–88.

REHBERG, RICHARD A., AND M. COHEN
1975 "Athletes and scholars: An analysis of the compositional characteristics and image of two youth culture categories." *International Review of Sport Sociology* 10: 91–107.

REHBERG, RICHARD A., AND WALTER E. SCHAFER
1968 "Participation in interscholastic athletics and college expectations." *American Journal of Sociology* 73 (May): 732–40.

REHBERG, RICHARD A., AND D. WESTBY
1967 "Parental encouragement, occupation, education, and family size: Artificial or independent determinants of adolescent educational expectations." *Social Forces* 45 (March): 362–74.

REICH, CHARLES A.
1970 *The Greening of America*. New York: Bantam Books.

REVZIN, PHILIP
1980 "TV picture blinking, sliding, zigzagging? Relax, your set's OK." *The Wall Street Journal*, December 19, 1980, p. 1.

RICHARDSON, D.
1962 "Ethical conduct in sport situations," in the Proceedings of the National College Physical Education Association for Men.

RICHMAN, MILTON
1977 "Reggie gives credit to the man." *Bowling Green Sentinal Tribune*, September 15, 1977, p. 16.

RIESMAN, DAVID, AND REUEL DENNY
1954 "Football in America: A study in culture," in David Riesman (ed.), *Individualism Reconsidered*. Glencoe, Il.: Free Press.

RIORDAN, JAMES
1977 *Sport in Soviet Society*. London: Cambridge University Press.
1978 *Sport under Communism*. Montreal: McGill-Queen's University Press.

RITZER, GEORGE
1975 *Sociology: A Multiple Paradigm Science*. Boston: Allyn and Bacon.

ROARK, ANNE C.
1976 "Federal sex-bias forms seen inviting dishonesty." *Chronicle of Higher Education* 13 (December 6): 8.

ROBBINS, JAMES M., AND PAUL JOSEPH
1980 "Commitment to running: Implications for the family and work." *Sociological Symposium* 39 (Spring): 87–108.

ROBERTS, KENNETH
1970 *Leisure*. London: Longman.

ROBERTS, MICHAEL
1977 "The separation of sport and state." *Skeptic* 21 (September/October): 16–19, 50.

ROBERTS, RANDY
1975 "Jack Dempsey: An American hero in the 1920's." *Journal of Popular Culture* 8 (Fall): 411–26.

ROBINSON, JOHN P.
1967 "Time expenditure on sports across ten countries." *International Review of Sport Sociology* 2: 67–84.

ROBINSON, JOHN P., P. E. CONVERSE, AND A. SZALAI
1972 "Everyday life in twelve countries," in A. Szalai et al. (eds.), *The Use of Time: Daily Activities of Urban and Suburban Populations in Twelve Countries*. The Hague: Mouton.

ROBINSON, JOHN P., AND PHILLIP R. SHAVER
1969 *Measures of Social Psychological Attitudes*. Ann Arbor: University of Michigan, Institute for Social Research.

RODMAN, HYMAN
1963 "The lower-class value stretch." *Social Forces* 42 (December): 205–15.

ROHRBACHER, R.
1973 "Influence of a special camp program for obese boys on weight loss, self-concept, and body image." *Research Quarterly* 44 (May): 150–57.

ROONEY, JOHN F., JR.
1974 *A Geography of American Sport: From Cabin Creek to Anaheim*. Reading, Ma.: Addison-Wesley.
1975 "Sports from a geographical perspective," in D. Ball and J. Loy (eds.), *Sport and the Social Order*. Reading, Ma.: Addison-Wesley.
1981 "Football and the new southwest (1958-1976): A geographical approach." *Journal of Regional Cultures* 1(1): 149–61.

ROPER ORGANIZATION, INC.
1980 The 1980 Virginia Slims American Women's Opinion Poll.

ROSENBLATT, AARON
1967 "Negroes in baseball: The failure of success." *Transaction* 4 (September): 51–53.

ROTHMAN, SEYMOUR
1977 "TV sports alive and well and living in luxury." *The Toledo Blade*, March 26, 1977, p. 4.

RUDOLPH, FREDERICK
1962 *The American College and University*. New York: Random House.

RUNFOLA, ROSS
1974 "Sport and the mass media: The myth of objective transferral." Paper presented at meetings of Popular Culture Association. May 2-4, 1974.

RYAN, ALLAN J.
1973 "Philosophy of athletics at the junior high school level," in Robert A. Cobb and Paul M. Lepley (eds.), *Contemporary Philosophies of Physical Education and Athletics*. Columbus, Ohio: Charles E. Merrill.

SABO, DONALD, JR., AND ROSS RUNFOLA
1980 *Jock: Sports and Male Identity*. Englewood Cliffs, N.J.: Prentice-Hall.

SABOCK, RALPH

1973 *The Coach*. Philadelphia: W. B. Saunders.

SACK, ALLEN, AND ROBERT THIEL

1979 "College football and social mobility: A case study of Notre Dame football players." *Sociology of Education* 52 (January): 60–66.

SADLER, WILLIAM A.

1976 "Alienated youth and creative sports' experience." Paper presented at the Annual Meeting of the Philosophic Society.

SAGE, GEORGE H.

1973 "Occupational socialization and value orientation of athletic coaches." *Research Quarterly* 44 (October): 269–77.

1975 "An occupational analysis of the college coach," in D. W. Ball and J. W. Loy (eds.), *Sport and the Social Order: Contributions to the Sociology of Sport*. Reading, Ma.: Addison-Wesley.

1980a "Socialization and sport," in George H. Sage (ed.), *Sport and American Society: Selected Readings*. Reading, Ma.: Addison-Wesley.

1980b "Humanistic theory, the counterculture, and sport: Implications for action and research," in George H. Sage (ed.), *Sport and American Society: Selected Readings*. Reading, Ma.: Addison-Wesley.

1980c "Orientations toward sport of male and female intercollegiate male and female intercollegiate athletes." *Journal of Sport Psychology* 2 (4): 355–62.

SAGE, GEORGE H., AND SHERYL LOUDERMILK

1979 "The female athlete and role conflict." *Research Quarterly* 50 (March): 88–96.

SALAMINI, LEONARDO

1979 "Gramsci and Marxist sociology of knowledge: An analysis of hegemony–ideology–knowledge." *Sociological Quarterly* 15 (Summer): 359–80.

SALVAN, J.

1962 *To Be and Not to Be*. Detroit: Wayne State University Press.

SAUNDERS, E. D.

1976 "Sociology, sport and physical education." *Review of Sport and Leisure* 1 (Fall): 122–38.

SAXE, DAVID B.

1977 "Help for sports fans? They need plenty of it." *The New York Times*, October 30, 1977, p. 2.

SCHAFER, WALTER E.

1969 "Some sources and consequences of interscholastic athletics: The case of participation and delinquency." *International Review of Sport Sociology* 4: 63–79.

1970 "Sport and subculture in American secondary schools." Paper presented at the meeting of the World Congress of Sociology, Varna, Bulgaria.

1971a "Sport, socialization and the school: Toward maturity or enculturation." Paper presented at Third International Symposium on the Sociology of Sport, Waterloo, Ontario.

1971b "Sport and youth counterculture: Contrasting socialization themes." Paper presented at Conference on Sport and Social Deviancy, State College of New York at Brockport.

1975 "Sport and male sex-role socialization." *Sport Sociology Bulletin* 4 (Fall): 47–54.

1976 "Sport and youth counterculture: Contrasting socialization themes," in Daniel Landers (ed.), *Social Problems in Athletics: Essays in the Sociology of Sport*. Urbana: University of Illinois Press.

SCHAFER, WALTER E., AND MICHAEL ARMER
1968 "Athletes are not inferior students." *Transaction* 5 (November): 21–26, 61–62.

SCHAFER, WALTER E., AND R. REHBERG
1970 "Athletic participation, college aspirations and college encouragement." *Pacific Sociological Review* 13 (Summer): 182–86.

SCHLENOFF, DAVID
1980 "The role of a therapeutic running program in rehabilitation." *Rehabilitation Literature* 41 (March–April): 76–77.

SCHNEIDER, JOHN, AND D. STANLEY EITZEN
1979 "Racial discrimination in American sport: Continuity or change?" *Journal of Sport Behavior* 2 (August): 136–42.

SCHNEIDER, LOUIS
1975 *The Sociological Way of Looking at the World*. New York: McGraw-Hill.

SCHWARTZ, BARRY, AND STEPHEN BARSKY
1977 "The home advantage." *Social Forces* 55 (March): 641–61.

SCHWARTZ, J. MICHAEL
1973 "Causes and effects of spectator sports." *International Review of Sport Sociology* 8 (No. 3-4): 25–43.

SCOTT, JACK
1969 *Athletics for Athletes*. Berkeley: An Otherways Book.
1971 *The Athletic Revolution*. New York: Free Press.
1972 "Sport: Scott's radical ethic." *Intellectual Digest* 11 (July): 49–50.

SCOTT, MARVIN, AND STANFORD LYMAN
1968 "Accounts." *American Sociological Review* 33 (February): 46–62.

SCULLY, G.
1974a "Discrimination: The case of baseball," in R. Noll (ed.), *Government and the Sports Business*. Washington, D.C.: The Brookings Institute.
1974b "Pay and performance in major league baseball." *American Economic Review* 64 (December): 915–30.
1978 "Binding salary arbitration in major league baseball." *American Behavioral Scientist* 21 (January/February): 431–50.

SECORD, PAUL, AND S. JOURARD
1953 "The appraisal of body-cathexis and the self." *Journal of Consulting Psychology* 17 (October): 343.

SEGRAVE, JEFFREY, AND DONALD CHU
1978 "Athletes and juvenile delinquency." *Review of Sport and Leisure* 3 (Winter): 1–24.

SENATE COMMITTEE ON COMMERCE
1972 Federal Sports Act of 1972. Hearings on 5.3445, Ninety-Second Congress. Washington, D.C.: U.S. Government Printing Office.

SEPPANEN, PAAVO
1981 "Olympic success: A cross-national perspective," in G. Lüschen and G. Sage (eds.), *Handbook of Social Science of Sport*. Champaign, Il.: Stipes.

SEWELL, WILLIAM H.
1964 "Community of residence and college plans." *American Sociological Review* 29 (February): 24–38.

SEWELL, WILLIAM H., A. HALLER, AND G. OHLENDORF
1970 "The educational and early occupational attainment process: Replication and revision." *American Sociological Review* 35 (December): 1014–27.

SEWELL, WILLIAM H., A. HALLER, AND A. PORTES
1969 "The educational and early occupational attainment process." *American Sociological Review* 34 (February): 82–92.

SHAW, GARY
1972 *Meat on the Hoof*. New York: Dell.

SHECTER, LEONARD
1969 *The Jocks*. Indianapolis: Bobbs-Merrill.

SHERIF, CAROLYN
1976 "The social context of competition," in Daniel Landers (ed.), *Social Problems in Athletics: Essays in the Sociology of Sport*. Urbana: University of Illinois Press.

SHERRIFF, MARIE C.
1969 *The Status of Female Athletes as Viewed by Selected Peers and Parents in Certain High Schools of Central California*. Masters thesis, Chico, California State College.

SIEBER, SAM
1974 "Toward a theory of role accumulation." *American Sociological Review* 39 (August): 567–78.

SIEGFRIED, JOHN, AND C. E. HINSHAW
1977a "The professional sports television anti-blackout law," in House Select Committee, Inquiry into Professional Sports. Hearings before Ninety-Fourth Congress, Appendix III-E-1. Washington, D.C.: U.S. Government Printing Office.
1977b "Professional football and the anti-blackout law." *Journal of Communication* 27 (Summer): 169–75.

SIMMEL, GEORG
1950 *The Sociology of Georg Simmel*, trans. K. Wolff. Glencoe, Il.: The Free Press.

SINGER, ROBERT N.
1969 "Reaction to 'sport and personality dynamics'." In Proceedings of the National College Physical Education Association for Men.
1972 *The Psychomotor Domain: Movement Behaviors*. Philadelphia: Lea and Febiger.
1976 *Physical Education: Foundations*. New York: Holt, Rinehart and Winston.

SLUSHER, HOWARD S.
1967 *Man, Sport and Existence: A Critical Analysis*. Philadelphia: Lea and Febiger.

SMELSER, NEIL J.
1962 *Theory of Collective Behavior*. New York: The Free Press.

SMITH, GARRY
1973 "The sport hero: An endangered species." *Quest* 19 (January): 59–70.

SMITH, MICHAEL D.
1975 "Sport and collective violence," in D. Ball and J. Loy (eds.), *Sport and the Social Order*. Reading, Ma.: Addison-Wesley.
1976 "The legitimation of violence: Hockey players' perceptions of their reference groups' sanctions for assault," in Richard S. Gruneau and John G. Albinson (eds.), *Canadian Sport Sociological Perspectives*. Reading, Ma.: Addison-Wesley.

SNYDER, ELDON E.

1969 "A longitudinal analysis of the relationship between high school student values, social participation, and educational-occupational achievement." *Sociology of Education* 42 (Summer): 261–70.

1972a "High school athletes and their coaches: Educational plans and advice." *Sociology of Education* 45 (Summer): 313–25.

1972b "Athletic dressingroom slogans as folklore: A means of socialization." *International Review of Sport Sociology* 7: 89–102.

1973 "Aspects of social and political values of high school coaches." *International Review of Sport Sociology* 8 (3-4): 73–87.

1975 "Athletic team involvement, educational plans, and the coach–player relationship." *Adolescence* 10 (Summer): 192–200.

1981 "A reflection on commitment and patterns of disengagement from recreational physical activity," in S. Greendorfer and A. Yiannakis (eds.), *Sociology of Sport: Perspectives*. West Point: Leisure Press.

SNYDER, ELDON E., AND LUCKY BABER

1979 "A profile of former collegiate athletes and nonathletes: Leisure activities, attitudes toward work, and aspects of life satisfaction." *Journal of Sport Behavior* 2 (November): 211–19.

SNYDER, ELDON E., AND JOSEPH E. KIVLIN

1975 "Women athletes and aspects of psychological well-being and body image." *Research Quarterly* 46 (May): 191–99.

1977 "Perceptions of the sex role among female athletes and nonathletes." *Adolescence* 45 (Spring): 23–29.

SNYDER, ELDON E., AND ELMER SPREITZER

1973 "Family influence and involvement in sports." *Research Quarterly* 44 (October): 249–55.

1974 "The sociology of sport: An overview." *The Sociological Quarterly* 15 (Autumn): 467–87.

1974a "Orientations toward work and leisure as predictors of sports involvement." *Research Quarterly* 45 (December): 398–406.

1974b "Involvement in sports and psychological well-being." *International Journal of Sport Psychology* 5 (Number 1): 28–39.

1976a "Correlates of sport participation among adolescent girls." *Research Quarterly* 47 (December): 804–9.

1976b "The collegiate dilemma of sport and leisure: A sociological perspective," in Proceedings of the National College Physical Education Association for Men, Department of Physical Education, University of Illinois at Chicago Circle.

1977 "Participation in sport as related to educational expectations among high school girls." *Sociology of Education* 50 (January): 47–55.

1978 "Socialization comparisons of adolescent female athletes and musicians." *Research Quarterly* 49 (October): 342–50.

1979a "Orientations toward sport: Intrinsic, normative, and extrinsic." *Journal of Sport Psychology* 1 (2): 170–75.

1979b "High school value climate as related to preferential treatment of athletes." *Research Quarterly* 50 (October): 460–67.

1980 "An ironic perspective on sport." *Journal of Popular Culture* 13 (Spring): 609–17.

SNYDER, ELDON E., JOSEPH KIVLIN, AND ELMER SPREITZER

1975 "The female athlete: An analysis of objective and subjective role conflict," in Daniel Landers (ed.), *Psychology of Sport and Motor Behavior*. University Park: Pennsylvania State University.

SOBEL, LIONEL
1977 *Professional Sports and the Law.* New York: Law-Arts Publishers.

SPADY, WILLIAM G.
1970 "Lament for the letterman: Effects of peer status and extracurricular activities on goals and achievement." *American Journal of Sociology* 75 (January): 680–702.

SPAULDING, MARC
1975 "Superstition and sport." Unpublished paper, Department of Sociology, Bowling Green State University.

SPINRAD, WILLIAM
1981 "The function of spectator sports," in G. Lüschen and G. Sage (eds.), *Handbook of Social Science of Sport.* Champaign, Il.: Stipes.

SPREITZER, ELMER, AND MEREDITH PUGH
1973 "Interscholastic athletics and educational expectations." *Sociology of Education* 46 (Spring): 171–82.

SPREITZER, ELMER, AND ELDON E. SNYDER
1975 "The psychosocial functions of sport as perceived by the general population." *International Review of Sport Sociology* 10 (No. 3-4): 87–93.
1976 "Socialization into sport: An exploratory path analysis." *Research Quarterly* 47 (May): 238–45.

STAFF, PRESIDENT'S COUNCIL ON PHYSICAL FITNESS AND SPORT
1979 "Situation on exercise in the United States." *Newsletter* (July): 7.

STEBBINS, ROBERT A.
1979 *Amateurs: On the Margin Between Work and Leisure.* Beverly Hills: Sage Publications.

STERBA, JAMES P.
1976 "In Dallas, football is bruising for fans as well as players." *The New York Times,* October 16, 1976, p. 30.

STEVENSON, C. L.
1975 "Socialization effects of participation in sport: A critical review of the literature." *Research Quarterly* 46 (October): 287–301.

STINCHCOMBE, ARTHUR
1964 *Rebellion in High School.* Chicago: Quadrangle Books.

STOKES, RANDALL AND JOHN HEWITT
1976 "Aligning actions." *American Sociological Review* 41 (October): 838–49.

STONE, GREGORY P.
1965 "The play of little children." *Quest* 4 (Spring): 23–31.
1969 "Some meanings of American sport: An extended view," in Gerald S. Kenyon (ed.), *Aspects of Contemporary Sport Sociology.* Chicago: The Athletic Institute.
1973 "American sports: Play and display," in J. T. Talamini and C. H. Page (eds.), *Sport and Society: An Anthology.* Boston: Little, Brown.

STRAUB, WILLIAM F., AND STANLEY E. DAVIS
1971 "Personality traits of college football players who participated at different levels of competition." *Medicine and Science in Sports* 3 (Spring): 39–43.

STRENK, ANDREW
1979 "What price victory? The world of international sports and politics." *Annals of the American Academy of Political and Social Sciences* 445 (September): 128–40.

STRUNA, NANCY
1977 "Sport and societal values: Massachusetts Bay." *Quest* 27 (Winter): 38–46.

STRUTT, JOSEPH
1903 *The Sports and Pastimes of the People of England.* London: Methuen and Company.

SUBCOMMITTEE ON COMMUNICATIONS
1977 *Cable Television.* Oversight Hearings on Cable Television, U.S. Senate, Ninety-Fifth Congress, Serial No. 95-32. Washington, D.C.: U.S. Government Printing Office.
1978 *Sports Anti-Blackout Legislation.* Hearings before the Subcommittee on Communications of the Committee on Interstate and Foreign Commerce, Ninety-Fifth Congress, Serial No. 95-185. Washington, D.C.: U.S. Government Printing Office.
1979 Amendments to the Communications Act of 1934. Hearings before the Committee on Commerce, Science, and Transportation, U.S. Senate, Ninety-Sixth Congress, Serial No. 96-45. Washington, D.C.: U.S. Government Printing Office.

SUBCOMMITTEE ON CONSUMER PROTECTION AND FINANCE
1977 Consumer Product Safety Commission: Oversight. Ninety-Fifth Congress, Serial No. 95-52. Washington, D.C.: U.S. Government Printing Office.

SUBCOMMITTEE ON INTERNATIONAL ORGANIZATIONS
1977 The 1984 Summer Olympic Games. House of Representatives, Ninety-Fifth Congress. Washington, D.C.: U.S. Government Printing Office.

SUBCOMMITTEE ON MONOPOLIES AND COMMERCIAL LAW
1975 Rights of Professional Athletes. House of Representatives, Ninety-Fifth Congress, Serial No. 59. Washington, D.C.: U.S. Government Printing Office.

SUBCOMMITTEE ON MONOPOLY POWER
1952 Organized Baseball. House Report 2002, Eighty-Second Congress. Washington, D.C.: U.S. Government Printing Office.

SUBCOMMITTEE ON TRANSPORTATION AND COMMERCE
1976 The 1980 Winter Olympic Games. House of Representatives, Ninety-Fourth Congress, Serial No. 94-78. Washington, D.C.: U.S. Government Printing Office.
1980 Alternatives to the Moscow Olympics. House of Representatives, Ninety-Sixth Congress, Serial No. 96-130. Washington, D.C.: U.S. Government Printing Office.

SUBCOMMITTEE ON TRANSPORTATION AND FINANCE
1976 The 1980 Winter Olympic Games. Hearings before the Ninety-Fourth Congress, Serial No. 94-78. Washington, D.C.: U.S. Government Printing Office.

SUGDEN, JOHN, AND ANDREW YIANNAKIS
1980 "Politics and the Olympics." *Newsletter of the North American Society for the Sociology of Sport* Volume 2 (No. 1, January).

SURFACE, BILL
1977 "A national controversy: How much are sports arenas costing the taxpayer?" *The Pittsburgh Press Parade*, November 27, 1977, pp. 10–13.

SUTHERLAND, EDWIN H.
1939 *Principles of Criminology*, 3rd ed. Philadelphia: J. B. Lippincott.

SUTTON-SMITH, BRIAN
1975 "The useless made useful: Play as variability training." *School Review* 83 (February): 197–214.

SUTTON-SMITH, BRIAN, AND JOHN M. ROBERTS
1970 "The cross-cultural and psychological study of games," in Gunther Lüschen (ed.), *The Cross-Cultural Analysis of Sport and Games*. Champaign, Il.: Stipes.

SUTTON-SMITH, BRIAN, JOHN M. ROBERTS, AND ROBERT M. KOZELKA
1963 "Game involvement in adults." *The Journal of Social Psychology* 60 (June): 15–30.

TALAMINI, JOHN T.
1973 "School athletics: Public policy versus practice," in J. Talamini and C. Page (eds.), *Sport and Society*. Boston: Little, Brown.

TALAMINI, JOHN T., AND CHARLES H. PAGE
1973 *Sport and Society: An Anthology*. Boston: Little, Brown.

TATUM, JACK
1980 *They Call Me Assasin*. New York: Everest House.

TAYLOR, JIM
1978 "Kubek–Steinbrenner argument threatens journalistic integrity." *The Toledo Blade*, May 5, 1978, p. 3.

THIRER, JOEL
1978 "Politics and protest at the Olympic games," in Benjamin Lowe et al., (eds.), *Sport and International Relations*. Champaign, Il.: Stipes.

Toledo Blade
1976 "Agase joins growing list of grid coaches 'looking'." November 27, p. 7.
1976 "Cost no factor for Oklahoma football fans." December 12, Section D, p. 7.
1977 "Vandy coach bemoans cage violence." February 20, Section E, p. 7.

TURNER, RALPH
1964 *The Social Context of Ambition*. San Francisco: Chandler.

TURNER, RALPH, AND L. M. KILLIAN
1957 *Collective Behavior*. Englewood Cliffs, N.J.: Prentice-Hall.

TUTKO, THOMAS, AND WILLIAM BRUNS
1976 *Winning Is Everything and Other American Myths*. New York: Macmillan.

ULLRICH, EDWIN
1971 "System-Environment Relationships in American Universities: A Theoretical Model and Exploratory Study." Ph.D. dissertation, The Florida State University.

U.S. News and World Report
1977 "The boom in leisure: Where Americans spend 160 billions." May 23, pp. 62–63.

VAN DEN BERGHE, PIERRE
1963 "Dialectic and functionalism: Toward a theoretical synthesis." *American Sociological Review* 28 (October): 695–705.

VAN DER LEEUW, GERARD
1963 *Religion in Essence and Manifestation.* New York: Harper and Row.

VANDERZWAAG, HAROLD J.
1972 *Toward A Philosophy of Sport.* Reading, Ma.: Addison-Wesley.
1977 "Ball games: The heart of American sport." *Quest* 27 (Winter): 61–70.

VANNIER, MARYHELEN, AND HOLLIS F. FAIT
1975 *Teaching Physical Education in Secondary Schools.* Philadelphia: W. B. Saunders.

VANNIER, MARYHELEN, MILDRED FOSTER, AND DAVID L. GALLAHUE
1973 *Teaching Physical Education in Elementary Schools.* Philadelphia: W. B. Saunders.

VAZ, EDMUND
1974 "What price victory." *International Review of Sport Sociology* 9 (2): 33–55.

VEBLEN, THORSTEIN
1918 *The Higher Learning in America.* New York: Sagamore Press.

VOIGT, DAVID Q.
1966 *American Baseball.* Norman: University of Oklahoma Press.
1974 "Reflections on diamonds: Baseball and American culture." *Journal of Sport History* 1 (Spring): 3–25.
1977 "The changing dimensions of sport." Unpublished manuscript, Department of Sociology, Albright College.

VOLTMER, EDWARD F., AND ARTHUR A. ESSLINGER
1967 *The Organization and Administration of Physical Education.* New York: Appleton-Century-Crofts.

WALLER, WILLARD
1932 *The Sociology of Teaching.* New York: Wiley.

WEBB, HARRY
1969a "Professionalization of attitudes toward play among adolescents," in Gerald S. Kenyon (ed.), *Aspects of Contemporary Sport Sociology.* Chicago: The Athletic Institute.
1969b "Reaction to the Loy paper," in Gerald Kenyon (ed.), *Aspects of Contemporary Sport Sociology.* Chicago: The Athletic Institute.

WEBB, MAX
1974 "Sunday heroes: The emergence of the professional football novel." *Journal of Popular Culture* 8 (Fall): 453–61.

WEBER, MAX
1946 "Class, status, party," in H. Gerth and C. W. Mills (eds.), *From Max Weber: Essays in Sociology.* New York: Oxford University Press.

WEISS, PAUL
1969 *Sport: A Philosophical Inquiry.* Carbondale: Southern Illinois University Press.

WEXLER, HENRIETTA
1979 "Myths about women sports." *American Education* 15 (August–September): 38–39.

WHITFIELD, SHELBY
1973 *Kiss It Goodby*. New York: Abelard-Schuman Ltd.

WHITING, ROBERT
1979 "You've gotta have 'wa.' " *Sports Illustrated* 51 (September 24): 60–71.

WILBER, CHARLES G.
1975 *Contemporary Violence: A Multidisciplinary Examination*. Springfield, Il.: Charles C Thomas.

WILENSKY, HAROLD
1960 "Work, careers, and social integration." *International Social Science Journal* 12: 543–60.

WILLIAMS, BRIEN R.
1977 "The structure of televised football." *Journal of Communication* 27 (Summer): 133–39.

WILLIAMS, ROBIN
1970 *American Society*. New York: Alfred A. Knopf.

WILMORE, JACK
1980 "Exercise's role in promotion of health among adults." *Newsletter, President's Council on Physical Fitness and Sports* (March): 5.

WILSON, WAYNE
1977 "Social discontent and the growth of wilderness sport in America: 1965-1974." *Quest* (Winter): 54–60.

WINTHROP, JOHN
1947 *Winthrop Papers*, 6 vol. Boston: Massachusetts Historical Society.

WOHL, ANDRZEJ
1966 "Conception and range of sport sociology." *International Review of Sport Sociology* 1: 5–15.

WOLFE, TOM
1972 "Clean fun at Riverhead," in G. Lewis (ed.), *Side-Saddle on the Golden Calf*. Pacific Palisades, Ca.: Goodyear.

WRONG, DENNIS H.
1961 "The oversocialized conception of man in modern sociology." *American Sociological Review* 26 (April): 183–93.

WYRICK, WANEEN
1974 "Biophysical perspectives," in E. Gerber, J. Felshin, P. Berlin, and W. Wyrick (eds.), *The American Woman in Sport*. Reading, Ma.: Addison-Wesley.

YABLONSKY, LEWIS, AND JONATHAN BROWER
1979 *The Little League Game*. New York: Times Books.

YETMAN, NORMAN
1980 "Racial participation and integration in intercollegiate basketball." Paper presented at the North American Society for the Sociology of Sport.

YETMAN, NORMAN, AND D. STANLEY EITZEN
1971 "Black athletes on intercollegiate basketball teams," in Norman Yetman and C. Steele (eds.), *Majority and Minority: The Dynamics of Racial and Ethnic Relations*. Boston: Allyn and Bacon.

1972 "Black Americans in sports: Unequal opportunity for equal ability." *Civil Rights Digest* 5: 20–34.

YINGER, MILTON
1970 *The Scientific Study of Religion*. New York: Macmillan.

YOUNG, RICHARD A.
1975 "A study of the relationship between organizational structure and athletics within state assisted universities as measured by four success criteria," Ph.D. dissertation, Bowling Green State University.

ZAJONC, R. B.
1965 "Social facilitation." *Science* 149 (July 16): 269–74.

ZEITLIN, IRVING
1968 *Ideology and the Development of Sociological Theory*. Englewood Cliffs, N.J.: Prentice-Hall.

ZIJDERVELD, ANTON
1979 *On Clichés: The Supersedure of Meaning by Function in Modernity*. London: Routledge and Kegan Paul.

ZION, L.
1965 "Body concept as it relates to self-concept." *The Research Quarterly* 36 (December): 490–95.

ZOBLE, J.
1973 "Femininity, achievement, and sports," in Dorothy Harris (ed.), *DGWS Research Reports: Women in Sports*. Washington, D.C.: American Association for Health, Physical Education, and Recreation.

ZUCKERMAN, MARVIN, SYBIL EYSENCK, AND H. J. EYSENCK
1978 "Sensation-seeking in England and America: Cross-cultural, age and sex comparisons." *Journal of Consulting Psychology* 46 (February): 139–49.

Index

t

u

v

w

y

z